D0834737

Hip Hop Hypocrisy

Also by Alfred "Coach" Powell

Message N/A Bottle: The 40oz Scandal (vols. 1 and 2)

Hip Hop Hypocrisy

When Lies Sound Like the Truth

Alfred "Coach" Powell

iUniverse, Inc.
New York Lincoln Shanghai

Hip Hop Hypocrisy:
When Lies Sound Like the Truth

Copyright © 2006 by Alfred Powell

All rights reserved. No part of this book may be used or reproduced by any means, graphic, electronic, or mechanical, including photocopying, recording, taping or by any information storage retrieval system without the written permission of the publisher except in the case of brief quotations embodied in critical articles and reviews.

iUniverse books may be ordered through booksellers or by contacting:

iUniverse
2021 Pine Lake Road, Suite 100
Lincoln, NE 68512
www.iuniverse.com
1-800-Authors (1-800-288-4677)

Allow me to apologize in advance for the language we must use throughout this book. To explain commercialized gangsta rap and gangsta Hip Hop, we must deal with the actual words that are used in rap lyrics and daily conversation in the Hip Hop community.

ISBN-13: 978-0-595-41909-8 (pbk)
ISBN-13: 978-0-595-86256-6 (ebk)
ISBN-10: 0-595-41909-7 (pbk)
ISBN-10: 0-595-86256-X (ebk)

Printed in the United States of America

To all frontline educators, counselors, parents, ministers, institutions of faith, peace officers, Hip Hop artists, good people, and mentors dedicated to saving and improving the lives of our children and their families no matter what others think.

In Loving Memory

Ahmad Rashad Reynolds
Born January 3, 1978
Killed July 17, 2005

You are with us in spirit, and we feel your presence. You are missed but not forgotten. From your football coach and all your teammates, this one is for you, baby boy. R.I.P. (**R**ise **I**n **P**raise), for you are in the place where praise and glory rule.

Acknowledgments

On behalf of the children of Hip Hop, I extend my gratitude to the defenders and healers of the village: the staff of Human Motivation Council (Chicago, Illinois), Urban Minority Alcoholism and Drug Abuse Outreach Program of Ohio, Black Alcoholism and Addiction Institute Council, Inc., Black Cops Against Police Brutality (East Orange, New Jersey), Khepera & Associates Networking Services, Nia Committee/Harambe Na Nguzo Saba Cobbala Productions, Bobby E. Wright Comprehensive Behavioral Health Center, Partnership for a Smoke-Free Chicago, Office of Multicultural Ministry (Louisville, Kentucky), and Turner Mandley & Turner, Inc. (Louisville, Kentucky).

I respectfully salute the leadership and staff of Visionary Leaders Institute (Columbus, Ohio): Ako Kambon, Donna Anderson, Cynthia Johnson, and Gwendolyn Napper.

Likewise, many thanks to:

- Ms. Anna Taliaferro, President, New Jersey Association of Parent Coordinators, Inc.
- Jah Sun Lamarr, Wanda Jones, Kira Jackson, Carol Russell, Nina Thomas, and Detective Rochelle Bilal
- Mentors Ron Allen and Richard Green (a million thanks for your teachings on how to be effective with youth)
- Black Brothers & Sistas Involvement (Dayton, Ohio)
- Chalena Mack and 4 Sho 4 Kids (St. Louis, Missouri)
- Angela Cornelius, Project Linden, Inc. (Columbus, Ohio)
- The Peters Group, Inc. (Orangeburg, South Carolina)
- The best coaching crew: Peter Pullen, Sidney Booker, James Lacking, David Caldwell, and Dave Hackett
- Tamara Henry, Kathleen Hauck, Alfred Gladden, Mamie Gladden, and Minister Leila Thomas

- C. Vincent Bakeman, PhD, Founder and President Emeritus, Human Resources Development Institute, Inc. (Chicago, Illinois)
- Patricia A. Newton, MD, MPH, MA (Nana Akosua Akyaa), President and Medical Director, Newton & Associates, PA (Baltimore, Maryland)
- Terra Thomas, PhD, President/CEO, Human Resources Development Institute, Inc. (Chicago, Illinois)
- Edie Lundgren, John Robertson, PhD, Dr. M. Leon Seard II, Eddie Young, Maxine Womble, Susan James-Andrews, Judge Karen Freeman-Wilson, Bertha Murphy, Judge Robert Russell, and Allison Robbins
- Big Blue connection (Dunbar High School alumni)—Dan Wilkinson and NaShan Goddard
- Sista Helen Salahuddin and Brotha Ali Salahuddin, D'Zert Club, Philadelphia, Pennsylvania

For your research and insights on the complex world of Hip Hop, big ups and much love to the scholar-activists who make me appreciate who we are in the midst of this continuous struggle: Cashus D, Minister Yusuf Muhammad, Suzan Bradford-Kounta, Leo Hayden, Deborah Styles, Dr. Tyrone Powers, Dr. Amos Wilson, Dr. John Henrik Clarke, Dr. Wade Noble, Dr. Yosef ben-Jochannan, Dr. Asa Hilliard, Chuck D, Davey D, Sista Soldier, Mark Bartlett, Cedric Muhammad, Kevin Powell, Bakari Kitwana, Nelson George, Haki Madhubuti, Dr. Mutulu Shakur Straight, Dr. Eric Dyson, Dr. Michael Williams, Steve Harvey, Stan "The Man" Scofield, Calvin Mackie, PhD, Dick Gregory, Kwame and Chavunduka, Damu Smith, Dr. Gloria Peace, Bishop Lance Davis, Anthony Browder, Makani Themba-Nixon, Donna Scrutchins, Barbara Clayton, Rev. James Anyike, Baba Hannibal T. Afrik, Dr. Conrad Worrill, Dr. James Dobbins, Dr. Lance Williams, Stephen MacDonald, and Elder Olumenji.

special thanks

To my many colleagues, students, friends, family members, and workshop participants who gave of their intellectual properties, research expertise, and time to this five-year project, I find no words adequate enough to express the depth of my gratitude. Space permits me to list only a few: Stephanie Mwandishi Gadlin, Crystal Harris, Kevin Britton, Dr. Didra Brown-Taylor, Victor N. Taylor, Mary K. Early, Dr. Guy Wheeler, Robyn L. Price, Kevin Britton, Michael Williams, Laura Williams, Monica Owens, Dr. Cassandra Jones, Frank T. Gipson, Dr. William Waymer, Aaron Williams, Dr. Ron Lewis, Kwesi R. Harris, Onjewel Smith, Sherri Watson Hyde, Felix Adeyeye, Kelvin Little, Darren Powell, Marlon C. Shackleford, Pam Shackleford, Devin Price, Hunter Adams III, Jerrica A. Mack, Albert Eugene Packett-Powell, Cherie Andrews, Stephen Peters, Dr. Angela Peters, Derrick Davis, Peter Hayden, Dr. Llaila Afrika, Cousin Jeff (a real voice in real times), Dr. Cassandra Jones, Keidi Obi Awadu, LeeRoy Jordan, Dr. Gloria Long, Pam Lightsy, Dr. Carlos Vidal, Detective Calvin Hart, Valerie Robinson, PhD, Chike Akua, Tavares Stephens, Dr. Rev. Jamal-Harrison Bryant, Bishop Eddie L. Long, Boddie (Tank) and Margaret Sims, Willie Howard, Frances Winborn, Iona Jefferson, and students of Dayton Paul Lawrence Dunbar High School, H. D. Woodson Senior High School (Washington, DC), and Detroit Kettering High School.

On behalf of Hip Hop, I'd like to thank Treel Beatz Records and Huggable Beats Productions for challenging every word of this project.

Big ups to my brothers in the struggle. Sgt. DeLacy Davis and Dr. Tyrone Powers, thanks for having my back. Believe me, I've got yours. To the crazy "40 crew," E-Dub Aka 165 and Bruz, thanks for helping to close the gap. I hope we will continue to learn from each other.

To my dean and mentors, Dr. Frances L. Brisbane and Dr. Na'im Akbar, thank you for your criticisms and support of my projects.

special kudos

Thanks so much to everyone who prayed for my wife and to every doctor and medical professional who aided in her recovery. Much love to our neighbors for the food, encouraging words, and acts of kindness. They truly live the creed, "Love thy neighbor as thyself." Shelly, your illness may have robbed you of your sight but not your vision or courage. You are our daily reminder that God is still in the miracle business.

To "four the hard way," our children Natasha, Terrea, Al J, and Tiara Powell: you continue to be the wind beneath our wings. I can never repay you for your loving support during your mother's prolonged illness. Your sacrifices have been invaluable.

To our grandchild: there's a reason why your name is Destiny. Know that My-U and Papa love you. To our extended grandchildren and godchildren: we are blessed because you chose us. To all my loving siblings and in-laws: thanks for keeping me upright in my days of challenge. To my uncles, cousins, nieces, and nephews: our life experiences continue to be a learning tree providing shade for others.

To my twin brother Albert and his faithful wife Darlene, my big brother John and his loving wife Jacqueline: a million thanks will never do, so let me just say I love you and there's nothing you can do about it! To my big sister Shirley (BeBe) and Aunt Dorothy: thank you for giving up everything to help me nurse my wife. To Barbara Canty, Jeff and Paula Woodson, Carrie Lane, Kwesi Ronald Harris and Donna F. Edgeworth-Harris, Roy and Brenda Hollis, John and Patricia Rickman, Jay and Karrie Ann Chase, Keith and Katherine Rakestraw, Stephen and Angela Peters: your friendships are invaluable. Thank you all for being there beyond the call of friendship. You're God sent.

Beyond words, I am grateful to my business partner and editor, Donna Marie Williams. Your diligence behind the scenes continues to be irreplaceable. Your words of encouragement and assistance have helped me persevere. You constantly go over and beyond the call of duty, and the project and I are better for it. I am forever indebted.

Contents

Acknowledgments vii

Preface: My People Are Destroyed for Lack of Knowledge........xiii

Introduction: A Unique Generation 1

Part 1: Get the Hell out the Hood
Chapter 1   Framework for Understanding Hip Hop Youth....19
Chapter 2   Types of Rap 31
Chapter 3   The 10 Commandments of Hip Hop............. 34
              By Stephanie Mwandishi Gadlin

Part 2: Trapped in the Matrix
Chapter 1   **Hypocrisy 1—Keeping It Real //
              Flippin' the Script**.. 45
Chapter 2   Making Lies Look Like the Truth 51
Chapter 3   Hip Hop Mind Control................................. 63
Chapter 4   Words of Deadly Persuasion.......................... 73
Chapter 5   Poetry in Motion.. 96

Chapter 6   **Hypocrisy 2—Bling Bling //
              Poverty in the Hood**................................... 111
Chapter 7   Africa: The Origin of Bling 115
Chapter 8   Ghetto Life: Not So Fabulous 119

Chapter 9   **Hypocrisy 3—Role Models //
              Pimps, Hos, Pushers, & Spies**.................... 138
Chapter 10   Fear of a Gangsta Planet.............................. 143
Chapter 11   The Intoxication of the Hip Hop Generation.. 162
Chapter 12   Spies Among Us 188
Chapter 13   Who's the Boss?.. 204

Chapter 14 **Hypocrisy 4—Grown Folks Business //
            Tricks Are for Kids** 219
Chapter 15 Sex in the Hood 225
Chapter 16 Lyrical Felonies & Misdemeanors in Hip Hop .. 245
Chapter 17 Dirty Dancing & STDs 251
Chapter 18 Parent'Hood: A Divine Mission 265
            By Crystal Harris & Alfred "Coach" Powell

Chapter 19 **Hypocrisy 5—The Cross // The Beast** 276
Chapter 20 Hip Hop @ the Cross................................. 281
Chapter 21 St. Hip Hop 300

Part 3: Rescuing Our Children
Chapter 1   Redefining the Revolution 315
            By Kevin Britton
Chapter 2   Hip Hop Survival.. 319
Chapter 3   SugarStrings: Music Education for the
            Hip Hop Generation.................................... 335
            By Donna Marie Williams
Chapter 4   Gateways to Heaven: Enhancing Prevention
            Programs... 342
Chapter 5   Raising Hip Hop Scholars........................... 351
Chapter 6   Welcome to Nellyville 370

Endnotes 381

Index 405

Preface

My People Are Destroyed for Lack of Knowledge

"My People Are Destroyed for lack of knowledge. Because you have rejected knowledge, I also will reject you from being priest for Me; Because you have forgotten the law of your God, I also will forget your children." **Hosea 4:6**

For the record, when it comes to the healthy development and safety of our children, I have always been in it to win it. But over the past 20 years, I have witnessed the invasion and occupation of the African American community by an enemy so powerful that it seems invincible.

This enemy comes against parents, educators, ministers, social service providers, and all others who work with youth. No matter where I go to give my motivational workshops and lectures—schools, colleges, universities, detention centers, recreational centers, church-sponsored youth camps, parks, street corners, and all places in between—the rules of gangsta Hip Hop are large and in charge. Commercialized, pornographic, violent gangsta rap/Hip Hop have taken over the traditional African American community. The young are running the elders, and the hood is out of control.

Gangsta rap/Hip Hop is one big viral marketing scheme to deprive consumer-driven youth (and their parents) of their money and minds. Viral marketing refers to:

"... marketing techniques that seek to exploit pre-existing social networks to produce exponential increases in brand awareness, through viral processes similar to the spread of an epidemic. It is word-of-mouth delivered and enhanced online; it harnesses the network effect of the Internet and can be very useful in reaching a large number of people rapidly."[1]

"Viral" comes from the word "virus." The last I heard, a virus is a sickness, a disease. In my next book, *Caterpillars in the Hood: A Survival Guide for Hip Hop Youth*, we'll deal with the viral nature of Hip Hop in more depth. Suffice to say for now, gangsta Hip Hop is a virus, a cancer that has mutated, thanks to infusions of capital, into a global youth pandemic of misperceptions, misinformation, racial and gender stereotypes, and anti-life values.

Let's pause and think for a moment. People who were 10 and 20 years old when Hip Hop was born some 30 years ago are now 40 and 50. This same group can't believe what has become of the music and movement they unconditionally loved in such a short period of time.

The carefree gangbanging, sexual escapades, drug dealing, and substance abuse of the 1980s and '90s served as the creative engine of gangsta rap. After three decades of allowing our children to mentally intercourse with these promiscuous artists, the entire African American community is suffering the consequences.

No one can say they are hypocrisy free, including me. I'm a substitute father and role model to many children in my community, but I'm not perfect. I'm aware that when I point a finger in this book, three more will point back at me. This truth motivates me to reach and teach all concerned about the need to rescue the children who are born into the Hip Hop/ghetto matrix.

Music is supposed to help us escape the cares of the world, but in the case of gangsta Hip Hop, the music has trapped an entire generation. Gangsta rap/Hip Hop has blood on its hands. With its smoke and mirrors, its words, symbols, images, and other WMDs (weapons of mass destruction), gangsta rap has lyrically sold drugs and alcohol to our children and it has done nothing to reverse their academic demise and poverty.

Black males have learned how to kill one another and treat their sisters like pieces of meat from lyrical infomercials (rap tunes). Black females have learned how to objectify and commodify their own bodies.

Hip Hop moguls say they're simply giving the people what they want, and somehow we accept that bull. Who are these people? Are they black, brown, or white? Where do they live? Did they explain why they have a death wish for their children and community? Did they say they can't get enough of juvenile acting men and whorish acting women?

Unfortunately, Hip Hop has left a lasting impression on our children. Elementary and middle school principals, including my wife, have shared their stories of students as young as eight and nine years old who wanted to perform inappropriate dance routines or songs in the school talent show—and of young Hip Hop parents who couldn't understand why the dances and songs were not allowed.

High school principals dread junior and senior proms. "Coach, have you seen how this generation of hip hoppers dress for the prom? They dress as if they're going to the playa's pimp ball. It's simply too painful to watch." I've heard these comments from coast to coast.

In the present era of Hip Hop bling, Hip Hop hasn't done much to help our children. I'm tired of Hip Hop moguls talking about how powerful Hip Hop is as a movement. If Hip Hop is so powerful, then why has it yet to bring those historical barriers that impede our social mobility to its knees? The only thing Hip Hop has brought to its knees is grieving parents.

A few have prospered in the Hip Hop game, but the masses remain trapped, blinded by the illusion of their bling. Seemingly, we're satisfied with being consumers and not owners. The institution of Hip Hop has yet to purchase one hotel chain, airline, school, college, or medical institution. We seek riches instead of wealth, information instead of knowledge. Some have collected a few Grammys and other music awards (and an Oscar). Others have purchased plenty of mouth jewelry, tire rims, and a couple of basketball teams.

Hip Hop is no longer for us or about us. Have you noticed that the experts on TV dance shows who judge Hip Hop routines have no expertise in Hip Hop? All the movies featuring struggling Hip Hop dancers feature white actors. What's up with that? Clearly, Hip Hop has been commercialized and has left the hood for good.

For 10 years, the so called adult leaders of Hip Hop have been meeting with inner city youth only to announce that they will meet again in six months and until then, buy the new CD of the brotha or sista who just happens to be sitting on the stage. Hip Hop has no agenda other than its own financial interests. Hip Hop moguls spend more time in mediation with other rappers who can't refrain from shooting one another. Across the board, they behave like fourth and fifth graders.

Will the real men and women of Hip Hop please stand up?

Those brave civil rights warriors, freedom fighters of the 1960s who fought to make life easier for the Hip Hop generation, continue to rot in jail cells as forgotten political prisoners while the richest of the Hip Hop rich sip expensive champagne (and in some cases soak their feet in it). Hip Hop can afford to pay for the defense of those freedom fighters, but in the true spirit of the gangsta, no one cares because selfishness rules.

If I sound upset it's because I am. Sometimes I think we need a check up from the neck up. Now, thanks to BET, we're celebrating hard core gangsta Hip Hop celebrities going to prison. BET has made their prison trek into a prime time viewing experience. These types of programs only confuse children and young adults.

Instead of producing lyrical porn and lyrical drive-bys, Hip Hop should be taking on the many problems facing the African American community. As Yolanda Young writes in a *USA Today* editorial slamming 50 Cent's latest literary project to publish graphic novels,

"A 2004 study by the National Endowment for the Arts found that Hispanic and black males had the lowest rates of literary reading, at 18% and 30% respectively. Though reading rates are falling for all groups, from 1992-2002 African-Americans had the largest decline, from 45.6% to 37.1%.

"Reading literature is important because it expands one's vocabulary, perspective and intellectual capacity. And though some might argue that any reading is better than none, the reader ingests poison when metaphor and imagery are replaced with sex, violence and expletives."[2]

Where is the lyrical outrage? Rap used to be called the "CNN of the streets," but I have yet to hear the following reported in any recent top 40 Hip Hop hit.

"In 2000, 65 percent of black male high school dropouts in their 20's were jobless—that is, unable to find work, not seeking it or incarcerated. By 2004, the share had grown to 72 percent, compared with 34 percent of white and 19 percent of Hispanic dropouts. Even when high school graduates were included, half of black men in their 20's were jobless in 2004, up from 46 percent in 2000.

"Incarceration rates climbed in the 1990's and reached historic highs in the past few years. In 1995, 16 percent of black men in their 20's who did not attend college were in jail or prison; by 2004, 21 percent were incarcerated. By their mid-30's, 6 in 10 black men who had dropped out of school had spent time in prison."[3]

This book is the body bag, coffin, nails, and obituary of gangsta Hip Hop, a movement that grew out of a more socially conscious value system, but somewhere along the line became so corrupted that no child under its influence is safe from spiritual, psychological, and social harm. Through its lyrics and video images, gangsta rap has strived to leave no child from the hood behind—in alcohol, tobacco, and drug use, STDs, unwanted pregnancies, crime, violence, and pornographic sex.

I love Old School and rap, and if I'm not careful, I'll start tapping my feet to a tune that has inappropriate lyrics. In my blood are African rhythms that resonate to drums and strong bass lines. The music sounds good until you listen to the lyrics. How many times have you loved the music but hated the lyrics? You hate to love it, and you love to hate it. That's the contradiction I constantly face. But I refuse to give in, and I teach children how to resist.

Although you may not believe it after reading this book, I love the artists of Hip Hop, from the profound to the profane. My fight is not with them, but with the demon spirits that influence them (Ephesians 6:12). I love their creativity, energy, and genius. We are from the same place. I ain't mad at them for wanting to get the hell out the hood. I ain't mad at them for wanting to get paid. I'm proud of the fact that they've peeped the economic game of the PTBs (powers that be) and are playing it better than they do in some ways.

So how can I write this book criticizing commercialized gangsta rap when I'm guilty of hypocrisy myself? I ask you, who among us can question anything? How can the preacher preach when she is not always godly? How can the teacher teach when he doesn't know everything? Not one of us is perfect. So with my imperfect, sometimes hypocritical self, I'm taking a chance that you are ready to question with me how this fallen music came to exist and represent the black community on a global scale.

These are the days of Hip Hop capitalists, not Hip Hop activists. The capitalists allowed commercialized gangsta rap to take the spotlight without conscience or social consciousness.

Their time is over. We've got God on our side, and we cannot lose. We're tired of what's happening to our youth. We're tired of commercialized gangsta rap getting airplay over socially conscious Hip Hop/rap because of the deep pockets and payola of the PTBs.

We're tired of African American queens being called bitches and hos. We're tired of African American kings lyrically assassinating one another. We are sick and tired of our children digesting lewd and vulgar Hip Hop lyrics and images as if they were candy or aspirins to ease their pain. We're tired of our circumstances being the source of entertainment and not change.

We're tired of nigger/nigga being used to describe African American men, women, and children.

We're creating a new cultural space for the true, original voice of Hip Hop to be heard. We want to hear raps about spirituality, marriage, educational reform, sobriety, nonviolence, economic empowerment, peace from the East Coast to the West Coast, and Black-on-Black Love.

Am I blaming all of society's ills on Hip Hop? No! Am I attacking or demonizing all Hip Hop artists? A million times *no*! But if the shoe fits wear it. In this book I confront the many critical issues that I and other educators, parents, ministers, social service providers, and activists are facing in our work with children. Gangsta rap/Hip Hop has made raising, healing, and educating African American children extraordinarily difficult. Not since slavery and institutionalized racism has there been such a violent force designed to take us out. But while institutional racism has a white face, Hip Hop's face is black. Can you say confusion?

We failed to stop the monster when it first reared its ugly head, and now we are paying with the blood of our children. Corporate, commercialized gangsta rap/Hip Hop has sown seeds of discord into the hearts and minds of children trapped inside the Hip Hop/ghetto matrix. What harvest will we reap in the future? Sometimes the problem seems impossible to fix. But if we say or do nothing we will lose our children forever. Jesus said to His disciples, "The harvest truly is plentiful, but the laborers are few" (Matthew 9:37). There is so much work to be done. Let it begin with us.

~ ~ ~

I hope that *Hip Hop Hypocrisy* will make you pause and think outside the box. I realize that some folk I mention in this book will fight back, but "No weapon formed against me shall prosper" (Isaiah 54:17). My prayer is that they will see the truth of what they're doing to our children and begin to change.

In the words of Hip Hop, I'm not punking out. What about you?

Introduction

A Unique Generation

"Any kingdom divided against itself will be ruined, and a house divided against itself will fall." **Luke 11:17**

In the beginning, Hip Hop was conceived and birthed in the hood (neighbor**hood**, ghetto). It learned to crawl and walk in the hood, was nurtured in the hood, fought, played, skinned its knees, and perfected its hustle and pimp game in the hood. But quick as a flash of bling in the spotlight, Corporate America did a drive-by and jacked Hip Hop on the way to the bank, just like it did Grandma Blues and Papa Jazz.

Despite the ownership movement in Hip Hop, Corporate America still pulls the strings. Our cultural raw material is sold back to us as CDs, clothes, and music videos. We created it, but Corporate America sells it and we consume it—repackaged, remixed, and biggie sized.

After the jacking of blues and jazz, we should have known better. A people who don't know their history are doomed to repeat it. Isn't that what our elders have been trying to teach us? Will we ever learn? Better yet, do we want to?

Historically, black music and the black spoken word have been the powerful, hypnotic WMDs (weapons of mass destruction) against injustice, the great equalizers in our ongoing battle against oppression, and the instruments that speak for the underserved and the forgotten.

1

ghetto export

Rap music has its origins in African oral poetry and West African rhythms. West Africa is where prisoners of war (slaves) were first kidnapped. As it evolved (some would say devolved), rap fused with rock, R&B, jazz, and even gospel.

Hip Hop grew out of the harshness of ghetto life. Poverty, broken families, high unemployment, miseducation, disease, crime, self-hatred, and violence were the legacies of slavery and the soil where Hip Hop grew.

Hip Hop is more than just rap music. It's a complete culture that includes entertainment, warfare, fashion, art, values, economics, communications, unique styles of relating, mating, and parenting, and, of course, rap music.

As we'll see in *Hip Hop Hypocrisy*, Hip Hop's complex interrelationship with ghetto culture, Corporate America, mainstream society, the media, and the global economy have formed a tightly woven matrix in which our children live, dance, play, and struggle to survive. The negative elements of this matrix have trapped their minds, souls, and spirits in a *deliberately designed* web of destruction. We must rescue our children, and in this book, parents, educators, service providers, street counselors, and ministers will find the weapons to do battle.

once noble

Hip Hop wasn't always negative. In fact, it started out as a positive, revolutionary movement, a party with a purpose. For many of us, rap was our theme song, and every warrior, solider, superhero, and crime fighter needs a theme song.

It's often said that history is written by the people who won the war. In Hip Hop, the war is still raging and the histories and timelines vary, depending on who's writing the book, column, or article. Many timelines completely overlook the influence of Africa and the 1960s black arts movement (cousin to the black power movement) on the evolution of Hip Hop/rap. The seeds of the Hip Hop spirit were planted in the 1960s by The Last Poets, Gil Scott-Heron, Don L. Lee (Haki Madhubuti), Sonia Sanchez, Nikki Giovanni, Dick Gregory, and others who recorded, self-published, and performed their revolutionary spoken word poetry on street corners, college campuses, and in small clubs.

There are many theories about the origins of the terms "rap" and "Hip Hop." According to Africana.com, black nationalist H. "Rap" Brown "gave both his name and his oratory style to rap music."[1]

Within the black lexicon, rap connotes many things. Rap is a means of expression. When mastered, you can talk your way in or out of any situation. This is the trademark of the pimp, mack, playa, hustler, politician, and yes, I hate to say it, the preacher.

During the 1960s, my older sisters would say of their male admirers, "Girl, his rap was smooth." My mother would warn them to not listen to those boys pimp talk (rap). In those days, the pimp was known to have a smooth, sweet, convincing way with words (rap). He would weave rhymes and lines with a distinct cadence as in, "You know what I mean, sweet jelly bean?"

If a brotha's rap was weak, he was called a "jive talker" (also a "jive turkey"), meaning he couldn't back up anything he said (rapped about). He was told to "stop jiving."

Rap also referred to crime or trouble as in, "Man, whoever did it better own up 'cause I'm not taking the rap" or "I got a bad rap."

My grandparents called rap "signifying" and told us not to do it because it could get you killed. In the Black Church it's known as "testifying," but it sounds like rap to me. On the streets, rap was the same as playing the good old dozens. My childhood friend Otis (a.k.a. Jughead) was a master at the dozens. Whenever I was on the losing end of a verbal battle I'd solicit his help. We all did. The brotha's rap was so good it would make you want to run home and kiss your mama. You just couldn't win against him.

African Americans have always enjoyed verbal gymnastics involving rhythms and rhymes. To survive in the black community, you'd better have a good rap or you'd better *get* one.

The term Hip Hop is more difficult to track down. Afrika Bambaataa credits his brother, Lovebug Starski, with first coining Hip Hop back in the late 1970s. Umar Bin Hassan, member of the 1960s pre-rap group The Last Poets, remembers,

> "We used to have hops or dances back in the day. We all used to go to them in the schools, churches, and dance halls. If we went to a hop that was really fun and afterwards we talked about it saying 'that was really a hip hop we had last night.'"2

I can recall on many Sunday mornings as we were getting ready for church, my brothers and cousins would discuss the hop (sock hop) from the night before.

"How was the hop?"

"Man, it was hip [cool]. I'm going to slip out to another hip hop next weekend."

the movement takes shape

Lovebug Starski may have first coined Hip Hop, but it was DJ, rapper, and street entertainer, Afrika Bambaataa, who shaped the movement during the mid-1970s. Bambaataa's creation gave voice to a generation that had no connection to disco and was on the fringes of R&B and funk.

Bambaataa's vision was divine. He taught a generation how to be architects and builders of a new culture. His dream of creating a musical force that would educate, unite, incite, and uplift his people became the conscience and drive of Hip Hop. Bambaataa drew loyal followers with his unique performances.

In 1973, Bambaataa founded an umbrella organization called the Universal Zulu Nation, a group of DJs, MCs (masters of ceremony), rappers, dancers, and graffiti artists. The organization was an important influence on rap music and Hip Hop culture in the early years.

A Jamaican DJ named Clive Campbell (a.k.a. DJ Kool Herc) should also receive credit. At the age of 12, Herc moved from Kingston, Jamaica, to the West Bronx in New York.

In Jamaica, DJs would improvise (toast) spoken word poems over recorded music. During the Herc era, rap was a poetic call-and-response between the DJ and the crowd in the club. Herc also introduced the double turntable scratching technique that rappers use in their acts to this day.

With DJ Herc the party never stopped. After finishing his set at a club, he would take the party to the parking lot or another joint. His music was infectious, turntable skills masterful, and the party would last until the early hours of the morning—thus the saying, "party to the break of dawn." Herc was the original Pied Piper of Hip Hop.

My first experience with this new sound was on the dance floor at Central State University back in the day. The DJ would shout, "Can I do my thing boogie down [New York] style?" We corn-fed Midwestern students would shout in unity, "Hell yeah!" and it was on like popcorn. This is how call-and-response between the DJ and the crowd became an integral part of the Hip Hop scene.

Like the civil rights movement of the 1960s, the first rap tunes were a battle cry against ghetto conditions. They celebrated black people as royalty and honored the ancestors (e.g., "The Crown," by Gary Byrd).

The courageous voice that once spoke of the hardships of ghetto life today openly promotes black-on-black crime, drug use, drug dealing, alcoholism, violence, hating on women, and promiscuity. Once rap stood boldly against racism and other social ills; now it promotes the denigration of black children and women, the pimpism of black men, materialism, and our unresolved light-skinned/dark-skinned self-hatred issues.

Those of us who loved Hip Hop's original purpose long for her return. We miss her truthful and revolutionary tongue, sassy walk, bold demeanor, broad and strong shoulders, and unconditional love for the oppressed and underserved. Unfortunately, she has been upstaged by commercialized gangsta rap, which has been blessed and approved by the PTBs (powers that be) of the music industry.

Can you believe it, but rap is now so established that there's a genre called Old School Rap (mid-1970s to mid-1990s). Although many dance tunes emerged during the Old School era, there were still echoes of the original conscience and consciousness. Public Enemy ("Fight the Power") and Queen Latifah ("U-N-I-T-Y") had some positive things to say.

As I drive the highways of America, I often surf the radio dial in search of Old School Rap. Thanks to satellite radio, I've been able to find some of the lost treasures of Hip Hop: the Sugar Hill Gang, Whodini, and Grand Master Flash & the Furious Five.

When conscious Hip Hop degenerated into commercialized gangsta rap in the 1980s, I had to divorce myself from the music I loved. So today I find it therapeutic to go down memory lane to remind myself how far we have come and how far we have to go.

The history is being rewritten as I write these words. There is an attempt to reclassify the early commercialized gangsta rap tunes that were produced after 1984 as Old School Rap. This is the biggest crime ever in Hip Hop, even bigger than removing MCs from rap. The true classics are being buried, out of sight, out of mind, out of our history.

a tower of babel

According to Teen Research Unlimited, the total Hip Hop market is worth $155 billion, and its impact is felt around the world.[3] Sixty percent of rap CDs are purchased by whites. Hip Hop is a global economic force.

"In fact, hip-hop music sales made up 89.2 million, or 11.7%, of the 762.8 million albums sold in the U.S. in 2001—ranking it the third bestseller behind rhythm & blues and alternative music, according to SoundScan, a White Plains, New York-based firm that monitors U.S. album sales. At an average of $12 per CD, that's more than a billion dollars in hip-hop music sales alone. The Hip-Hop Economy slumped in 2001 when the U.S. slid into recession, but sales were more robust in 2000, totaling 101.5 million of the 785.1 million albums sold in 2000 for a total of $1.2 billion. When these revenues are combined with clothing, film, and television revenues, the market grows exponentially."[4]

How did Hip Hop become such an economic power? *TV and music videos.*

Popular music video programs on MTV, BET and now FUSE are considered the best, and most seductive, in the world of music. Many are downright pornographic. Unfortunately, the bump-and-grind and revealing fashions appeal to adolescents and teens, the primary audience. For better or worse (mostly for worse), rap artists are role models and idols, and young people worship them without question.

Try this experiment: criticize your child's favorite rapper. He will probably ...

1. Roll his eyes.
2. Say, "Oh, ma! I don't listen to the lyrics. I just like the beat!"

Now what sense does that make? Hip Hop fans are the most loyal in the world. Not only do they defend their rapper gods, they buy their CDs and fashions, and they imitate rapper behavior, even down to wearing glass (fake) bling.

This lost generation is the soul and engine of Hip Hop. The entertainment industry possesses, finances, markets, and distributes this soul to the world. That's their job, and they're excellent at it. Gangsta rap stars are packaged as the bad boys and girls of the industry, the self-proclaimed dogs/doggs/dawgs/bitches who engage in mental intercourse with the Hip Hop generation. They lyrically hit on our teens, leaving them pregnant with hype and no hope.

As you'll read in this book and nowhere else, Hip Hop has a forked tongue. It is filled with hypocrisies, and the rap star is the master of communicating confusion and mixed messages. Wearing a crucifix made of gold, platinum, and diamonds, he gives thanks to God for making his violent, sexually explicit tunes go triple platinum. He glorifies street violence and the drug culture while telling kids to be all they can be. He shouts "fight the power" without really understanding the historical roots of the battle. He says his art is about keeping it real, but for some reason refuses to show young fans more real realities that would get them the hell out the hood.

With their total immersion in this culture, is it any wonder our teens become dysfunctional on so many levels? I would never blame commercialized gangsta rap alone for turning our children inside out, but it definitely has had a strong influence. This is the culture where most African American youth live. With pornographic lyrics set to hypnotic beats, our young people have found a friend in Hip Hop. The aggression, rage, and anger they often feel toward themselves and others are echoed and celebrated in the music, and the music fuels their developmental urge to rebel against authority in harmful, destructive, and sometimes lawless ways.

What our children don't know is that they are being played big time. They are pawns in a game. They are creative fodder for a global industry from which they receive no profit and no love.

rule of thumb

You don't watch TV. TV is watching you. African American families watch approximately 75 hours of television per week, compared to just 52 hours by their white counterparts. Black children watch on average 20 to 25 more hours of TV than their white counterparts.

The PTBs are aware of this, so they created the following programming rule of thumb: since black children seemingly need more visual reminders of how to become thugs, murderers, victims, and vixens, gangsta rap must be aired during prime time homework and dinnertime hours. Children can sneak and watch uncut, pornographic versions of videos around 2:00 am and 3:00 am when their parents are asleep. They can even get 90 minutes worth of hypersexual eye candy via videos before school.[5]

Remember the double entendres in cartoons and songs that held the attention of parents and children alike? Double entendres seem innocent to children who lack knowledge and experience to understand their deeper meanings. The jokes or lyrics can only be understood by those who have a clue. The Old School music I grew up on was full of double entendres. Remember "Why must I chase the cat/ Nothin' but the dog in me" from George Clinton's "Atomic Dog?"[6]

Nowadays, the PTBs cleverly use all the tricks and techniques of grammar, Ebonics, and slanguage, including onomatopoeia, irony, allusion, metaphor and simile, context clues, word manipulation, hyperbole, hypnotic rhythm, symbolism, sound, alliteration, and Haiku styling. These work together with provocative images to push more than one idea or storyline into our minds, creating a host of emotions that can be both beautiful and painful.

How I long for the good old days of double entendres! I guess rappers and their bosses aren't creative enough to hide adult content beneath the surface. It's just all out there. Even innocent kid topics like candy, candy shops, ice cream, milk shakes, and magic sticks are turned into obvious sexual symbols.

This is the musical diet fed to our children day and night. It's okay to play songs that glorify crime, violence, and pornography on radio shows with high black and Latino listenership. It makes me wonder, are the PTBs doing this on purpose? As you think in your heart, that's how you'll be. Are they actually trying to criminalize black and Latino youth? Are they trying to retard their social, mental, and spiritual growth? Hmmm …

Culture, through the spoken word and literature, carries all the values by which a people are known in history and society. We saw this with our African ancestors, whose voice was silenced via the prohibition against speaking African languages, the cruel cutting of tongues, and the physical breaking of the African drum, the ancient mode of communication. By learning to speak English, they were forced to take on a new culture and values that were foreign to their communal way of life.

Controlling the voice of young people is a war tactic. The goal is to conquer minds and manipulate consumer spending. Revelations 18:23 (Amplified) says, "Your businessmen were the great and prominent men of the earth, and by your magic spells and poisonous charm all *nations* were led astray—seduced and deluded."

The reference was to Babylon, but this is also a perfect description of commercialized gangsta rap's all-consuming influence on young people.

The powerful voice of Hip Hop has been captured and co-opted. Without this prolific voice working to heal the community, genocide on many levels looms ahead, not just for blacks but for all groups who have become mute. For the black voice has always served as a global blueprint for liberation. You'd betta recognize.

hip hop hypocrisies

In *Hip Hop Hypocrisy*, I deal with at least five major hypocrisies that directly contradict the "keeping it real" creed of Hip Hop, and through their mixed messages, create confusion in the minds of youth and chaos in the hood. Hip Hop gangstas ...

1. ... say they're "keeping it real" while constantly flippin' the script—i.e., changing the meanings of words to confuse and confound youth perception.
2. ... love to promote the bling bling lifestyle in their music, but the hood they supposedly represent is characterized by poverty and unemployment.

3. ... are promoted as role models for youth even though, in reality, their rap personas and jobs as pimps, hos, pushers, and spies serve their masters, the PTBs of the music industry.
4. ... rap about adult themes while denying the tricks they play on youth to seduce them into the gangsta lifestyle.
5. ... wear the diamond-encrusted crucifix and Jesus heads and say "Thank you, God" when they win awards, but their lyrics and values promote evil themes.

Hypocrisies are those difficult obstacles we are all bound to encounter on the road of life. A hypocrisy is when you say you believe one thing but act in opposite ways. There's a double standard.

Hip Hop hypocrisies are more than just immoral lies that affect one or two people. They are WMDs (weapons of mass destruction), powerful and effective tools that control young people, their identity, and their money. It's my belief that many of the front men and women of Hip Hop, as well as those operating behind the scenes, can't be trusted. They're hypocrites. The lifestyles of these rappers are nothing like what they portray in their music. Nothing is as it seems under the spotlight.

Interestingly, according to the American Heritage Dictionary, hypocrisy comes from the Greek word *hupokrisis,* meaning "to play a part, pretend."[7] As we'll see throughout this book, some commercialized gangsta rappers play the role of the rapper thug as they live out their real lives as husbands and wives, concerned parents, and entrepreneurs. The Bible says, "Therefore, rid yourselves of all malice and all deceit, hypocrisy, envy, and slander of every kind" (1 Peter 2:1).

In Part 2, I explore five hypocrisies that appear to be most prominent in Hip Hop; you may uncover more. If you want to understand why young people seem like a lost generation, meditate on the hypocrisies. Through the power of words, imagery, music, money, media, and ghettocentric culture, these rapper and PTB hypocrites push opposing thoughts into the minds of their fans at once and to a beat. The psychiatric term for this phenomenon is "cognitive dissonance." The brain gets overwhelmed, blows a fuse, and you end up believing that the two ideas go together. Because they really don't, the brain becomes as moldable as clay, and that's when mind control is highly effective.

In my first book, *Message N/A Bottle: The 40oz Scandal,* I explored how one alcohol ad will often carry at least two opposing ideas, e.g., alcohol will make you sexy even though, in males, it causes chemical castration (premature ejaculation or the inability to get an erection). Yet billions of dollars are spent to work up a feeling that can't exist when you're drunk.

Things are not what they appear to be in Hip Hop. If young people only knew just what went on behind the scenes, they would realize how much they're being played. And young people hate to look stupid. In this war for their minds, we can use this to our advantage. **The hypocrisies are the weakest links in the power matrix**. To blow up a building, you put explosives at the weak points in the structure, then pull the trigger and the entire building falls down.

So it is with the hypocrisies of Hip Hop. Interestingly, the words "hip," "hop," and "hype" are embedded in hypocrisies. Commercialized gangsta rap is Hip Hop hype. Think about it.

A house divided against itself cannot stand, and as we talk and work with our children, this house will fall. We must tell our children what we know about the hypocrisies. Don't keep this valuable information a secret. Don't let their back talk, defensiveness, and ridicule stop you. When you hear an offensive song, deconstruct it and explain it to your child. When they roll their eyes and protest, "It's only a song!" remind them that art shouldn't smell like a fart! If it stinks you should retreat.

Commercialized gangsta Hip Hop/rap is everywhere, but the situation is not hopeless. We must, and we will, rescue our children from its destructive influence. The first step in any revolution is to spread the word. Up until now, the negative elements of Hip Hop have virtually drowned out all dissenting voices. That means our resolve must be stronger and our voices louder. We will put pressure on the weak points in the Hip Hop matrix by counseling young people, teaching them, demonstrating what we know, turning off the TV, exposing them to positive music, and demonstrating the concepts put forth in this book. We must do this until they get it.

I often say that Corporate America understands us better than we understand ourselves. The manipulation of our children's minds for the purpose of financial gain is cold and calculated. Hip Hop has proven to be a willing and powerful instrument.

I believe that rap artists possess a secret to success, but for some reason they refuse to share their knowledge with fans. For these are no ordinary fans. Much has been made of white suburban kids buying most of the hard-core gangsta rap CDs, but the heart, soul, and creative engine of Hip Hop are African American youth, the underserved, impoverished, and poorly educated.

Rap artists owe their success to these young people, and giving back would be the moral way to go. Instead, lies, lies, and more lies. And black youth continue to live below the American ideal.

As we'll see in this book, ghetto culture, mainstream society, Corporate America, the media, and the global economy have formed a tightly woven matrix within which the Hip Hop generation lives. Not all Hip Hop is negative, but over the past 25 to 30 years, corporate and media entities in the matrix have asserted their power and greed. As a result, the negative sub-elements of rap have taken center stage in the theater of war against our children. Keep in mind that as a generation is biblically defined as 25 to 30 years, Hip Hop, as of the writing of this book, will soon be hitting 30. As we'll explore in the chapters that follow, the children of this generation are imitating the behaviors of their gangsta idols. If only they knew that their idols' personas are just illusions.

not all bad

Not all Hip Hop is bad, but the bad is out front, fully armed, and loaded with images and messages children, adolescents, and teens should never have been exposed to.

Other authors and scholars have written on the more positive aspects of Hip Hop/rap. I have chosen to deal with the negative because this appears to have a much more persuasive power over our children. Unfortunately, the negative has, in the language of scripture, become host to principalities and powers. Our war is not with rappers per se, but with the evil alliances they have made and evil ideas they rap about.

With the billions of dollars that are generated by this movement, it's easy to feel overwhelmed and powerless when trying to work with young people. Don't give up on our young people. This book will give you the information you need to help them see the lies for themselves and to achieve maturity in one whole and healthy piece.

It's true that some rap artists have done positive things in a highly corrupted climate. In the mid-1990s, pop star Prince declared himself Sony's slave. That was no joke, nor was it an exaggeration. Today, many of the biggest and brightest stars are nothing more than well paid slaves working as overseers for the promotion of corporate Hip Hop.

As you'll read in this book, the multinational entertainment corporations have Hip Hop on lockdown. Still, artists and producers such as P. Diddy, Master P, Missy Elliott, Nelly, Dr. Dre, Lil' Kim, Ice Cube, Jay-Z, and Russell Simmons have created empires with their own record labels, fashion lines, and more.

But in the greater war, Corporate America still controls global manufacturing, media, marketing, and distribution channels. As a result, they control what rap has to say and who gets to hear it.

In my work in the trenches with this Hip Hop generation as a counselor, certified violence prevention specialist, and educator, I have noticed that few scholars and thinkers dare deal with the damage commercialized gangsta rap and Hip Hop culture have done to the psyche of young people, particularly children of poverty. There seems to be a fascination with the movement in the Ebony Towers of America. Members of the black intelligentsia have become star struck apologists who, with their rose colored glasses, know all about the history of rap music but are strangely silent on what gangsta Hip Hop is doing to the fans, the true victims of this war.

Some scholars have dealt at length with the misogynistic and pornographic themes in rap, and they are to be applauded. *Hip Hop Hypocrisy* digs even deeper into the subliminal and entrainment aspects of why the music is so successful.

In Part 3, I offer strategies to rescue our children and blow up commercialized Hip Hop's destructive influences. This book is a challenge to rap artists to reconsider the product they're putting out and to use their money, energy, and influence to help empower African American youth to become economically self-sufficient and psychologically whole.

Those of us who work with and love young people must be strong in our resolve to speak the truth and expose the hypocrisies because only the truth will set our children and community free.

If our goal is to help children and youth grow into healthy, productive adults, then we had better recognize that there is a force to be reckoned with out there that is opposed to this goal. It is my strong belief that commercialized Hip Hop/gangsta rap means our children no good, and children are blind to this fact. The messages and images promoted in this music are completely contrary to what's needed to develop healthy minds and spirits.

We must question how overexposure to degrading images and lyrics has impacted the welfare and pathology of a generation. For example, how has commercialized Hip Hop contributed to the decline of educational achievement among children of color? The high rate of incarceration? Violence and intoxication?

We must critically examine all hooks in Hip Hop songs and argots that double as subliminal instructions to destroy self, property, and life. We must question the collective pathology that enables us to dance to this music.

Why do the PTBs promote prison culture as fashionable and acceptable to our youth? We must question the bosses of the wannabe bosses. There was a time when rap music was proudly referred to as the CNN of the Hip Hop nation. Now it is seen as the comedy central of black pathology.

Part 1

Get the Hell out the Hood

Chapter 1

Framework for Understanding Hip Hop Youth

"We ... estimate that aggregate expenditures by 15-to 24-year-olds in the 15 urban areas with the highest concentration of multicultural youth will total $203 billion in 2007. This represents cumulative growth of 26.7%."[1]

"Gangsta Hip Hop is not childproof." **Alfred "Coach" Powell**

Brothers & Sisters, Hip Hop is a $155 billion industry, and its primary consumers—African Americans, Afro-Latinos, and other youth—are measured by the amounts they spend. I have a problem with this. Our young people are souls to be rescued, not units to be counted.

Although Hip Hop appeals to all nationalities and races, in this book I focus primarily on African American and Latino youth because they are the groups most blatantly exploited by the principalities and powers of Corporate America.

We must learn all we can about Hip Hop youth. Marketers say they're the 15 to 24 year-olds who have access to billions of dollars in disposable income. Voter registration campaigns target the 18 to 30 year-old segment of Hip Hop because they know their votes can determine the outcomes of political battles.

However, from the perspectives of education, ministry, social services, and parenting, Hip Hop youth are all that and more.

Those of us who work with youth know that Hip Hop captures children as young as two years old. They love rap, and although they can barely talk, they can repeat the lyrics of some rap tunes.

Two, three, and four-year olds are dressed by their Hip Hop parents in baby gangsta gear. I've heard toddlers curse you out before saying "da da" or "mama." That's their genius and our challenge.

Urban babies are born into the Hip Hop matrix and they will live there until possibly 40 or 45 years old (due to Prolonged Adolescent Syndrome, which will be explained later in this chapter). They may even die there. It makes you wonder what tunes the future elders of our communities will fondly hum as they remember the good old days of juking and other types of dirty dancing. Will they still be saggin' or showing their g-strings at 65, 70, or 80 years old?

The negative elements of Hip Hop are dangerous because they influence children during the most critical stages of emotional and cognitive development. Psychologist Erik H. Erikson identified eight stages that are dependent on social interactions with parents, teachers, etc.; developmental biologist Jean Piaget identified four. While both Piaget and Erikson are concerned with childhood development, Erikson also looks at the future impact of current conditions on the psychological health of adults and elders.

My concern is for children and youth ages two to 18. Although they're old enough to drive and go to war, 18 year-olds still lack the maturity to handle this fallen music, even though they listen to it 24/7. The following tables list the stages I consider most relevant to African American children ages two to 18 and beyond who live in the Hip Hop/ghetto matrix. Through this framework, we can begin to understand the detrimental effects of gangsta Hip Hop culture on the hearts and minds of our children.

I'm a student of Afrocentric scholarship, but I will present the models of Erikson and Piaget since many of the psychologists, educators, and counselors who work with our target population have been trained to use their models.

TABLE 1. PIAGET'S STAGES OF
INTELLECTUAL DEVELOPMENT[2]

Developmental Stage & Approx. Age	Behavior	Hip Hop Concerns
Sensory Motor Period *0–24 months*	Evidence of an internal representational system symbolizing the problem-solving sequence before actually responding. Deferred imitation.	• Does a pornographic rap video on TV help develop internal representational system? • Are parents/siblings playing x-rated rap music in the home/car? • Does baby ever hear music (e.g., classical, jazz, gospel) that stimulates cognitive/spiritual development?
Preoperational Phase *2–4 years*	Increased use of verbal representation, but speech is egocentric. The beginnings of symbolic vs. simple motor play. Transductive reasoning. Can think and talk about something without object being present.	• Will child prefer rap lyrics (egocentric) or spiritual/gospel lyrics (other-centered)? • As symbolic skills develop, how will child internalize diamond-encrusted cross hanging on neck of rapper and other symbols of materialism?

Intuitive Phase *4–7 years*	Easy to believe in magical increase, decrease, dis-appearance. Reality not firm. Perceptions domi-nate judgment. In moral-ethical realm, the child cannot show prin-ciples underlying best behavior. Only uses simple do's and don'ts imposed by authority.	• Since child doesn't yet have a firm grasp on reality, how will rap phallic symbols (e.g., magic stick) be internalized and acted upon later? • Is the child being taught values via rap videos? • Does rap idol serve as child's moral author-ity?
Period of Concrete Operations *7–11 years*	Child is capable of concrete problem solving.	• How do rap videos portray critical think-ing skills (e.g., in a police chase)? • How does rap teach problem solving?

| Period of Formal Operations

11–15 years | Abstract thought. Thinking becomes less tied to concrete reality. Prepositional logic, as-if and if-then steps. | • How do subliminals embedded in rap CD tracks, music video frames, and alcohol ads impact abstract, logical thinking?
• What kind of logical as-if and if-then statements are children deducing when they see three barely clothed females in a hot tub or when they see black males rapping in front of a prison? |

TABLE 2. ERIKSON'S STAGES OF HUMAN DEVELOPMENT[3]

Developmental Stage & Approx. Age	Behavior	Hip Hop Concerns
Stage 1: Learning Basic Trust vs. Basic Mistrust (**Hope**) *First 1 to 2 years of life*	If well parented, baby develops trust, security, and basic optimism. If not, he learns not to trust others.	As rap music plays during baby's nap time, will the discordant, minor tones affect his ability to have secure and restful sleep and less waking irritability? Will this affect his trust for parents to keep him safe?

Stage 2: Learning Autonomy vs. Shame (**Will**) *18 months–2 years to 3½–4 years of age*	The purpose of this stage is to develop self-confidence so that toddler can be proud vs. ashamed. This "terrible two's" stage is full of tantrums and no's.	• Young Hip Hop parents often begin harsh discipline at this stage. Will toddler emerge from this stage ashamed or proud? • Do toddlers learn to feel pride or shame when they juke dance at family reunions and church picnics? Are they praised for their ability to dance this way?
Stage 3: Learning Initiative vs. Guilt (**Purpose**) *3½ to 5 years of age*	This stage is about play. The healthy child learns to fanta-size, cooperate, lead, and follow. At-risk children are paralyzed by guilt, are fearful, loners, dependent on adults, and under-developed in play skills and fantasy.	• How do sexual and materialistic themes in gangsta rap help feed fantasies? • Since rap content often conflicts with traditional cultural values, do rap-inspired fantasies lead to confusion and guilt?

Stage 4: Industry vs. Inferiority (**Competence**) *School age (K–middle school)*	In school, children learn to master academics and social rules relating to peers, progressing from free play to rules-bound team play. Successful children learn to be industrious. At-risk children experience failure, defeat, and inferiority.	• What are children learning about the value of education, the work ethic, and cooperation from rap music and videos? • Upon what foundation is child building self-esteem: the mastery of reading or the watching of rap videos? • Are children's peer relationships being monitored?
Stage 5: Learning Identity vs. Identity Diffusion (**Fidelity**) *13–14 to 20 years of age*	Develops a sense of self in relationship to others and to internal thoughts and desires. This is when children ask "Who am I?" Sexual identity is established.	• With 24/7 TV watching, how are rap videos influencing youth's evolving identity? • How does gender bending in rap videos influence gender development?

Stage 6: Learning Intimacy vs. Isolation (**Love**) *Young adult years*	Develops ability to give and receive love. Begins to make long-term commitments to relationships.	• How does gangsta rap influence views of the opposite sex? • How does rap's portrayal of love/sex influence the ability to commit to long-term relationships? • Given that children are our future and that our children love Hip Hop, how will rap impact the black family of the future?
Stage 7: Learning Generativity vs. Self-Absorption (**Care**) *Adulthood years*	Generativity—the ability to unselfishly look beyond self and care for others—is developed in this stage. There is also concern for the next generation(s).	• Will egocentrism and instant gratification themes in rap prevent Hip Hop adults from caring for others and the future of the community? • Will elders, children, and the disabled be able to depend on the generativity of Hip Hop adults?

Stage 8: Integrity vs. Despair (**Wisdom**) *Elder years*	If all previous stages have been resolved successfully, then the elder years will be the peak of adjustment, integrity, and wisdom. Otherwise, elders will suffer disgust and despair.	When they look back, will Hip Hop elders be proud of the legacy that was Hip Hop? Will they desire that their children, grandchildren, and future generations live according to Hip Hop values?

In addition to Piaget's and Erikson's works, my own theories of African American child development have evolved. In my 20 (plus) years of work in the trenches as a coach, certified violence prevention specialist, and parent, I have discovered two highly disturbing behavioral trends that are creating major obstacles to the healthy maturation of African American youth: Prolonged Adolescent Syndrome and Psychomedia Perpetrator Disorder.

Prolonged Adolescent Syndrome (PAS). This is also known as the Peter Pan Syndrome or arrested development but with pathologies that are unique to African American culture. For example, Michael Jackson's Neverland was about staying a child and the disaster that can occur when an adult refuses to grow up.

Hip Hop appeals primarily to children, but many rap icons are fully grown adult men and women. While some in the rap game grew up and went on to other endeavors (Queen Latifah, Jay-Z, Will Smith, etc.), others just don't want to grow up. Some rap icons hitting 40 years old are still saggin' their pants, wearing pony tails, and using adolescent speech patterns and slanguage.

When young children worship rap stars, they're idolizing everything about them. They want to imitate them. Remember all the Michael Jackson look-alikes from the *Thriller* and *Off the Wall* era?

Grown men and women with Prolonged Adolescent Syndrome act like children, and they influence young fans during critical stages of development (see Tables 1 and 2 above).

Middle-aged men with Prolonged Adolescent Syndrome refuse to act their age. So what age are they acting? I asked my editor, Donna Marie, for her opinion and she remembered that it was in the fourth grade when she saw her first pornographic picture. A boy in her classroom had drawn a picture of a penis. He shoved it at her, thinking it was funny.

That was back in the late 1960s. Today, a fourth grade boy might drop his already saggin' pants to expose himself to a girl. In fact, one inner city teacher told me that four boys were recently caught in her school's bathroom simulating a sex act.

But these are extreme behaviors. Mostly boys at this age are fighting, wrestling, playing the dozens, and playing video games with each other.

Still, they are beginning to get curious about girls. They don't *want* to like girls, but they can't help it. They feel more comfortable (and safer) bonding with other boys, but they can't deny their awkward feelings. Girls have been flirting with them since kindergarten, and they're finally starting to get it. A pack mentality emerges as a defense against girls—and rappers in full-blown Prolonged Adolescent Syndrome show them how to put girls to the side and stay bonded with their "boyz." Further complicating this situation is the fact that most black boys are being raised by their mothers (fathers absent), which means they have few models of healthy male-female relationships to learn from in the hood.

Take a look at a rap video, any rap video. Nine times out of ten you'll hear sexually explicit lyrics—grown men telling young females what they want sexually. Hardly ever will you see a man and woman in a loving, adult relationship, and forget marriage. The purpose of females in rap videos is to dance sexually and serve as a member of a playa's/pimp's stable. Usually one or two females will have starring roles in the video while many others dance suggestively in the background. In the world of rap videos, females serve no other purpose.

With more than 70 percent of African American children being raised in single parent homes (father absent), who's teaching young boys how to relate appropriately to girls? Rap videos? Gangstas, pimps, and playas in the hood? Lord, help us.

Interestingly, experts say that fourth and fifth grades are academic make-or-break years for African American boys. When was the last time you heard a rap tune celebrate getting good grades? Hmmm …

What about the women of rap? How old are they acting? Girls seem to intuitively know a lot about male-female relationships from early ages. Watch them play with dolls. But black girls are also suffering from the lack of fathers in the home. They begin to get aggressive about the pursuit of boys at 12 and 13 years of age, because that's what they see older females in the community doing. As their bodies fill out in adolescence, their clothes get tighter because society and rap videos say this is the way to dress. Their Hip Hop mothers also may be dressing this way. With their sexually explicit lyrics and one-track themes ("get the boy," "I got your man," or "I'm better than other girls"), the women of rap seem to be acting out the pre-teen and teen years.

Psychomedia Perpetrator Disorder (PPD). African American youth view more TV than any other racial group. This has created a widespread epidemic of PPD in the Hip Hop/ghetto matrix. PPD is media addiction, which, as many studies are discovering, can lead to media copycatting, i.e., the imitation of behaviors viewed in cartoons, sitcoms, movies, video games, music videos, etc. How are underserved African American youth processing images of sparkling bling and shaking behinds in music videos from their less-than-perfect circumstances? When they watch rap videos, what behaviors are they fantasizing? Since they can't yet separate fantasy from reality, what is the 24/7 viewing of videos and TV in general doing to their value system, especially if parents and the church are no longer the primary influences in their lives? How will 24/7 viewing of videos shape goals and dreams and actions taken?

Among African American youth (and the community at large), there is a disproportionately high rate of Psychomedia Perpetrator Disorder that directly correlates to high risk behaviors and low academic performance. More research needs to be done in this area, but my educated guess is that the pathology shows up in at least 75 percent of African American youth that overindulge in gangsta/Hip Hop culture.

Perhaps the most important question of all is this: Does Hip Hop promote a mature African American racial and cultural identity to youth? Hip Hop shows only one way to be black, one way to be a man, and one way to be a woman. The sub-realm of Hip Hop presents confusing and distorted African American and gender identities. As African American youth are so thoroughly immersed in this culture, my fear is that they can't even begin to understand what a real loving relationship is or what it means to be a producer (vs. a consumer).

At least one industry exec understands why children should be protected from the music he himself produces:

> "I have a 7-year-old daughter, and she can't listen to my music. She can't listen to it in the car, not in the room, and she can't watch videos. Right now she loves Usher. His music is good, but the lyrics are a bit much for her—especially once she starts to understand what he's saying about adult relationships. So I went and bought her the Hip-Hop Bears CD, and we listened to it together, and she loves it. I gave Usher's CD to her mother."[4] **Jay "Icepick" Jackson,** senior vice-president, A&R, Ruff Ryders Records

Chapter 2

Types of Rap

"I rap in such a way where the hood can respect it but I can sit right in front of a white executive and spit the exact same verse and he'll understand at least 80% of it."[1] **Kanye West**

"When you talk about rap you have to understand that rap is part of the Hip-Hop culture."[2] **Afrika Bambaataa**

"I like to make music, I like rap music. Even if I'm white, I support that music. If I want to support it or any other white kid wants to support it more power to them."[3] **Kid Rock**

There are different types of rap that serve different purposes and reach different audiences. Each type of rap features critical thinking and creative communication skills, which can be used for good or destruction.

Where once rap was our weapon in the fight for justice and freedom ("fight the power"[4]), now our rap has no power left for the fight. Rap has become commercialized and cheapened by grown men and women. Have we forgotten that rap is the vernacular, feelings, spoken passion, and culture of African people throughout the Diaspora? Rap conveys our conditions, spirituality, and history. It vividly illustrates our dramas and traumas, collective mood, and political agenda. Rap is the word, the alpha and the omega and everything in between.

I love playing with words, and in rap I see a powerful acronym: the **R**evelations of **A**frican **P**eople.

Rap is also the **R**eevaluation of **A**frican **P**eople.

Rap is the art of storytelling, a skill mastered by the elders or griot of the village. These masters of memory are held in high esteem for they keep the stories and history of our people alive via the oral tradition. Our historical struggles as African people demand that the words we rap/speak should help author our emancipation and manifest our love for our community. Words that demean, slander, and wound others can never be considered true rap because they create chaos, violence, and filth.

The eloquence of rap is exquisite when used properly—it builds us up and doesn't tear us down. Its true intent is to heal, raise consciousness, and give us some peace.

I see another acronym in rap: **R**eaching **A**fter **P**eople. Rap has the power to reach many groups of people, which is why there are so many different types of rap. The following are just a few styles of rap. Keep in mind that in her quest to reach the world, rap constantly changes. My definitions may differ from yours; no one definition can accurately capture the essence of any style of rap. But if you will, allow the following list to provide a common basis for discussion in this book.

- **Rap or Hip Hop Rap.** A combination of styles, such as classical, jazz, R&B, and reggae, mixed with human beatbox rhythms and turntable scratching. Although rap is meant to be spoken, many tunes feature back-up singers.
- **Political or Conscious Rap.** Promotes the black power struggle. Offers intellectual criticism of the police, government, systemic racism, poverty, and oppression. A dying art form.
- **Soul or R&B Rap.** An adult Motown soul sound with a Hip Hop flavor.
- **Poetry or Spoken Word Rap.** A smooth, poetic, personal dialogue pertaining to family, personal struggle, Black-on-Black Love, and intimacy.
- **Gangsta Rap.** Contains graphic and derogatory language and advocates black-on-black gang violence, sex, and the sale and use of drugs.

- **Misogynist Rap.** Contains lyrics and video images that demean women as sex objects. Advocates violence against women. Some of these tunes have referred to females as chicken heads, hood rats, pigeons, hos, and bitches.
- **Gospel or Holy Hip Hop Rap.** Signals the arrival of Hip Hop in the church. Features the rhythms and bass of funk, rock, R&B, and gospel while lyrically praising the Lord.
- **Commercial Rap or Crossover Rap.** Black culture goes mainstream. Used in ad jingles, movies, etc. to sell clothes, food, alcohol, vehicles—anything. Uses black stereotypes under the guise of humorous entertainment.
- **Crunk Rap.** Simplistic but aggressive up-tempo bass club beats with repetitive Ebonics (a.k.a. country) lyrics. Themes in crunk, gangsta, and misogynist rap are sometimes used lyrically with call-and-response. Drenched in old racial stereotypes. Sexually explicit.
- **Rock (Hop) Rap.** Fuses rock or Heavy Metal with rap. Includes human beatboxing and turntable scratching.
- **Hippie-Hop Rap.** A fusion of 1970s funk with 1960s retro in both sound and look. Lyrics feature slang hooks.
- **Hick Hop.** Racial slang for white country artists who rap their stories instead of singing traditional Country Western style.
- **Reggaetone Rap.** With its strong dancehall beats, this tropical style of reggae fuses Jamaican and Latin music and can be heard throughout the Caribbean and Latin America. Like its U.S. cousins, the lyrics are sexist and misogynist.

Chapter 3

The 10 Commandments
of Hip Hop

By Stephanie Mwandishi Gadlin

*Before you begin reading the hypocrisies in Part 2, please take
the time to read the following 10 Commandments of Hip Hop.
Veteran researcher Stephanie Mwandishi Gadlin has brilliantly
deciphered the hidden tenets agreed upon by rappers and the
PTBs (powers that be) in principle (if not in reality).* **Coach**

The more I think about it, I am convinced there must be a Hip
Hop constitution that mandates how rappers represent musically.
The mandate, in the form of a recording contract, is actually a set of
commandments authored by the "music establishment," otherwise
known as the "industry," to ensure the artist's marketability in an
already saturated genre.

COMMANDMENT I

Thou must dis' black women (and other women of color). You
are allowed to distinguish between bitches, hos, and "real sisters" only
during interviews when asked to clarify your statements. You must
talk about beating a woman up at least once on your CD or demo.
On at least four (4) but no more than five (5) singles/demos you must
talk about having rough and unprotected sex with a woman. You
must also refer to your girlfriend or wife as a "bitch" in an endearing way. All music videos must reflect the aforementioned notions.
You can talk about doing things to other people's mothers as acts of

creative expression. You may also refer endearingly to an unplanned child as a "bastard," "shorty," "lil nigga," or "Lil G." By honoring this commandment you vow to never rally behind black females or support a strong family bond. You see her only as an object for sex and to reap the repercussions of your rage. You also believe she is only out to get you.

Supplement for females: Thou must dis' black men. Female rappers are allowed to distinguish against niggas, bustas, scrubs, and punks. You must lyrically emasculate them in every way possible. On at least one (1) CD or demo you must destroy his character by either calling him a homosexual or talking about his lack of money. You are allowed to refer to your boyfriend or husband as your "nigga" in an endearing way. All music videos must reflect aforementioned notions. By honoring this Commandment you vow to never identify with the black male's struggle against white supremacy. You vow to never support a strong family bond. You also uphold the tenets that all of his problems are of his own doing. You see him as only an object for sex and money. You believe he is only out to get you.

COMMANDMENT II

Thou must kill. You must lyrically take the life of at least one other black person in order to secure a hit CD. This law does not promote the physical killing of another person. However, it is not against the law to assassinate another person on record. You must only talk about killing your own kind, however, or other cultures may sue you for inciting racial violence. You must express pleasure in the kill. The kill must be graphic and extensive in detail. The consumer must always be left with the feeling that taking a person's life (lyrically) was justified. Most of the lyrical murders must be done by guns; however, creativity allows for poisoning, stabbings, beatings, stomping, and suffocating. You do not distinguish between male or female kills. By keeping this Commandment you vow to never claim acts of genocide publicly even when you are a victim of violent repression yourself.

You also agree to lyrical acts of black-on-black violence, as well as prolific incidents of brutality.

COMMANDMENT III

Thou must covet. Thou must talk about lusting after things that do not belong to you. You must have an unusual craving for things that do not belong to you. Your desire must be so strong that you unwittingly uphold Commandment II. This law does not advocate that you physically go after the material possessions of someone in your community. By keeping this Commandment you vow to never promote a strong work ethic in your music or to speak against greed, lust, and impulsive behavior. In fact, you now believe greed is healthy.

COMMANDMENT IV

Thou must have a lot of sex. You must have no fewer than three (3) songs on your CD or demo that promote sexual intercourse with one or a group of individuals. You cannot express a deep sense of love or marriage. Thou shalt not talk about commitment, bonding, and intimacy. You can only talk about sex in its purest and rawest terms. Do not use "make love," "provide pleasure," or "procreate." You must never mention a sexually transmitted disease in the context of these records. You can, however, discuss the use of contraceptives, but only if you're referring to sexual intercourse with a ho. (See Commandment I).

If you are under age 16, you may substitute sex with flirting and fantasies about being intimate with your teacher, neighbor's child, or another rapper. You must be creative in your graphic details of sexual intercourse so to leave nothing to the imagination. The details can be slightly skewed in order to circumvent radio censors. However, this does not excuse radio edits from removing references to sex. Therefore stay ahead of the game by using clever phrases with dual and triple meanings. By keeping this Commandment, you vow to never promote unconditional or agape love in your community, promote the black family in a positive light, or uplift male/female relationships.

COMMANDMENT V

Thou must celebrate the drug culture. Thou must condone and identify with the proliferation of drugs in the black community. You should create endearing lyrical expressions to identify various narcotics and mind-altering substances. Though you are not to personally distribute or purchase illegal substances, you may allude to it lyrically. (To protect industry investment, we discourage musical confessions to crimes where the statute of limitations have not run out.) You may allude to a war on drugs, but only as justification to carry out Commandment II. You must continually suggest that selling drugs or "slangin'" produces the only legitimate income for impoverished black people. All music videos must either glamorize this lifestyle by showing the "success" of the narcotic trade, or glamorize prison living. You should refer to drug addicted citizens in comical terms that illicit disgust, laughter, fear, pity, or retribution. You are never to question U.S. drug policy. You can never promote healthy living and thinking. Nor can you advocate moderation in tobacco and liquor consumption. By keeping this Commandment you vow to never discuss the impact of drug addiction among people of color, on the community's overall health, on the prison industrial complex, or on the black family.

COMMANDMENT VI

Thou must rarely talk about God and spirituality. You must lyrically condone atheism and a false belief system that negates the existence of a higher being. You must routinely question the existence of a god by lyrically challenging him/her/it to take your life or to grant you three wishes. You are to refer to yourself as a god who gives and takes life.

You may lyrically create your own religion (see Commandment X) based on a ghetto belief system. Thou shalt not talk about life and death as it relates to spirituality or a sense of purpose. You should never speak of scripture or religious texts. You are prohibited from acknowledging any spiritual beliefs that may have been instilled in you by family. However, you may identify with a Jesus by wearing a large, diamond encrusted piece whereby you may brag about its cost. Under no circumstance are you to promote prayer, reflection, meditation, atonement, redemption, sacrifice, mercy, or grace. The consumer fan base must identify with your lack of spiritual grounding by believing that the only gods are sex and money. By keeping this Commandment you vow to limit your personal spiritual growth and development. You also vow to never be seen publicly in a church, synagogue, mosque, temple, or other house of worship and reflection.

Commandment VII

Thou must promote capitalism. On no fewer than four (4) singles or demo records you must talk about money as if it were a living, breathing thing. You must talk about making it, taking it, and the love of it. Your lyrics must always place money over love, over women, over religion (see Commandment VI). You must never talk about saving and investing. You can, however, say the words "currency exchange," "welfare check," "first of the month," and "food stamps." You must never talk about the pooling of resources. You can never equate capitalism with poverty. You must never mention the IMF, WTO, or Federal Reserve. In fact, never mention banking or the stock market at all. Do not mention technology. Do not discuss taxing. Do not discuss the federal budget (see Commandment V). You must promote individual wealth over community wealth.

You should talk about all of your purchases, specifically naming makers/distributors of expensive jewelry, cars, clothing, and liquor. Once you become a successful entertainer you should purchase a very big house and no fewer than three (3) expensive cars. Publicly, you should live within a lavish lifestyle in order to please your consumer fan base that now lives vicariously through your music. Your lifestyle should include, but not be limited to: living in exclusive communities, catering to huge entourages, routinely eating at expensive restaurants, flying to Europe for fashion shows, purchasing designer clothing only, ordering platinum and diamond encrusted jewelry for your body and teeth, purchasing expensive weapons and devices, frequent partying, and purchasing big quantities of expensive liquor and tobacco/cigars. Thou should consistently ridicule those who cannot afford the afore-mentioned items. By keeping this Commandment you vow to always promote a consumer culture vs. a producer culture.

COMMANDMENT VIII

Thou cannot have a sense of history. Never ever refer to any historical event that may cause the consumer to think about his/her relation to history. Your role is to entertain, not educate. Thou art prohibited from speaking of the following: Trans-Atlantic slave trade, African holocaust, Reconstruction, the civil rights movement, the black power movement, the "real" Harlem Renaissance, and so forth. You can never mention the following people: Martin Luther King Jr., Hannibal, Mansa Musa, Harriet Tubman, Sojourner Truth, David Walker, Nat Turner, George Jackson, El-Hajj Malik Shabazz (Malcolm X), Jesse Jackson, Patrice Lumumba, Nelson Mandela, Winnie Mandela, Steve Biko, Louis Farrakhan, Booker T. Washington, W.E.B. DuBois, Huey Newton, Fred Hampton, Bobby Seale, Kwame Ture, Ida B. Wells, Assata Shakur—unless you are making fun of their names, causes, or crusades (e.g., Rah Digga's Harriet Thugman). Do not mention Africa, Brazil, the Caribbean, or Asia unless to disparage. By keeping this Commandment, you vow to never promote a sense of awareness, knowledge of self, or the con-sumer's global relationship to kindred spirits.

COMMANDMENT IX

Thou must not advocate. Thou art prohibited from advocating anything that has a socially redeeming value. Your lyrics must reflect a detachment from the social, political, and economic reality of your community. Your lyrics can occasionally ridicule people who march, protest, and advocate social causes. The consumer should never assume that you read newspapers, magazines, or books. In other words, it must appear that nothing that happens in the "real" non-entertainment world has any personal affect on your thinking. Nor should the consumer of your CD or demo walk away with the belief that you care about anything other than Commandments IV and VII.

Never talk about the "industry." By keeping this commandment, understand you must never appear at a non-entertainment-related event, unless of course you are entertaining. You must never donate money, resources, or materials to needy organizations, families, or causes. When questioned about this you must defend your position by claiming you are an entertainer and that's all. You can never discuss relevant social issues during interviews.

Thou art not responsible for the behavior encouraged by your music because thou art not responsible for marketing and sales to minors, unstable individuals, or mentally ill citizens. You understand that you cannot attend rallies, sermons, marches, picnics, festivals, or workshops that have nothing to do with entertainment or the recording industry.

Commandment X

Thou must promote all things ghetto. Thou may never define the word ghetto or discuss its creation. You must uphold its principals and create new creeds. You must lyrically create a fictional account of ghetto living that inspires comradeship and a sense of pride among its residents. Your lyrics must create a ghetto dweller that is proud to live in the ghetto and takes offense at others moving into it. You must celebrate ghetto life by reminiscing about days in poverty and your mothers on welfare and your fathers who were not there. Also, your lyrics must offer the mainstream a rare glimpse inside a "socio-economic matrix" while allowing them psychologically off the hook for the ghetto's creation.

You must celebrate ghetto language, ghetto living, ghetto housing, ghetto clothing, ghetto hairstyles, ghetto sexual habits, ghetto education, ghetto economics, and ghetto self-hatred. You must romanticize poverty with tales of sex, drugs, money, creed, and fear. The ghetto must become a magical place. By keeping this Commandment you vow to create and then instill pride in a false culture of poverty, crime, drugs, illegitimacy, ignorance, and apathy. You also vow to attribute the ghetto only to black people.

You vow to never leave the ghetto matrix psychologically, even when your economic status changes (see Commandment VII). In other words, you will remember to "keep it real."

By keeping the aforementioned Commandments, we, "the industry," guarantee the following:

1. Unlimited marketing success and crossover appeal.
2. A guaranteed income.
3. Fame beyond your wildest dreams.
4. Unlimited (but recoupable) industry resources.
5. Several music awards, citations, and honors.
6. Protection from community repercussions.

Part 2

Trapped in the Matrix

Chapter 1

Hypocrisy 1—

Keeping It Real//
Flippin' the Script

"As a parent, I place restrictions on my son [Lil Romeo]. And, while creativity is a must for this industry, we have to keep it real." **Master P** speaking to the 2002 Congressional Black Caucus and performer of "F**k a Bitch Cause I'm Paid"

"Image is what colonizes the mind." **John Hendrick Clarke**

When rappers are confronted about the lyrics in their songs they love to say "I'm just keeping it real." In other words, they're just telling the truth as they see it. Keeping it real is a Hip Hop value. If you're not keeping it real, you've sold out. But I have problems with keeping it real as it's played out in Hip Hop.

Reading the above quote, Master P seems to be a concerned, loving father who protects his son, rapper Lil' Romeo. (By the way, what's a young person doing with the name Romeo, which in the hood implies that he's a playa? Lil Mack, which is just as bad, suggests a pimp or sexual predator. Also, why does a growing *male* teenager have baby hair? We'll talk about gender bending, the hyper sexualization of youth in rap, and Prolonged Adolescent Syndrome throughout the book.)

As a father, I want to know what restrictions Master P placed on his son. Maybe he banned his son from watching his own videos. No concerned, loving father in his right mind would let a child watch gangsta and misogynistic rap videos, especially the uncut versions. Yet these rappers, who may be concerned, loving fathers, consistently produce such filth for *your* children.

On the BET program *Blueprint* (2005), rap superstar Nelly stated, "I monitor what my child watches on TV and I'm gone most of the time. I don't understand why people who are home with their children can't control what their children watch."

Nelly's right. It's parents' responsibility to protect their children. But in the interest of keeping it real, hard core rap tunes are shot at African American children like drive-bys 24/7. What happened to protecting our children? You think your child's safe watching a cartoon during primetime when suddenly an inappropriate commercial for the latest rap CD or Hip Hop video game flashes images that no child should see. Behind your back he may sneak and flip to BET, MTV, or one of a half dozen other video programs. If you have children, you know what I'm talking about. They may go to their cousin's house where negative rap is in the air all day. You can't watch your children 24/7, that's unrealistic. In the hood, media is all around them, and you can't turn off the atmosphere. Hip Hop/gangsta rap is like alcohol billboards in the hood; it's everywhere. You can't take a walk down the street without passing a car playing rap so loud that the windows shake.

Not to pick on Master P and Nelly, but I believe they are typical of many rappers who promote pornography and materialism/consumerism through their music. There's a lot of hypocrisy going on. Their secret lives would shock and disappoint their young rebellious fans. I bet you fifty cent that many rap artists are spiritual people who attend church, mosque, or temple, or at least believe in God, a Higher Power, a Supreme Being. Rap artists are constantly thanking God at the Grammys, Source Awards, Soul Train Awards, American

Music Awards, BET, MTV, and Image Awards, so they must have some sort of spiritual belief.

True spirituality is the antidote to ghetto conditions, and our children need it. Unlike the original rap tunes that were trying to change conditions in the hood, today's artists refuse to teach spiritual truths. They hold up the cross but deny the mission. They seem to have a form of godliness while denying its power (2 Timothy 3:5). *This is hypocritical.*

What's really confusing is when Hip Hop keeps it allegedly real in their word choices. My generation led the way when we flipped bad to mean good, and we've been calling our loved ones nigga since the plantation.

African Americans have mastered this right-brained ability to flip words, which is why playing the dozens and other word games is so popular. This ability also enables youth to improvise rap lyrics on the spot (battling, spittin'), rhymes and all. It's a gift.

But it can be a trap, too. Within the Hip Hop matrix, where the negative elements have taken over, everything has to be reexamined if we are to rescue our children.

Later in this section, we'll look at how our youth's gift at word-play has been exploited in a negative way. Take the word "pimp," for example. "Pimp, pimping, pimp juice, pimp paraphernalia like goblets and canes, the pimp lifestyle, ethos and 'code of honor' have permeated hip-hop culture and beyond."[1]

Back in the day, a pimp was a man who sold women's bodies on the street for money. Pimp was a word with a very specific definition. The pimp was NOT a role model in the African American community. He was not someone to be admired and imitated. He was someone to be avoided at all cost. Parents aggressively protected their daughters against him.

Of all the words to flip, pimp was deliberately chosen to confuse and water down the idea of sexual responsibility and morality and substitute it with sexual power and sex with no boundaries. In rap, the pimp is a sexual predator with cash money, materialistic values, and "stables" of near-naked women. We may never see authentic acts of prostitution in music videos, but the suggestion is always there.

These images impact African American youth in all stages of development, especially during adolescence ("Who am I?") and young adulthood (formative period for developing commitments in love relationships).

Back in the day, the playa was just beneath the pimp. Playas didn't sell women's bodies, they were just sexual predators. Today, to be a pimp is to be a playa, playboy, mack daddy, etc. Playas are pimps and pimps are playas, and no doubt our daughters are confused. We may all be confused. In fact, according to 50 Cent, our daughters can be pimps, too. Even a car can be pimped (e.g., *Pimp My Ride* TV show).

Am I paranoid, as some have suggested? When you compare images of new school pimps (Snoop Dogg, 50 Cent) to old school pimps (Huggy Bear on the old TV series *Starsky and Hutch*), they look the same. If it quacks like a duck, it's a duck. In fact, didn't Snoop Dogg play Huggy Bear in the remake of *Starsky and Hutch*, the movie? Hmmm ...

New school pimps look like real pimps, but they say, "Don't get it twisted, it's only a look. Pimping today is all about the mack." Hypocrites! This lie has been cleverly flipped to make it seem like the truth. When it's repeated often enough, we begin to believe it. A pimp sells women's bodies for money. This is exactly what's going on behind the scenes at video production sets and athlete parties. We have to wonder, of all the looks to choose from, why did rappers choose to look like feminine pimps? If they're not directly involved in pimping women for money, why are they pretending to be in this line of business? Interesting, but none of the Hip Hop leaders, such as Russell Simmons, will stand up on behalf of the black community, specifically black children, on this issue. Makes you go hmmm ...

Did Nelly know the true meaning of pimp when he named his energy drink Pimp Juice? Nelly's name choice has caused a stir in the black community. It's tough for me to take a shot at this brotha because to be fair, he has contributed huge sums of money to programs for the underprivileged. Nelly is one of the few who gives back without being asked, and he has worked hard to raise awareness about bone marrow disease in the black community.

But to whom much is given much is required, and that includes respecting the community at large. Together with Fillmore Street Brewery, Nelly created the **P**ositive **I**ntellectual **M**otivated **P**erson (Pimp Juice) Scholars Program, which gives $5,000 scholarships to one male and one female student each year. Love the scholarship, hate the name.

We are to believe that P.I.M.P. stands for **P**ositive **I**ntellectual **M**otivated **P**erson? What was Nelly thinking? Couldn't Nelly have chosen more appropriate names for his scholarship and energy drink?

I guess now when we hear pimp we're not supposed to think about Bishop Magic Don Juan, Huggy Bear, The Mack, or Flavor Flav on *Flavor of Love.*

I'll admit Nelly's acronym is clever, but it's too abstract and completely divorced from its true meaning and impact on society.

On the other hand, if we take the acronym out of the Hip Hop box and look at it from an African-centered point of view, pimp is everything the acronym implies on every level of social awareness—and more. Using Nelly's basic idea, allow me to clarify the true meaning of pimp.

P = **P**ositively able to procure customers to purchase p**y and punanny (i.e., sex from women)

I = **I**ntellectual, as in street smart

M = **M**otivated by cash, sex, and power

P = **P**erson who appears as a saint (Sweetness, Huggy Bear) but is really devilish

Now that's a pimp for you. We all know that every pimp must have mack abilities (i.e., manipulation skills smooth enough to convince you that the piss on your face is really rain). Perhaps this explains why, at three different funerals of young black males all under the age of 20 in 2005, a can of pimp juice lay in their caskets. That was a deep symbolic statement of their lives. Don't tell me that pimp doesn't mean what it used to mean, what it has always meant!

I assume the winners of the P.I.M.P. scholarship don't mind being associated with the original, deeply embedded meaning of the term as the world knows it. The first male winner of the scholarship, a Howard University student and self-confessed Bible reading Christian man, has bit on the flip. He states:

> "In this culture, a pimp is no longer someone who takes advantage of people for selfish or unethical reasons. A pimp is now to be known as an individual who takes advantage of opportunities to better their communities, and someone who brings a positive reputation that reflects their culture, heritage, and people they represent."[2]

You've got to be kidding. Now that's some Hip Hop hypocrisy. Sorry, I must have missed the memo that announced: PIMPS AIN'T WHAT THEY USED TO BE. I hope and pray this brotha doesn't graduate from one of our elite educational institutions with this misinformation. According to his definitions, all of us who work to improve the conditions that plague our communities are pimps—not civic leaders, community activists, or revolutionaries. Say it ain't so, bro!

Many words have been flipped like this. Nigga/nigger and dog/dogg are only a few. Snoop Dogg has even flipped the script on the word "preach." Is nothing sacred?

Our children love word games. As educators and parents, it's our job to channel this gift into more positive directions. The following chapters will arm you with the information you will need to deal with flipped scripts and the hypocrisies that go with them.

Chapter 2

Making Lies Look Like the Truth

"Up, up you mighty race! You can accomplish what you will." **The Honorable Marcus Garvey**

In the aftermath of Hurricane Katrina, the American media machine went into overdrive to make lies look like the truth. Their weapons were words and images. The racist double standards that persist in the American mind rose with the flood waters of New Orleans.

African American citizens were called refugees. I've never heard the word refugee applied to American survivors of any catastrophe until the mostly black citizens of New Orleans fell victim to nature and governmental neglect. Blacks were looters; whites were feeding their families. Blacks were called everything but a child of God; whites were given the benefit of the doubt.

CNN reporter Wolf Blitzer reported live on air, "Almost all of them that we see are so poor and so black." So black? Did he mean so dark or so African American? Was this a racist Freudian slip of some sort? Once again, African American stereotypes were used as a convenient way to define and categorize us. Recycled stereotypes only hurt African Americans. They justify the injustice, inferior education and health care, high unemployment, poverty, violence, and crime that plague urban communities.

The world deals with us based on historical and modern imagery created by the mass media propaganda machine, which never sleeps. It's the job of media to make lies look like the truth, so the PTBs (powers that be) pay rappers huge sums to promote crime, irresponsible sex, social ignorance, and questionable ethics in the music.

Even though Hip Hop arose out of the poverty of ghetto life, ironically, today's Hip Hop videos seldom show young people in poverty, and they sure don't show them with the beneficiaries, creators, and owners of the ghetto. This is a lie being made to look like a truth. As a result, society blames the victims for their plight without fully understanding the complexities that cause ghetto conditions.

Since gangsta/Hip Hop videos run on average eight hours more per day on TV than any other form of music, my colleagues and I decided to actually count how often certain themes reoccur in the videos. Interestingly, it was from these reoccurring themes that Ghettopoly creator David Chang openly admits he gathered his market research for his racist board game.[1]

My colleagues and I work with youth on a full-time basis (we're also parents), so we had a vested interest in discovering the truth. Although the study was unscientific, it still proved enlightening. We looked at 350 gangsta rap videos released between March 1985 and March 2005. The themes that had the highest reoccurrence rates were, without a doubt, the following:

- Sex—simulated orgies, gyrating buttocks, oral and anal sex simulations, masturbation, fondling of the crotch and breasts
- Drugs/Substance Abuse—using and selling marijuana, cocaine, crack, alcohol, cigarettes, cigars
- Crime/Violence—shooting and guns, gangs and gangbanging, drive-bys, prison life.

What we didn't find was even more interesting than what we found. For example, most gangsta rap videos feature some kind of black-on-black crime but hardly any black-on-white crime. Nigger/nigga was rapped and rhymed in just about every tune, but not one "wigger" (white nigger) was uttered. Few scenes of marriage, love, social activism, or doing well in school could be found. Hmmm ...

Long Beach, California, research genius Keidi Obi Awadu states,

"To me these videos are designed and used to socially engineer people in and outside the ghetto matrix, to uphold and
reinforce long held racist stereotypes first seen in the movie
Birth of a Nation. The process of repeatedly viewing hundreds of videos is a painful one for me. Quite simply, it is
difficult to watch one's own people wallowing in the swamp
of self-debasing detrimental behavior on the TV tube as if
real life is not tough enough."[2]

Over the past 20 years, the black community has been consuming
a video diet consisting of synthetic garbage, death, destruction, and
unhealthy self imagery and self concepts. It's like watching a long
rerun—the movie never ends.

With all this video viewing, there's a collective psychological price
to pay. Such repetitive viewing can and often does have an entrainment affect akin to a social engineering program. We think we're
being entertained when we're really being "entrained"—i.e., psychologically bonded to the negative elements. With repetitive ingesting
of rap, our children's thoughts and emotions become aligned with
the lyrics and video images. When this happens, children begin to
imitate the behavior they've entrained to.

That's why young females wear thongs above their pants in broad
daylight and young males sag their pants. Entrainment explains why
parents, educators, and ministers have less influence over children
than rappers, gangstas, thugs, and pimps.

Have you noticed how our children (and many adults) can't
ride one minute in a vehicle without changing the radio or CD 10
times? Need I mention our behavior when it comes to a TV remote?
We are constantly in search of that mood altering vibration we've
become accustomed (entrained) to. We're not satisfied until we hear
a song lyrically immersed in nigga/ho/bitch this or that. Hooked but
ashamed to admit it, we may all be victims of what Dr. Kobi Kambon
calls "psychological misorientation."

Often people ask me during my lectures, "Why do children, especially children of color, act the same from coast to coast? They appear to have the same attitudes, tastes, and habits. There is no sense of individuality whatsoever."

While this may or may not be true, our children do appear to be under the influence of what I call "artificial intelligence"—i.e., the repetitive indulgence and belief in lies and propaganda. As we read earlier, this all leads to Psychomedia Perpetrator Disorder, which is an epidemic in the black community (see Framework for Understanding Hip Hop Youth in Part 1). Youth are acting alike in large part because of their media conditioning. Even when they disagree, they may be too intimidated by their peers to say so.

In music, harmony is created by the playing of different notes all at once. "Artificial harmony" or "social entrainment" within the ghetto/ Hip Hop matrix is created by prolonged exposure to misinformation and miseducation about self and culture. This influences groups to move in unison and act as one entity in negative ways, to the exclusion of common sense and traditional values.

The Hip Hop creed of "no snitching" is one example of artificial harmony in the hood. The saying goes, "Snitches get stitches, they come up missing." Who are we protecting with the no snitching rule? Gangstas and criminals, people who don't want to get caught. Doing what? Selling drugs and committing sex crimes and other violent acts. Even though the no snitching rule puts our children, friends, and family in danger, the creed continues to rule the streets and most everyone in the hood buys into it.

Because our realities are constructed from lies, our children are hyper-suspicious and hyper-skeptical of anything an adult says. They readily respond to our critical statements with:

"Keep it real."

"Stop lyin'."

"What's going on?"

"For real, doe."

"Oh no you didn't!"

Hypocrisy 1—Keeping It Real//Flippin' the Script

The late Dr. Bobby Wright suggested that the purpose of manipulating the black mind is to disorient the reality of African Americans. He called this phenomenon "mentacide," which is "the planned and systematic destruction of a group's mentality aimed at the destruction of the group."[3] Thus alienated from their culture and history, brothas and sistas eventually lose their sense of purpose and direction. These are the symptoms of mentacide.

Self-knowledge and expression laid the foundation for the black arts movement, the nationalist movement, the civil rights movement, and all other movements designed to raise our consciousness. Everyone from the Honorable Elijah Muhammad to James Brown stressed that knowledge of self was the key to liberation. Elijah Muhammad said that without knowledge of self, we're victims of amnesia or unconsciousness. How can our community ever move forward if we refuse to wake up?

tv 'programming' of the hip hop mind

Infomercials are long winded commercials that substitute true information (knowledge) for persuasive communication to sell products. Could there be a better metaphor for rap videos and rap tunes than the infomercial? Commercialized Hip Hop entertainment is one big infomercial designed to sell young fans certain concepts and values (materialism, irresponsible sex, substance abuse, violence, crime, misogyny, etc.). Hip Hop infomercials use powerful symbols and themes to subliminally communicate racial stereotypes to a global audience.

Hip Hop talk shows are also infomercials. They substitute knowledge that could help young viewers improve their lives for celebrity chit chat that often reinforces gangsta values. The following programs on Viacom-owned, teen oriented BET and MTV illustrate this point. These video countdown shows regularly feature Top 10 videos and hypersexual rap stars that appeal to young people.

Hypocrisy 1—Keeping It Real//Flippin' the Script

1. *Total Request Live* (MTV) airs live weekdays in the afternoon. The audience is made up of teens (16–19) and young adults (early 20s). TRL has a racially mixed audience, but the show is skewed toward the 18 year-old white middle-class females who make up the majority of the call-in requests and viewing audience. Artists are introduced to thunderous applause, screams, cat calls, and teary-eyed girls. The host takes the artist to a large window that is high above an even more enthusiastic crowd standing below on Broadway, the street in the heart of New York City's famed Times Square. The show has a carefree feel.

2. *BET's Rap City: The Bassment* (as in the basement of a house) airs weekdays in the late afternoon. The host of the show is a young black male who gives the impression that he's living in his mama's basement. His guests are mostly grown black males and an occasional female who stop by to kick the knowledge and talk some smack. In the background is a visiting DJ who mixes phat beats. The visitors eventually get off the couch and go into a small recording booth for an impromptu freestyle rap session. Some repeat guests make me wonder if any of these brothas have a steady job. The show has an urban gangsta boyz-only bonding vibe.

3. *106 & Park* (BET) airs weekdays in the late afternoon. This popular 90-minute video countdown show is hosted by two adults, one male and one female. The audience is mostly young black teens and 20 something adults. 106 & Park is located in the Hell's Kitchen section of Manhattan. Hip Hop artists and movie stars are introduced to a cheering, mostly female audience. The show has an urban middle-class feel with occasional dips into ghettofabulism.

In TV programming, the set plays an important role in delivering subliminal cues. In *TRL*, the New York City skyline is featured, connoting to the viewer a sense of success and superiority. Being high up or on top connotes instant feelings of grandeur, the idea that you have finally arrived. The big window opens out to Broadway below, the toughest street in the world. As the saying goes, "If you can make it on Broadway, you can make it anywhere."

Artists are always ushered to the window where they look down on their adoring fans, "the people below me" or "the people beneath my feet." They literally tower over fans. The fans, standing on Broadway, in all types of weather, look up to their kings/queens—"the people above me"—like loyal subjects.

Black Hip Hop artists who appear on this show throw their gangsta/hood demeanor out the window (so to speak) and seem to bend over backwards to thank the mostly white audience—unlike their visits to the BET video countdown shows (can you say Hip Hop hypocrisy?). Clearly, appearing before *TRL's* mostly white audience connotes the idea of having arrived, success. We all have been conditioned to associate success with any and all things white. So a guest appearance on *TRL* means the artist has arrived, as in moved up and out. Which begs the question, moved up and out from where?

Perhaps the answer is up and out of the basement, as in your mama's basement. BET's *Rap City: The Bassment* takes place in the basement, the lowest room, the bottom of the house. Psychologically, emotionally, and socially, the basement connotes failure to the subconscious mind of the viewer, reinforcing long held stereotypical views of black men.

The Bassment is a true Hip Hop infomercial. The guests have nothing of substance to say as it relates to the condition of self and community (other than a brief, occasional visit from knowledge dropping Cousin Jeff). For the most part they discuss risqué topics, blinging, and making it in the rap game—in other words, moving up. Judging from the way these grown black men dress, behave, and sound, they appear to be displaying symptoms of Prolonged Adolescent Syndrome. This is a profoundly debilitating image being exported to a global TV audience. The message is clear: "As black men, we're still living with and being cared for by our mama (woman)." Shameful.

Hypocrisy 1—Keeping It Real//Flippin' the Script

While *The Bassment* is about moving up, BET's *106 & Park* suggests the need to get off of something. The name of the show, combined with its hypersexual themes, suggests that Hip Hop is on the corner (as in "get off the corner"). In the hood, the corner is a gathering place, often in front of a liquor store. Brothas on the corner drinking out of brown paper bags are often unemployed, do drug deals, and just hang out.

106 & Park is a video countdown program. Most top ten rap videos featured are hypersexual and openly promote the pimp agenda. Who else dominates the corner in the hood? The pimp and the prostitute. Hip Hop is the hard working ho on the corner, working nightly from 6:00 pm to 7:30 pm, making big money for the entertainment pimps. This show is Viacom's most popular Hip Hop video countdown program.

These infomercials are expert at numbing the mind and blinding our cultural eye. The set designs, guest artists, topics, and music videos combine to make lies look and sound like the truth. After all, that's the name of the game.

hitting the mark

Hip Hop videos are created from tested and proven formulas. Every video has an actor/performer/rapper, director, writers, and producers. Their goal is to manufacture a hit. "Hit" connotes "strike" as in "strike the target." The production team must connect with the target on the following levels:

H = Heart (strike the emotions, pull at the heart strings)
I = Intellect (elevate or dummy down the intellect)
T = Tongue (repeat it, speak it; the tongue has the power of life and death)

It's the job of the production crew to program you. That's why TV shows are called programs.

Another formula that's used is SAWV, in which material possessions, the degradation of women (specifically women of color), hypersexual activity, and criminal activities are glorified. The ingredients in SAWV are:

S = **S**ex
A = **A**ddictions
W = **W**ealth
V = **V**iolence

SAWV is the hugely successful formula used in nearly all rap videos. Some elements of SAWV can be found in 100 percent of uncut, black Hip Hop videos.[4]

In the reoccurring themes study mentioned earlier, we studied and compared substance abuse references in different music genres. Not surprisingly, substance abuse references were more common in gangsta/crunk Hip Hop music. References to sexually lewd and graphic acts are commonplace in crunk/gangsta rap.[5]

Clearly, Hip Hop videos are a classic Sigmund Freud mix of sex and aggression.

According to Hunter Adams III, watching music videos accelerates the process of thinking in images rather than logic. The repetitive flashes of color and images overwhelm the visual senses and dull critical thinking.[6]

What are our children thinking when they see and hear so much bitch this and nigga that in their favorite music? Remember, children can't always tell the difference between fantasy and reality.

hip hop scamola

According to the Federal Communications Commission (FCC), "It is a violation of federal law to air obscene programming at any time. It is also a violation of federal law to broadcast indecent or profane programming during certain hours" (www.fcc.gov). Federal law also forbids radio programmers from accepting gifts, cash, or anything of value in exchange for playing specific songs on the air.

So how is it that some of the lewdest music known to mankind got airplay, despite FCC regulations against obscene programming?

I hate to say I told you so, but since 1995 I've been saying in my lectures that the global popularity of gangsta Hip Hop is the result of payola. After all, propaganda is no good if it's not heard, right? The PTBs of Hip Hop have been doing what many of us on the outside have long suspected—paying to have their deadly messages played.

Your favorite radio station may be nothing more than a big juke box. When money is put into a juke box, only the song paid for is played. Yet another dirty truth about Hip Hop has come to light. DJs and others with the juice have compromised their position of trust by doing favors for favors.

How many times have you called or written your local radio station to complain and they told you the only reason they play certain music is because it's what the people request? Now you know Mr. Charlie has lied once again. These songs are pumped into the minds of young people with the help of your trusted DJ and programmer. Can you say spies in the house?

"Our investigation shows that, contrary to listener expectations that songs are selected for air play based on artistic merit and popularity, air time is often determined by undisclosed payoffs to radio stations and their employees," said New York Attorney General Eliot Spitzer.[7]

Sony BMG got caught and had to pay a $10 million settlement[8]; Warner Music Group had to pay $5 million.[9] Radio programmers and DJs were getting gifts like sneakers, tickets to high profile events, computers, free trips—even sex (surprised?)—in exchange for playing favored artists.

Why would programmers and DJs have to be bribed to play Hip Hop? I believe this is a bigger issue than some radio people getting paid. I believe that urban radio stations where R&B and rap are played almost exclusively have proven to be the perfect arena for the

PTBs to push the persona of the gangsta, the criminal, the ho, and the thug down the throats of African American and Afro-Latino toddlers, children, adolescents, teens, and young adults.

Payola ensures the delivery of words and beats that have the power to influence human behavior. This is social engineering on a massive scale—or in the case of gangsta rap, psychological warfare. The same songs of wanton sex, violence, and degrading terms are pumped into our children's psyche around the clock. Like a dripping faucet, the sound becomes a part of our existence. It no longer annoys, it just is.

The music industry is owned by big conglomerates in control of the airways, both radio and TV. They know good and well that the images the radio puts into your head are so powerful you'll want more. You'll want to see the "real" thing, and a video will suffice. Thus, Jamal Public starts craving to see butts shaking or black men acting childish, pretending to be Mafiosos. If you think the song is bad, wait until you see the video. The video must meet or surpass the song's message.

Hearing a 50 Cent jam over and over again may eventually persuade you that the song is good since the music experts (DJs) are playing it all the time. Your perception of what's good and bad has just been altered; reality has just been manipulated; lies have been made to look like the truth. That's why they call a song a hit, because it hit the mark. In street terms, mark = victim. Who's the victim? You. Our children. Our community. The music itself. Truth. You may feel like you pick the songs you like, but in reality they pick you. When a song is tagged a hit, it means more than you know. It's a scam on the psychology and emotions of the customer. Payola isn't a victimless crime.

Hip Hop is a $155 billion global industry. Our hard earned money leaves our pockets due in part to this trickery. This is Entrainment 101, Hip Hop style. Words evoke images, images provoke powerful emotions, emotions instantly trigger cravings, and cravings trigger behaviors. The behavior can be the innocent humming of a tune that's stuck in your head, the purchase of a CD, or to the extreme,

Hypocrisy 1—Keeping It Real//Flippin' the Script

the imitation of gangsta themes in real life. As you'll read later, studies are emerging to show that music does have the power to influence behavior.

The PTBs have put a hit on black and brown youth, and with white youth being the biggest consumers of rap, they're a target as well. Don't believe me? All you have to do is listen closely to most rap lyrics and watch most rap videos, and you'll know something is deadly wrong.

The PTBs have yet to apologize to the community/village for such actions and never will because they know the victims love their abuser more than they love themselves—so much so that they will defend those who call them nigga/bitch/ho. This is mentacide and making lies sound like truth on the grandest of scales.

Chapter 3

Hip Hop Mind Control

"Who is to say that robbing a people of its language is less violent than war?" **Ray Gwinn Smith**

"Disinformation is most effective in a very narrow context ... You take a fraction of reality and expand on it. It's seldom totally at odds with the facts...It's shaving a piece of reality off." **Frank Snepp**, former CIA agent (1985)

"The basic tool for the manipulation of reality is the manipulation of words. If you can control the meaning of words, you can control the people who must use the words." **Philip K. Dick**, *How to Build A Universe That Doesn't Fall Apart Two Days Later* (1978)

Subliminal symbols and themes can be found everywhere in Hip Hop. In *Message N/A Bottle: The 40oz Scandal (vols. 1 & 2),* I dealt extensively with the subliminal advertising of alcohol to African American youth. I decoded hidden satanic and pornographic themes and symbols in malt liquor ad campaigns.

"Subliminal perception is a subject that virtually no one wants to believe exists, and—if it does exist—they much less believe it has any practical application. Doubtless, it would be far more comfortable to simply ignore what is going on. Every person ... has been victimized and manipulated by the use of subliminal stimuli directed into his unconscious mind ... The secret has been well kept. The average citizen, as well as most … scientists, simply do not know what is going on."[1]

Mind control is the name of the game in Hip Hop. The payola scams have taught us that there is a deliberate movement among recording industry PTBs to spotlight certain songs that go against every traditional African American value, every moral code of the church, every sane behavior of human beings. The PTBs have made raising and working with Pookie, Peaches, and Puddin' extremely difficult.

Brothers & Sisters, there's a beast creeping through Hip Hop, and we've allowed it to grow into a monster. Its mind control tools are words, images, and musicology. We'll address musicology and imagery later in the book. To understand the hypocrisies, especially the hypocrisy of keeping it supposedly real while flippin' the script, we must first understand the power of the word in Hip Hop/rap.

John 1:1 reads, "In the beginning was the Word, and the Word was with God, and the Word was God." God created everything via the Word. Furthermore, God made us in His image, so if His Word has power, then our words have power. In the current state of Hip Hop/rap, we're dealing with principalities and powers, and unfortunately they too know the power of the word.

Hip Hop/rap is a spoken word art form. In the beginning of Hip Hop, the word was used for good. Today, in commercialized gangsta rap, it is used for evil.

"C'mon, Coach, you're going off the deep end here. Rap is just about kids acting out in music and on the dance floor. Harmless fun," you may be thinking. Bear with me, Brothers & Sisters. In this chapter, you'll see how the word in commercialized gangsta rap has become the mind control tool of choice. Toward what end? You be the judge.

cussin'

"Precious Lord, take my hand before I smack the taste out of these kids' mouths!" Sound familiar? Everywhere I lecture, parents complain to me about the filthy words their young children repeat verbatim from gangsta rap tunes. The most profound Hip Hop scribes unfortunately dip their pens into inkwells of profanity as they script their lyrics. Profanity is often "blessed" by some of our brightest and most visible artists from the Hip Hop genre.

> "Not to pick on Puffy … but right now he's the largest one out there … I recall going to his concert in San Jose and watching him get 15 thousand people to raise their hand middle finger and say 'F**k You Bitch' … Right afterwards L'il Kim came out and got everyone to yell 'F**k You Nigga' … The majority of that audience was non-Black. It sure was strange hearing a whole bunch of white and Asian kids, some as young as 10 yelling 'F**k You Nigga' … But hey we're in the last days … and Jerry Springer rules."[2]

Songs are written in major and minor keys and so are Hip Hop lyrics. My student athletes love to debate me on what is and is not profanity. They like to divide profanity into two categories they call majors (really bad words) and minors (bad words, but not so bad):

Majors = motherf**ker, sh**, pu**y, di** head, cunt, bitch
Minors = butt, cock, hell, SOB, bastard, damn it, goddamn, asshole, nigga

In 2004, Black Brothers and Sisters Involvement, Inc. of Dayton, Ohio, asked 185 fifth graders (90 males and 95 females) the following questions:
1. Do you understand words that are bleeped out of gangsta rap songs? *94 percent responded yes.*
2. Do you listen to the unedited versions of Hip Hop songs that include profanity? *90 percent responded yes.*

3. Have you ever watched the TV show *BET Uncut* (contains near full nudity and sexual reenactments)? *77 percent responded yes.*

4. —If yes, have you ever watched the entire show from 2:30 am to 3:30 am? *75 percent responded yes.*

5. Have you ever watched *BET Uncut* in its entirety more than five times? *82 percent responded yes.*

6. Have you ever watched *BET Uncut* with an adult (someone 18 or older)? *56 percent responded yes.*

7. Do you sing or rap the bad words with the CD or video? *96 percent said they do.*

8. Do you know what "explicit lyrics" means? *29 percent responded yes.*

9. Do you think that rappers are real gangsters? *85 percent responded yes.*

10. Of the following three choices listed, which do you think about the most after watching a rap video or hearing a rap song: (A) the opposite sex; (B) fighting; or (C) fashion? *60 percent chose A; 30 percent chose C; and 10 percent chose B.*

11. Below are 20 sets of CD covers. Within each set is both a clean and a dirty version of the CD. Review each artist or group then circle the version you would like to listen to. *92 percent selected the dirty versions.*

Explicit warning labels were introduced in 1985, and artists have been only too happy to comply, figuring youth ages 10 to 14 will see the sticker as an incentive, not a deterrent, to buy the CD. Believe me, the sticker is not there because the artists want to fulfill their moral obligation to warn and inform parents. They're seeing bling bling.

Urban radio is the main pipeline into the souls of young people. This is where new songs are market tested, marketed, and sold. According to my friend Marlon Shackleford, rappers use profanity to rejuvenate old beats and rhymes in otherwise dead rap songs, and these songs are then given air time.

Radio stations across the nation play profanity-laced rap with the bad words barely bleeped out. We must work to limit children's access to sex and violence on TV, and we must target urban radio stations for their anything goes daily line-up of vulgar songs and talk.

The issue of profanity is not new for youth caught up in poverty and violence. Profanity has always been a way to express in the hood. Profanity is used to express the pains and tribulations of poverty and violence. When it hurts, you cuss.

For young people, male and female, profanity is common. In fact, to not hear it on the streets is the exception, unfortunately. It's just part of the culture and environment of the ghetto.

When I was growing up, we were foul mouthed, too, but at least we would cuss behind the backs of adults. We respected and feared them so much that no way would we cuss in front of our parents, teachers, and church elders. Today, young people cussin' in front of adults is no big deal. It's gotten so bad, they don't know what they're saying is wrong.

The vocabulary of our children is minimal, so they have to resort to foul language to express themselves. Public school systems and the village must be held accountable for allowing this deep linguistic ignorance to take root and flourish in our community.

Black comedy has helped desensitize youth to the offensive nature of profanity. Black comedians such as Chris Rock, Eddie Murphy, Steve Harvey, and Dave Chappelle have made cussin' funny and uniquely black, unfortunately. Pioneers in this style of entertainment were Richard Pryor and Redd Foxx. They used profanity to connect to their urban audiences. Bill Cosby and Sinbad are truly geniuses because they figured out how to be funny and profound without using profanity.

Youth will use profanity to emphasize a joke or to stress their point of view, particularly in a rap song. Profanity plays a major role in ghetto games like dissin' and playing the dozens. Some folk build their reputations on their ability to think fast while cussin'. Freestyling heavily depends on profanity. The goal is to "spit" the best raps, the "colder," the more vulgar, the better.

Free speech, Brothers & Sisters, was one of the few things that made the United States a better place to call home than a lot of other places. Today, this high principle has been so twisted that the original purpose can no longer be detected. Cussin', swearing, nasty language, and four letter words are shouted on school playgrounds, basketball courts, in shouting matches between girls, and between thug lovers.

We all know that gestures like flipping the finger are obscene and routinely used in Hip Hop videos viewed by children. In middle schools, profanity is one of the main reasons, second only to fighting, for referrals to detention.

the 'p and l theory' of rap

The P and L Theory of rap is that male rappers use P words constantly, and females use L words. Below are two lists containing popular words and subjects you'll hear over and over again in rap. The list is in no particular order; however, I often ask my high school and college students to rank the lists in order of importance. The lists shown below reflect, on average, how the words are usually ranked by males and females.

Females: L Theory	**Males: P Theory**
1. Love/lover	1. Pimps/prostitutes
2. Luxury/liquor	2. Penis
3. Lust	3. Pu**y
4. Lying	4. Prison
5. Looks	5. Pistol
6. Leaving/liberation	6. Pseudo power
7. Listening	7. Parole/probation
8. Lord	8. Prayer
9. Like	9. Profanity
10. Law	10. Pregnancy

Hypocrisy 1—Keeping It Real//Flippin' the Script

Male rappers use profanity to exaggerate the importance of **pimp**-ing, **p**enis, and **pu****y (sex). Females focus on **l**iving **l**arge (luxury), drinking expensive **l**iquor, stealing men from other women (lust), buying designer clothes, and getting their hair and nails done (looks).

To listen to these rappers you'd think there was nothing more to life than selfishness, irresponsible sex, and bling bling. These issues are expressed through profanity, and young fans love to repeat this garbage word for word. For better or worse, parents are the first teachers, and in our workshops, young people say that their parents or siblings first exposed them to profanity. Rap music then takes over.

The P and L words are used to make Hip Hop lies sound like the truth, specifically on the issues of prison, lust, pistols, prostitution, pseudo power, pregnancy, and love.

Black men are frequently portrayed as promiscuous, savage, animalistic, destructive, and criminal. Our perpetual use of "pimps," "prostitution," "pu**y," and "penis" works to project us as sex fiends and sociopaths. Rappers are guilty of perpetuating centuries old racial propaganda via the average video (both uncut and so-called "cleaned up") that deals with our desires from the waist down, as if that's all that matters to African men.

The L theory is just as troubling. When I reviewed female Country Western artists, I didn't find many L words. Instead I found the following M words:

1. Men
2. Money
3. Memories
4. Motherhood
5. Mistakes
6. Mistress
7. Matrimony/marriage
8. Melodramas
9. Meekness
10. Mothers-in-law

Female Country Western tunes may feature M words, but they're similar to the L words of Hip Hop females. L words supposedly represent women of color. Media continues to portray black women as sexually lascivious, bitchy women who desire to be kept in bling bling by their niggas. Hip Hop videos depict the black female with hips thrusting, cleavage exposed, and minimal clothes, and she readily answers to ho, skeezer, and bitch. In contrast, although M words are similar to L words, M words ensure that white women will be portrayed as committed lovers and wives who fall victims to love. White women are portrayed as obedient, faithful mothers, and silent and suffering caretakers. Quite a different picture from the black female.

Here's your homework assignment (this is a good one for students): review ten Country Western music videos and ten Hip Hop videos that feature female performers. Analyze and compare content, contexts, fashions, and the portrayal of the female. Note their similarities and differences. It won't be long before you realize that Lil' Kim and Shania Twain project very different images and messages to their fans. Then write an essay that explains why this difference between black and white females exists in music videos.

The PTBs are slowly moving to close the gap. Country artists are starting to borrow elements from Hip Hop. Country singer Trace Adkins hit the big time with his 2005 bootylicious "Honky Tonk Badonkadonk," the third song from the *Songs About Me* CD. Its risqué imagery and lyrics have all the sexual elements of a Hip Hop video. After the release of "Honky Tonk Badonkadonk," the CD leaped from gold to platinum in 60 days.

Gold means that 500,000 copies of the CD were shipped to retail outlets; the CD goes platinum when one million units are shipped. This proves that the booty, whether black or white, is worth its weight in gold.

the formula for killing your own

"If now isn't a good time for the truth I don't see when we'll get to it." **Nikki Giovanni**

Hypocrisy 1—Keeping It Real//Flippin' the Script

During the past 20 years, there have been too many rap lyrics that promote misogyny and sexual assault against females. For example, there are numerous rap songs that glorify "running trains," "gang-banging" females, and telling females to "suck my d**k." The original kings of such vulgar writing were 1980s megastars Too Short and Luke of 2 Live Crew.

In the reoccurring themes study, we discovered several formulas that rappers use to write misogynist rap. Seldom do songs written outside of these formulas get airplay on radio and television. I call one such formula DOGS:

D = **D**emean and denigrate
O = **O**ffend and objectify
G = **G**lorify gangs, guns, and grass (marijuana)
S = **S**ell and sensationalize sex

The nature of a dog is to hunt, and in Hip Hop, black males are always hunting for young females. Remember George Clinton's "Atomic Dog?"

The hunt is celebrated in the lyrics of the songs and the visuals of the videos. The hunt is purely sexual, violent, and predatory, and the dogs/doggs are going for the kill.

In addition to the DOGS formula, all commercialized gangsta (dog/dogg) videos follow the BITCH formula:

B = **B**elittle blacks, specifically women
I = **I**ndoctrinate, intoxicate, and indulge in insanity
T = **T**each thugs and tots to target and torment
C = **C**ause casualties, cheat, and cuss out people of color and Caucasians
H = **H**urt, hustle, and humiliate humans

You'd be hard pressed to find any of the BITCH formula elements absent from a gangsta video. Young men who buy into the dog/dogg mentality have no problem dogging (mistreating) females, particularly sexually. This is why we must stress to young men to not greet others with or accept being called dog/dogg. You may become what you claim to be.

By nature, the dog (male) chases the cat (female). When the dog catches the cat and forces her into a corner, their relationship becomes violent. In fact, they repeat the violence over and over again, as if they both believe she has nine lives.

How many of you know females who stay in violent relationships? Sometimes, a female will use sex out of fear to negotiate with her abuser/dogg (sex out of fear is still rape). When the female tells the father/dogg she's pregnant, the father/dogg runs away (a.k.a. "dogg-gone").

How many of you know any absent fathers? The offspring, let's say it's a male child, is called a bastard by society. The mother has been verbally abused by the father/dogg, and he's called her a bitch over and over. She in turn has internalized the word and now calls her own male child a "son of a bitch" (SOB). The mother tells the SOB that he looks and acts just like his "no good father" who was a "low down dirty dog." Unconsciously she transmits this animalistic mentality to her own son.

The SOB grows up hating his **m**other and all **f**emales and goes on to mistreat females—like father like son. When a male physically assaults a female or emotionally scars her, she verbally responds by calling him a motherf***ker (MF). An MF is a **m**an who mistreats **f**emales, thus a real MF. Subconsciously, she knows he hates his **m**other and all **f**emales, and by abusing her, the cycle repeats. It's true, you really can't teach an old dog new tricks—not unless he wants to change.

In Hip Hop/ghetto culture, the mind control is intense and the cycle of producing victims seems to be unending, but we MUST break it. Scripture tells us to be transformed by the renewing of our minds (Romans 12:2). It's going to take an act of God, faith, and determination to reverse the curse of Hip Hop brainwashing. And as the next chapter shows, we've got a long way to go.

Hypocrisy 1—Keeping It Real//Flippin' the Script

Chapter 4

Words of Deadly Persuasion

"At its core the n-word is connected with linguistic violence and the subjugation of black people. For older black Americans, the word still conjures up memories of the degradation of segregation and racial discrimination." **Yvone Bynoe**

"Fifty years ago we'd have you upside down with a f**ing fork up your ass. He's a nigger! He's a nigger! He's a nigger! A nigger, look, there's a nigger!" **Michael Richards** (a.k.a. Cosmo Kramer of *Seinfeld*) insulting black audience members (Laugh Factory, West Hollywood)

Hip Hop runs through my son's blood. His mother and I have no real problem with that because we raised him right. There are times, though, when he becomes philosophical like his old man and tries to get me to come around to his Hip Hop point of view. One of our more interesting debates was when he defended Hip Hop's constant use of nigga/niggas/niggaz.

"Nigger's not what it used to be," he said. "Nigger is now nigga. We flipped it to mean something positive."

At times he can be as deep as Malcolm X, poetic as Tupac, and as philosophical as Dr. Michael Eric Dyson all rolled into one. I was truly impressed, but not convinced, by his rationale. I responded to his monologue with one of my own.

Pop's Soapbox

Hip Hop has flip flopped on nigga for too long. The attempt to rebirth and socially engineer nigga into the social matrix as a positive thing has been psychological and cultural suicide for our people. Nigga is an obvious attempt to alter the collective psychosocial memory and reality of blacks as it relates to our historical trauma associated with nigger.

The PTBs (powers that be) in the entertainment industry are experts at altering our perception and, thus, our reality. Hyping negative sexual, materialistic, violent, and misogynistic images with nigga/niggas/niggaz reinforces the slave/ Jim Crow meaning of its surname, nigger. This is insulting and an act of psychological warfare. Nigger is so steeped in American tragedy that media censors itself by using the euphemism "N-word" instead of keeping it real with nigger/niggas/niggaz.

In the documentary *Tupac: Resurrection,* Tupac Shakur explains, "Niggers were the ones hanging from the trees with the rope around their neck ... Niggas are the ones hanging in the clubs with the gold ropes around their necks." Yet there is no mental transition from nigger to nigga to N-word that eases the suffering and imagery the terms conjurer up. The overuse of nigga/niggas/niggaz in Hip Hop has desensitized an entire generation of youth to the inflammatory aspects of the word.

When you hear N-word you think nigger. If you say nigga, I think nigger! Rappers have sold youth out and are too much the coward to admit it. Only black people are sick enough to allow the poisoning of their children to occur without outrage!

Now we read in Wired.com that for close to a year and a half, actor Damon Wayans has been trying to trademark nigga. Why? To get paid, of course. He wants to put the mark on everything—clothing, books, music, and general merchandise.

The U.S. Patent and Trademark Office turned him down (for now), citing a law that prohibits marks that are "immoral or scandalous."[1]

Son, tell the truth. How would you feel if your baby's disposable diapers had the nigga mark? Nigga is simply the commercialization of nigger, and rappers can't afford to get rid of the word because their income depends on it.

Non-black rap artists are waiting in the wings for Hip Hop's endorsement and approval of their use of the word. Once a non-black rapper drops the nigga/niggas/niggaz bomb on wax, digital, or www, he will instantly go triple platinum and generate billions. Black producers will be out searching for the next great white Hip Hop hope, and they will pimp him like they pimp black artists now. It's going to happen one day, and your Hip Hop generation will be reminded that you made it a politically and culturally correct thing to do because you conveyed to the world that nigger ain't what it used to be.

My son said he would get back to me later.

In fact, the day may be already upon us when white rappers use nigger/nigga in their lyrics. As I write these words, the hottest tune out is "Miss New Booty" by white rapper Bubba Sparxxx. In an interview in *XXL* magazine, Bubba refers to his collaborator on the tune as "My nigga Kaine."[2] This is all good? It was only a matter of time. I'm not hating on Bubba Sparxxx, but the institution of Hip Hop cannot continue to permit the disrespect of the painful journey of black people.

I would be remiss if I didn't mention the one attempt that was made to correct centuries of pathology and injustice created by nigger. The NAACP was informed in March 2004 that a landmark decision was made at Merriam-Webster Dictionary. They have recognized the error of their ways. Nigger will no longer be synonymous with African Americans. It will be duly noted that nigger is a racial slur, not what African Americans are. This wasn't just a victory for African Americans but for everyone, for knowledge is power.

Now if we can only get Hip Hop and the community at large to stop using the term. A nigga is still a nigger, and as a man thinks in his heart, so is he.

the birth of the negro and nigger psyche

"History is a clock that people use to tell their time of day. It is a compass they use to find themselves on the map of human geography. It tells them where they are, and what they are." **John Henrik Clarke**

"In 1600 I was a darkie, until 1865 a slave. In 1900, I was a nigger, or at least that was my name. In 1960, I was a negro …"[3] **Gil Scott-Heron**, Evolution (and Flashback) (1999)

The word "nigger" may have been spun off from "Negro." The origins of Negro are the early English words *negar, neegar, neger,* and *niggor.* Nigger is probably the white southern phonetic mispronunciation of Negro. Whatever its origins, by the early 1800s, nigger was firmly established as a negative description, and the Western world became obsessed with fearing, hating, catching, selling, raping, humiliating, imprisoning, maming, and killing all Africans and people of African descent

The so-called nigger is an early Eurocentric creation. The nigger was created in order to serve, please, and obey its master, even at its own expense. For just a handful of rations (bling, toys, and things), he will spiritually, psychologically, and physically kill his own.

During slavery, nigger was a common name for pets of the master that had darkly colored fur, especially dogs and cats. The slave master referred to his stud bulls and stud horses as his prize niggers, and this is why black athletes are called horses, bulls, and animals to this day.

African psychologist Dr. Na'im Akbar says that Negro "comes from a Greek origin meaning something that is dead."[4] Does that mean we're a race of dead people with a dead history and no hope for resurrection? Perhaps this is why Europeans had no problem enslaving and killing black people. Dead things are powerless, useless, and not important. In the European mind, the Negro is like the living dead. The ultimate deadbeat, a nigger was stereotyped by the slave master as shiftless and lazy, which is ironic considering Africans did all the work!

The nigger/nigga phenomenon continues via gangsta rap and good old fashioned racism. The question remains: why do we call each other niggers/niggas/niggaz, and why does Hip Hop reinforce this self-hatred? As nigger was spun from Negro, nigga is spun from the low expectation the world has of the so-called nigger.

Judging by the lyrics of Hip Hop's brightest stars (Jay-Z, Nas, Dr. Dre, Tupac, Master P, Snoop Dogg, Ice Cube, 50 Cent, Notorious B.I.G.), the word is used most effectively in phrases such as "Kill niggaz," "Roll up on a nigga," "Shut a nigga down," "Shoot a nigga," and "F**k a nigga up." The message is clear: whatever a nigga is, it's to be destroyed.

Some artists have tried to assign nigga a new meaning in order to justify its use in Hip Hop music. The late rapper Tupac Shakur created an acronym for nigga: "**N**ever **I**gnorant **G**etting **G**oals **A**ccomplished." That was an attempted word flip, but it didn't work. Nigga still means nigger, and not even the most creative Hip Hop artist can strip the word of its painful meaning. Using this word today is a slap in the face of all those black men who protested in the 1960s with signs that read "I Am A Man" and all the Africans, both men and women, who died because they refused to answer to the term.

The original text of the Constitution of the United States stated that an African was three-fifths of a man. It's ironic that we were valuable only when we were three-fifths, not when we achieved our full

Hypocrisy 1—Keeping It Real//Flippin' the Script

potential as human beings. The less human we are, the more valuable we become. The more we use words of deadly persuasion that diminish our humanity in gangsta rap, the more valuable we become.

evil images

"They saw themselves as others had seen them. They had been formed by the images made of them by those who had had the deepest necessity to despise them." **James Baldwin**

"In my music, my plays, my films, I want to carry always this central idea: to be African. Multitudes of men have died for less worthy ideals: it is even more eminently worth living for."[5] **Paul Robeson**, 1934

Paul Robeson made that bold statement when being African wasn't popular. We were under constant attack via imagery manipulation on every front—art, toys, music, film, advertising. In fact, today, vintage black collectables are a hot commodity in the antiques market. Visit Ebay.com to get an insight, not into the culture of African people, but into the degenerate minds of those who thought this way.

For example, in 1817, the American Tobacco Company had a NiggerHair (smoking tobacco) redemption promotion. A 1916 magazine ad, copyrighted by Morris & Bendien, showed a black child drinking ink. The caption read, "Nigger Milk."[6]

In 1874, the McLoughlin Brothers of New York produced a puzzle game called "Chopped Up Niggers."[7] Can't you just picture little Peggy Sue and Jim Bob sitting next to the fireplace, playing with their board game, unaware that they were being trained to hate other human beings?

Apparently, some things never change.

"New anti-Black images are also found in the popular children's games *Pokemon* and *Dragonball Z.* The Pokemon character Jynx has jet-black skin, large protruding pink lips, gaping eyes, a straight blond mane, and a full figure, complete with cleavage and wiggly hips. Carole Boston Weatherford, a cultural critic, described Jynx as 'a dead ringer for an obese drag queen.' Mr. Popo, a Dragonball Z character, is a rotund genie, dwarfish, with pointed ears, jet-black skin, and large red lips. He is a loyal servant."[8]

You may remember Agatha Christie's 1939 story, *Ten Little Niggers.* Later, the book went through a few name changes, including *Ten Little Indians* and *Then There Were None.* The original story was full of violence against African American boys ("Seven Little Nigger Boys chopping up sticks; one chopped himself in halves, and then there were six."[9]) *Ten Little Niggers* reads like a blueprint for gangsta rap.

The African American Registry® (www.aaregistry.com) provides a short list of nigger terms that you can easily find in old dictionary editions in the libraries of mostly poor schools. My grandfather used to tell us that the following names formed the language of hate spoken by the Ku Klux Klan near his home in Eutaw, Alabama, in the early 1900s.

1. Niggerlover: derogatory term aimed at whites who lack the necessary loathing of blacks.
2. Nigger luck: exceptionally good luck, emphasis on undeserved.
3. Nigger-flicker: a small knife or razor with one side heavily taped to preserve the user's fingers.
4. Nigger heaven: designated places, usually the balcony, where blacks were forced to sit—for example, in an integrated movie theater or church.
5. Nigger knocker: axe handle or weapon made from an axe handle.[10]

These terms are still in our national consciousness. To prove it, I sometimes give the following test to my students to measure their level of exposure to nigger/nigga. Take the test to assess your own level of exposure. Some questions have several answers. (The answers are provided at the end of this chapter.)

1. Niggas get on my last _____.
2. Niggas can't do _____ right.
3. Niggas are _____.
4. Niggas are always _____.
5. Niggas _____ for everybody.
6. Don't let a nigga work on your _____.
7. Don't pay a nigga _____.
8. Please fix it; don't _____ it.
9. Niggas can _____ like no one else.
10. If you want to go to jail, get a _____. If you want to go to the graveyard, get a nigga _____.
11. Niggas are always _____.
12. Every time a nigga makes it they always _____ outside their race.
13. Niggas are natural _____.
14. Niggas love to get _____.[11]

I hope that bothered you so much that you'll do your part to remove these spiritually and socially destructive words from our language. Obviously we have a long way to go.

that's my ...

Remember when we used to greet one another with "Whatz up, pops/cuz/blood/brotha/sista?" We would claim a person by saying things like, "That's my people," "Whatz up, soul brotha/sista," "She's my play cousin," and "We're family." Those sayings said a lot about our consciousness at the time. We were striving to move away from the individualistic Western culture to the communal, African way of life. We went from Negro to nigger to colored to Black to African American in a few short years following slavery because we were determined to shake off the old labels and create a new identity that was based on our African heritage.

One day, my high school football team was returning from a road game, and we stopped to eat at a popular fast food restaurant in a small town. As we were waiting for our food, a fan (a 20-something black man) said in a loud voice, "Can a nigga get sumthan to eat?" Sadly, there was some laughter by a handful of our ball players and others. Bystanders (all white) stared in disbelief as did a few ball players and coaches.

I approached him and asked that he not speak like that in the presence of self and our team. He replied, "My bad, Coach. That's how I talk. I keep it real, dogg, cause I'm a real nigga for sho."

naming ourselves

"I got nothing against no Viet. No Vietnamese ever called me 'nigger'." **Muhammad Ali,** former Heavy Weight Champion (1967)

The first person who ever called me a nigger was black. The first person I beat up for calling me nigger was a white classmate in the seventh grade at Shoup Mill Middle School in Dayton, Ohio. I don't advocate violence, but the fact that I didn't beat them *both* up speaks to the level of confusion I was under.

It was common for my twin and me as children to be described as "the baddest [as in good] dancing little niggers in town" by family and friends. Still, somehow I knew that if a white person ever called me nigger I was to handle my business.

I have been educated, miseducated, and reeducated about who I am and where I come from. As a child I learned I was colored because my grandmother always complained about colored people, and colored people looked just like me. No one sat my twin and me down and told us we were Negros, yet I learned I was a Negro when my white fourth grade teacher told us before each field trip to behave like good Negro children.

My memory of becoming black is clear. It happened when James Brown sang, "Say it loud, I'm black and I'm proud." I admired my older brother Stevie's big afro and black leather Black Panthers jacket. Suddenly I knew I wasn't a Negro or colored anymore. I was a Blackman, a certified fist pumping soul brotha, and man was I ready to fight the revolution. I had no idea what a revolution was, but I knew it wouldn't be televised.

I stayed a Blackman for a long time. I was a Blackman longer than I was a soul brotha, which if memory serves, went the way of the greasy jheri curl. In fact, I was willing to be a Blackman for life, as long as I didn't have to wear a bone in my nose like those brothas in the Tarzan movies. (Little did I know at the time that I was paying $1.25, a fortune back in the day, to be trained in self-hatred.)

All that changed for me in high school after the series *Roots* premiered on TV. After watching the first episode, I became an African living in America. Over the next few years, I became a bonified African American with no clue about my African tribe or country of origin. It didn't matter. At least I could find Africa on the map. I couldn't and still can't to this day find Coloredland, Negroland, Blackmanland, or Soulbrothaland on any map.

My black history teacher shared with us the following Truth that I never forgot:

> "You're not an African because you're born in Africa. You're an African because Africa is born in you. It's in your genes … your DNA … your entire biological make up. Whether you like it or not, that's the way it is. However, if you were to embrace this truth with open arms … my, my, my…what a wonderful thing." **Marimba Ani**

Hypocrisy 1—Keeping It Real//Flippin' the Script

saggin'

"When our young people wear their pants down claiming it's Hip Hop, this symbolizes that as a people, we have been caught collectively with our pants down. We have failed to instill the social values that would make our children pull their pants up and uphold them with the belt of cultural pride." **Alfred "Coach" Powell**

Believe it or not, many of our young males wear niggas on their rear ends. Thanks to my dyslexia it occurred to me sometime during the mid-1990s that there's more to those infamous saggin' (sagging) pants than meets the eye (see *Message N/A Bottle, vol. 2*). I began to suspect that this "fashion" was disguising a deep, subconscious pathology. Then it hit me. Saggin' spelled backwards is, that's right, *niggas*! Could the message here be that niggas are backwards and ignorant? I wonder if the CEOs of Sony, Vivendi Universal, Bertelsmann AG, and AOL Time Warner are aware of this subliminal trick.

Where did saggin' start anyway? Urban legend says that saggin' started in prison. The truth is that sagging pants can be traced back to the slave plantations. Black male field hands (captured Africans) were not allowed to wear their pants in a respectable manly fashion. Field slaves might have been given a piece of rope to hold their pants up. In the latter days of slavery, field hands mostly wore overalls.

Only the slave master was allowed to wear his pants like a man with a belt or suspenders, thus the phrase, "Only the man wears the pants around here."

If wearing pants up and belted symbolizes manhood, then one trip around the block in the hood will have you quickly asking, where did all the real men go? The Hip Hop male's refusal to wear his pants up and belted in a manly, respectable fashion is a symptom of Prolonged Adolescent Syndrome.

If a symbol of manhood is pants up and belted, then pants down and un-belted (saggin') must mean "boys" or in Hip Hop, "boyz."

Boyz are men who refuse to grow up. If pants up and belted is a symbol for manhood and responsibility, then wearing them down must connote "not wanting the responsibility that comes with adulthood, manhood, brotherhood, and fatherhood (i.e., supporting your own children); not wanting to care for, protect, and provide for the community." Perhaps we drop our pants because we have dropped our collective effort to be real men.

The fact that saggin' has received the blessing of the PTBs suggests that the historical relationship between slave master and field hand is playing itself out in their descendants, the music industry execs and the boyz of Hip Hop. Furthermore, the boyz of Hip Hop who show their behinds are symbolically telling all those brave African ancestors who gave their lives for us to wear our pants up like men to kiss their sorry asses.

If pants up and belted symbolize a man's self-esteem and self-worth, then perhaps the Hip Hop gangsta who sags his pants subconsciously sees himself as defeated and enslaved.

This indecent exposure has gotten so far out of control that some school districts and city lawmakers are considering introducing bills and passing laws to criminalize the wearing of pants that sag below the waist. If these bills become law, police officers can then ticket citizens and students who wear their pants too low.

The boyz of Hip Hop brought this on themselves. We told them to pull their pants up, but they arrogantly refused.

On the other hand, the so-called "house nigger" was allowed to wear a belt or a pair of suspenders occasionally to keep up appearances before guests and the residents of the house. Belts became status symbols and a subtle yet powerful way to stir up jealousy among the field slaves and turn all Africans against one another.

Whatever a nigga is, it's expected to wear its pants down low, which begs the question, *Is he?* Don't trip. I'm just saying that since most women say they don't find saggin' pants attractive on men, who are these supposedly tough gangstas revealing their backsides to? Considering that gangsta males hang out with other gangsta males,

Hypocrisy 1—Keeping It Real//Flippin' the Script

it's a fair question. Down low pants could be a low down (slick) way to communicate one's sexual preference. Why wear pants that don't fit? Why put on pants and literally not wear them? The style is not comfortable, socially acceptable, or culturally correct. Call me crazy, but there is something to it. Seldom is anything what it appears to be inside the gangsta Hip Hop/ghetto matrix.

act of war

It's an act of war to take away a human being's identity, culture, and language. Ever wonder what black people called each other before nigger was invented and introduced into our consciousness?

I've found the Hip Hop "nigga for life" creed of self-hatred written on the walls of boys locker rooms and rest rooms in dozens of middle schools and high schools around the country.

I was stopped in my tracks by the lyrics of Nas and Scarface in their gangsta rap collaboration, "Favor For A Favor" from Nas' *I Am* CD. I was walking toward my school's locker room when I heard the song bouncing off the walls. When I came into the locker room, my football players scrambled to change the song. I said, "Hold up." We discussed the meaning of the song beyond its entertainment value.

In the chorus, Nas raps, "You wet who I want wetted, I'll wet who you want wetted/Any nigga can get it."[12] What does wet and wetted mean? My athletes decoded the words to mean kill/killed.

I said, "So the bottom line is that as a favor, I'll kill who you want killed and I expect you to do the same?" They said yes.

I couldn't help but ask, "Who's a nigga?" One young man said, "You know, somebody who gets on your nerves or gets in your way."

All I can say is that the mind is a terrible thing to waste and easy to manipulate. Could these instructional CDs and videos (urban infomercials) be well orchestrated, new millennium, COINTELPRO (Counter Intelligence Program) instructional hooks? This is a fair question considering that gangsta rappers are endorsing and providing instructions on how to kill African American men in their music.

n.w.a.

One day our son was listening to what he called an oldie but goodie.

"What's the name of that group?" I asked.

"N.W.A., Pops. It stands for Niggaz With Attitude." He showed me the CD cover. The title read Efil4zaggin. My dyslexia kicked in immediately. Efil4zaggin read backward is "Niggaz 4 Life." My son thought Niggaz 4 Life spelled backward was slick, as if they had gotten away with something.

Of course I had to put in my two cents and inform him that niggaz/niggers appearing in music wasn't new (or slick) to the music world. Nigger has been in everything from vaudeville to Broadway musicals. Audiences have been entertained with lyrics such as "Niggers will be niggers," "Niggas git on de boat," and "Run nigger run."

Today, gangsta rap is running with the baton. Consider these rap titles: "Trigga Happy Nigga" (The Geto Boys), "Killa Hilla Nigga" (Cypress Hill), and "Sucka Nigga" (A Tribe Called Quest).

Remember this old school indoctrination rhyme?

Eeny-meeny-miney-mo!
Catch a nigger by the toe!
If he hollers, let him go!
Eeny-meeny-miney-mo!

Nigger was a standard word in our daily vocabulary, and as kids, we would use it on each other all the time. We didn't even have the sense to be offended, it was that common. Today's child is bombarded via gangsta Hip Hop. He'll often hear in his home, school, and on the street, "You bad ass little nigga." To add to the confusion, this may be a compliment or an insult.

Hypocrisy 1—Keeping It Real//Flippin' the Script

I now encounter children as young as three years old saying nigga, among other things. Out of the mouths of babes. Pookie, Peaches, and Puddin' are saying words they shouldn't and don't understand. In fact, they are asking, "What's a nigga?"

'wiggers' not allowed

Nigger is the ultimate American insult used to offend other ethnic groups. Jews and Irish people are called "white niggers," "Arabs, "sand niggers," and Japanese, "yellow niggers." No other label carries as much purposeful malice.

Back in the 1930s, '40s, and '50s, white teens who enjoyed black music (jazz, blues, rock & roll) had to sneak away to listen to it, and that included Elvis himself. They were called "nigger lovers" by other whites. Any white person who admires black culture is subject to ridicule, specifically from other whites.

Hip Hop has sold itself as the one and only racially inclusive genre in the music matrix. With white kids as the real financial source of Hip Hop, the industry can't afford to ignore them. Business is about giving people what they want, and white youth want nigga.

In the mid-1990s, when Hip Hop went commercial, white youth started using wigger as away to insult other white kids who were into Hip Hop/black culture. The brain makes no transition from wigger to nigger. When you hear wigger you think nigger/black person.

Rebellion is part of the teen years. It's a part of growing up. Today, Hip Hop gives all youth, especially whites, a way to rebelliously express themselves.

In the song "White America," Eminem speaks to suburban (white) kids. Actor and comedian Jamie Kennedy introduced the world to his version of a wigger in the 2002 movie *Malibu's Most Wanted*. His character was loud and full of ghetto stereotypes. The plot revolved around his father trying to reprogram his ghetto ways.

Young whites from the suburbs who act out in this way can never fully understand what it means to survive day to day in black skin in the ghetto/hood. For them it's a game of pretend and a way to rebel against authority (parental) figures. When they get tired of the game, they can always go back to their white privilege, protected by the forces and institutions of racism and sexism.

Until white Americans experience the same atrocities that were committed against Rodney King, James Byrd, Amadou Diallo, Abner Louima, and their forefathers, their love of rap will only be a passing fad. When the wigger experiences those evil forces, he quickly drops the façade and takes full advantage of his white skin privileges. In other words, he can play the race card and get a free pass out of niggaville (racism, poverty, and the ghetto).

Interestingly, wigger never made it into mainstream media. It's as if the PTBs of the music industry sent out a cease and desist order concerning the term. Can you say Hip Hop hypocrisy?

Black Hip Hop artists will rhyme nigger with figger, digger, jigga, trigger, and just about anything else—but not wigger. Not one white rap star has yet to promote themselves as a wigger to the world and never will. It's okay to promote the idea that blacks are niggers, but white children must be protected at any cost. Words have power and can manipulate self-image. Wigger can't enter the consciousness of the world because it could cause psychosocial damage to white children.

Rapper icon Ice-T, in his 2006 VH1 reality show *Ice-T's Rap School,* teaches mostly white affluent youth about the Hip Hop/gangsta game. I predict that Ice-T will never have them rhyme wigger or any lyrics that promote the killing, pimping, or rape of another white person. I won't be surprised if the children learn to rhyme nigga under the Hip Hop guise of keeping it real. Viewers will accept this as harmless Hip Hop entertainment and business as usual.

One nigger image on television can cause self-loathing, a crisis in identity, and smear the entire black race. The same could happen to white children. Because the term nigger is known and applied to blacks globally, black children suffer and have yet to heal. This cannot happen to white children, the future rulers of industries and governments. How can wiggers grow up to rule if they are not respected? No one will groom a wigger to run Microsoft, IBM, or the government.

In my 25 years of coaching at predominately black schools, I've coached my share of white student athletes. I could tell you funny stories about each and every one of them. They tag each other with some of the most memorable nicknames I've ever heard. There was Powder, Ice Cream, Pretty Boy Nelson and his brother Dirty Willie, Shadow, White Bread, Chop-Shop, Forest G, Big Vanilla, Lil Country, Country Dogg, Billy Bob, Biscuit, and Smooth Tom Cruise. Not once have I heard wigger used against one of them or among them. That's because they're going off the meaning of the original word, nigger.

I first became aware of wigger around 1994 when my white student athletes complained to me about the ridicule they were taking from their white peers in their neighborhoods. They were being accused of acting black. One of my players said he was told by a white church member that his walk was black. Now I didn't notice if his walk was black (whatever that is), but he could out battle (rap freestyling) 98 percent of the team. Was that acting black? I think not. Dirty Willie just loved Hip Hop.

Interestingly, many of my white athletes were pained by the ugly hurl of nigga among black teammates. I can't tell you the number of times Chop-Shop and Lil Country would ask their black teammates, "Why do you guys call each other that?" Sadly, my black athletes would reply, "I don't know man, we just do."

Whites romanticizing black culture is nothing new. However, the embrace of the ghetto lifestyle by white youth speaks to a new pathology. Just know this: If Negro/nigger = death, then wigger = death. The worst death imaginable for a people is the slow, painful death of one's culture, heritage, spirituality, and self.

bitches & doggs

At the beginning of a fifth grade workshop, I asked one of the boys to introduce himself. He said, "My name is Rico, bitch!" To the backdrop of laughter and high fives, his peers gave their approval. Mind you, this was in the basement of a church. (Thanks a lot, Dave Chappelle!) To flip the words of Jay-Z ("99 Problems"), we got ninety-nine problems and the word bitch is one. You can rest assured I handled my business with Rico, and the other 45 boys introduced themselves respectfully.

The following is a historical snapshot of why I discourage the Hip Hop generation from using nigger/nigga/dogg/bitch:

1. Every dog/dogg has a master who teaches him tricks.
2. Every bitch has a master/pimp who makes him or her turn tricks.
3. Every nigger/nigga has a master who knows a nigger/nigga can be tricked.
4. Every master/pimp has the power to sleep with, train, and/or kill his nigger/nigga/dogg/bitch.
5. The master makes his nigger/nigga/dogg/bitch dependent on him so that it will never seek freedom, identity, or its true nature. The master convinces the slave that he is his one and only god.
6. The master trains his nigger (slave), dog/dogg (pet), and bitch (woman) to obey. He uses psychological manipulation and physical punishment to accomplish his mission. He trains his dogs/doggs/niggers to fight and kill their own kind on command. The programming ensures that the master will never be attacked.

Niggaz, dogs/doggs, and bitches: apparently these are the three magical words every rapper is contractually obligated to use to increase sales. I have no doubt that a study has been done to find out which words touch nerves and wallets the most. These three words have been used in every way imaginable in Hip Hop, from the profound to the profane.

The Hip Hop viewpoint seemingly is rooted in the Western psychology of Sigmund Freud. As Dr. Na'im Akbar points out, sex and aggression form the core of Freud's psychological theory. When you reduce a person to his lowest element you essentially have an animal whose primary orientations are pleasure seeking and violence.[13] Not surprisingly, typical rap lyrics are filled with pleasure seeking and animal-like aggression.

The portrayal of the bitch and dog/dogg archetypes in Hip Hop produce what I call the "Lady and the Tramp" syndrome. Female rappers consistently rap about their desire to have a dog/dogg type man, and the males call the females bitches. For reasons that are as complex as the ghetto matrix these terms arose out of, our youth identify with these archetypes. I appreciated it when Queen Latifah called them all to task in her 1993 Hip Hop hit "U.N.I.T.Y." She said, "Who you calling a bitch?"[14]

If nigga is the number one word uttered in Hip Hop songs, then bitch and dog/dogg are close seconds. Many young blacks accept being called dogs/doggs and bitches; this is disturbing on all levels. A bitch is a female dog, so when young women are called bitches, they are really being called dogs. Is Hip Hop a culture of dogs, animals, subhumans?

Historically, the slave owner called his female slaves "negress bitches" or "wenches" (which closely rhymes with bitches). Not only does Hip Hop now promote the language of the old slave masters but the street pimp as well. Young males are taking out their hatred and fear of women in their lyrics. In Eminem's 2004 song "Bitch," he uses the word so many times you begin to wonder if he likes women at all.

What men don't realize is that when they call their sistas a bitch, they point the pistol of self-hatred at themselves. Let's use the power of wordplay to educate ourselves. Consider the following: the first three letters in **bit**ch is **bit**; the last two letters are **ch**. When males say "bitch," maybe what they're really talking about is a little **bit** of themselves that they can't **ch**ange. A man will often call a woman a bitch when he loses control—when the woman refuses to obey him, especially on the issues of money, sex, abortion, and God.

Hypocrisy 1—Keeping It Real//Flippin' the Script

Every man has a little **bit** of female in him, and every wo**man** has some male in her beyond simple symbolism. Young men and women must get in balance and in touch (in a healthy, respectful way) with their feminine and masculine sides. For fun, let's see how some common words can help you get in touch with your other side. (Worry not, men. This exercise will not emasculate you.)

1. Fat**her**: you are a good fat**her** because of the **her** in you.
2. Brot**her**: you are a strong brot**her** because of the **her** in you.
3. Mot**her**: perhaps **he** is in mot**her** to remind men that to respect our mot**her**s is to respect ourselves and that our mot**her**s have the strength of any man.
4. Fe**male**: **male** anchors **female** to remind us that the **male** comes through the **female**.
5. W**oman**: **man** anchors **woman** to remind us that **man** is connected to **woman**.
6. **She** and **Her**: reminds us that for every time **she** loves us and we love **her**, we men learn to love ourselves, and this can't be done without **her**. Now that's deep.
7. **Lad**y: only a **lad**y can birth a **lad** (boy), and a **lad** (man) is meant to be with a **lad**y. It is what it is, my man.

Symbolically, using bitch means that you're in touch with your dog/dogg side instead of your God side. God is in every human being. God spelled backward is dog. Divine symbols that are inverted, read backwards, or are turned upside down have satanic connotations.

The master referred to his male slave offspring as puppies (young dogs). The so-called dog side of man is also known as his demon/de-man side. In some Christian art, demons are depicted with the body of a dog and the face of a man and vice versa. In the word Good is the word God. In Hip Hop subculture, only the dog (demon/de-man) side of man is celebrated and recognized, not the good (God) side. Can you say demented?

Decoded, DOG means **D**elusions **O**f **G**randeur. Because rappers have large egos, they compete with each other for the most women, the most bling bling, the biggest mansions, and the most money. DOG also defines Satan, whose fall came after pride and his patho-logical idea that he was more powerful than God (a.k.a., delusions of grandeur). You'd better recognize.

A woman who sleeps with a dog/dogg accepts on some level of consciousness that she is his equal, a bitch. Some believe that oppo-sites attract. Maybe that's why the good or God-fearing girl often falls for the dog/dogg/de-man (bad boy).

In the ghetto/hood, the dog/dogg persona is a title not given but earned—sadly via violence and coldness. The term "dirty dog" describes a man who causes emotional pain, usually in love relation-ships and the abandonment of his children.

Dirty dogs are sexual predators. They are also called "players/pla-yas." Dirty dogs overpower their victims by using date rape drugs, manipulation (charm), and brute strength. They don't care about putting their female victims at risk of unwanted pregnancies and exposure to HIV/AIDS and other STDs.

Since Hip Hop is about deep thinking, let's take this theory to the next level. In biology, the X chromosome all by itself indicates female; thus a woman is a woman without a man. The XY chromo-somes indicate male (mother's X and father's Y). Perhaps the symbolic message here is: "It takes a woman to complete a man." Holla at me. Now that's deep, but it gets deeper.

Wordplay helps us understand why we should respect our elders, something that's missing from the Hip Hop generation in general. Let's look at the words "grandmother" and "grandfather" to see what pearls of wisdom and knowledge they have to offer.

Grandmother   Grandfather

Notice the letters AND in both words; they spell "and." Rearranged, these letters also spell "DNA"—deoxyribonucleic acid—the very thing that makes us connected to each other, that special little bit that makes us a bit like our parents and grandparents and all those gone before us.

According to biological law, species reproduce after their own kind. Thus a bird can't produce a rat; a fish can't produce kittens.

This means that if a male's mother and sisters/sistas are bitches, then the male is a dog/dogg. Species can only reproduce after their own kind, which means that a bitch can only produce a dog/dogg.

The same is true for females who celebrate having a dog/dogg for a man. He can only reproduce after his own kind, which would make the female a bitch. I got you, sistas! You thought you were off the hook.

lil' doggie

Children are conditioned early in life via fairytales, folklore, fables, nursery rhymes, myths, legends, and the classics to love the "little doggie in the window." Outside the Hip Hop/ghetto matrix, the little doggie is probably a real little doggie (poodle, German Shepherd, etc.). Inside the Hip Hop/ghetto matrix, however, the lil' doggie may be a brotha/dog/dogg looking out of the bars of a prison window.

real men, stand up

Nothing but God can defeat this de-man/de-mon.

Young black males must desire within their hearts to rise above the dog-eat-dog animal state of being. They must want to be transformed from dogs/doggs to men.

In Hip Hop, rap tunes glorify the dirty dog, not the man who stays with and provides for his family. Unfortunately, young female Hip Hop audiences have been conditioned to love the dirty dog (the bad boy). They dance to his music and fantasize about being his bitch. This is on display big time in "Soldier," the 2004 pop hit by Destiny's Child.

In the video, the good girls of Destiny's Child are shown walking three large black dogs, the subliminal cue for three vicious black men. Thus our brains decode soldier to mean dogg/playa/street hustler/gangsta.

In the Hip Hop mindset, keeping it real means using these words constantly. Now that you know their history and symbolic associations, you're responsible for the words you speak, especially to children.

Answer Key
1. Niggas get on my last **nerves**.
2. Niggas can't do **sh*t/nothing** right.
3. Niggas are **lazy**.
4. Niggas are always **late/beggin'**.
5. Niggas mess **it up** for everybody.
6. Don't let a nigga work on your **car/house**.
7. Don't pay a nigga **before the job is done**.
8. Please fix it; don't **nigga rig** it.
9. Niggas can **lie/steal** like no one else.
10. If you want to go to jail get a **nigga lawyer**. And if you want to go to the graveyard get a **nigga doctor**.
11. Niggas are always **broke**.
12. Every time niggas make it they always **marry** outside their race.
13. Niggas are natural **athletes.**
14. Niggas love to get **high**.

Because many people score at least 90 percent or better on this test, I start most of my workshops with my national anthem, "I Want to Free the Afrikan in Me." It's more of a chant than a song. The chant is designed to psycho-surgically remove the ugly stereotypes embedded in our minds and to counter all the self-hate in the community. Interestingly, whites readily sing the chant more so than many of my black students at first. Oh boy, what a sight.

Chapter 5

Poetry in Motion

"Music is a world within itself with a language we all understand." **Stevie Wonder**, "Sir Duke"

"Rappers such as Snoop Dogg and Jay-Z have professed a liking for the music of Tony Bennett and Tom Jones, and Sean 'P. Diddy' Combs has said he listens to Sinatra and Elton John."[1] **Brian Ballou**

My editor, Donna Marie, learned to play classical piano at an early age, but she also loves Old School (Earth Wind and Fire, Stevie Wonder, Marvin Gaye, George Clinton, Parliament, the Emotions, etc.). So she thought she knew something about music—until she had a baby boy who was born into the Hip Hop matrix. It was all good until around fifth grade when he gave up *Teenage Mutant Ninja Turtles* for gangsta rap, rap videos, saggin', and freestyling. Donna felt like the victim of a home invasion.

Donna's story is typical. There was a generation gap to bridge, and blocking the way was her son's favorite music—gangsta rap. As time went on their relationship began to suffer. She felt offended by the lyrics, and he thought she was trippin'. Telling him not to listen would, of course, make him sneak around. Interestingly, he wanted her to give the music a chance, so finally, she put her ego aside, held her nose, and dived in.

What makes the music so attractive to a young black male? Half-naked women on the videos was easy to see, but with her music background, Donna wanted to know what was in the construction and structure of the music itself that made it so seductive to young people.

Music is a power. All types of music, from rap to gospel to jazz, have the power to affect how you feel. The manipulation of rhythm, harmony, and melody can make you feel good or bring you down. Music can make you laugh and cry. When you walk into a store, the music is designed to make you want to buy something. Music can make you want to have sex, and it can make you want to worship God.

1 Chronicles 25:1 says that music can inspire prophecy. I've spoken at many churches around the country, and all of them had some sort of music program. Some do simple praise and worship while others have multi-million dollar sound systems, orchestras, and choirs.

They say that music soothes the savage beast, but in gangsta Hip Hop, it's the opposite. It stirs up the beast, or hostility, in our youth. The work of Dr. Paul MacLean at the National Institute of Mental Health explains why. Dr. MacLean says that the human brain is three brains in one:

1. Reticular formation (RF)—five percent of the brain. RF lets in most sensory input. It also maintains automatic body processes, such as circulation and respiration.
2. Limbic system (LS)—10 percent of the brain. LS controls emotions, certain kinds of memory, and glandular functions.
3. Cerebral cortex (CC)—85 percent of the brain. The CC is about higher order thinking.

According to MacLean, the LS is so powerful that it can literally facilitate or inhibit learning and higher order thinking. He also discovered that positive emotions such as love and tenderness (which are anti-gangsta Hip Hop), facilitate higher order thinking skills. Negative emotions, such as anger, hostility, and fear (which characterize rap performances, lyrics, and music) "downshift" the brain to basic survival thinking.[2]

Gangsta rap's obsession with sex, cash, status, weapons, and substance abuse is tied to the basic survival thinking of the LS. When so many African American and Latino youth in the Hip Hop/ghetto matrix are fighting for their survival everyday, it's easy to see why they connect to the music.

Our African ancestors knew about the power of music. An important part of life, music was integrated into every ceremony because of its power to create high, spiritual states. It's important to understand our connection to African music. Slavery tried to strip us of our culture, but our music and our African DNA are the two things they couldn't take away. African music can be felt in blues, jazz, gospel, reggae—and rap. Rap rhythms are African rhythms. Rhythms can imitate and complement the beat of our hearts, and this connects us physically to the music.

I think it was a pastor who once said, "In the beginning was the Rhythm, and the Rhythm was with God, and the Rhythm was God" (John 1:1 paraphrased). When the Rhythm and the Word come together, this is music's power, the essence of Divinity.

For young people in the secular world, music is for dancing and doing homework to. In the hood, listening to music helps young people tune out what's going on around them. With headphones on, they don't have to hear their parents arguing or the gunshots in the alley. Rap takes them to a place where they think it's all good.

To many adults, rap sounds like noise with no real melody, harmony, or instrumentation. Although some rappers have sophisticated orchestration to back them up, many are making millions with little more than a couple of pieces of equipment and Dr. Seuss-like poetry (we'll get to that later). This is the creativity and genius of Hip Hop.

Rap evolved as it reached back to Old School, reggae, and even rock. The music of each generation samples (borrows) from the ones before. Old School borrowed heavily from jazz, blues, gospel, and even classical.

Youth don't know that their favorite rap tunes are often sampled from the bass riffs, lyrics, and melodies of James Brown, Chaka

Khan, Michael Jackson, the Jackson 5, Chic, Kool and the Gang, Parliament Funkadelic, Rick James, DeBarge, K.C. and the Sunshine Band, Ohio Players, Diana Ross, Sly and the Family Stone, and even TV theme songs (*Welcome Back, Kotter*).

Although this mother and son didn't agree on everything about rap, they at least were talking, and the mother-son relationship began to heal and harmonize like an Old School/New School remix on the Tom Joyner Show. Donna's son began to understand the funk roots of his favorite music, and Donna began to appreciate the fact that once again, black folk with little more than a couple of pieces of equipment and their speaking voices (not even singing) generated a worldwide movement.

keys to rap

All songs are written in either major or minor keys. Many Old School songs were written in major keys. That's why they sound upbeat, happy. Major keys make you feel good. For example, *One Nation Under A Groove*, the funk anthem, was written in a major key. I challenge you to listen to that song and not feel good.

Rap, on the other hand, is usually written in minor keys. Halloween music and music written for horror movies or dramas are written in minor keys. Minor keys make you feel suspenseful, scared, moody, depressed, violent, aggressive, angry, frustrated—basically the lower emotions which, according to MacLean, keep us focused on survival thinking vs. higher order thinking. Remember the theme music to the Alfred Hitchcock thriller *Psycho*? Every time I hear those violins I can see the knife blade going down, and I can hear the screams.

Which leads me to my next point: *memory*. Music not only stirs us up emotionally, it's tied to memory.

"Ballard and Coates (1995) researched nonviolent, homicidal, and suicidal heavy metal and rap songs and their effects on college students. The purpose of Ballard and Coates'

Hypocrisy 1—Keeping It Real//Flippin' the Script

study was to investigate the effects of the lyrical content of heavy metal and rap songs on mood. The participants were randomly assigned to six groups. Each group listened to a different type of song: nonviolent rap, homicidal rap, suicidal rap, nonviolent heavy metal, homicidal heavy metal, and suicidal heavy metal. Each group listened to their song twice and took a memory test in order to evaluate how well they could remember the lyrics to the song. The State-Trait Anger Inventory showed that lyrical content did affect the participants' scores; those listening to the homicidal heavy metal songs scored higher than those listening to nonviolent heavy metal songs."[3]

That's why, when you hear a slow jam from back in the day, you remember who you were with, how you were feeling, and whose basement you were in when you heard the song. Might even remember the furniture, the clothes you were wearing, and the perfume she had on. Now that's deep.

Given the negative subject matter of most rap, minor keys make sense. Life in the hood is not in a major key. Combine the minor keys and hypnotic rhythms with the negative word, and this matrix our children are plugged into is not healthy and could possibly lead to antisocial behavior.[4]

If rap tunes were written in major keys, maybe our youth would feel more hopeful about the future. Think about it.

rap and sex

In this book I talk a lot about how rap sees women as sexual objects and men as pimps and playas, which are all throwbacks to slavery. The white slaveholder's slaves worked the land, kept his house, created/bred more slaves, and satisfied his sexual lust. Rap has misguidedly taken on the role of the slave master in its sexual orientation and put down of women. I ask you, can such a music be sexy or romantic?

Hypocrisy 1—Keeping It Real//Flippin' the Script

Music has the power to stimulate sexual feelings. Romantic/erotic songs can be written in either major or minor keys, but it's the attitude of the performer that creates the powerful feelings. Old School slow jams no doubt contributed to the high rate of teenage pregnancies. "Our song" was the one that stimulated that first kiss (and maybe more), and every time you hear it, you remember. Music is connected to the memory of strong romantic and sexual emotions.

When our teens grow up, will they remember "our song" as "Beat the Bitch with a Bat?" Will they remember that first kiss when they revisit "Sunshine" by Lil' Flip ("I need a lady in the streets but a freak in the sheets")?[5] Will they remember their first love when they hear Juvenile's sweet lyrics, "If you going through your cycle, I ain't with it, I'm gone" ("Slow Motion").[6]

While we can appreciate the creativity, we must check all lyrical content when it comes to our children's healthy development. Donna constantly talked to her son about the sexual perversion in rap music. He tried the "it's only music" response that all young people give, but she kept talking anyway. She gave examples. She showed how commercialized gangsta rap goes against the family's values of respecting women, respecting self, and putting sex in the context of love, commitment, and marriage.

Even if it feels like you're not getting through, keep planting those seeds anyway. One day, when they're raising their kids, they'll finally understand.

rap poetry

Scholar and civil rights activist Dr. William Waymer proposes the following theory:

> "The pattern of speech used by William Shakespeare and some other writers of his era was written in iambic pentameter. Each pair of syllables in poetry is a foot. Another word for a foot in poetry is 'iamb.' Hence, writing that fits

Hypocrisy 1—Keeping It Real//Flippin' the Script

this pattern has five feet (pentameter) in each line, with the emphasis on the second syllable. An example of this is as follows:

Ta Dum ta Dum ta Dum ta Dum ta Dum
Ta Dum ta Dum ta Dum ta Dum ta Dum

"Shakespeare and other writers of Middle English did not rhyme their lines.

"The beat and rhythm of iambic pentameter is also that of Hip Hop. As a matter of fact, it is the same or very similar cadence as that used by Martin Luther King, Jr., Jessie Jackson, and other prominent speakers."[7]

There are some generally accepted rules of poetry, but rap turns all rules inside out:

- **Imagery**—Shaking booties, bling bling, pimp gear, tattoos, sexual acts, violent acts.
- **Similes, metaphors, symbols**—In Old School music, the lyrics were often symbolic, creating layers of double entendres as in George Clinton's *Atomic Dog* (dog = man, cat = woman). Not surprisingly, in rap, the tools of poetry are used to serve the sexual and violent content. No one can accuse rap of being subtle like most poetry. What you hear is what you get. But rappers are the masters of wordplay. Language is clay. Not only do they use similes, metaphors, and symbols, they use homonyms, antonyms, wild rhyming schemes, and anything else they can twist to suit their purposes. This is their genius.
- **Meter (rhythm)**—Lyrics go with the beat, and the beat (rhythm) is repetitive. Without repetitive rhythms, there can be no music composition or pattern in poetry. Our two year-olds know all the lyrics to 50 Cent's "P.I.M.P." because repetition aids memory.

- **Tone/attitude**—Gangsterish, sexual, violent, selfish and cold-hearted, self-promoting, and sometimes humorous.

what they talkin' 'bout?

Lyrics are the most important issue we must deal with in rap. For me and many parents, there is no negotiating room. Wrong is wrong. The lyrics in commercialized gangsta rap are irresponsible and harmful to the psychosocial and spiritual development of youth.

Earlier we talked about the words of deadly persuasion (nigger, bitch, dog/dogg, etc.) rappers love to use in their lyrics. But in rap, it's not just about what you say but how you say it that creates the attraction.

Without rap's rhyming schemes and bold, comical performances, rap would be as dry as dirt.

New York Times reporter Margo Jefferson says that "Hip-hop is the ethnic vaudeville of our day, and it doesn't hesitate to stage minstrel shows, either."[8]

I wonder how rappers like being compared to minstrel performers. Are they proud, or can they begin to see the harm they're causing? Maybe they don't care how they look, as long as they're getting paid. Have they forgotten how hard black artists fought for the right to perform with dignity? Don't they know or care that what they do in public reflects on all of us as black people?

Rap is a spoken word poetry. Spoken word poetry came out of the black arts movement, which was the creative engine of the civil rights movement. Back in the 1960s, poets such as Haki Madhubuti, Sonia Sanchez, Amiri Baraka, and Nikki Giovanni experimented with poetry that was both performed and written down. In the late 1960s, the Watts Prophets of Los Angeles and the Last Poets of Harlem were the earliest group pioneers of spoken poetry (rap).[9]

Spoken word poetry was about uplifting the consciousness of black people. This is where rap departs, unfortunately, from its roots.

Hypocrisy 1—Keeping It Real//Flippin' the Script

One of the biggest rap tunes to come out in 2004 was Juvenile's and Soulja Slim's "Slow Motion." It was number one on the Billboard charts. Why was this song such a hit? Decode the poetics of "Slow Motion" and you'll discover one of the secrets to rap's seductive power.

You may not know the lyrics to the entire song, but you probably know the line that is hypnotically repeated throughout: "I like it like that/she working that back/slow motion for me."[10] Clearly this is a sexual act, but toddlers, adolescents, and teens don't care about that. All they care about is rhyming "that" and "back" over and over throughout the song. "Back" is also rhymed with "that" in "Your pu**y throw back and you know that" and with "neck" in "Her neck and her back hurting."[11]

In rap, words don't have to rhyme exactly. Neck and back are close enough. Like my friend Larry Whitman once said, "Rappers are so creative they rhyme words that were never meant to be rhymed." That's the genius of these performers.

Back and *that*. If it wasn't for the subject matter you'd think you were listening to a Dr. Seuss book on tape. Rhyming is critical in rap. Many modern poems don't rhyme, but that would never work in rap. Even when freestyling and battling (on-the-spot improvisation), you've got to spit rhymes.

Rhyming poems, songs, and stories are exciting to children. In early education, the first words children learn to read and write are taught in lists of rhyming words (bat, cat; hill pill; play, stay). Gangsta rap takes cues from Dr. Seuss, Mother Goose, and *Sesame Street*. Rap rhymes are like the Pied Piper to children; they're a major part of rap's attraction and power.

In addition to the all-important rhyming schemes, performance is extremely important. When Juvenile raps that infamous line, he accents "back" and "that" like a slap across the face. When youth repeat the line, they do the same thing. It gives them pleasure to rhyme "back" and "that" to a beat. They're not dealing with the sex act. All they care about is rhyming "back" and "that." It's fun. The problem is that these lyrics are inappropriate for children.

The 12 year-old daughter of a friend loved the line so much that for awhile, she would rap it over other songs to see if it fit. It did. In fact, the meter (rhythmic pattern) of that line fit into just about every song, slow or fast, that played on the car radio.

My friend talked to her daughter about the lyrics. She explained in detail what the song was really about. Her daughter was shocked. She said, "I didn't know what they were talking about." She hadn't paid attention to the lyrics as a whole, just the "back and that" line.

Brothers & Sisters, a formula is used to compose popular tunes. The tunes that deviate from the formula seldom get air time.

The formula requires that rap tunes be written in 16 bar cycles and a 4:4 time signature. Snoop Dogg was being interviewed on a VH1 program when he let out that piece to the puzzle. He said he used to write in 52 bar cycles, but Dr. Dre taught him how to write in the formula.

4:4 time, also called "common time," is most often used in classical, rock, country, pop, and Hip Hop. DJ Waxy Fresh says, "If you listen to a lot of music, you'll realize that the whole world turns in 4/4 time" and that "... the repetitive elements in the song tend to repeat every 4 beats."[12]

In 4:4 time you can count along with a song, "1-2-3-4, 1-2-3-4." "Slow Motion" fits perfectly within this scheme.

What's the significance of the 16 bars Snoop referred to? Why is the formula so effective with children? Why wasn't 52 bars effective? I suspect it has to do with the shortening attention spans of us all. Marketers know that African American youth, who watch more TV than any group in the country, have been programmed to stay interested for limited periods of time. However, more research needs to be done in this area.

power of rap images

You can't separate rap music from rap videos, and you can't separate Hip Hop from mainstream media. Corporate America found a goldmine in Hip Hop. This highly profitable partnership has contributed to the widespread pandemic of Psychomedia Perpetrator Disorder in the Hip Hop/ghetto matrix (see Framework for Understanding Hip Hop Youth).

Turning music videos into brainwashing infomercials is an art and a science. There are times in rap videos when the music and imagery do not go together. For example, the lyrics suggest a love song but the video is all about drive-bys. This confuses the brain so much that it shuts down and merely accepts what it is seeing and hearing. Brainwashing or mind manipulation is most effective at this point.

This approach to making videos is engineered to overwhelm and manipulate the autonomic nervous system (ANS). The ANS has two subdivisions: the sympathetic nervous system and the parasympathetic nervous system. When the sympathetic nervous system is stimulated, the heartbeat starts pumping, adrenalin flows, and blood pressure is raised. The body is ready to fight or run, even if it's only a rap video and not a real event.

At least we adults can question (hopefully) our autonomic responses to violent and scary visuals. Children can't always distinguish fantasy from reality, especially when their autonomic responses to violent video images *feel* so real.

Even if they never took a science class, all good musicians, movie directors, and music video directors are aware on some level of these basic biological and physiological facts. Music has always been deliberately designed to create emotions, regardless of genre. In the hood we know it as that good feeling you get from listening to R&B, gospel, jazz, funk, and rap. Major and minor keys combined with flashing lights, rhythms, rhymes, simplistic bass riffs, hypnotic drum beats, repeated musical themes/loops (with virtually no improvisation as in jazz and some Old School), sexual and violent lyrics—these musical tools work together to trigger strong autonomic responses.

This is why rapper Lil Jon is so successful with his shouting technique (crunk) and how the Ying Yang Twins and David Banner created a hit song using only a whisper. (By the way, Lil Jon's shouting technique also mimics some forms of mental illness and mental retardation.)

Autonomic responses may explain why our children appear to be getting more sexual at earlier and earlier ages. The sexually-oriented music and visuals are stirring up sexual feelings.

It's been said that commercialized gangsta rap may have been the first music to be specifically created for television. This is a problem given our addiction to TV. We think we're too smart to be fooled, but judging by our spending habits, we act like we believe everything TV sells us. We consume TV like the gospel truth, especially gangsta rap videos.

According to Hunter Adams III,

> "TV controls our reality. For those stuck in the cycle of generational poverty, TV is a violent instigator. People in poverty tend to indulge in the world of make believe, and TV feeds the imagination. Watching gangsta rap videos may help a young person cope with poverty and violence the way soap operas and game shows help stay-at-home moms cope with their lives."[13]

Adams says that people who watch a lot of TV act like substance abusers. They even go through withdrawals when they try and stop watching.

Repetitive TV viewing leads to copy cat behaviors. Hip Hop video editors often use rapid, chaotic editing techniques, such as quick cuts from scene to scene and zooms in and out, which overload the viewer's brain. It's impossible to follow what's going on, but it's so fascinating that you keep watching anyway. What's more, the quick cut technique enables producers to hide even more offensive images frame by frame to have a subliminal impact. Likewise, during the production of a CD, offensive lyrics can be secretly inserted in tracks.

Young people haven't yet developed the ability to sort out fantasy from reality. Children act out the scenes they see on TV. Boys will play war games after watching violent cartoons, movies, or video games.

With all the quick cutting, blurry focusing, and repetitive shots going on in music videos, you won't consciously remember every-thing that's happened during those few short minutes. However, the subconscious mind remembers all, and it's at this level that the desire to act out is stirred.

Rap videos are like infomercials, selling and instructing our youth on ways to squander wealth, roll blunts (marijuana cigars), do drive-bys, and flash gang signs. With prolonged viewing, young fans will romanticize, glamorize, and identify with the thug image. This will prioritize their behaviors. They recognize that thugging and mugging have status in the hood. During the critical "Who Am I?" adolescent phase of self-discovery, youth may become wannabe gangstas as they imitate their Hip Hop role models.

The social scientist working in TV programming knows all about the mind control game. MTV perfected video and audio techniques that are designed to dull the mind's cognitive powers. In the book *Rocking Around the Clock*, author Anne Kaplan says that

> "MTV hypnotizes more than others (other television pro-grams) because it consists of a series of short (four minute) texts that maintain us in an excited state of expectation. [Viewers are] trapped by the constant hope that the next video will finally satisfy, and lured by the seductive promise of immediate plentitude, we keep endlessly consuming the short texts. MTV thus carries to an extreme a phenomenon that characterizes most of television."[14]

Robert Pittman, a co-founder of MTV, wrote:

> "We make you feel a certain way as opposed to walking away
> with any particular knowledge … What the kids can't do
> today is follow things for too long. They get bored and dis-
> tracted, their minds wander. If information is presented to
> them in tight fragments that don't necessarily follow each
> other, kids can comprehend that."[15]

Maybe they can, but maybe they can't.

Do you know what your child is watching?

Today's parents let their toddlers watch Hip Hop videos all day
long. The April 2004 Pediatrics report states that "Children who
watch significant amounts of TV between the ages of one and three
are more likely to have attention problems."[16] With each hour of television preschoolers watch, attention problems will probably increase
by 10 percent later on.

Lest you think Robert Pittman is unaware of the social impact his
creation has had, here's what he told *The New York Times*: "When you
are dealing with music culture, music serves as something beyond
entertainment. It is really the peg that people use to identify themselves. It is representative of their values and culture."[17]

During the minstrel era, black performers could only create negative images of themselves that were humorous to whites but devastating to us. Some of those performers, like Bert Williams, were comic
geniuses, but at the time they were not allowed to perform with dignity. In novels, movies, advertisements, newspapers, and magazines,
we were shown as clowns, as "lazy, ignorant, pleasure-seeking, powerful, childlike black men who needed to be supervised and controlled
by powerful, competent, responsible white males."[18]

Today's youth across the globe are being exposed to images of black
manhood and womanhood that reinforce all the ugly stereotypes. For
example, Redman and Method Man, who once performed with the
conscious political rap group Wu-Tang Clan, sank low in the sum-

mer of 2004 when they appeared in their Fox TV show *Method & Red*. This sitcom reduced black men to clowns who wanted to live in master's house. They were pleasure seeking, buffoonish, and immature.

Children may know all the words to a rap tune, but that doesn't mean they understand how it was constructed and for what purpose.

Many progressive educators are using rap in the classroom to teach. Let's now take this a step further. Just as we teach grammar, poetics, and music theory, let's begin to develop rap literacy in our youth by teaching them:

1. How rap is constructed.
2. The musical formulas used in rap.
3. The poetic connection to Dr. Seuss and *Sesame Street* (that alone may wake up teens).
4. How to decode the overt and covert meanings in gangsta rap tunes.

Chapter 6

Hypocrisy 2—

Bling Bling // Poverty in the Hood

"This is God's world, and instead of trying to be the best producer or record company executive, I'm constantly just trying to be the best person I can. When I wake up, that's the mission I'm on. Money doesn't buy you happiness, and success doesn't buy you happiness. It doesn't make you better than anyone else." **Sean "P Diddy" Combs**

Which one is keeping it real: bling bling on rap videos or poverty in the hood? What's the perspective of the rap artist—streets littered with broken glass and empty syringes or the mansions, gated communities, and private schools rappers send their children to? With the money some of these brothas have, do you think they're keeping it real from a street perspective? They might have come from the street, but with all that money, I guarantee they don't live there anymore, and they probably need a writer to help them write their rhymes about the street.

If rappers were keeping it real about their lives, they'd be rapping about their investment portfolios, their marriages, their children's private education, and paying the IRS. They may still have gang affiliations, but from the safe, quiet confines of their gated communities, so what?

I ain't mad at these brothas and sistas for peeping America's economic system, but I am mad at them for keeping the secret to

111

themselves and feeding our children poison instead. Why are they promoting the "reality" of the streets instead of information that could help them? The hypocrisy is that these rappers are living one way but pretending through their music that they're living another way. This keeps our youth believing the lie, that the ways out of poverty are drug dealing, golddigging, and pimping.

I've been searching the country for the ghetto because to look at Hip Hop videos, there is only ghetto fabulous. According to rappers, black folk are now living large with mansions, luxury cars, fur coats, designer clothes, and diamonds. Brothers & Sisters, this is a lie made to look like the truth.

In the mid-1990s and into the new millennium, a few rappers got hood rich by exploiting our desperation and seducing our children with promises of wealth and things. They tease and tempt with this picture, but what you see ain't necessarily the truth.

Hip Hop wealth is concentrated in the hands of a few. In the true spirit of capitalism, the money of the Hip Hop poor flows straight to the pockets of the few Hip Hop rich—the rappers, entrepreneurs, and their owners. This is unacceptable considering that the multibillion dollar Hip Hop industry originated in communities where there are no jobs, substandard housing, poor education, and low quality health care. Ghetto residents, who wealthy rappers say they represent, are poor, broke, and in debt.

While rappers live in mansions in gated communities (watch *MTV Cribs* and BET's *How You Living*), their young black fans are living in substandard housing and dodging bullets. There are gates all right, but they're on windows and double bolted doors.

While rappers, producers, video directors, and investors drive around in their Bentleys, black youth are taking the bus.

While rappers send their children to private schools, black youth attend substandard public schools and are falling farther and farther behind in reading and math. The drop out rate for young black males is as high as 70 percent in some urban communities.

Hypocrisy 2—Bling Bling//Poverty in the Hood

While rappers dine at the best and most expensive restaurants and drink expensive bottles of Cristal, black youth in the ghetto are eating unhealthy greasy fast food and drinking cheap, lethal 40oz malt liquor.

While rappers like P. Diddy are featured in the pages of *Vogue*, sporting their designer clothes, black youth in the ghetto are paying top dollar for clothes that will fall apart after one time in the washing machine.

The irony is that many rappers come from middle-and upper-income families. Lil' Romeo and Lil' Bow Wow didn't come from the street. Like many top Hip Hop artists, they are educated and have never ever lived in the projects, went to bed hungry, stomped on a cockroach, or cleaned a mouse trap. They are nothing like the fourth and fifth generations of black children who are still trying to pick the padlock that their parents and grandparents could not unlock. The ghetto consumers of Hip Hop/rap who are struggling to achieve and maintain self-respect receive no help from the rap artists they love.

At this point, young people should be waking up. They should be asking themselves, with friends like gangsta rappers, who needs enemies?

Some Hip Hop entertainers come from working-class backgrounds. You'd think they'd want to help uplift those they left behind. Instead, they create songs and videos that disrespect black women and promote the gangsta agenda and lifestyle.

The original voice of Hip Hop protested ghetto conditions with a vengeance. Today, rap lives in la la land while a disproportionate percentage of their African American and Latino fans are suffering in subhuman conditions. Rap videos keep our youth spending precious dollars on the latest consumer fad rather than promoting the entrepreneurial spirit and skills that made some rappers multimillionaires.

One of the latest fads to hit high schools is pinning birthday money to white tee-shirts with big diaper pins. White tee-shirts are like a uniform in the hood because you can get them cheap at the Korean beauty supply store, two for $5. The diaper pin is an early warning sign of Prolonged Adolescent Syndrome.

I was taught to hide my money in my shoes, underwear, and socks so no one could steal it. The visible display of cash across the heart is a sad, love-sick identification with rappers.

While our youth spend the few dollars they get as a birthday gift or from working a minimum wage job (if they can get one), the smart rapper is investing his/her millions of dollars in energy drinks, fashion lines, recording companies, and other ventures. Our children only see the visible bling bling, but it's the invisible investments made behind the scenes that generate the real money. Last time I looked, they weren't sharing the money or knowledge with their fans.

Gym shoes featured in rap videos cost about as much as a month's income from a minimum wage fast food job, but that doesn't stop our children from buying the gym shoes their rap idols promote. Males and females in the hood wear fake glass and plastic bling as earrings, necklaces, rings, and belt buckles while a rapper's diamond tennis bracelet may cost hundreds of thousands of dollars.

Young people have always imitated their idols, and they say that imitation is the sincerest form of flattery. Rappers ought to feel very flattered—and ashamed of their hypocrisy in the face of unrelenting ghetto poverty. In the quote that led off this section, Sean "P Diddy" Combs says that money doesn't buy you happiness and it doesn't make you better than anyone else. Do his fans believe that? Do his fans know that Combs was once an altar boy who studied business at Howard University and that he launched his career with an unpaid internship?

In his 2004 hit "Why," Jadakiss said that "Rappers lie in 85% of [their] rhymes."[1] Do their young impressionable fans know that? It's true that money can't buy you happiness, but as we in the hood would say, it's better to be sad and rich than happy and broke. It's hypocritical of multimillionaires to say that money doesn't buy you happiness when all they show are the "joys" of consumption, materialism, and bling bling.

Hypocrisy 2—Bling Bling//Poverty in the Hood

Chapter 7

Africa: The Origin of Bling

"Good Morning, this ain't Vietnam still
People lose hands, legs, arms for real
Little was known of Sierra Leone
And how it connect to the diamonds we own."[1]
Kanye West, "Diamonds from Sierra Leone (Remix)"

"Cruise the diamond district with my biscuit
Flossin' my Rolex wrist
S**t I'm rich
I'ma stay that bitch."[2]
Lil' Kim, "Queen Bitch"

Bling bling is the most visual symbol of the wealth-poverty hypocrisy. Bling bling is jewelry made from expensive precious stones and metals. It can also mean all forms of showy style. Bling bling was coined by New Orleans rap family Cash Money Millionaires back in the late 1990s. Cash Money's BG gained national awareness with the song "Bling Bling."

Bling bling is also associated with the term "hood rich." Let's break it down:

Hood + Rich = Local Wealth

Hood rich is wealth made off the backs of the poor. It can also mean the appearance of wealth. The bling bling creed is, "If you've got it, flaunt it." But let's keep it real. Showy displays actually cover up feelings of low self-worth that are caused by poverty.

A mental health definition of bling bling could possibly read: "The unhealthy fascination with celebrating and/or pretending to be the wealthiest member of the poorest group to the detriment of one's own psychological, economic, social, cultural, and spiritual well-being."

While rappers can afford to have the top jewelers in the world custom make their diamond dollar sign necklaces, black youth wear cheap imitations made of plastic, rhinestones, glass, cubic zirconias, or cheap gold and silver purchased from the dollar store, Korean hair store, or Arab jewelry cart at the mall.

Hip Hop jewelry, also known as gangsta jewelry, thug jewelry, iced out jewelry, or bling bling jewelry, feature large gold, sterling silver, and platinum chain necklaces, medallions, dog tags, watches, rings, and tooth caps.

I have witnessed students, from fifth graders to high school seniors, fighting over their fake bling. While rappers' bling might be valued at hundreds of thousands or even millions of dollars, the bling of black youth is usually valued at 50 cents. Clearly, it's not about the monetary value of the jewelry but the perception of having something that *appears* valuable. The symbol of prosperity is what's important. In the hood, bling bling creates status, self-esteem, identification with rappers, and Hip Hop group membership.

Black youth are so creative and resourceful. They buy cheap and worthless junk, put them together in new ways, and the result is ghetto fabulous, a global fashion phenomenon that ripples throughout the retail industry. Ghetto fabulous is considered an art because not everyone can pull it off. Fashion designers, such as Tommy Hilfiger, put their egos aside to cash in. One Hilfiger ad shows a white male model in big, baggy clothes, saggin' pants, and underwear showing. Hilfiger's red, white, and blue colors combined with Hip Hop to form Urban Prep. The line revived his company.[3]

Brothers & Sisters, buying bling bling here in America literally means that an African brother, sister, or child will bleed for our greed. The diamond game has created a battle field in Sub-Saharan Africa, the the Democratic Republic of Congo, Sierra Leone, South Africa, Liberia, and Angola.

When diamond mastermind Cecil Rhodes landed on African soil in 1871 and saw children playing with diamonds like marbles, he launched what would become a multibillion dollar, bloody, global enterprise. The sale of African diamonds to the West and the rest of the world is financing brutal dictatorships and wars, African against African. Young boys are abducted from their homes to fight, girls are raped, and their parents are killed.

According to Rep. Tony Hall, the U.S. is the world's largest diamond consumer. Sixty-five percent of gem quality diamonds are bought here, and "DeBeers provides 70 percent of the world's uncut diamonds."[4]

Some of the biggest supporters of racist diamond mine owners are rappers, with their six-carat earrings, 42-carat diamond studded crosses, 42-carat Jesus head figures, 48-carat bracelets, 11-carat rings, and 27-carat Jacob watches.

Rapper Kanye West helped to educate the world with powerful visuals in his 2005 "Diamonds from Sierra Leone" video (*Late Registration* CD). He raps about the conflict Hip Hop has with the diamond trade.

> "I thought my Jesus Piece was so harmless
> 'til I seen a picture of a shorty armless
> And here's the conflict
> It's in a black person's soul to rock that gold
> Spend ya whole life tryin get that ice
> On a polar rugby it look so nice
> How could somethin' so wrong make me feel so right, right?"[5]

In a *USA Today* interview, Kanye explained how recording "Diamonds Are Forever" marked the beginning of his spiritual awakening regarding diamond lust:

"When I was saying 'Throw your diamonds in the sky' on
the original, I was talking about the symbol fans throw up
(thumb to thumb, index finger to index finger) at Roc-A-
Fella concerts. But God led me down this path. He put
angels in my road to give me all this information. I didn't
know I would wind up talking about blood diamonds."[6]

The Hip Hop community can contribute to the healing of Africa
by refusing to purchase African diamonds. First, they must learn about
the evil enterprise they're supporting. Hip Hop artists should launch
a worldwide movement to educate the world about the Belgians,
Germans, and other European diamond mine owners. A Miners Aid
Concert would generate millions of badly needed dollars for black
African miners and their families.

Then let's just give up diamonds altogether, for what will a man
gain if he loses his soul (Matthew 16:25)?

Chapter 8

Ghetto Life: Not So Fabulous

"My mom is from Jamaica and she was going to school in the morning, and in the evening she was working, and at night she would go to night school and then come in and go to sleep. So she would never watch the news and stuff like that and she didn't know what crack was. She didn't know nothing about it, but when I told her I was selling crack, she threatened to kick me out of the house. And then I just started paying for stuff—paying her bills and giving her money, so she'd just tell me to be careful because there was nothing she could do to stop it."[1] **Notorious B.I.G.**

"Poverty is the worse kind of violence." **Jewish proverb**

I did a Google search for the phrase "you know you ghetto" and got 443 websites of ghetto jokes. There's even a Christian "you know you ghetto."

Black comedians have made a fortune from ghetto jokes that often come from personal experience. Ricky Smiley talks about the spinners in the casket at the "drug dealer funeral." Remember Eddie Murphy's alcoholic uncle who nearly burned the house down at the family barbeque and the kid who couldn't buy ice cream because his family was on welfare?

Chris Rock loved black people but hated "niggas." Nikki Parker's (Mo'Nique) "hey!" and Bernie Mac's parenting skills are straight ghetto. Richard Pryor's standup characters were created from the people he grew up with in the ghetto. J. Anthony Brown, Cedric "The Entertainer," and Steve Harvey are country ghetto. Shows like

In Living Color and *Def Comedy Jam* were revolutionary because they revealed the secret life of the ghetto.

I'm not going to lie, I've laughed at the jokes, but I've laughed as one who knows ghetto life firsthand. Sometimes if you don't laugh you'll cry. I've lost loved ones to drug addiction, alcoholism, and violence in the ghetto. I've struggled as a parent to keep my son and daughters safe from the streets in the ghetto. As an educator, I've worked with young people who were succeeding despite having drug-addicted or incarcerated parents, and I've also mourned the violent deaths of athletes I coached in the ghetto. I work with kids who are stuck in foster care in the ghetto. I've known girls who got pregnant in their early teens and boys who became fathers much too soon in the ghetto.

If you don't laugh you will cry. These things can happen to anyone caught inside the ghetto matrix. Now you know why Master P's (Percy Miller) first CD in 1991 was entitled *The Ghetto is Tryin to Kill Me.*

Like black comedians, gangsta rappers (those who grew up in the hood) have gotten hood rich off of their ghetto experiences. Unlike many black comedians who have some race consciousness, gangsta rappers glorify the plight of the ghetto.

The Western concept of ghetto first sprung up in European cities to restrict Jews to certain areas. Today, ghettoes in this country are occupied by members of minority groups who live there because of economic and social pressures and restrictions. According to Rodger Doyle in *Rise of the Black Ghetto: How to Create An American Version of Apartheid,*

> "The modern ghetto, with its sharply defined racial lines, generally did not begin to form until blacks in substantial numbers migrated north beginning in 1916. There they found themselves competing for jobs and housing with immigrants from Europe. The competition was often violent, as in the Chicago riot of 1919, when 38 people were

killed. Violence and the threat of violence, together with agreements among white homeowners not to sell to blacks, increasingly left African-Americans in separate neighborhoods and worlds."[2]

There may be no laws or gates preventing movement to other parts of the city, but the restrictions are still felt on the residents. Many public housing projects are located near high-income neighborhoods. While whites come to the hood to purchase their drugs and solicit prostitutes, black folk in the hood seldom journey beyond the tracks. Downtown—where all the jobs and wealth are—may be close by, but the mental prison here is strong. Better grocery stores may be across the tracks, but we prefer to shop at stores that are not owned by us, sell spoiled milk, and are not kept clean.

City PTBs (powers that be) like us staying in our place (unless there's a plan to "revitalize" the neighborhood, which means entire populations will be displaced). But we also do it to ourselves. I'm a strong advocate of the black brain trust staying in the hood to improve conditions, but there's also a big world out there. The mental prison prevents us from seeing what's out there, so we live vicariously through characters in movies and of course, rap videos.

There are many racial and ethnic ghettoes in this country, but the most fascinating, creative, and energetic is the black ghetto. Most black folk come from the ghetto, still live there, play there, go to church there, teach there, fight fires there, break the law there, fight crime there, eat ribs there, sit on porches there. This is where Hip Hop was born, flourishes, and is exported to the world via rap and music videos. Hip Hop is a ghetto product, but the ghetto doesn't profit. Young people keep coming up with new dances, fashions, language, and more to export, but they don't benefit.

poverty

> "According to the National Center for Education Statistics, 30 percent of children who attend urban schools live in poverty, and 40 percent of urban students attend a high-poverty school—one that has 40 percent of its students eligible for free or reduced-price lunch."[3]

It's not all good in the hood. Families are trying to make ends meet under entrenched poverty. Despite media portrayals, welfare recipients aren't trying to be dependent. People aren't trying to be poor or unemployed. Have you ever been so stuck in a negative place in your life that if it hadn't been for the grace of God, you may have never escaped? Our children are trapped in the hood.

Poverty is violence against humanity. In a nation as wealthy as ours, it is inhumane that children of all races, but especially African Americans, don't get to eat a good dinner because a single mother has to make a choice: the high heat bill, the high bus fair—or food. Medicine or food. School fees or food. It's official: a single parent making minimum wage can't afford rent in most urban areas, not even the worse areas. Thus, homelessness has an African American face.

Some of the strange behaviors we see coming from our next door neighbors or from our own homes make sense when you consider this unbearable situation.

In the hood, hunger competes with the fear of violence, the po po, and crime. How can a child come to school ready to learn under these conditions? In fact, take a walk through the halls of just about any urban school in America and you'll notice that schools have begun to mimic prisons in many ways. The school-to-prison pipeline is real, as are the similarities between schools and prisons. Which one is becoming more like the other?

SIMILARITIES BETWEEN SCHOOLS AND PRISONS

Prison	Schools
Metal detectors	Metal detectors
Surveillance cameras	Surveillance cameras
Intercom used to buzz people in and out	Intercom used to buzz people in and out
Security guards with weapons (guns)	Security guards with weapons (guns)
Drug culture	Drug culture
Drug searches by drug sniffing dogs	Drug searches by drug sniffing dogs
Climate of fear, gangs, bullying, cliques	Climate of fear, gangs, bullying, cliques
Poor libraries	Poor libraries
High illiteracy rate	High illiteracy rate
Disproportionately high rate of minorities in prison	Disproportionately high rate of minorities in special education
Hostile staff	Hostile staff
Hostile inmates	Hostile classmates
Sexual assaults, inappropriate relationships with prison personnel (sex life mismanagement)	Sexual assaults, inappropriate relationships with school personnel (sex life mismanagement)
Upon release, poor financial prospects	Upon graduation, poor financial prospects
Understaffed (more nurses, psychologists, counselors needed)	Understaffed (more nurses, psychologists, counselors needed)
Poor lighting, inmates exposed to little sunlight, which contributes to mood swings	Poor lighting, students exposed to little sunlight, which contributes to mood swings
Serves fatty, sugary foods	Serves fatty, sugary foods
Some inmates monitored by electronic ankle bracelets	Some students monitored by electronic ankle bracelets
Identified by a number	Identified by a number

Inmates upon release have parole officers	Many students have probation officers
Placed in "time out" (the hole, isolation)	Placed in "time out" (in-school suspension, isolation)
Life changing experience	Life changing experience
Psychotropic medications issued	Psychotropic medications issued
Strict schedule	Strict schedule
High levels of mental stress	High levels of mental stress
Jailhouse mentality	Jailhouse/schoolhouse mentality
Rising recidivism/continue to come back	Rising retention/continue to be held back
Badge of honor for acting out against authority	Badge of honor for acting out against authority
Many facilities are in poor condition, overcrowded	Many facilities are in poor condition, overcrowded
Supported by tax payers	Supported by tax payers
TV is used as a tool of privilege and electronic babysitter	TV is used as a teaching aid, tool of privilege, and electronic babysitter
Hustling, gambling, betting, playing cards, shooting dice	Hustling, gambling, betting, playing cards, shooting dice
Daily head count, all visitors must sign in and out of the building	Daily head count, all visitors must sign in and out of the building
Self imposed racial segregation	Self imposed racial segregation
Nationally, minorities are convicted at rates of two to three times that of other groups	Nationally, minority students are suspended at rates of two to three times that of other students
On average it takes about $140,000 a year to incarcerate a young person	On average it takes about $9,000 to $10,000 a year to educate a young person

Hypocrisy 2—Bling Bling//Poverty in the Hood

Annually, prison construction is a billion dollar industry	Annually, school construction is under funded by $1 billion
Criminals are unfairly called animals; prisons are often called zoos	Students are unfairly called animals; schools in the hood are called zoos

teen sex & pregnancy in the hood

Poverty is entrenched in the hood for many reasons, including teen pregnancy. Brothers & Sisters, we need to wake up and realize that sex and economics are intimately connected. My editor calls this "sexonomics," which is the impact of irresponsible sex on cash flow in the hood.

> "When the court makes you pay to support a child that was conceived during a loveless one-night stand, that's sexonomics. When you spend money on a date to get her into bed, that's sexonomics. When you get on the pole and shake your money maker to make him pay, that's sexonomics. When you spend money on medical care because of an STD that came from having unprotected sex with a person you didn't know, was down low, or low down, that's sexonomics. The impact of sexonomics is felt at both the micro and macro levels. The best way to build wealth is to have sex with one husband or wife for the rest of your life. In the African American community, love and money are more on the liability and loss side than the profit and assets side of the ledger." **Donna Marie Williams**

We must continue to educate our teens on the consequences (negative and positive) of their sexual behavior, perhaps by tapping into their Hip Hop values of materialism, consumerism, and getting paid. If we show them how sex and pregnancies outside of marriage contribute to poverty, we may see their behavior change. In the meantime:

1. Black teens are more likely than white or Hispanic youth to have had sexual intercourse, to begin sexual activity at an earlier age, and to have had more than four sexual partners.

2. Although pregnancies for black teens (aged 15 to 19) declined 23 percent between 1990 and 1997, they still have the highest pregnancy rate among all major racial and ethnic groups and are more likely than other adolescents to have children outside of marriage. (Hispanic teens have the highest teen *birth* rate.)[4]

ghetto games

David Chang (not to be confused with Jeff Chang, author of *Hip Hop Can't Stop, Won't Stop*), a Taiwanese immigrant who has been tagged an authority on all things ghetto, created Ghettopoly, a parody of Monopoly. A 28 year-old graduate of the University of Rochester with degrees in Economics and Psychology and a minor in Marketing, Chang has created several board games that exploit the plight of the ghetto and promote racist stereotypes.

Chang's game references malt liquor addiction, money laundering, loansharking, and paying protection fees, among other ungodly things. Ghettopoly players move around the board with interesting pieces: pimps, machine guns, 40oz bottles of malt liquor, a basketball, a marijuana leaf, and rocks of crack cocaine. One game card reads, "You got yo whole neighborhood addicted to crack. Collect $50."[5] Players buy stolen properties, pimp hos, build crack houses and projects, and try not to get carjacked.

Once again, it's business as usual in the hood, and it ain't all good. We counter the likes of Mr. Chang in our rites of passage programs with "Ghetto Child," a song by Hip Hop/R&B artist Joe.

"Just because I'm a ghetto child
I won't live down to your expectations
Just believe that a ghetto child
Can rise in the highest celebration."[6]

Black folk were mad at Chang, not only because of the way he portrayed us but because he blasphemed the names of some of our most revered historical figures. Malcolm X is spelled "Malcum X" and Dr. King is "Martin Luthor King Jr." Rev. Glenn Wilson, pastor of Enon Tabernacle Baptist Church, said, "This is beyond making fun, to use the caricature of Dr. King in this regard. There's no way that game could be taken in any way other than that this man had racist intent in marketing it."[7]

But Bob Herbert, *The New York Times,* also has a point. He says,

"How can you march against a game and not march against the real-life slaughter on the streets and in the homes of inner cities across America? Violent crime, ignorance and disease are carving the very heart out of America's black population. Instead of using their influence to help stop the slaughter, certain truly twisted elements of the Hip Hop culture encourage it, celebrating it in songs that not only glorify murderous violence, but also degrade black people to a degree that should leave any sensible person stupefied, trust me, we've got some problems that are bigger than Ghettopoly."[8]

Murray Forman, a communications professor at Northeastern University, weighed in from his far-removed ivory tower:

"What might have Ghettopoly told us about the ghetto? It could have been an opportunity to discuss a guy selling crack on the street corner, just trying to put diapers on his kid's bottom …"[9]

Hypocrisy 2—Bling Bling//Poverty in the Hood

Please. Ghettopoly is just another in a long list of racist products designed to denigrate black people and exploit the ghetto, just like *Ten Little Niggers* by Agatha Christie and the McLoughlin Brothers' *Chopped Up Niggers* puzzle game.

ghetto colonization

Through mass media, ghetto/Hip Hop culture is exported all over the world. The formula for ghetto colonization is as follows:

Hip Hop Culture (values, style, art) + PTB Money/Power + Mass Media = Ghetto Colonization of the World

We know the ghetto doesn't profit from the culture it exports and that conditions remain the same. Does the same hold true for other colonies of Hip Hop: small towns, high-income neighborhoods, and suburbs? Have they seen an increase in unemployment, low academic performance, or a decrease in their local economies?

Absolutely not. They'd like to blame all their problems on black people, but they can't. These problems exist across the board.

Segments of white communities have become ghetto not in substance but in style. Developmentally, teenagers of all races begin to stretch beyond the family. These are the rebellious teen years and the communications and values gap between adults and young people is a problem with every generation. White teens rebel via punk, heavy metal, rock, and goth music. So when you see them on the street with multi-colored hair, piercings, black clothes, and other strange fashions, they're stretching. It's what the hippies did back in the 1960s.

Just when white parents were coming to terms with these different styles, along came Hip Hop, and they had a collective fit. Their children were acting black and *turning* black. They were bringing home their one black friend, listening to rap music, braiding and locking their hair, saggin' their pants, wearing baggy clothes, gyrating, and talking the talk (you know what I'm saying?).

There are so many ways to be black, but the only way that caught the attention of young whites was the ghetto/Hip Hop way. The term "wigger" (white nigger) comes from whites who accuse other whites of acting black, or as some of us would say, whites *wanting* to be black.

For white males (young and middle-aged, believe it or not), rap's gangsta persona is a testosterone rush. But for all teens of all races and nationalities, the bottom line is the music.

ghetto, hood, or village?

How we see/perceive our community will determine our direction in the next few years. In this section, I'll decode our three perceptual communities: "ghetto," "hood," and "village." As you read through this section, search your soul to assess how you truly feel about the ground out of which our children are growing. If we only see rocks and weeds, then there's no hope. But if we see good soil, sunlight, and clean water, then a garden will grow.

Ghetto($) Decoded

Before the hood, there was the ghetto. Ghettoes are not new to black folk. We've been trying to escape them since our capture by the Portuguese in 1441.

I sometimes spell ghetto/ghettoes as "ghetto($)" or "ghettoe$." Why? Because billions of dollars are made off of African American ghettoe$. This is ironic considering they are some of the most impoverished places in the world.

To decode ghettoes, I'll use only the letters in the word, sometimes more than once in a phrase or sentence. When I initially played around with the word, I found concepts that are highly associated with ghetto living, stereotypes, and thinking. The following are some basic words I found that are associated with ghetto life:

Hypocrisy 2—Bling Bling//Poverty in the Hood

- **Ethos:** The basic and unique character of a group, social context, or period of time typically expressed in attitudes, habits, and beliefs.
- **Ego:** The part of self that is tied to identity and feelings of superiority in relationship to others.
- **Ghost:** 1. The supposed spirit of someone who has died; appears as a shadowy form, causes sounds, moves objects, or creates a frightening atmosphere in a place. 2. Nonexistent person or thing. 3. In religion, someone's soul or spirit (archaic). (Give up the ghost to die.)[10]
- **Ho:** 1. A taboo, slang, and insulting term for a prostitute, woman. 2. Late 20th century pronunciation of whore.[11]
- **Hot:** 1. Causing much discussion, disagreement, or controversy (a hot topic). 2. Unpleasant or uncomfortable because of antagonism, trouble, or danger (informal).
  3. Quickly angered, easily provoked, or aroused. A hot temper (It got too hot for him to handle.). 4. Intense or violent. 5. Hot to trot: eager and willing (slang). 6. Extremely infectious, lethal, or containing infectious viruses. 7. Physically attracted or aroused (slang); exciting (slang); desire (informal).
  8. Something stolen, obtained illegally (slang) (hot jewels).
  9. On the run: wanted by the police (slang) (a hot suspect).[12]
- **Host:** 1. Someone who invites, welcomes, and entertains guests, often providing them with food and drink. 2. A military army (archaic). 3. A human, animal, plant, or other organism in or on which another organism, especially a parasite, lives. (14th century. Old French from Latin *hostis*, "stranger, enemy"; in medieval Latin, "army"; source of English "hostile.")[13]
- **Sot:** An offensive term for someone who habitually drinks alcohol to excess (dated insult). (Pre-12th century. Old French "fool," from Medieval Latin *sottus*.)[14]
- **Tot:** 1. A small child (informal). 2. Small amount of something, especially liquor.[15]

Hypocrisy 2—Bling Bling//Poverty in the Hood

- **Tote**: 1. To carry or haul something, especially something heavy. 2. To carry something, especially a gun, on your person. 2. A heavy load that is hauled or carried. (Late 17th century. Origin uncertain. Perhaps originally a dialect form of Gullah *tot* "to carry," probably from a West African language.)[16]
- **Toot**: 1. A bout of heavy drinking. 2. A quantity of an illegal substance, especially cocaine, taken by inhaling through the nose (slang).[17]

Now, Brothers & Sisters, let's put these words from ghettoes into sentences. The following may not be grammatically perfect, but the story these sentences tell is chilling.

1. **The tot** (child) **got to go** (sounds like ghetto in rap poetic style).
2. **The ho** (sexually promiscuous person) **got to go**.
3. **The sot** (drunken fool) **got to go**.
4. **He** (black man) **got shot**.
5. **She** (black woman) **got shot**.
6. **The tot got shot** (small children are victims of stray bullets and drive-bys).
7. **The ho got shot** (with a dirty HIV needle).
8. **The sot got shot** (by the police).
9. **Get to he** (via educational system, entertainment, gang jump-ins).
10. **Get to she** (via welfare system, sex industry, sexual predators).
11. **Get to tot** (addict them while in the womb, eliminate parents via incarceration).
12. **Get to ho** (via STDs, HIV/AIDS).
13. **Get to sot** (via alcoholism, cheap 40 ounce malt liquor, and fruity wine coolers).
14. **He's hot** (attractive, wanted by police, infected).
15. **She's hot** (attractive, promiscuous, infected).
16. **The tot's hot** (angry, hostile).

17. **The ho's too hot** (infected, angry, wanted by police).
18. **The sot's hot** (fool on the run).
19. **He totes** (carries a gun).
20. **She totes** (carries a load).
21. **The tot totes** (is stressed out).
22. **The ho totes** (is stressed out from heavy lifestyle).
23. **The sot totes** (pulls others down with him/her).
24. **The ghettoes host** (parties, armies/gangs, parasitic diseases).
25. **The ghetto toots; he/she/tots toot too** (cocaine, other illegal drugs).
26. **The ghettoes host ghost too** (the ghetto has a spirit, the ghetto is dead).
27. **The ghetto got teeth too** (teeth bite, chew things up before spitting them out!).
28. **The ghetto goes to soothe the tots** (eases the pain of the children).
29. **The ghetto ethos** (culture, beliefs, and practices of the ghetto).
30. **The ghetto got shoes** (every rapper or sports star from the ghetto gets a shoe deal).

As we'll soon see, there's a sense of pride when you live in the hood. However, ghetto shows us the flip side (perceptually) of the same community. There's a stigma highly associated with being from the ghetto. It's common to hear parents warning their children to not "act ghetto" (meaning loud and disrespectful without shame). If someone says, "You so ghetto," you've just been insulted. By the same token, being called "ghetto fabulous" is an honor. Since this book is about hypocrisy, allow me to 'fess up now. I experienced just about all things ghetto at one point or another during my youth.

Grandmaster Flash's ominous 1982 hit, "The Message," with its chorus, "It's like a jungle sometimes, it makes me wonder how I keep from going under,"[18] marked a change in how we began to perceive the ghetto. That song taught us to see with different eyes. We've been *hood*winked. Ghetto life is not fabulous. It is profoundly desolate.

Hood Decoded

Hood: 1. Neighborhood (slang). 2. A hoodlum (slang). 3. To cover.[19]

One of the many meanings of hood is cover. When something is covered its movements are restricted—in other words, trapped! When you feel trapped, restricted, and limited physically, mentally, and spiritually, you become physically and mentally exhausted. Residents of the hood give up trying to escape and accept "it's all good in the hood" as a means of pacifying themselves, never realizing that the real world is bigger than the hood.

Hood is short for neighborhood, but if you think about it, hood is missing neighbor. A hood, therefore, is a place without neighbors, a.k.a. people, and as we all know, people make the world go round. The Bible says, "Love thy neighbor as thyself" (Mark 12:31), but when you don't love yourself you can't love your neighbor.

The hood has its rules. For example, you have to know how to fight in order to live in the hood. You have to watch your back in the hood. Certain territories are off limits in the hood—or suffer the consequences. Don't trust the po po in the hood. You've got to wear your colors in the hood. Avoid the blinking blue police cameras in the hood. You live in the hood, you die in the hood.

Hoodlum comes from hood; hoodlums (criminals) make life in the hood dangerous. Hip Hop youth are often instructed to not act hoodish, which can be translated as thuggish or criminal. Poverty and violence create a bitter taste that never satisfies and leads to black-on-black and black-on-brown tensions.

As rapper Jezzy says in his 2005 hit "My Hood" (from the *Let's Get It: Thug Motivation 101* CD), "Every time I do it I do it for my hood ... It's understood I do it for the hood."[20] Unfortunately, what he's doing is creating havoc in the hood. Gangstas in the hood fight over turf/land they rent and don't even own.

Based on stereotypes and realities of life in the hood, the decoded meaning of hood reads as follows:

H = **H**ustle
O = **O**bey
O = **O**r
D = **D**ie

One must hustle in order to survive in the hood. Obey the unwritten rules of the hood (e.g., snitches get stitches) or else live in fear or die from random acts of violence.

The hood consists of hard working people trapped by classism and institutional racism. The projects, rental properties, gutters, vacant lots, and foreclosed, abandoned houses and storefronts serve as shelter for families, the homeless, and the drug addicted. Ironically, the worse the conditions, the stronger the rep (reputation). A reputation can be so strong that a resident can get instant respect by saying, "I'm straight up out of the hood" or "I'll ride and die for the hood."

With hood values such as "no snitching" and "it's all good in the hood," we are indirectly inviting the criminal to move in next door to our families.

To prove my point, I ask students in my workshops to make a list of everyone who lives in their home. Most lists include parents, siblings, little nieces, and nephews.

Then I have students list their neighbors to find out who else lives in the so-called hood. The typical list includes grandparents, aunties, cousins, friends, and new strangers. Generational poverty doesn't often permit residents to move outside the boundaries of the neighborhood where they were raised. Thus, many of the people you grew up with in your house now live down the street, which was the case with my family.

I then ask students, "Do you respect and/or love the people on your list?" They overwhelmingly respond "yes"—except for the new strangers.

I ask students, "If you were a criminal (rapist, murderer, pedophile, or drug dealer), where would you live to avoid detection—in a community where the neighborhood watch program will turn you in with a quickness or where the rule is "no one snitches" (tells on the criminals)? Overwhelmingly students respond, "Where people don't snitch." Why? "Because they're not trying to go to jail."

So in fact, when we support the "no snitching" and "it's all good in the hood" mentality, we put the very people we claim to respect and love in harm's way. We put the needs of criminals (rapists, murderers, pedophiles, drug dealers) ahead of our family, children, elders, and neighbors. Holla at me if I'm wrong.

We've been played, pimped, and hoodwinked by the criminal. This is why we have an overabundance of parolees (strangers) living in the hood. They move in and do what they do best—kill, steal, and destroy everyone and everything, thus reducing the neighborhood to a hood. Perfect for hoodlums. In the case of the hoodlum, "Home is where the crime is." Children in the hood see criminals as role models and before you know it, they succumb to the Roman Law Syndrome: when in Rome (the hood), do as the Romans (hoodlums) do. Thus, it's all good in the hood.

Hoodology 101 is the essence of gangsta Hip Hop psychology. This hard core persona contributes to the authenticity of the Hip Hop artist. Rappers who come from middle-class neighborhoods might take a ride through the hood one time and think that gives them enough experience to write and rhyme fake lyrics on behalf of the people. That's **hood**winking the people.

To be good or to be hood, that's the question. Being good (soft) in the hood could get you killed. So many of our children elect to be hood (hard) strictly for survival reasons. Inner-city living is no joke. Consider Tupac's take on the issues of hood survival. In his fourth CD, *Me Against the World* (1995), the titles of his tunes tell the story of what it's like to live in the hood. "If I die 2nite" and "Death Around the Corner" describe the danger and paranoia of living in the no-mercy, no-peace hood. "Me Against the World," "So Many Tears," and "F**k the World" tell the truth about it. Although gangsta rappers like to romanticize life in the hood, in truth, the rest of us are trying to get the hell out of the hood.

Village/Wholevillage Decoded

"It takes a whole village to raise a child." **African proverb**

Hillary Clinton popularized the above African adage for mainstream America during the early 1990s. "It takes a whole village to raise a child" quickly gave way to President Bush's "Leave no child behind."

When spoken by people who have never lived in the village, the proverb leaves me cold. The village is in a state of disrepair, which is why there are so many troubled youth. We must take care when we speak this proverb. In its current state, I wouldn't want the village raising my child. Would you?

Commercial Hip Hop/rap promotes values that are directly at odds with village philosophy. Gangsta Hip Hop artists refuse to consider the fragile psyche of the children of the village when they pump their views into their minds.

The whole village has been profoundly impacted, so we will combine "whole" and "village" to read as "wholevillage" for a maximum learning experience. Listed below is a short list of words abstracted from the term. Feel free to add to the list and discuss with others.

Love = Life sustaining, faith, culture.
Level = Equal treatment and access.
Leave = Hip Hop generation has left the village to die.
Gave = Justice, liberation, safety, healing.
Lie = Business as usual, practiced by governmental, educational, and banking institutions.

Hypocrisy 2—Bling Bling//Poverty in the Hood

Who	=	We the people of the village need to remember where we come from.
Ill	=	Sick, as in drug and alcohol addictions, STDs, diet, and mental disorders.
Live	=	To live long and healthy lives.
Eve	=	The black mother of all the children of the village (world).
Age	=	Children trying to be grown and adults acting like children!
Evil	=	Violence, abandonment, police brutality.
Hole	=	Social traps (poverty).
Veil	=	Media, political cover ups.
Hell	=	Racism, sexism, adultism, homophobia.

Love and **evil** co-exist in the village.

The village is **ill** (sick) and has an **age** (maturation) problem. Children are acting and dressing like adults, and adults are dressing and acting like children.

The producers and owners of Hip Hop take dramatic license with their portrayal of the hood, ghetto, and village. Why would speakers for the hood teach their young fans to perceive themselves and their elders as pimps, gangstas, and hos? It's time for the Hip Hop generation to stand up and deliver. Don't be scaaared. If a man won't protect his own children then he ain't much of a man at all.

Although the village is ill, there are resources, a sense of community (common unity), traditional values (*nguzo saba* and *ma'at*), and love here. Thus, of the three perceptual communities (hood, ghetto, and village), it's the village that holds the most promise and potential for our individual and collective well-being.

Hypocrisy 2—Bling Bling//Poverty in the Hood

Chapter 9

Hypocrisy 3—

Role Models//Pimps, Hos, Pushers, & Spies

"A role model should be someone closest to you. I don't feel it should be someone that the only time you see them you know of their success. When people see Nelly, all they know is my success ... As far as being a role model, no, because you don't know the whole role ... You should know everything going on. I don't call actors and entertainers role models. That's what they are, entertainers. They are there to entertain."[1] **Nelly**

What is a role model? I always teach students in my rites of passage classes that a role model is one who models the role when no one is watching. Within the Hip Hop/ghetto matrix, the rapper role model is the object of intense love, adoration, and worship by fans. Young people will defend their rapper role models *especially* when their behaviors are out of order.

When Nelly says he doesn't want to be a role model, this is like a child of poverty getting his favorite game for Christmas only to discover that batteries weren't included. The child is appreciative but also hurt because he can't enjoy something that doesn't work.

Where's the love? How can rappers turn their backs on their fans? Whether rappers want to be role models or not, they have been drafted. It comes with the game. You can't tell fans who adore you not to adore you while taking their money. You can't have it both ways.

Back in December 1996, Snoop Dogg was asked how he felt about letting his then two-year-old son listen to gangsta rap. Since parents are role models to their children, I include his response here to give you an idea of how at least one gangsta rap artist thinks about his responsibility to youth.

> "Whatever I play at my house, he listens to. Whether I show it to him or not, it's going to be out there in front of his eyes every day. The streets don't have no love for him. They're not going to teach him. I'm going to love him and show him the right way of going about it. I didn't have no father in the home to stop me from gangbangin', but he does."[2]

So Snoop's goal was to keep his son from gangbanging? Then why is his music about gangbanging and why does he let his son listen to it? Can you say confusion and hypocrisy?

In the interview, Snoop revealed that he was living in Chino Hills, California. He described it as a "nine-to-five, upper-class, Republican" community. I wonder how much gangbanging his son saw living next to those Republican voters? Would it compare to what a black boy growing up in Harlem, the West side of Chicago, or Compton sees?

Reluctant rapper role models are only too happy to take the cash of their adoring fans while caring less about the effect gangsta/pimp/ho images have on children, adolescents, and teenagers. What are youth getting for their money, except for some lyrical rage and sex? Those lower emotions don't even stimulate the higher order thinking that could get them the hell out of the hood and into a nice Republican community like Chino Hills. Tunes like Snoop's "Drop It Like It's Hot" keep them in survival mode, perfect for life in the hood.

I don't have a problem with rappers living in gated communities and mansions, but to keep perpetrating such a limited picture of life to young fans from their mansions on the hill, that's hypocrisy. How is this keeping it real?

role models for girls

Video girls, a.k.a., video hos or video vixens, are now role models to young females. The Ricki Lake Show (cancelled in 2004) sometimes featured video girl competitions. Audience members got to shake it and humiliate themselves before a national audience. Remember when girls wanted to be doctors, astronauts, lawyers, and homemakers when they grew up? Now they aspire to be strippers and video vixens. This is what we have come to.

BET UnCut is simply scandalous.

> "It's three o'clock in the morning, BET, the premier cable channel for airing hip-hop videos, broadcasts BET UnCut. The program features music videos in which many of the girls are wearing lingerie and doing the sorts of acrobatics usually reserved for bachelor parties. There's a bikini-clad woman shaking her booty and grinning wildly while holding one leg high in the air in Nelly's *Tip Drift*. Another woman, standing on her head, provides the backdrop to Ludacris's rhyming, with his head between her naked, open thighs while she flexes her buttocks in *Pussy Poppin'*. There are women on all fours, women writhing on the ground, women grabbing their ankles, all poppin' to the beat."[3]

Video girls don't like to think of themselves as role models, but too late! Unfortunately, they are stars in the eyes of many young girls. Pamela Weddington, Motivational Educational Entertainment Productions (MEE), says of the classic video girl moves,

> "These are dances young girls didn't used to know about. Now it's something that they aspire to. Even if they are not

staying up until three in the morning to watch BET UnCut, everyone can set up a VCR." [4]

MEE surveyed thousands of low-income African American teens between the ages of 16 and 20. They were asked about sex, the media, and music videos. Weddington says that "'They are learning that what's important about a woman is her body, not her mind. So that means, 'I am a commodity, therefore I'm going to use that commodity to get what I want.'"[5]

If young girls are seeing their bodies as a commodity, then it's a short distance to offering sex to get what they want. That means risky sexual behaviors.

> "In 2003, in Alabama, 522 African-American girls in rural and poor neighborhoods were asked about their consumption of hip-hop videos, then their behavior was tracked for a year ...' We divided the group into girls who watched fewer than 21 hours a week of music videos and girls who watched more,' explains Ralph DiClemente, Ph.D., associate director of the Center for AIDS Research at Emory University ...' We found that girls who watched more videos were 60 percent more likely to have contracted an STD during the year, twice as likely to have multiple sex partners and 60 percent more likely to use alcohol and drugs.'" [6]

African Americans believe in giving back to the community. We have forced companies that do business in the hood to give back to the hood—in jobs, money, scholarships, and vending contracts. We should demand as much from rappers who refuse the mantle of role model while getting hood rich off the youth that idolize them. And if they refuse to give back more positive lyrics, images, grants, and seed capital, then as parents we have the power to slow their role—by any means necessary.

Wouldn't it be amazing if one of these rappers did a dance tune about high self-esteem? That would be a refreshing change from the bump and grind. Wouldn't it be great if a tune was released about a young male or female who made it out of the hood via a good education and entrepreneurism? Instead of Kanye West's *College Dropout,* I would like to see a CD entitled *My BA, My MBA, My PhD!*

Speaking of Kanye, his breakout hit tune, "Jesus Walks," was a revelation. He proved that if rap artists take the high road, they can still make a fortune.

Nearly all rappers deny that rap has an impact on youth development. "It's only entertainment," they say while perpetrating the biggest Hip Hop hoax of all. It's not just entertainment for young people who are still in Piaget's and Erikson's vulnerable stages of development. It's entrainment for youth who haven't yet learned how to tell the difference between fantasy and reality.

Eric Berman asked Snoop Dogg if rap influences children and the decisions they make in the hood. Here's what Snoop had to say:

> "No, I don't. It's an expression. And it's a legal way out for those who don't have opportunities. A lot of times, people don't see all the positivity inside of this gangsta-rap thing. We all come from violent backgrounds, but yet and still we find time to do the right thing for Mother's Day. We look out for the homeless. We look out for people who don't have anything. Rappers Against Violence is a group that I'm a part of—we work to unite with real gang members who are trying to stop the violence. I made it from a community that doesn't expect people to make it. My job is to make sure I'm doing the right thing, and that's the best example in the world."[7]

Are we confused yet?

Hypocrisy 3—Role Models//Pimps, Hos, Pushers, & Spies

Chapter 10

Fear of a Gangsta Planet

"It's healthy for the children of the village/community to fear the elders. The elders should never have to fear the children. The gangsta Hip Hop agenda has sabotaged this long held cultural philosophy and now, for the first time, many of our cherished elders fear the children. From this no wisdom can ever flourish." **Alfred "Coach" Powell**

Comedian Bernie Mack says in his famous punchline about children, "I ain't scared of you!" For the first time in history, black parents, adults, educators, and leaders are scared senseless of gangsta frontin', pants saggin', profanity talkin', lips smackin', eyes rollin' Hip Hop youth. Our youth fear each other like never before. When, why, and how did this come to be?

Every generation has its fads. My generation had big afros, Earth, Wind, and Fire, the P funk, Superfly, and the conviction that education would lead to prosperity. In the 1960s, young black men raised their fists as a sign of protest at the Olympic Games. That generation smoked weed at Woodstock and watched Jimi Hendrix play the National Anthem.

Our parents and grandparents didn't understand us just like we don't understand Hip Hop. Communication breaks down, which is why they call it the generation snap.

Some would say Hip Hop is just another youth fad and that they'll grow out of it. Maybe they will, but *how* will they grow out of it? We should be concerned because of the gangsta behaviors and values they've grown up with and relate to. We weren't left untouched by our youth culture, nor will they be.

One of the most negative and influential figures to emerge in African American culture was the pimp. Snoop Dogg's persona came straight from the 1970s pimp with his stables of women, long, flowing hair, top hat, cane, and chalice cup. From the hard core pimp who sold women on the street for sex emerged the player/playa (white version: playboy). The player/playa helped to bring about the destruction of black families so that now around 72 percent of black families are headed by one parent, usually a female.

The player/playa idea flourishes in the imaginations of black boys as they mature through childhood, puberty, the teen years, and young adulthood. Unfortunately, for many youth, especially black males, the player/playa is a role model and hero who provides a loveless strategy for dealing with girls and women, including their mothers, sisters, cousins, and lovers.

Boys look up to this power figure who rules the streets. They want to be like him because he seems to have it all: clothes, cars, women, and respect. Players/playas (a.k.a. "mack daddies") may not sell women on the street, but they engage in multiple sex partners without any sense of responsibility for the children they produce, the hearts they break, or the diseases they spread. With the emergence of the player/playa, marriage became less of an option for young African American women in their childbearing years. Few in the black community have escaped the predatory sexual exploits of the player/playa.

the power figure

Psychologists say that children will imitate or react against the most powerful adult in the home, male or female. Today in Hip Hop, the power figure that young fans respect the most is the gangsta. Like the 1970s pimp, the gangsta is the man with the most money, jewelry, fur coats, women, and respect. He's living the American Dream. Many young African American and Latino males feel drawn to gangs because there is seldom a power figure in the home they respect.

Gangs always have been in existence. The word thug dates back to 1200 AD in India where the Thugz, a gang of criminals that roamed the country, did the ancient version of drive-bys. Thugz had their symbols, hand signs, rituals, and slang, and modern day thugs have continued the tradition.

> "With considerable cultural currency, this mindset of wanton lust, meanness and vulgarity has been conflated as 'authentic black cultural heritage' as in 'keeping it real.' It gets worse. Thug life play-acting plays out in the streets and schools in bravado, bullying, sexual excess and exploitation, criminal behavior and arrests. Recall the pompous East Coast/West Coast rapper feud escalated to tragedy in execution-style deaths of super-stars, Tupac Amaru Shakur (died September 1996) and Christopher Wallace (a.k.a. Biggie Small, The Notorious B.I.G., died March 1997). The line between worlds—pretend and real—was blurred and breached."[1]

As I write these words, I mourn the recent death of a friend, Derrick Ali, a community activist and *Dayton Daily* newspaper reporter. Brother Ali was murdered by a 16 year-old black male who had been refused entry into a party just before the party was about to end. On that same tragic weekend, within the same hour and less than two miles away, yet another young man, another 16 year-old former football player of mine, was killed by gunfire. His murderer was yet another 16 year-old male.

Those are only a few examples of what some of our young people are becoming. Hard. Cold. Dog-eat-dog. What's yours is mine. I deserve. You better not dis (disrespect) me. Stop looking at me.

In my day we had our problems, too, but at least we saw education as a way out of poverty. During slavery, the ancestors learned how to read under the literal threat of death. After slavery, they went after education with a vengeance because they understood that it could help them escape poverty and ignorance. Today we are witnessing a backlash against education. In urban areas around the nation, dropout rates (or what I call "pushouts," because youth have been pushed out by a failing educational system) are sky high. Statistically we know that dropouts/pushouts often end up in prison, and most inmates are illiterate. Some education is better than none, but this Hip Hop generation doesn't buy it.

It's true that public education leaves a lot to be desired in this country, but that doesn't mean we should give up and give in. In the 1960s and '70s, disgruntled parents and educators created independent black schools to provide a quality education for their children. Compared to that powerful movement, gangsta Hip Hop is part of the problem rather than the solution. The gangsta is Hip Hop's Pied Piper, and as our children follow his seductive rap tunes, their hearts are hardening and their souls are dying.

perpetrating the mob

Snoop Dogg, the pimp of Hip Hop, says black males are infatuated with the lifestyles of Italian mobsters: "Blacks and Italians have a mutual love for the same things. We're infatuated with how the Mafia punks America."[2]

Rappers use the movie *Scarface* as a blueprint for the rap game. The documentary on the *Scarface* DVD features rappers P Diddy, Snoop Dogg, and Scarface (yes, a rapper gave himself the name of one of the most notorious criminals in cinematic history), discussing how the film connects to Hip Hop culture. They say gangstas and rappers portray the American Dream, from rags to riches.

In the book *Style over Substance*, the authors state that "African American teen culture parallels the European American gangster subculture of the roaring 1920s. Both cultural groups were fueled by the catalyst of the American dream that was stagnated by racism."[3]

Hip Hop took a wrong moral turn when it adopted Mafia values, codes, and styles. Rappers couldn't just dress the part; they had to act like their role models and heroes. Enter crime, drugs, sexism, violence, and racism (internalized): the Mafioso way of life.

HIP HOP GANGSTA PATHOLOGY: LINKS TO MAFIA AXIOLOGY

Mafia	Gangsta Hip Hop
Dons	Producers
Godfathers	Playas, pimps, kingpins
Hit men	Rappers (MCs)
Cartel/family	Posse/entourage
Unique nicknames	Mafia nicknames
Territorial beef (global)	Territorial beef (East Coast, West Coast, Dirty South, etc.)
Push drugs (heroin, alcohol, cocaine, Ecstasy)	Promote drugs (marijuana, alcohol, crack, Ecstasy)
Appearance of legitimacy (music industry, restaurants, construction)	Appearance of legitimacy (music industry, car detail shops, hair shops)
Beat justice system	Beat justice system
Weapon of choice: gun	Weapon of choice: gun
Pornography, strip clubs	Pornography, strip clubs
Victims: anyone	Victims: black community
Talk very little	Talk too much
Investments (children's education, real estate)	Investments (cars, music, drugs, bling bling)
Tactics: intimidation, violence	Tactics: intimidation, violence
Under surveillance by FBI, CIA, DEA, IRS, ATF, FDA, CSI, DOJ	Under surveillance by FBI, CIA, FCC, DEA, IRS, ATF
Luxury lifestyle	Bling Bling
Informants	Snitches
Gangsters	Thugs

Sense of racial pride	No sense of racial pride
Cultural heroes	National scapegoats
Work for the family	Work for everyone
Loyal to the family	Loyal to other gangstas
Molls	Bitches, hos

Snoop said the mob played America, but in reality, the mob punks the black community with all the drugs and crime they import into our streets. Richard Martin, former Assistant U.S. Attorney, said, "The Mafia has no goal other than to enrich itself and get power."[4]

Let's be clear: mobsters are not our friends. In fact, they can be just as racist as the white supremacist corporate structure that they are often in league with. Clearly, gangsta rappers are suffering from Stockholm Syndrome, where the victim identifies and sympathizes with his abuser.

Snoop Dogg's comment speaks to the psychological damage done to the black psyche via slavery, prejudice, and discrimination. I believe it was psychologist Frantz Fanon who said that colonized minds desire to preserve the very social structure that oppresses them.

No rapper portrays the gangsta/pimp persona as fresh as super rapper Jay-Z. "When XXL magazine asked Jay-Z how much of the industry was 'real,' he groused, 'Two%? Ten at most, but closer to two."[5]

Why is it natural to put Hip Hop and gangsta together? Jay-Z's former Roc-a-fella partner Damon Dash used the mogul/tycoon/gangsta/boss persona for his 2005 BET show Ultimate Hustler, which features him in a Donald Trump wannabe power-broker role. Dash teaches contestants how to be swindlers, cheats, and crooks. Instead of saying, "You're fired!" he boldly snatches a gold Roc-A-Fella pendant off the neck of each losing contestant. Just what we need to teach our youth.

In 2003, UPN introduced Platinum, a short lived Hip Hop soap opera produced in part by famed Godfather director, Francis Ford Coppola. The show featured the drama and trauma of everyday gangsta Hip Hop, street warfare, drugs, promiscuity, and black-on-black violence. In 2006, BET continues this sad trend with shows such as *American Gangster and Beef.*

According to Cedric Muhammad,

> "It has been an error in judgment for Hip-Hop artists to glorify violence and celebrate guns, and for the Hip-Hop media—the fourth estate and conscience of the culture—to project these images for profit and endorse only a segment of the community for magazine covers and prominent features."[6]

Without a doubt, many gangsta rappers are talented and gifted performers. Wouldn't it have been great if, instead of identifying with Italian mobsters, they had continued the legacy of Afrika Bambaataa and The Last Poets and rhymed about the African builders of history?

what's in a name?

Gangsta and mafia names dominate Hip Hop culture. Our most prominent artists on the world scene today have proudly tagged themselves with loaded names like Gambino Family, da Corleone Family, Ghetto Mafia, Uptown Syndicate, The Family, Three 6 Mafia, South Central Cartel, Black Mafia, Jr. Mafia, Murder Squad, Infamous Mobb, O.G. Felony, F.U.P. Mob, Death Row, Murder Inc., and Speedknot Mobstaz.

And then there's CorMega, Scarface, Young Gotti, Don Cartagena, Roc-A-Fella, Crime Boss, Capone-N-Noreaga, Nas Escobar, Cormega, Bossalinie, Beanie Sigel, Tha Boss King, Irv Gotti, Don Corleone, Crime Boss, The Last Don—the list is endless.

All of the above names are connected to crime and violence. There's something tragic about adopting the names of criminals who oppressed and suppressed our community.

Hypocrisy 3—Role Models//Pimps, Hos, Pushers, & Spies

The social behaviors of many of these rappers have blurred the line between their gangsta image and their real selves. Their aliases/stage names make it even more confusing. Are they real gangstas, or is it just an act? For artists whose creed is "keep it real," why do they work so hard to pretend to be somebody else?

> "'Mafioso' rap, which boomed in the mid-1990s, is an extension of East Coast 'thug' rap as well as West Coast 'gangsta' rap. Whereas gangsta and thug rappers tell tales of life on the ghetto streets, Mafioso rappers spin imaginary fantasies of rappers as Mafiosis, drug kingpins, and organized crime figures … Usually, artists who perform gangsta/thug rap are byproducts of the ghetto life that they portray … On the other hand, Mafioso rap is based virtually on pure fantasy and interpretation."[7]

What's in a name? Our African ancestors chose names carefully. Each name had meaning and gave a clue to the bearer's future destiny. In the Bible, Abram became Abraham and Saul became Paul after life-changing encounters with God.

Names carry meaning and vibration. Some of our people name their children after great ancestors while others are named after cars and alcoholic drinks. A name is powerful. It contains a prophecy of the person's destiny and the seeds of self-image, for better or worse.

This imitation of Italian mobsters is evidence of our compelling need to assimilate into white society, even at the lowest levels. Clearly, there is a lot of cultural miseducation taking place within Hip Hop and the black psyche.

kkk wannabes?

While Italian mobsters were firing the imaginations of gangsta rappers, more violent and racist archetypes from American culture emerged in gangsta Hip Hop. Observing young brothas across the country, I began to notice many similarities between gangsta Hip Hop and the KKK.

"No way, Coach. You've really gone off the deep end this time." If you don't believe me, check out the following chart and tell me where I'm wrong. And feel free to add to the chart.

PSYCHOSOCIAL LINKS BETWEEN:

KKK	Gangsta Hip Hop
Wears long white robes with hoods	Wears long white tee shirts with hoodies
Carries guns, shoots, beats, kills black men	Carries guns, shoots, beats, kills black men
Committed rape, sodomy, and abuse against black women and children; impregnated/abandoned	Via rap lyrics, promotes rape, sodomy, and abuse against black women and children; impregnates/abandons
Outlaws	Thugs, gangstas
Good ole boys	Home boyz
Ride bys/drive-bys	Drive-bys
Sold drugs, stole, robbed blacks	Sells drugs, steals, robs blacks
Burns and wears crosses	Sports crosses
Established along racial lines	Established along racial lines
Openly hates blacks; calls blacks niggers and animal terms (beasts, herds, puppies, monkeys, bulls, etc.)	Symbolically hates blacks; calls blacks niggas/niggaz and animal terms (hoodrats, chickenheads, dogs, bitches, etc.)
Uses propaganda to promote stereotypes about people of color	Uses propaganda to promote stereotypes about people of color
Openly defies the law	Openly promotes defying the law

Calls black women wenches and whores; respects, honors, protects, and upholds white women in high esteem	Calls black women bitches and hos; respects, honors, protects, and symbolically upholds white women in high esteem
Puts on a front in public (double lives)	Puts on a front in public (double lives)
No snitching allowed	No snitching allowed
Practiced physical castration against black men only. Acceptable entertainment for some parts of white society.	Practices lyrical castration against black men only. Acceptable entertainment for some parts of white society, the #1 consumers of Hip Hop.
Obsessed with genitals of black men. Lynching involved: • castration • putting penis in victim's mouth after lynching • putting penis on public display in jars in stores	Obsessed with own genitals. This involves: • constantly touching penis • referring to penis in rap lyrics • lyrically insisting that people taste, lick, suck, etc. penis • public display of CDs about penis in record stores
Practices mob violence	Promotes mob violence
Mind control and manipulation via intimidation	Mind control and manipulation via intimidation
Dogs attack black children and hunt black people	Dogs (pit bulls, rottweilers) attack black children and hurt black people in the hood
Disrespectfully addresses grown black men with the monikers Uncle, Son, Big, Boy—never man or mister	Disrespectfully addresses grown black men with the monikers Nephew, Son, Lil, Boyz—never man or mister
KKK = Ku Klux Klan	**KKK = Kids Killing Kids**

Hypocrisy 3—Role Models//Pimps, Hos, Pushers, & Spies

the gangsta agenda

The gangsta's goal is to gain power, status, luxury items, and cash. If he has to kill his own mother or step on his own children to accomplish his goals, he'll do whatever it takes.

In Hip Hop culture, the gangsta promotes his agenda and values (unquestioning loyalty) through gangsta rap and music videos. Not only do these videos exert influence over youth, but society at large feels the impact as well. The ideas and visuals in one video can spread faster than a cold (and can make you feel just as sick). Videos can shape attitudes, change opinions, and control fads, fashions, and sexual appetites. In the beginning, the times influenced videos. Now videos change the times.

As the gangsta raps about his agenda of domination and power, copycats and fans of the thug lifestyle carry out the violence, irresponsible sex, and other problem behaviors. Teen pregnancy, STDs, death, incarceration, illness, poverty, and mental illness are the consequences.

The gangsta rapper would say he's not creating the conditions. He's only reporting on what already exists in the hood. Although these problems have always been present in our communities, the gangsta rapper must still be held accountable.

> "While African Americans comprise 12% of the U.S. population, 45% of all murder victims in 2002 were African American, 91% of whom were killed by African Americans. Nationally, homicide is the leading cause of death for black men and second leading cause of death for black women ages 15-24."[8]

In the early 1980s, the voice of rap was healthy, political, pro-black, and anti-crack. Rappers proudly dressed in red, black, and green. In the late 1980s, when Hip Hop walked into the boardrooms of the major record labels, that once proud voice became violent against other brotha rappers.

How did street violence bleed into lyrical and rapper-on-rapper violence? Rumors are always hot in Hip Hop. Insiders say that *Vibe* magazine allegedly had something to do with the East Coast vs. West Coast war. In a now infamous interview, Tupac stated his belief that members of the Bad Boy Records camp had something to do with his getting shot. Before you knew it, it was on between the Death Row and Bad Boy labels. The fact that Biggie Smalls was killed while leaving a *Vibe* party only contributed to the rumors.

The resumes of many Hip Hop gangstas list multiple convictions for drug dealing and gangbanging. Some of the biggest names in the business openly brag about their past criminal escapades. Rumors abound that the sale of crack cocaine and other drugs have launched many a rap career and independent record label. This sends the message to youth that it's okay to deal drugs until you get enough money to start your music career.

most wanted

Gangsta Hip Hop is in the sites of the NYPD and other law enforcement organizations. It has been widely reported that dedicated police units have put Hip Hop under surveillance to investigate alleged violence and other crimes. Can you guess who might end up on Hip Hop's Most Wanted List?

last days?

Thugging on CD may be on its way out. Death Row changed its name to Tha Row Records, and Murder Inc. dropped the word Murder from its name (too little too late). Suge Knight filed bankruptcy to try and save Death Row. Are we seeing the end of an era?

Hypocrisy 3—Role Models//Pimps, Hos, Pushers, & Spies

Rappers know that thugging won't last forever. That's why many have successfully used gangsta rap to launch themselves into other areas of entertainment, mainly movies, television, even religion. As they reinvent themselves, their profane lyrics, arrest records, and acts of violence are swept away into the subconscious memories of our children.

I'm not hating the sinner, just the sins. Gangsta rappers don't want the responsibility of being role models, but they are, for better or worse. The violent messages of gangsta rap have an enormous affect on impressionable youth. Our youth idolize gangsta rappers because they make crime look glamorous and exciting in music videos, self produced DVD movies, and now billboards that pollute the air in the hood.

not on my block

In November 2005, the PTBs of Paramount Pictures came out in big time support of 50 Cent's new movie, *Get Rich or Die Tryin.* Paramount Pictures is a division of Viacom—the same Viacom that owns BET, scheduler of gangsta/pornographic rap videos during children's prime time viewing hours.

One way they tried to push the super violent *Get Rich* down the throats of black and brown men, women, and children was via billboards in the hood, many of which appeared near schools.

With a gun in one hand, a microphone in the other, and his back to us, 50 Cent's arms are outstretched, like a poor imitation of Christ on the cross. *Get Rich* is a somewhat biographical depiction of his former life as a heroin/crack dealer and prison inmate. What's the real message on the billboard? "If I can't beat you with the mic/words/ rap game, I'll shoot you" or "Violence is a part of the rap/Hip Hop game."

According to Errol Louis, son of a retired NYPD inspector and former associate editor of *The New York Sun*, some New Yorkers refused to accept the billboards in their neighborhoods. Louis wrote that "Under community pressure, including protests, Paramount has already agreed to yank a half-dozen of the offensive billboards from Los Angeles."[9]

Louis makes the following excellent point:

> "50 Cent is free to sell lies to his mostly suburban audience about a mythical ghetto where guns, violence and dope-dealing are glorified and respected. We must also hold accountable the entertainment corporations that treat real-world tragedies such as murder, robbery and the soul-destroying degradation of drug addiction as cultural commodities to be sold for cheap laughs and a fast buck."[10]

Big ups to all those who fought for their children. We don't have to accept the media pollution over our homes, schools, churches, parks, and businesses.

Gangsta rap affects adults, too. Repetitive reenactments of violence desensitize the public to the seriousness of the crimes occurring within the ghetto matrix. People who live in poor communities learn to accept violence. We become immune to guns and drugs. We feel helpless because young people are armed, and they're roaming the streets.

For those of us who live in the hood, thugging is real and not a source of entertainment. Rappers, specifically gangsta rappers, are created and employed by entertainment executives to deify pimping, drug dealing, promiscuity, and violence. They are trained to professionally deliver a duel message that entertains white children while persuading children of poverty, particularly children of color, that violence and hustling is a viable employment option.

Remember the movie *Toy* starring Richard Pryor and Jackie Gleeson, in which the rich father bought his child a black man for entertainment? Pryor's job was to be with the child 24/7. Rappers also serve this babysitting function, whether they like it or not.

Hypocrisy 3—Role Models//Pimps, Hos, Pushers, & Spies

The street doctor of urban psychology, LeeRoy Jordan, Jr. of New York City, founder of the Afrikan American Men United to Save Our Lives, Inc., says:

> "In some respects, the gangsta rap game is a damn rerun running out of time and stunts. Young brothas are killing and dying just because, not for a cause. They are suffering from 'Autoimmune Homicidal Syndrome' (will automatically kill you for stepping on his shoe or dissin' him). They need to give up this deadly game of urban cowboy and Indians. This form of nostalgia for a criminal lifestyle is completely unhealthy and unproductive for us."

gangsta economics

It's hard to start a business in this country with no money. You've got to beg and borrow just to get started because the banks won't help. In the meantime, the criminals are stealing, selling drugs, pimping, prostituting—whatever it takes to get the money. Then they launder/invest the dirty money through a front, like a hair salon, funeral home, liquor store, or record label, and become legitimate.

This is a time honored tradition in America. President Kennedy's daddy did it. He sold alcohol during prohibition. When drinking became legal, he got paid big time.

You can take the gangsta out the ghetto, but you can't take the ghetto out the gangsta. Gangsta economics is a lot like Wall Street and Corporate America. The same rules of marketing, distribution, sales, special promotions, and collections apply.

Laws of supply and demand exist in the ghetto just like in any other economy, but because there are so few jobs here, most of the money generated is illegal and underground. The ghetto is an underground economy. In Hip Hop, you can't separate gangsta or ghetto economics from the music and images. They are bound together.

It's a documented fact that some Hip Hop producers, DJs, and artists received seed money from criminal activities, but the relationship between the music industry and crime didn't start with gangsta rap. Remember Frank Sinatra? Historians say the mob's relationship with the music industry started in the 1920s.

> "A brief overview of *Who's Who* in the record business leads one to the unmistakable conclusion that the recording industry, as far as the production, distribution, and popularization of rock and rap, is under the control of a syndicate representing a marriage between organized crime networks and high-level fixers on Wall Street."[11]

In mainstream society, artists are proud of not linking their art to financial concerns. This is where the term "starving artist" comes from. Struggling artists have to take second and third jobs just to make ends meet.

This is not the case with rap. Not only does money pay for production expenses and artist salaries, *money is the message*. Money symbols infuse the music like no other type of youth music—not grunge, punk, rock, or heavy metal.

Rap was tailored made for capitalism. I've yet to hear any gangsta rapper deal with *ujamaa* (cooperative economics) or *ujima* (collective work and responsibility). And they say they speak for the hood.

fear factor

> "There is nothing more dangerous than to build a society with a large segment of people in that society who feel that they have no stake in it; who feel that they have nothing to lose. People who have stake in their society, protect that society, but when they don't have it, they unconsciously want to destroy it." **Dr. Rev. Martin Luther King Jr.**

Why do we love to be afraid? We go to horror movies to the tune of billions. We love the rides with the scariest dip at the amusement park.

Gangsta rappers and their producers build their careers on looking, talking, and acting intimidating. We buy their CDs and go to their concerts because they're scary and exciting. The more we fear gangsta rappers, the more we support them. Marketers know that people subconsciously love things that are taboo. This is why white youth monetarily support gangsta rap against their parents' wishes.

A special March 2004 edition of *Source* magazine featured ten of Hip Hop's musical pioneers in prison mug shots on the cover. The article was titled "Hip Hop Behind Bars." In the July 2004 issue of *Source,* the cover article, "The Takeover," showed five black males dressed in Hip Hop gear and jewelry and flashing bundles of money.

Then, in its November-December 2005 issue, *Source* took another look at Hip Hop behind bars. This time rapper Lil' Kim joined the boyz on the cover. Soon there'll be another article about rappers behind bars, and the industry is banking that the five brothas appearing on the "Takeover" cover will do something to place themselves behind bars down the road.

As of this writing, one of the featured artists on the "Takeover" cover is facing murder charges and two others assault charges. Guess you can say the game works. Those who were selected to take over have been taken over. The playa has been played! When rap stars fall, no worries. The PTBs know there are other young black men willing and eager to take their place.

Around 1990, gangsta rap scared white middle-class Americans, and the issues that we in the community had been dealing with all along finally were revealed in the media. Fear generated by NWA's *Straight Outta Compton*, Ice-T's *Cop Killer*, and Ice Cube's *Death Certificate* solidified gangsta rap's presence in the homes of white suburbia. These gangstas tapped into white youth's developmental need to rebel against their parents and other authority figures. This is both a micro (private) and macro (public) social problem, existing on national, state, and local levels.[12]

Vibe magazine has sold many issues thanks to gangsta rappers, and there is a violent vibe in every gangsta lyric. Within Hip Hop/ghetto culture, vibe stands for:

V = **V**iolence
I = **I**nfiltrating
B = **B**lack
E = **E**ntertainment

From 1989 to 1996, the media tuned us to the ongoing war in Los Angeles between the Crips and the Bloods. Those brothas and sistas claimed to be fighting against white supremacy, but one symbolic look at their colors and you'll realize they were actually aligned with their enemy. The Crips wore the color blue and the Bloods wore red—colors of the American flag. They fought at night, under the stars, and competed to be the stars of the hood. Stars are also on the flag, their symbolic enemy.

Close your eyes and visualize the American flag. What happens when all the blue kills (removes) all the red and all the red kills (removes) all the blue? What color is left to enjoy the spoils (booty) of that war? That's right, white.

Could the Crips and Bloods have been playing into somebody's hands?

If we're to believe local and national news, since September 11, 2001, gangs have all but disappeared. America is no longer obsessed with Crips and Bloods, Lords, Kings, Queens, Folks, Disciples, or People. Those of us living here in the hood know they still exist. We see and hear them every day and night. But since America is fighting a new war against a much bigger enemy, Al Qaeda, the Taliban, Osama Bin Laden and the boys, street gangs apparently aren't as interesting as they once were. We must tune into gangsta rap to get the news.

america has no hip hop idol

American Idol judge Randy Jackson greets contestants and audiences with the question, "Whatz up, dogg?" Now many from the Hip Hop nation are asking the same question: "Whatz up, dogg? Why is there no Hip Hop category on the number one music show in America?" With Hip Hop being a multibillion dollar industry and the most popular of all musical forms, why has it been left out of the *American Idol* competition?

I know you want to believe that America loves Hip Hop, but deep down folks still believe that rap is just noise. Some suspect that the corporate sponsors of *American Idol* have rejected rap music because rap performers are overwhelmingly black and brown.

The first four years of *American Idol* has come down to race. Every contestant who finished second or third, in their supporters' minds, lost due to race, not lack of talent.

Most importantly, contestants on *American Idol* must have clean backgrounds. The March 2004 cover of *Source* magazine features the mug shots of some of the most prolific Hip Hop rappers. To compete in *American Idol,* performers can't be in the middle of a felony case. There goes the rapper, who typically has been through the revolving doors of the justice system. All contestants undergo a background check and are asked to fill out a personal history. While having a felony/criminal background is a requirement for rappers nowadays, few would qualify to compete on *American Idol.* 50 Cent, C-Murder, Mystikal, Tupac, and Biggie Smalls would have never gotten the chance to launch their careers on *American Idol.*

How many votes do you think a swearing MC would receive? How would Simon respond to nigga being repeated 50 times in a short two-minute gangsta rap? What advice would Paula give to rappers who call women hoodrats, bitches, and hos? Now you know why Hip Hop will never get its 15 minutes of fame on *American Idol.*

Chapter 11

The Intoxication of the Hip Hop Generation

"Yeah, they want reality, but you will hear none/They'd rather exaggerate a little fiction."[1] **N.W.A.**, "Express Yourself"

Hip Hop enters its third decade, the coming of age of its first generation, not claiming victory but in surrender to the sub-elements of the culture. Battle fatigued, teary-eyed, mistrustful, and world weary, Hip Hop has turned to alcohol, tobacco, and drugs to dull the pain, a suicidal move if ever there was one.

Hip Hop and rap videos insidiously link symbols of sex and success (mansions, money, cars, bling) to symbols of intoxication (expensive alcohol, blunts, pipes, cigars). Unfortunately, this has entrenched substance abuse as a fixture in the getting paid Hip Hop culture. Because alcohol, tobacco, and drugs are placed so craftily in rap tunes and music videos, it's difficult for our children to separate the symbols of success from the symbols of intoxication. They all go together, which is what makes the lie so deadly, confusing, and seductive. When a rapper wearing a mink coat drinks alcohol from a jeweled "pimp cup" or is smoking a blunt while in a hot tub with women, the lie is that intoxication is a *natural* part of a wealthy lifestyle. This idea, dropped slyly like a stealth bomb on the community, has had devastating consequences for youth in the hood.

hurricane cracktrina

Around 1983 or '84, it was rumored that some drug addicts in the San Francisco Bay Area were doing something new: smoking free base cocaine. Soon, in Dayton, Ohio, my athletes were telling me horror stories of parents, siblings, and loved ones being strung out on this new thing or who had been caught selling it.

Cocaine, the rich man's drug, had been chemically transformed into a much cheaper drug called crack. At the $2 introductory price, crack became widely and quickly available in ghettoes from New York to L.A.

Crack hit us like a hurricane, bringing death and destruction. With no warning, it dropped a bomb on families and uprooted homes from their once solid foundations. This new drug cracked the potential of our future, our hopes and dreams. It launched evil careers, fears, and tears.

Addicts were nicknamed "crackheads," which I've decoded as follows:

Crack	=	to split or shatter
Head	=	thinking, thoughts, where dreams live
Crackhead	=	split thinking, shattered thoughts and dreams

Take a walk through the hood with me where crack has ruined once beautiful neighborhoods. Empty lots, alleyways, and abandoned subway cars are the homes of empty-eyed addicts. Colorful pills, syringes, and vials litter the floors of vacant buildings like a thousand M&Ms.

Black folk have never had any luck with anything that sounds like cane/cocaine. During and after slavery, we were forced to plant and chop sugar cane. Blacks were beaten with the cane and in old age are forced to walk with a cane. Now brothas and sistas are taking crack cocaine.

Although the CIA and DEA (Drug Enforcement Administration) predictably denied any role in the cocaine trade, in August 1996, we learned from reporter Gary Webb of the *San Jose Mercury News* that the CIA allegedly protected the delivery of tons of powdered cocaine into the U.S., specifically into African American communities. The CIA had allowed the Nicaraguan Contras to sell millions of dollars of Columbian cocaine to supposed members of the Bloods and Crips. The CIA protected the Contras from investigation so that they could freely raise the money they needed to fund their war against the Sandinistas.[2]

The poster child for crack was a monster with a black face. Thousands of addicts were driven to desperate acts, including prostitution and robbery, to feed their pipes. Children were orphaned, abandoned, and abused. Babies were born addicted. Pushers and users fought unholy wars to stake claims in lucrative territories in the hood and to pimp indirectly for the U.S. government.

Crack criminalized inner city Hip Hop youth. From 1986 to 2002, I lost 18 students and athletes to death, prison, and/or addiction; combined with family and friends, that puts my personal total at about 45. What's your count?

Crack addiction is not limited to Hip Hop youth—grandparents and even great grandparents have succumbed. The drug takes no prisoners.

> "I have done crack with people 65 years old and seen middle school children hold and run dope for their parents and/or project dealer. Most people become addicted to crack cocaine because of its power. Every fiend will tell you the first high is the best and every fiend will search for this first high repeatedly, with no success. Crack becomes a means of escape for those who are looking for a crack to simply crawl into from the pains of yesterday, today, and tomorrows yet to come."
> **John "Herkie" Early**, born again Christian street counselor, Dayton, Ohio

Hypocrisy 3—Role Models//Pimps, Hos, Pushers, & Spies

Webster's definition of crack is, "To break into pieces, to make a sharp sound, to split apart and/or to fracture." My definition, based on experiences with family, friends, and students, is slightly different. I define crack within the ghetto matrix as:

C = The conscious conspiracy committed upon communities of color via the use of cheap cocaine in order to cause confusion, chaos, and communicide.

R = A radical form of racism to reduce, remove, and redefine a race of people to repress the ideals of revolution, reparations, and religion.

A = The attempted assassination of all African Americans and Latinos and all those associated with them via AIDS and academic suicide. (Is this the American way?)

C = Cold, calculated, chemical, biocidal, psychological, physiological warfare committed against people of color and Caucasians to keep them going in circles.

K = The killing of the soul, the dream, the dreamer, the belief, the believer, the kings and queens of Kemet, which you know as Egypt on the continent of Africa whose true name is Alkebulan. How is it that the people who fell through the crack got up smoking the crack?

Streets named after Dr. Martin Luther King, Jr. became the stage for crack deals, crack houses, and gang wars. What would he say today to this legacy of violent intoxication?

cracked out

The term crack refers to the crackling sound heard when the cocaine mixture is heated with sodium bicarbonate (baking soda). This is a highly sophisticated process. The science behind crack cocaine is complex and took trial and error to perfect. Yet we are expected to believe that Pookie and Peaches had both the knowledge of chemistry and the resources of an industrial manufacturer to produce, market, and distribute tons of the white power each month. Hmmm ...

The DEA estimates that crack rocks are between 75 and 90 percent pure cocaine. Dosages of crack are smaller, so there is no need to dilute the cocaine with various substances. Because of the smaller dosages, crack is highly profitable for the dealer. The opportunity to make quick money is tempting for many young black and Latino youth caught inside the perpetual cycle of poverty.

Zero tolerance is no joke for urban youth caught using or selling crack; sentencing laws for crack offenders are much harsher than for cocaine offenders. Clearly, this has racial overtones. Further, the U.S. Sentencing Commission found that "nearly 90 percent of the offenders convicted in federal court for crack cocaine distribution are African-American while the majority of crack cocaine users is white."[3]

Whether crack cocaine is injected with a syringe or smoked, the drug creates great harm to the body. A user might become addicted more quickly if he smokes (vs. snorts). Smoking delivers quick, high doses of cocaine to the brain and brings an intense and immediate high. Crack cocaine can be instantly addictive. During the early days of crack cocaine folks used to say that crack was God sent. They would say "I love crack" just as easily as you would say "I love my child."

go west, young brotha

In the early days of Hip Hop, rappers rhymed against drugs. "White Lines," by Grandmaster Melle Mel, educated listeners about the dangers of drug use and abuse.[4] Drugs were not accepted in rap music like they are today. Clearly, the PTBs have shifted their agenda into high gear.

The most effective marketing tool for the widespread delivery of crack has been gangsta rap/Hip Hop. West Coast rappers introduced an attitudinal shift of defiance and rebellion into the crack selling game that was an instant hit with youth culture. Like a deployed military force, the rap industry moved quickly and strategically to digitize the message of drug glorification onto CDs and tapes. They rapped covert and overt rhymes about grams, kilos, and keys as if they were teaching a *Sesame Street* lesson. Rappers lyrically explained how to use crack, measure it, cut it, package it, and push it. They included instructions on how to roll primos (crack cocaine sprinkled in cigarettes and marijuana joints).

Rappers should be outraged, not on stage trading our collective pain for a wage. Kanye West is one of the few rappers speaking to the issue. He flips the script of the PTBs with his take on the crack tragedy in "Crack Music."

ecstasy

In an interview, rapper Eminem was asked if he was still writing songs while taking Ecstasy. He said,

> "A couple of the songs on the new record were written on X. It exaggerates s**t. Somebody will be just looking at me wrong and I'll just flip a table over, like, what the f**k are you staring at?! If you're in a good mood you love everybody, but if you're in a bad mood and you got s**t on your mind, you're gonna break down and s**t. The hardest s**t that I've f**d with is X and 'shrooms."[5]

Trick Daddy, Dr. Dre, Eminem, Missy Elliot, Big Tymers, Xzibit, Bone Thugs-n-Harmony, and Jay-Z have all willingly loaned their voices to promote addiction to their young followers. They openly speak of Ecstasy's sexual promise, never its deadly potential. This reinforces the myth that blacks are only about getting high and having sex.

In his hit "Nas Is Like," superstar Nas says, "I like ecstasy for ladies."[6] I challenge readers to try and find a Hip Hop/gangsta rap CD that does not mention blunts, alcohol, and Ecstasy (a.k.a. XTC).

Missy Elliott used her genius in "X-Tasy" to rap, "Ecstaacyy, I'm willing to do the things I said I wouldn't do/On ecstaacyy, the feeling makes me feel like I'm in love with you."[7]

Missy's lyrics leave little to the imagination. This infomercial openly promotes Ecstasy as a love drug. This is a lie made to sound like the truth. Ecstasy's not a love drug. It'll kill you.

In her *Love Is Pain* CD, Missy does it again in a duet with Ecstasy lover Ja Rule. Sex and getting high is what it's all about. They even use Lord in the song. Makes you wonder which lord Ja Rule is referring to. Perhaps the lord of evil, Satan himself. You better holla, brotha.

While Missy's description of Ecstasy's high is precise, she fails to mention how many young people have died taking the drug. She seems to be advertising Ecstasy the same way a drug dealer would, pushing the high but none of the pain. Compare her lyrics to the medical and forensic facts and holla back at me if I'm wrong.

rhyming other drugs

Three Six Mafia's hit "Sipping on Some Syrup" pushed the Southern fad of mixing Nyquil® cough syrup with a can of strawberry soda on the national scene. This brew is also known as "Barre," "Candy Paint," or "Lean." Slim Thug raps, "Barre sipping car dipping" on rapper Mike Jones' song "Still Tippin."[8] Decoded, this line reads: "driving under the influence" (DUI). I suspect someone bought a lot of stock in cold syrup because when a product is placed in a rap tune, it sells like crazy in the hood. What do you think?

Hip Hop reintroduced the 1960s hippy LSD trip in the early 1990s (at the height of the Million Man and Million Woman marches and a renewed political black consciousness) with rap songs about mushrooms (a.k.a. psilocybin, 'shrooms). Rapper Xzibit's tune "Shroomz" is one of many examples: "don't get it twisted like a nigga coked up and druggied down/see cannibus and mushrooms be comin from the ground all natural."[9]

Drug cocktails such as Sextasy (Viagra and ecstasy mixed), chased with alcohol, were made popular at raves and are now popular at some Hip Hop events. Ecstasy, Sextasy, rohypnol ("roofies"), and GHB (gamma hydroxy butyrate), known as the date rape drugs, along with OxyContin (Oxy), are effectively being used as weapons of mass destruction on urban, rural, and suburban teens and communities. Drug use and lowered inhibitions are a gateway to unprotected sex, unwanted pregnancies, and STDs. Doctors warn that the real danger of these drug cocktails lies in their unpredictability.

Have you ever wondered why some Hip Hop videos feature teens and 20-something adults wearing pacifiers around their necks? Some are seen sucking their pacifiers and/or a toothbrush. This odd behavior is associated with the intake of Ecstasy and Sextasy, which causes the user to grind his/her teeth. Sucking a pacifier reportedly helps to minimize damage done to the teeth, even though it's quite childish for a teen or adult to suck on a pacifier or toothbrush. This behavior is symptomatic of Prolonged Adolescent Syndrome (refer to the Framework for Understanding Hip Hop Youth chapter).

I believe that if liberation soldiers such as Harriet Tubman, Fannie Lou Hamer, Amilcar Cabral, Rosa Parks, Sojourner Truth, Queen Mother Moore, Bobby E. Wright, Dr. Martin L. King, Marcus M. Garvey, and Malcolm X were alive to witness the travesty of subculture Hip Hop, they would declare these mercenary rappers traitors.

Is the goal to increase youth substance abuse? Is this the job rappers signed up for? Who benefits from making lies sound like the truth?

r.i.p. (rest in peace)

Robert Earl Davis, Jr., a.k.a. DJ Screw, was a star in the Houston rap scene. His contribution to the game was a technique of "screwing" a song, or slowing down the main tracks of a song as he was remixing it.

Hypocrisy 3—Role Models//Pimps, Hos, Pushers, & Spies

"Slowing down the song was supposed to recreate the effect of recreationally using Promethazine w/Codeine also known as 'lean' or 'purple drank' ... in Houston parlance ... DJ Screw often created 'chopped and screwed' versions of famous rap songs that rivaled if not improved upon the original songs. Some notable examples of these tracks include R. Kelly's 'I Wish' and Bone Thugs-N-Harmony's 'Budsmokers Only.'"[10]

In 2000, DJ Screw died of a heart attack, yet another genius in a long line of black entertainers claimed by the drug/music culture. It was rumored that the attack was caused by a codeine overdose or the long-term buildup of codeine in his system.

Hip Hop has followed the sad example of many great jazz, blues, rock, and R&B legends. The more things change, the more they stay the same. Addicted, intoxicated artists try to reproduce their high (drug experience) via their music. Some songs are never recaptured because the experience is lost forever. The PTBs look the other way or may even pay the artist with drugs. As long as they're producing hits, the PTBs don't care. Can you say big time exploitation?

chronic condition

Interestingly, according to the 2003 National Survey on Drug Use and Health, 17 percent of African American youth ages 12 to 17 reported being approached by someone selling drugs in the past month.[11] Apparently the Substance Abuse and Mental Health Services Administration doesn't watch BET or listen to urban radio because lyrically speaking, *100 percent* of our youth have been approached via rap infomercials *their entire lives*! One out of six (17.8 percent) African American youth ages 12 to 17 have used marijuana at least once,[12] thanks in part to the successful sales efforts of rapper pushers.

Unfortunately, the act of promoting drugs via music is nothing new. In 1932, Don Redman and his orchestra did "Reefer Man," a song about marijuana. If you keep a people intoxicated, they might riot for a few days, but they can't put up a sustained fight (revolution). What we need is a revolution, not a riot. Think about it.

Marijuana is the most popular of the illegal substances. The subliminal idea in gangsta Hip Hop seems to be that smoking weed is an authentic Hip Hop (black) thing. In 2004, during a workshop with high school students in Washington, DC, I asked the students to tell me at least one thing they enjoyed doing the most. Fifteen out of 40 girls told me they love to smoke and sip, which means smoking marijuana and drinking "yak," a.k.a. Cognac, Courvoisier, Remy, Hennessy, and Hpnotiq®. I've heard a lot over the years, but even I was shocked at the ease with which they shouted out their favorite drinks.

Like Kanye rapped in "Celebration," "I just thought you should know/We hit the liquor store/Got some Cris and some Mo."[13] I guess no rapper's perfect.

Compared to crack, marijuana may seem harmless, but it can damage short-term memory, judgment, perception, and problem solving skills. Thus, school performance suffers. Marijuana contains some of the same cancer causing chemicals found in tobacco smoke. You get double the dose of cancer causing agents when you wrap your marijuana inside a cigar. So smoking five joints per week puts you at the same risk as smoking a full pack of cigarettes per day. No wonder weed is called chronic; it can truly leave one in a chronic condition.

We used to call marijuana "weed" back in the day. Weeds kill those pretty things, those precious, tender young innocent things that grow in the garden of life. Tobacco and marijuana are both weeds that can kill. "They choke the young and rob them of their chance to bloom in the garden of life," says Ron K. Harris.

The hood at times appears to be playing a deadly game of Simon Says: Simon says get high and act stupid. Like Busta Rhymes says in "Get High Tonight," "Yo my whole squad smoking/aint straight unless we smoking at eight ... Weed smoking got me moving slow motion."[14]

more than a blunt, dunce!

"Smokin hydro-phonic and I'm high as a kite/Sippin on some crissy on a Saturday night."[15] **Big Tymers**, "Get High"

In recent years, public health specialists have tracked the rise of young people smoking cigars. In 2004, black middle school students were more likely than white students to smoke cigars.[16] There's a correlation between rappers smoking blunts and the popularity of blunt smoking in Hip Hop culture.

A blunt is a hollowed-out cigar that is filled with marijuana and other drugs, including cocaine, crack cocaine, PCP (phencyclidine), LSD (lysergic acid diethylamide), Ecstasy, Methamphetamine, heroin, GHB—even embalming fluid. These drugs are powerful and give a euphoric jolt. They can also cause paranoia and hallucinations. One bad blunt experience can lead to heart and lung failure, coma, convulsion, stroke, and death.

Blunts are popular for many reasons. Not only is it easier to work with large cigar wrappers (vs. cigarette papers to roll joints), blunts can be smoked over several sessions.

Some youth believe that smoking blunts (a.k.a. trees or branch) leads to a higher high than ordinary joints. They swear that cigar tobacco wrappers camouflage marijuana's distinctive smell, making it easier to smoke in public. Cigar wrappers burn more slowly than Tops cigarette papers, and this slow burn ensures the ingestion of an elevated dose of marijuana. Papers flavored with chocolate, candela, strawberry, vanilla, cognac, blueberry, watermelon, Jamaican rum, sour grape, passion fruit, black cherry, strawberry banana, peach, bubble gum, Pina Colada, butterscotch, cotton candy, and sweet cherry may disguise some of the drug's taste, but not the smell.

"Bust it then stuff it." This is what teenagers, usually males, say when they roll a blunt. Research shows that the Phillies cigar brand is the wrapper of choice among young users.[17]

Bragging about smoking blunts appears to be a requirement in the gangsta rap game. Try and find a gangsta rapper on the cover of a Hip Hop magazine without a blunt in his hand or mouth. Rappers convince their followers that smoking blunts is not a stunt; it's part of the fantasy of the wealthy Hip Hop lifestyle. They fail to tell their fans that 23 poisons, 43 carcinogens, and thousands of other harmful chemicals are in marijuana, tobacco, and cigar smoke.

Some of the more health-conscious rappers should come out and tell the truth about cigars, blunts, tobacco, and marijuana: that young smokers, especially African Americans, are at an increased risk of developing lung cancer, pulmonary and heart disease, esophageal cancers, oral cancer, and laryngeal cancer over nonsmokers.

blunt trauma

"Dem little niggas love to get high." **Convicted Drug Dealer**, Ohio Correctional Facility

Death by blunt trauma means to be struck on the head with an instrument heavy enough to cause death. Symbolically, placing a blunt cigar to your mouth (head) is blunt trauma. Gangsta rappers are striking Hip Hop youth upside the head with publicity photos, images in rap videos, and lyrics that push smoking blunts.

Platinum-selling artist Redman was featured on the cover of *High Times* lighting a blunt as was West Coast rapper Game. In this particular issue, Redman wrote an article about how to roll a blunt, clearly making him a mercenary.

An ad for Royal Blunts EZ Roll Tubes features nine semi nude women of different races sitting around a large dinner table with three 20-something black men strategically placed in the center of the picture. Containers of what appears to be wine are either held in the hands of the women or they sit on the table in front of them. There is a dish of fruit, one for each of the nine flavors of blunt papers being promoted. Two of the nine women are eating their fruit in an erotic manner. The ad is loaded with sexual cues as well as the spiritual theme of the Last Supper. The nine women plus the three men equals 12, the number of people at the last supper. Remember, one of the disciples was a traitor and another denied knowing Christ. Thus, smoking a blunt is highly associated with death, deception, and denial.

alcohol

> "The youth of hip hop are considered expendable. Their life expectancy is the shortest of any group on the planet. They have absolutely no rights Corporate America is bound to respect, so they are openly pursued by alcohol and tobacco companies and sacrificed, for they are the target as well as the market. No one expects them to live beyond 25. They are more likely to die just because and not for a cause." **LeeRoy Jordan**, master violence prevention specialist (Harlem 1999)

Every Hip Hop youth is a potential dollar for the alcohol and tobacco industries. That alone makes them targets right now. Today's youth are tomorrow's dollars, which means they're being courted and discussed in corporate boardrooms today.

Rappers endorse products with the promise and expectation of delivering youth in droves. Alcohol and tobacco companies love those adult artists that have a strong appeal and connection with youth. They look to partner with any rapper that has street cred and, via a criminal background or sexual reputation, considered authentic.

Unfortunately, alcohol is the drug of choice for African American youth.[18] The National Household Survey on Drug Abuse found that

19.8 percent of our young people between 12 and 20 used alcohol in the past 30 days, compared to 31.6 percent of whites; 10.5 percent reported binge drinking in the past month, compared to 21.7 percent of whites.[19] Although African American youth drink less than other youth, as we age, we suffer 31 percent more from alcohol-related diseases than other groups.[20]

Brothers & Sisters, alcohol use contributes to the three leading causes of death among African American 12 to 20 year-olds: homicide, unintentional injuries (including car crashes), and suicide.[21]

When rappers rhyme romantically about their favorite alcohol product, we must at least consider that they are part of the problem. A review of 1,000 popular songs from 1996 to 1997 found that rap had significantly more references to alcohol (47 percent) than other genres (Country Western, 13 percent; top 40, 12 percent; alternative rock, 10 percent; heavy metal, four percent). In addition, 48 percent of the rap tunes reviewed had specific alcohol product/brand name mentions,[22] and rap music videos also had the highest percentage of alcohol themes of any music genre appearing on MTV, BET, CMT and VH1.[23]

Corporate America knows that to gain the widest exposure possible for a product, buy time in a movie. Well, rappers got the same game. When alcohol companies seek to influence Hip Hop youth, they simply drop their product in a rap tune. In fact, they name drop every chance they get.

Interestingly, the Recording Industry Association of America rejected a recommendation to change how alcohol is marketed. They said, "75 percent of parents find the current parental advisory label program adequate."[24]

Obviously the recording industry doesn't want Hip Hop artists to stop rapping about alcohol products. The formula has proven to be highly profitable.

Hypocrisy 3—Role Models//Pimps, Hos, Pushers, & Spies

hooking the hood

> "I was gonna go to work but then I got high
> I just got a new promotion but I got high
> now I'm selling dope and I know why (why man?) yea heavy,
> cause I got high."[25] **Afroman**, "Because I Got High"

Fish won't bite if there's no bait on the hook. In the hood, gangsta rap has become the bait for addiction. Rappers name drop, hoping that companies will come bearing monetary gifts large enough to pay for production costs or an endorsement deal.

Coors has left the Rocky Mountains in search of inner city gold. The company paid for the title sponsorship of Nelly's summer 2003 U.S. tour and created a special edition Coors beer can celebrating 25 years of Hip Hop. Refer to *Message N/A Bottle, Vol. 1* for a peek into the racist practices of this company. Would rappers continue to lay down with these companies if they knew their history? Hmmm....

In the mega hit "Everybody Getting Tipsy," 17 year-old rapper J Kwon combined rough sex, alcohol, gunplay, and violence to make a top-of-the-charts urban Hip Hop hit.

> "Homeboy trippin' he don't know I got a gun,
> When it come to pop man we do s**t for fun, …
> Now i'm in the back gettin head from my hunz, …
> She smokin my blunt sayin she aint havin fun, …
> Now everybody in the club gettin tipsy."[26]

At the time of this release, J Kwon wasn't old enough to drink, and record executives used this fact to promote under aged drinking. Usher name dropped Hpnotiq and Alizé in his smash hit "Bad Girl." There ought to be a law.

I've never seen a rapper participate in a protest against tobacco and alcohol billboards in the hood or educate youth on the dangers of drugs, tobacco, and alcohol use. Contractually they can't; slaves can't and won't speak out against their masters for fear of financial retaliation.

hypnotic hip hop

(Thanks to Didra Brown Taylor, PhD, & Victor N. Taylor, who contributed "Hypnotic Hip Hop.")

The 40 ounce bottle of malt liquor hidden in a brown paper bag is still a thug staple, but some years ago, Hip Hop culture began to dress up its image. Female rappers put on designer dresses and furs and entire rap groups began sporting top-of-the-line designer suits. Gucci, Louis Vuitton, and other high-end labels became the new Hip Hop wear. This transformation in image was closely followed by new images of cigar smoking and expensive champagne drinking.

Hpnotiq has become a drink of choice for African Americans and under aged drinkers. Did the manufacturers of Hpnotiq create a product specifically for the African American Hip Hop lifestyle?

Hypnotiq is a tropical fruit liqueur. It's made from a blend of premium French vodka, pure cognac, and tropical fruit juices.

Ebonically and phonetically, Hpnotiq contains the "hyp" or "hp" sounds, which have subliminal connections to common rap words such as "hype," "hip," and "hop." Did the creators of Hpnotiq intentionally use the creative language of Ebonics to name their product?

The word "hypno," as in to hypnotize or to put to sleep, refers to how you're supposed to feel upon consuming the glowing blue beverage. The color blue is associated with sleep or the dream state and is used to induce a feeling of relaxation.

In "hypnotic," the correct spelling of the word, we find the word "not," which is a catchy buzz word in Hip Hop culture meaning "no" or "un-cool." "Tic" is the tick of the clock or what makes you tick. The tick-tock-tick-tock of a swinging pocket watch is used by the hypnotist to put a subject into a dream state. "Tic" is also found at the end of some interesting words, such as neurotic and psychotic, indicating the psychological suffering of a person not in touch with reality.

Marketing of alcohol products to Hip Hop youth has increased in intensity and cleverness. Product promotional nights at Los Angeles night clubs featured Hpnotiq sample bars, where the glowing, dark brew was served in long glass test tubes free of charge. It was as if the drink had been concocted in a science laboratory.

The creators of Hpnotiq took great care in naming the product, much like a master rapper creates a verse. At 17 percent alcohol by volume, the manufacturers ensure you will feel hypnotized. Given that African Americans consume 75 percent of all cognac beverages but make up only 12 percent of the U.S. population, it's little wonder that Hpnotiq was created and marketed to appeal to African Americans.

Young people are also attracted to the bright blue glow and sweet taste. After all, young African Americans set the trends for the world to follow.

If you look closely, you will see that Hpnotiq is simply: **Hip People Not** Having an **IQ.**

hip hop on the rocks

Biggie Smalls (a.k.a. The Notorious B.I.G.) name dropped just about everything he had ever tasted in his lyrics—ST Ides malt liquor, Cristal, Moet & Chandon champagne. Soon every rapper was following the leader. Cristal and other expensive drinks started popping up in the lyrics of Lil' Kim, Snoop Dogg, P. Diddy, Jay-Z, 50 Cent, and every Tom, Dick, and Harry in the rap game.

Courvoisier (cognac) duplicated the following successful advertising formula from the malt liquor era to revive sales:

Alcohol + Girl + Consumption = Sex

In 2002, thanks to Busta Rhymes' hit "Pass the Courvoisier," Courvoisier sales jumped 30 percent, the largest increase the 300-year-old brand had experienced since Napoleon III named it the "official supplier to the Imperial Court" in 1869.[27] Claire Coates, a spokeswoman for the Cognac National Interprofessional Bureau, says Hip Hop helped American sales reach more than 40 million bottles in 2002, worth $1 billion.[28]

The tune featured rappers P. Diddy and Pharell, actor Jamie Foxx, and a cameo by born again Christian actor Mr. T. This Hip Hop info-mercial received heavy rotation on BET and MTV. The phrase "Pass the Courvoisier" echoed throughout the hood as if it was all good. It was on the tongues of both the old and young, and when I say young, I mean third and fourth graders. Children really got into it.

The mastermind behind this successful strike against our youth was the self-proclaimed leader of the Hip Hop nation, Mr. Russell Simmons himself, the one and same who is so concerned about the condition of the Hip Hop nation and its youth. Can you say conflict of interest? Could it be that the godfather of Hip Hop is totally unaware of the effects alcohol has on children in the black community, even though he has children himself?

GlobalHue Advertising Agency named Russell Simmons its Vice Chairman and senior member of the Courvoisier Cognac Team, which pushes the product for its French parent company, Allied Domecq Spirits of North America. Allied Domecq hired Simmons' marketing firm, dRush, to boost Courvoisier's tired image.[29]

Simmons' campaigns were targeted to young adults, but of course, with the Hip Hop stamp of approval, under aged youth couldn't wait to try a sip. When you drop a bomb on a community, everyone suffers the effects of the mushroom cloud.

Hip Hop saved the cognac industry, much to the dismay of those who produce it. Jean-Marie Macoin, a 55 year-old cognac producer, said, "We weren't expecting cognac to be associated with those type of people."[30]

Excuse me, sir, what type of people? Niggaz? Considering that one of the lines in Busta's tune was "We gon' tell that nigga,"[31] I guess we can't really criticize Macoin for saying "those people."

shaken, not stirred

We in the black community have been shaken but not stirred out of our state of acceptance and passivity. The very people we've supported (rappers) now work on behalf of our enemy. Jay-Z has his own Armadale Vodka distributorship. Fellow rapper Jermaine Dupri is co-owner of his own liquor brand, 3 Vodka. Dupri states,

> "I became interested in the 3 Vodka Distilling Company after being amazed by its unique taste, as it is the only Vodka that is distilled from soy. I got involved cause I started seeing how much niggas in the club was watching what I used to drink. Then I started working out and stopped drinking and was introduced to this as a no carbohydrate vodka that I could drink and not get fat. I was like 'oh s**t, my people need to know about this,' so what better way to be introduced to them then [sic] through me? I got big plans for this."[32]

Let me see if I can make sense of what Dupri said. Vodka that won't make you gain weight but will still get you high/drunk. Is this supposed to be a health benefit? His people got to know about this? As if we need yet another intoxicant.

Our children love to nickname businesses in the hood, like Mikey D's for McDonald's. So it should come as no surprise that alcohol products also have their nicknames.

Hennessy is known as "Henn Dog," "Henn Roc," and "Henn" (a la Lil John & the East Side Boyz). Eminem celebrates "Henny" on his song "Just Lose It." In Jay-Z's song "Excuse Me, Miss," he raps, "You can't even drink Crist-OWL … you gotta drink Crist-ALL."[33]

Hypocrisy 3—Role Models//Pimps, Hos, Pushers, & Spies

Can't you just see it? As soon as teen Hip Hop heartthrobs Lil' Romeo and Bow Wow cross into adulthood, the alcohol and tobacco companies will be waiting for them, contracts in hand, using the likes of Jay-Z and Jermaine Dupri as role models. That should be enough to get a community stirred—in the sense of teaching youth the many tricks the alcohol and tobacco trades continuously use to get them hooked.

Jay-Z is the king of product placement in rap. With the power of Cristal, he's able to get the lady in his "I Just Wanna Love You" video to do things she otherwise wouldn't do. While sipping Cristal on his yacht, Jay-Z provides just the bad boy image alcohol and tobacco companies require from Hip Hop artists.

Jay-Z also connects images of sex and success (yacht) to drinking and smoking. This has made our prevention, intervention, and treatment work with youth extremely difficult.

Smoking Cigars/Blunts + Drinking Expensive Alcohol Products = Wealthy Lifestyle

The subtle lie here is that drinking expensive alcohol products puts you in the winner's circle. Drink this and you'll feel like a millionaire. This is similar to the old advertising con of linking alcohol to sexual power, even though drinking can cause chemical castration (impotence) in men and the loss of inhibitions (which can lead to STDS and unwanted pregnancies) in women.

Drinking 40s is straight ghetto, but drinking Cristal is Rodeo Drive. This is a lie made to look like the truth. Whether you spend hundreds of dollars on a bottle of booze or a couple of bucks, they both affect the body the same way. You're going to get drunk.

According to New York-based Scarborough Research, people who have attended a Hip Hop concert are 77 percent more likely than the general public to buy champagne.[34] DC-based New Media Strategies found that 60 percent of Hip Hop fans are likely to buy products pushed by rappers.[35] Man, a sucker is born every minute.

Hypocrisy 3—Role Models//Pimps, Hos, Pushers, & Spies

Interestingly, Jean-Marie Macoin, the cognac producer, wasn't alone in his views about Hip Hop's love of expensive alcohol products. It was widely reported that Frederic Rouzaud of Cristal said Hip Hop had brought the brand "unwelcome attention." Offended and viewing the comment as racist, Jay-Z decided to ban Cristal from his 40/40 Club sports bars.

when the smoke clears

(*Thanks to Ron K. Harris, who contributed "When the Smoke Clears."*)

"Hide nothing from the masses of our people. Tell no lies. Expose lies wherever they are told. Mask no difficulties, mistakes, failures. Claim no easy victories." Amilcar Cabral

When faced with the blatant exploitation and oppression perpetrated on the people by the merchants, politicians, and rulers, the Prophet Isaiah proclaimed boldly: "Woe unto them that call evil good, and good evil; that put darkness for light, and light for darkness; that put bitter for sweet, and sweet for bitter" (Isaiah 5:20).

Never in history have those words applied with more relevance than today. African Americans and other people of color carry a disproportionate burden of poverty, disease, and economic devastation. The American tobacco industry spends obscene amounts of money targeting the people of our communities with advertising and recruitment of replacement smokers—and African American teens will probably always be a target.

- Among African American teens, 61.3 percent prefer Newport, 10.9 percent prefer Kool, and 9.7 percent prefer Salem.[36]
- In 2002, 14.3 percent of African American high school students smoked. African American high school students were significantly less likely than white and Hispanic students to report current smoking. Among middle school students, rates

were relatively equal, with about one in 10 white (10.4 percent), African American (9.4 percent) and Hispanic (9.1 percent) students currently smoking. *However, African American middle school students had the highest level of current use of any tobacco products.*[37]

- The Brown & Williamson Tobacco Corporation ran a campaign for Kool cigarettes aimed at African American youth that featured Hip Hop icons. This appears to be in violation of a settlement between the industry and 46 states.[38]

The 1998 Master Settlement Agreement banned tobacco companies from targeting youth. However, according to a study published in the New England Journal of Medicine, this ban has not sufficiently accomplished its intended goal of curtailing tobacco exposure in children.[39]

We raise our hands in resignation and despair as more and more tobacco advertising blankets our communities. When we point out the racist nature of advertising that only targets our communities, we are accused of being anti-American, anti-business, or reverse racists—we can't win for losing.

The fact is, here in the Chicago area, you do not see cigarette billboards in Winnetka, Glencoe, or even in Lincoln Park; but you can't drive a block in Englewood, Lawndale, or Humboldt Park without seeing a tobacco billboard.

By comparison, alcohol, another deadly poison that is also unleashed criminally upon our population, is only one-fifth as lethal as tobacco. While alcohol kills more than 100,000, tobacco kills almost one-half million Americans per year.

Smoke & Mirrors

Sponsorship of black cultural events is the old smoke and mirror scam. Tobacco companies would love to have their products linked with the culture of Hip Hop and its four major themes, including art (graffiti), dancing (break dancing), MCing (rapping), and DJing (spinning records) at parties instead of emphysema, throat cancer, and suffering in the hospital.

What happens when a company endorses your program and gives you funding? They attach conditions and expect publicity and acknowledgment in your brochures and reports. How can we feel comfortable taking blood money and giving free publicity to the killers of our relatives? What has happened to our souls? Do we not hear the words of the prophet? Woe unto them that call evil good!

In the early 1990s, RJ Reynolds decided to create Uptown, a cigarette designed for and marketed to blacks. They learned a lot of things about us as they researched this product. For example, black smokers prefer menthol brands and they open their packs from the bottom. These idiosyncrasies and more were incorporated in the design and marketing.

Camel designed a Hip Hop Joe Camel campaign to introduce its new menthol cigarettes. The campaign targeted young black males.

In an effort to compete with Newports, Brown & Williamson did much the same thing in the spring of 2004 with their own well-established Kool brand by marketing collectible Kool Mixx boxes. The Kool Mixx National DJ Competition, the "special edition" packages, comes in four different styles. Full-cover illustrations feature a rapper saturated with gold jewelry, DJs working turntables, and Hip Hop dancers.

Perhaps KOOL stands for:

Killing
Off
Our
Leaders.

Now Brown & Williamson want to convince the black community that the Kool Mixx promotion is for adults. How many adults collect trading cards like a child, specifically cigarette box labels? The message is clear: "Collect 'em all, black kids, and trade 'em with your little black friends!"

The Master Settlement Agreement prevents Brown & Williamson from marketing and distributing brand name apparel or merchandise to youth. Yet, investigators found that brand-named merchandise was handed out at Kool Mixx DJ events in March 2004. "We shouldn't believe the hype that Brown & Williamson and other tobacco companies have ended youth marketing," said Sherri Watson Hyde, head of the Orlando-based National African American Tobacco Prevention Network.

Hip Hop is about mixing cultures, mixing tapes, and now mixing chemicals. Approximately 4,000 different ingredients have been identified in tobacco smoke, 43 of which are cancer causing. The main components are nicotine, tar, and carbon monoxide.

The most important ingredient in cigarettes is nicotine. Nicotine is the addictive agent in cigarettes and the reason why millions of people get hooked so easily and why they find it so hard to quit.

According to a report released in August 2006 by the Massachusetts Department of Health, the amount of nicotine delivered to the lungs of smokers, regardless of brand or type ("full flavor," "medium," "light," or "ultra-light"), increased by about *10 percent* during the past six years. The three most popular cigarette brands with young smokers—Marlboro, Newport, and Camel—delivered significantly more nicotine than they did in 2000. Nicotine in Kool cigarettes, a brand of choice among African Americans and Hip Hop youth, rose *20 percent.*[40]

Is there a label on cigarette packages warning smokers that nicotine content has been increased? Isn't that something that smokers should know about?

Smokers, if you've been wondering why quitting has seemed impossible, now you know why. Despite all the nicotine patches, chewing gums, hypnosis sessions, prayer and meditation sessions, detox programs, and sweat lodges, smokers are more hooked than ever before and are finding it harder and harder to quit. Could it be that tobacco companies, after having lost billions of dollars over the past few decades in lawsuits and mandatory statewide programs, had to find creative and sinister ways to continue to grow their revenue and market base? Quietly increasing the nicotine content in cigarettes has done the trick. Which tobacco scientist or corporate executive came up with this brilliant scheme to deepen addiction and, as a result, increase the risk of cancer and other related diseases?

Well, they may buy our politicians, but they cannot buy our silence! We will not shut up! *A Luta Continua Lazima Tushinde Bila Shaka*, or "The struggle will continue and we will conquer without a doubt."

It Tastes Like Candy

Sexual predators love to use candy/sweets to lure their victims, especially children, into their deadly traps. Seemingly, the tobacco industry has picked up on this hideous tactic.

Candy cigarettes were out when I was a child. You'd put a stick in your mouth and blow out a puff of sugar smoke, and then chew the gum. Today, the tobacco industry has created another trick to get children hooked on cigarettes early. Brown & Williamson Tobacco's new flavored versions of Kool cigarettes—Caribbean Chill, Midnight Berry, Mocha Taboo, and Mintrigue—cater to teenagers with their sugary names. These sugar cigarettes are especially appealing to members of the Hip Hop community, which has a sugar dependent diet. Let's be honest, what grown person is sitting around thinking, "Man, if only I could get my hands on a strawberry flavored cigarette!"

Since 1999, RJ Reynolds has been selling exotic blends of Camels: Crema (tastes like cream), Dark Mint (chocolate and mint), Izmir Stinger (brandy and crème de menthe), Mandarin Mint (citrus and mint), Twist (citrus), and Bayou Blast (berries). Malt liquor companies have long flavored their liquid crack products. I guess cigarettes are a bit late at the game.

African American teens have been less likely to become regular smokers during adolescence, and the tobacco industry (and their rapper front men) had to do something about that. According to the American Lung Association, tobacco use primarily begins in early adolescence. One-third of all smokers have their first cigarette by the age of 14. *Ninety percent* of all smokers begin before the age of 21.[41] Combine the sweet tooth of adolescents and teens and the sweet tasting tobacco and papers, which mask the nasty taste. Mission accomplished.

In addition, the National Institute on Drug Abuse released two studies that found that nicotine cravings appear to be linked to increased cravings for illicit drugs among drug abusers who also smoke tobacco.[42] This is a point of concern because the candy tasting cigarette/cigar products are similar to the sweet tasting Alcopops (alcohol products). With every puff you'll want a drink and with every drink you'll want a smoke. Diabolically brilliant!

Rappers front designer drugs, expensive alcohol, and designer candy cigarettes. What next? A designer bullet to the head?

Hypocrisy 3—Role Models//Pimps, Hos, Pushers, & Spies

Chapter 12

Spies Among Us

"Gangsta rap symbolizes a form of genocide prose, which has been encouraged and distributed by those in the industry who are driven by drugs, greed and racism. Rap in its purest form was an art form of pose and poetry which expressed life in the same sense that the spirituals did. Gangsta rap is a perverted form which has been encouraged by those who have always used the entertainment industry to exploit and project the negative stereotypical images to demean and depict African-Americans as subhuman, which is the antithesis of what we as African-American people are." **C. Dolores Tucker**, civil rights activist

They can say what they like about Dolores Tucker, but she inherently understands that rappers who spew ills about black women and promote the death of the black community are nothing less than symbolic spies working on behalf of a powerful machine that is dead set on suppressing the black community.

What is a spy? The Bible speaks of spies. Throughout history, all great battles and movements have had to deal with the spies in their own camps. Spies are essential in war; they are expected yet seldom detected.

Movies show spies, like James Bond, infiltrating countries and corporations, gathering information, reporting what they find to their bosses. They show them fighting and killing people. They show them having sex with the enemy. They show them living in a community, sometimes for years, getting married and having children as they await instructions to complete a mission.

In real life, spies, specifically agent provocateurs, were sent by the FBI to set up the Black Panthers and civil rights organizations.

A spy has been defined as an agent that steals the secrets of a country or corporation, but this definition doesn't begin to cover all the types of espionage that spies might be engaged in. In the Hip Hop/ ghetto matrix, the spies among us are engaged in so many different types of treasonous acts that in the African Court of Justice, many of your favorite rappers would be declared guilty of treason against the African American community and the global African Diaspora.

The following are five types of spies that work to undermine Hip Hop and the black community at large:

1. **Spy.** Secretly gathers intelligence (information). Market research firms specialize in providing intelligence on the buying habits of Hip Hop youth to the PTBs (powers that be). Reports can sell for thousands of dollars.

2. **Mole.** May or may not know he is a spy. Brainwashed/trained to believe he is a member of a community until activated to perform a task (assassination, sow dissension, gather intelligence, provide sexual favors) for the PTBs. May lay low in the community for years before activation.

3. **Agent Provocateur.** Embedded in groups to gather intelligence and sow dissension. Agent provocateurs infiltrated the liberation camps of Nat Turner, the Black Panthers, Martin Luther King, and Malcolm X. Once activated, a mole can become an agent provocateur.

4. **Economic Hit Man (EHM).** According to John Perkins, author of *Confessions of an Economic Hit Man*, EHMs "are highly paid professionals who cheat countries around the globe out of trillions of dollars."[1] EHM rappers are highly paid professionals who, through their seductive lyrics glorifying consumerism and materialism, cheat gullible fans around the globe out of billions of dollars.

5. **Assassins.** Kill on demand for money. No compassion, it's just a job. This is similar to the lyrical assassins who instruct

black youth on the many ways to commit violence against black men, women, and children.

We each have our role in this scenario, including me. But I refuse to be a pawn in this game, so long ago I decided that I would serve my community by being a code breaker and educator. Throughout this book I crack several codes which help clarify the hypocrisies and how our youth are getting played big time by spies who look just like them.

> "Cryptanalysis (from the Greek kryptós, 'hidden', and analýein, 'to loosen' or 'to untie') is the study of methods for obtaining the meaning of encrypted information without access to the secret information which is normally required to do so. Typically, this involves finding the secret key. In non-technical language, this is the practice of codebreaking or cracking the code, although these phrases also have a specialised technical meaning."[2]

spycraft: hip hop style

Spycraft within the Hip Hop community works on the level of symbolism and strategic communications. Hip Hop spycraft works on the subconscious, unconscious, and conscience of the target. Hip Hop agents/spies steal the state secrets of the Hip Hop/ghetto matrix and the African American community at large. The agents/spies— rappers and Hip Hop entrepreneurs—take these state secrets and transmit deep level programming and propaganda via music, fashion, video games, movies, and TV sit-coms to their target: global youth culture. This transmission occurs 24/7 via radio and TV broadcasts, cablecasts, the Internet, cell phones, billboards, and embedded moles and agent provocateurs. EHM rappers and Hip Hop entrepreneurs are contracted to cheat youth around the world out of billions of dollars. Lyrical assassins kill the dream, the dreamer, the hopes and future of African American youth. Video game assassins kill brothas and sistas with no compassion and with much pleasure and excitement.

Sometimes assassinations are real, possibly for marketing purposes. Many suspect that spies embedded in the camps of rappers Tupac Shakur and Notorious B.I.G. fueled the East Coast-West Coast war of words. Both rappers slandered one another with increasing brutality and frequency. Their bad blood eventually escalated from a battle of words to a bloody war which led to both of their deaths.

Whenever I tell my high school students and those who love gangsta Hip Hop that there are spies in the Hip Hop camp they say, "No way. This ain't the '60s. Nobody is selling out." They don't have to sell out. They only have to buy into the value system (inappropriate sexual behavior, consumerism-materialism, violence, drugs) that is promoted by commercialized gangsta rap/Hip Hop.

EHM rappers get airplay for their self-promoting tunes that glorify bling bling, alcohol products, drugs, and products that the black community, on average, cannot afford. Rap tunes that promote social issues seldom get air time or awards. In the words of rapper Jadakiss, "Why?" At least he had the guts to ask why in his 2004 rap, which was enlightening and thought provoking. Perhaps this is why he won no major awards.

Students always ask me to provide a list of the spies and for the longest I couldn't. So I began to ask the experts about what makes a good spy. First thing, good spies never get caught. You would never suspect they are working for hidden powers. They are able to throw off suspicion. Think about it. Who would ever suspect the following to be spies capable of selling out Hip Hop and black people with their lyrical bombs or entrepreneurial maneuverings: Russell Simmons, Damon Dash, Jay-Z, Jermain Dupree, Luke, Bob Johnson, Marion "Suge" Knight, Sean "P Diddy" Combs, Eazy-E, Snoop Dogg, Big Tymers, Master P, R. Kelly, Lil' Kim, Ma$e, Lil Jon, and 50 Cent. They look and talk just like you and me. This ability to blend in is the secret to the spy's success. In fact, the best spies are invisible and have names we will never know.

I'm sure that some of the above mentioned people would disagree they are spies. They may not recognize that they are acting as spies, and that's because there are many different types of spies.

I believe that most Hip Hop rappers, producers, and entrepreneurs are moles. Moles are trained to fit into a community before being activated to do whatever their bosses tell them to do. That could include going to jail or taking a bullet to drive up CD sales. I believe a handful of Hip Hop moguls have some limited knowledge about what's going on, but as in any spy game, information is compartmentalized, i.e., on a "need to know" basis.

I call some rappers spies because their history and influence within the Hip Hop/ghetto matrix is fairly consistent with the behavior of a good spy. They mean the youth of Hip Hop and the black community no good.

Most folk fail to realize or accept that Hip Hop artists and moguls report to higher ups. The lyrics, video imagery, and publicity (propaganda) tricks of these undercover spies must be pre-approved by the PTBs. According to former police Sergeant Delacy Davis, good undercover spies:

1. Don't get caught.
2. Can change an alias/cover story at a moment's notice.
3. Complete their missions at all costs.
4. Are expendable for the good of the mission (as are you!).
5. Develop the art of persuasion. They can persuade people to do anything.
6. Don't fall in love with their subjects/targets, even if they must have sex with them.
7. Trust no one.
8. Recruit other spies.
9. Rule out no tactic or strategy until carefully evaluated.
10. Protect the organization no matter what.

11. Use all of the target's weaknesses, vices, likes and dislikes, friends, family, and enemies against him.
12. Appear authentic (via walk, vernacular, fashion, e.g., bullet proof vests) to establish street credibility.[3]

In *The Art of War*, Sun Tzu discusses spying as a way to destroy enemies. To destroy an enemy (a community, a neighborhood, a people), effective spies must be entrenched in enemy territory.

A spy must be indistinguishable from the people he is infiltrating. He must be of the same race, ethnic group, and age group. He should be able to mimic the behaviors of those most intellectually vulnerable or those seeking something (spirituality, sex, etc.). This gives him the trust of the group and ready access to information.

According to author and ex FBI agent Dr. Tyrone Powers, spying is called the second oldest profession (after prostitution). Spying and prostitution include some of the same characteristics: money, power, secrecy, sex, and control. Based on his experiences in the field for several years, Powers concludes that:

1. A good spy must know the language and ways of the people.
2. Spies must have an established history that is consistent with the group, society, community to be infiltrated. This history can be real or manufactured, but if it is to be effective it should be embellished. The spy must rehearse and know it well.
3. A good spy must know the people and the popular locations, and they must be trained to know the history and major players in those locations.
4. A good spy must demonstrate a lack of fear under stressful situations.
5. To an extent, a spy must be attractive to the target population. If a spy is repulsive, it will be difficult to get targets to let down their guard and let the spy in. Physical attractiveness and an air of sexiness are the necessary assets of the effective spy.

6.   Good spies must be confident and able to force their will upon others without others knowing it.

7.   A good spy must be secretive and have the ability to disappear at times with explanation. The key to successful spying is keeping the whole matter as secret as possible.

8.   Spies must be able to operate without conscience, and they must be able to effectively suppress all ethical considerations. They must be willing to do whatever is deemed necessary to successfully complete their mission.

9.   A good spy must be able to effectively engage several clandestine operations at one time.[4]

50 cent

Compare the indicators listed by Dr. Powers and Sgt. Davis to prominent rappers and Hip Hop figureheads, and many will begin to look suspicious. If they're not real trench-coat wearing spies, then symbolic spies. Their mission? To answer that question, let's look at the strange case of mega rapper, *GQ*'s Man of the Year (2005), Curtis Jackson a.k.a. 50 Cent.

50 Cent is the product of a broken home and a drug involved parent. He was raised by loving grandparents, but for the most part, he took care of himself on the south side of Jamaica-Queens, New York. Those rough streets provide the backdrop for many of his lyrics about drugs, sex, money, crime, imprisonment, stabbings, and the infamous shootings. Unlike most rappers who fantasize about the thug life in their lyrics, 50 Cent (or Fiddy) actually lived his rhymes—and this has become his calling card.

"Now, Coach, that doesn't make Fiddy a spy. Lots of people in the hood have that type of background." True that. So let's see if we have a case.

First, a good spy must have at least some of the qualities and skills Dr. Powers and Sgt. Davis mention. Let's see how 50 Cent stacks up:

- He appears to be a member of the target group.
- He has established authenticity via his dress and vernacular.
- Because he fits in so well, he avoids suspicion and detection.
- He has earned the respect of the target.

"C'mon, Coach. A lot of people in the hood fit that description." True, but not everyone who fits that description is a multimillionaire with his own CDs, energy drinks, movies, video games—and access to the PTBs. But let's probe deeper.

Like many rappers, Curtis Jackson has an alias (fake name). This sends up red flags. An alias (like the Jackal) is a symbol of the bearer's personality, or it may provide a clue to the purpose of the bearer's mission. Never accept a rapper's alias at face value. Nine times out of 10, there's something going on beneath the appeal of being a gangsta (although that's bad enough).

What could the alias "50 Cent" symbolize? Let's crack this code together.

1. Write the number 5.
2. Spell the word five next to it (5 five).
3. Write the number 0.
4. Search the alphabet for the letter that looks like 0. Thus, 0 = O. (Often, when giving out a telephone number or address, we substitute "O" for "0.")
5. Now put the two new representations together and you have …

I will admit to taking symbolic license, but you skeptics have to admit, things are getting interesting. The number 50 decoded reads "Five-O," which is street argot for "police" a.k.a. "the po po." If not the po po, then could Jackson possibly be an informant for the police? Hmmm …

If you're like my students, by now you're thinking, "No way!"

It is well documented that Curtis Jackson/50 Cent, like a lot of popular rappers, is a convicted felon. Felons lose their civil rights, such as the right to vote, the right to bear arms, the right to hold a professional license, and the right to serve on a jury. The ACLU is working with state lawmakers to restore those rights when a felon's sentence is completed. But many states have yet to do so. I support the right of a felon who has done his time to vote and serve on a jury.

Convicted felon 50 Cent is often pictured on the cover of Hip Hop magazines holding a gun/weapon and wearing a bulletproof vest as part of his bad boy image—but wait a minute. Convicted felons can't wear bulletproof vests or carry firearms. This is a violation of the law! How is it that a convicted felon gets away with such behavior?

In the subjective arena of symbolism, everything matters and unlikely things are connected. 50 Cent gets away with his message of violence because the people continue to support him. There is no public outcry, not even in the community where his image is doing the most psychological harm.

In order for spies to avoid suspicion and detection, they must blend in with the people. They must have the ability to look, walk, talk, and act like the people.

50 Cent produced a series of ads for the sale of his clothing line. Each ad was unmistakably based on the drug trade, mainly cocaine. One disturbing ad features him in a basement with his jeans bundled like kilos of marijuana (or was it cocaine?). In 2005, he released *50 Cent: Bulletproof*, a profound DVD game, just in time for the holiday season and on the heels of his movie *Get Rich Or Die Tryin'*.

At least one country, Australia, chose to protect their children from this game.

> "A 3-member panel of the Classification Review Board has, after playing the game for a cumulative 42 hours determined, in a unanimous decision, that the computer game entitled **50 Cent Bulletproof** be refused classification.
>
> "Refused Classification means the game cannot be legally sold, hired, advertised or exhibited in Australia. Maureen

Shelley, convenor of the Classification Review Board said, *'The counter kills are enacted in detail, they are prolonged and take place in close up and slow motion. The most impactful of the counter kills involve knives and on-screen blood splatter. The Review Board determined that the impact of this mode was high and could not be accommodated at MA15+ classification. Therefore the game must be refused classification'.*"[5]

Supposedly, *50 Cent: Bulletproof* is loosely based on the gangsta rapper lifestyle. Keep in mind this convicted felon is allowed to promote and profit from the same lifestyle that got him in trouble with the po po in the first place.

The duty of a good spy is to report the cultural tastes, habits, strengths, and weaknesses of the target community to the PTBs. "There just aren't many celebrities who understand today's consumer as well as 50," says Marc Ecko, whose Ecko Unlimited manufactures and distributes 50 Cent's G-Unit clothing line.[6] I guess that's why Reebok contracted the rapper to do a line of shoes. He knows what youth want to wear and how much they will spend.

50 Cent: Bulletproof is produced by VU Games. It was rated M for Mature (Blood and Gore, Intense Violence, Sexual Themes, Strong Language, and Use of Drugs). The Entertainment Software Ratings Board believes that "Titles rated M have content that may be suitable for persons ages 17 and older."

Despite the rating, 50 Cent said that parents could use his game as a teaching tool for their children. "Just because it is rated Mature doesn't mean you shouldn't buy it for your kids. Play the game and explain to them what they are playing."[7] Can you imagine little Pookie and Peaches playing *50 Cent: Bulletproof* with Uncle Ray Ray?

A quick review of some 50 Cent tunes should prove enlightening:
1. Many Men (Wish Death on Me)
2. Candy Shop
3. In Da Club
4. Just A Lil Bit

5. Wanksta
6. P.I.M.P.
7. Magic Stick
8. Window Shopper
9. Hustlers Ambition
10. 21Questions
11. A Baltimore Love Thing
12. Porn Star

As an EHM, 50 Cent is king among rapper spies. His tunes use sex, bribes, drugs/alcohol, and power to help maintain a state of flux and chaos in hood consciousness. They employ strategies that contribute to the incarceration of the target, specifically the African American male population. They introduce words into the lexicon that reinforce the poor concept and self perception of the target group. They simulate assassinations, and they definitely cheat youth around the globe out of billions of dollars (remember, the Hip Hop market totals about $155 billion).

In addition to CDs, DVDs, movies, and video games, in 2007, 50 Cent will launch G-Unit Books in joint venture with MTV/Pocket Books, the publisher of his memoir *From Pieces to Weight*.

The public school system can't teach our youth to read, but 50 Cent may single-handedly raise literacy in the hood with his sexually explicit, violent tales of life in the street. Yes, it will get youth reading like Harry Potter got white youth reading, but couldn't we have found a better way?

gq scandal

With all the outstanding African American men in Hip Hop, business, social services, education, and ministry that serve the greater good, in 2005, *GQ* magazine decided to honor a convicted felon as a Man of the Year. You mean to tell me the editors couldn't find not one dedicated African American husband, father, provider, and community servant? Where's the public outrage?

GQ editor Mark Healy said, "[50 Cent] is one of those public figures we're endlessly fascinated by."[8]

Who's we? Interestingly, no mention was made of Fiddy's porn projects. According to AVN.com, in 2004, his G-Unit crew supposedly signed with video/DVD production company Digital Sin to release an "interactive" porno movie. 50 Cent will host a Hip Hop porno called *Groupie Luv* that will feature a glimpse into his XXX-rated lifestyle. "The viewer will be able to choose which girls have sex and where the sex will take place," Digital Sin director of marketing and media Jeff Mullen told AVN.com. "50 Cent is a marketing person and he understands this is another marketing outlet for him that will open him up to a bigger audience."[9]

Remember when Dr. Martin L. King (1963) and Nelson Mandela (1993) were voted Man of the Year by *Time* magazine? We were proud to have these men represent us. Today, 50 Cent represents African American men. This is what we have sunk to. Curiously, this is the same hard core thug rapper who ran to the aid of President George Bush by lashing out at fellow Hip Hop star Kanye West for his comment (in the wake of Hurricane Katrina) that Bush didn't like black people. As Dr. Powers says of the good spy, Fiddy creates and helps to maintain an atmosphere conducive to the psychological manipulation of the target. To protect his masters, he serves as an apologist, both overtly and covertly.

Now 50 Cent is jumping on Oprah for not having lewd rappers on her show. What is this really about? Who is he speaking for? The king of rap should beware that the queen of media has the juice to shut commercialized gangsta rap down if she wants to.

Spies do an excellent job of making lies look like the truth. When Fiddy told *GQ* magazine that President Bush was a "gangsta" and that he saw himself in him, was he kidding or was he telling the truth?

Is 50 Cent a Republican? Confused? You be the judge. The following is 50 Cent's widely quoted statement about the handling of the New Orleans crisis:

"The New Orleans disaster was meant to happen. It was an act of God. I think people responded to it the best way they can. What Kanye West was saying, I don't know where that came from."

15 minutes of fame

"In the Hip Hop culture everyone aspires to be a star. All over the United States of America we see young people achieving great feats in the music industry. Unfortunately, they only enjoy their fame for 15 minutes. They ride high on the backs of women, poor people and even the affluent under the guise of keeping it real. The music industry knows that they will only enjoy a few minutes in the limelight so the master manipulators of the industry ensure that those 15 minutes are the most profitable that any corporation could ever enjoy at the expense of the communities that the puppets (entertainers) hail from. Finally, the artist's 15 minutes of fame makes Luther Van Dross' request of 'Only for One Night' seem like a lifetime."[10]

Hip Hop doesn't have a retirement plan for its spies, moles, EHMs, agent provocateurs, and lyrical assassins. When their 15 minutes of fame are up, what will rap artists do? If they've been smart, they'll leverage their fame into their own businesses. A few may work in TV and film. A couple may produce other rappers or, like Jay-Z, get an executive job at a record company. If they're lucky, a couple may get an endorsement deal or two. They may become Hip Hop experts for media talk shows. And the rest will end up chasing dreams deferred.

Few rappers have managed to successfully brand themselves into a career. Longevity isn't a part of the 15-minute package. The truth of the matter is many never make the 15-minute mark. Back biting, incarceration, death, substance abuse, bling bling bankruptcies, and bad deals leave most rappers owing their record labels. Instead of pimping, they get pimped.

Hip Hop is approaching 30, and the list of stars that once rhymed in the bright lights reads like a Who's Who. The elders of Hip Hop (those who were in their teens or early 20s at its birth) are kicking 50 in the butt, hanging on a bit too long. Some of the men still sport curls and ponytails, backward hats, dangling earrings, and a juvenile lexicon.

Recently, my daughter's high school had a '70s day (1970s) during homecoming week. I couldn't believe the outfits the young people showed up in. Well, I guess I should say I couldn't believe my generation dressed like that back in the day, but we did. Our only saving grace is that as adults, we don't dress like that now. I often ask my high school students, "Do you think you'll be wearing the same fashions 25 years from now?" They often respond, "I hope not! I'm sure our clothes will be played out." Then I ask, "Will you be listening to Hip Hop and rapping 25 years from now?" Surprisingly they say, "Yes, why wouldn't we?"

There's an old saying that goes, "What you do now will become history for the rest of your life." Rappers do and say things seemingly without regret, and their 15 minutes of fame today will last a lifetime in the minds and memories of youth. Images of lust, violence, ghetto life—and the psychosocial damage—linger long after a rapper's 15 minutes are up.

One of my favorite workshop exercises is to have youth complete this lyric from an old school rap tune: "Rollin down the street—" Like clockwork they chime in with, "—smokin endo, sippin on gin and juice/Laid back with my mind on my money and my money on my mind."[11] Snoop Dogg's "Gin and Juice" is now a memory of youth, firmly set in their minds for the rest of their lives. Interestingly, even

Hypocrisy 3—Role Models//Pimps, Hos, Pushers, & Spies

the quiet ones complete the lyrics to "Gin and Juice." Youth who don't know each other instantly bond because they all know that song about drinking, smoking weed, and cash money. Sadly, it defines this generation. It's Hip Hop's coming of age tune.

What will a Hip Hop reunion concert look and sound like 30 years from now? Think about it, it's scary. A bunch of old gangstas in white tees and gold and platinum fronts in their mouths, covering what few teeth and rotting gums they have left. Ball caps sported backwards over bald spots and saggin' pants hanging under beer bellies. Thongs and pasties over flabby skin.

Can you imagine 65 and 70 year-old men on stage, smoking marijuana, holding their genitals (males) and shaking their booties (females) while spewing vulgarities at their senior citizen audience, throwing up signs for Roc-a-Fella, Westside, and Dirty South like they did when they were 16? Don't laugh, it could happen. Perhaps PBS is planning for it now.

In an effort to stretch 15 minutes into 16, legitimize Hip Hop artists, and gain national recognition, award shows have been passing out lifetime achievement awards to rappers like candy at a Halloween party. Rappers with less than three years in the business are receiving lifetime and legend awards!

Interestingly, Rock Hall of Fame voters have chosen to not extend another minute to any Hip Hop artist. Artists are eligible for nomination 25 years after releasing their first recording, but none of rap's senior citizens have been so honored. They continue to snub rappers, and I predict this will continue for years to come. The Run-DMC's and Public Enemy's of the Hip Hop world may eventually get there, but the majority white board will never rush to place the profane, misogynist rap playas next to the likes of Elvis.

Public Enemy front man Chuck D said, "It's blasphemous. We can't afford to have another piece of Black art history go undocumented."[12]

Speaking of Public Enemy, Flava Flav, the once revolutionary former rapper of the group, extended his 15 minutes of fame to about 20 on his big clock necklace when he was cast in VH1's reality shows *The Surreal Life* (2004) and its spin-off *Strange Love*. In *The Surreal Life*, Flava met and became romantically involved with Danish actress and Sylvester Stallone's ex, Bridget Nielsen. In *Strange Love*, Flav chases Bridget around the world like a brokenhearted puppy or sad clown.

Now airing on VH1 is *Strange Love's* spinoff, *Flavor of Love*, where a multicultural cast of females fight to spend time in the hot tub with Flav. The rapper once known as the greatest hype man in history has been reduced to having a woman defecate on his floor and another spit in the face of a fellow contestant. In the beginning of season two, we saw Flav meeting with his team of writers. Wait ... so reality TV is scripted? Are we surprised? Is this keeping it real?

Hoopz (Nikki Alexander), the "winner" of season one, may have ultimately "broken up" with Flav, but as she admits in *Black Men* magazine, she was hired to do a "job."[13]

Is *Flavor of Love* the honest attempt of an aging rapper to make a comeback? To come out of the cold? Was it all about getting paid—or was he activated for service by the PTBs? The career path makes no sense. To go from Public Enemy to *Flavor of Love*—it makes me wonder what we're really witnessing when we watch this show.

Does this fate await the Bow Wow's and Lil' Romeos of the Hip Hop world? God, I hope not.

Does this fate await other Hip Hop spies that have outlived their usefulness? Will more and more get outted like CIA agent Valerie Plame? (That would be a good thing.) God forbid, will they take a bullet? Lose recording contracts? Continue to work deep undercover for purposes we're only beginning to understand?

Chapter 13

Who's the Boss?

"One of the prevailing assumptions around Hip Hop is that it was...solely African-American created, owned, controlled and consumed. It's an appealing myth—but the evidence just isn't there to support it...I'd argue that without white entrepreneurial involvement Hip Hop culture wouldn't have survived its first half decade on vinyl."[1] **Nelson George**

"There are only about 10 to 20 rappers that are in the game making money with album after album."[2] **Jay-Z**

According to *Fortune.com,* the following Hip Hop entrepreneurs generate hundreds of millions of dollars via their business holdings:
- Sean "Puff Daddy/P Diddy" Combs: $315 million
- Jay-Z: $286 million[3]

According to *The New York Times,* 50 Cent earned $50 million in 2004, which included endorsement deals, films, a record label, and clothing and gym shoe lines.[4] The following are other top wage earners, according to VH1's 2002 "Rock's Rich List" (*Rolling Stone's* "Rock's 50 Richest 2003" also listed the following figures):
- Eminem: $28.9 million
- Jay-Z: $22.7 million
- Dr. Dre: $10.6 million
- Nelly: $6.6 million[5]

These names are repetitively and flashily promoted in the media, but the truth is that the billions of dollars generated by Hip Hop are consolidated in the hands of a few artist-entrepreneurs. And these are only crumbs compared to the real wealth of the PTBs.

What about the portfolio of the average rapper? A media industry has risen around "reporting" on the blingnomics (bling economics) of rap stars. Entertainment "news" shows report on the cars, mansions, pools, furs, and designer shoes of rappers. These geniuses appear to have it all. But do they really? Could our eyes be deceiving us? Or are lies being made to look like the truth? Are they really as rich as they appear?

MTV Cribs featured the lavish home of Ja Rule—only it allegedly wasn't his home. According to the *Miami Herald,* a woman claimed she rented it to the rapper for the Memorial Day weekend in 2001.[6]

Early in 2005, the home of Trina (*The Baddest Bitch* CD) was in danger of foreclosing. Apparently Trina was having a hard time keeping up payments. Hers was yet another rapper home featured on *MTV Cribs.* She paid only $157,000 for the home in 1999, not exactly the cost of a palatial mansion.[7]

Rapper Ricky Streetz says,

> "I don't pop bottles of Moët, I don't drink Cristal, and a lot of my friends can't afford that. A lot of time, they go in places and try to afford things that they can't budget, and that comes from trying to chase after a lifestyle that rappers lie about—being rich and being millionaires. I don't know anybody that's rich, but a lot of people start selling drugs to try and finance that type of lifestyle and live like a rapper."[8]

Those six and seven-figure development deals we hear about are supposed to cover the production costs of CDs and videos. Staff, group members, agents, managers, producers, and hangers on, not to mention the artist, have to be paid out of the advance. After the CD has been released, the artist receives only a small percentage (seven to 13 percent) off of each CD that sells. He receives the percentage only if record sales pay off the advance first.

What do rappers have to do to achieve real wealth instead of just the image of wealth? There's a difference. Within the framework of capitalism in America, are brothas and sistas in the rap game truly rich or do they just appear to be rich? Do they have mere spending change or the power to make social change?

Money + Power (influence) = Wealth in America

Some would say, who cares? As long as they're getting paid. This is the Getting Paid Syndrome, and it ignores the selling of your soul, the forming of unholy alliances, and the promotion of messages, themes, and images that harm black and Latino youth in the hood.

There is a fraternity of money men in this country. Just like gangs, they have their own secret rules, handshakes, meetings, and language. Their goal is to consolidate wealth and power in the world. That's why over the past few decades the number of major media outlets (radio, tv, print) has dwindled to a mere handful. Power is being consolidated. This has been especially hard on the rap music industry, because as power has consolidated in the hands of the few, only one theme of black hoodism, black promiscuity, black materialism/consumerism, and black buffoonery has been allowed to enjoy the global spotlight.

Are rappers true independent contractors or mercenaries? Or are they just high priced slaves? To those of us who may never see a million dollars in a year, that may be a "so what?" kind of a question. "They're getting paid," you may say.

But when it comes to the healthy development of our children, the question becomes all important. If these rappers are independent and are truly calling their own shots, then we can persuade them to change their lyrical content.

But if they are not independent, if they are owned by Corporate America, which I believe they are, then they don't have the power to make change. When a rap artist is called into an exec's office to talk about marketing, I imagine the scene goes something like this:

"How's that beef between you and Lil' Rapper going?"

"Ah, man, it ain't nothing. We cool."

"So you fellows kissed and made up?"

"We didn't kiss—."

"You know what I mean. Look, a magazine reporter called this morning, wanting an exclusive interview on the feud. Now, if there's no feud, there's no article. See?"

The street smart rapper slowly nods his head. "Yeah, man, I see what you mean."

And so it goes. The fight is on, and the rappers make it look good. It may be real or it may be staged. We know from history that Hollywood spin makers have staged all kinds of things, from feuds to love triangles. They'll accomplish their goals by any means necessary.

In the meantime, our young people are watching the feud in fascination. They take sides. As a coach and counselor, I've had to break up fights that were started by people they don't even know and for reasons they didn't understand.

So, who's calling the shots? Are rappers in charge of their own lives or are they high priced slaves? To answer that question, we'll have to follow the money trail. Income streams of top rappers include record sales, tour sponsorships, clothing lines, and licensing and endorsement deals.

At the height of his fame, Michael Jordan had endorsement deals in the millions. His ability to keep the deals depended on his clean image. This is not the case with rappers. Their ability to keep their deals apparently depends on their gangsta/thug/criminal image. This hurts us as a people.

When Lil' Kim is featured in an Old Navy (clean cut, All American) commercial, then you know something is up. Of all the black entertainers, why choose porn talking, pasty wearing Lil' Kim (who cleans up for the prime time spot but won't clean up for our children)? Could it be *because* of the character she portrays in her music? Hmmm....

Who's the boss? Who's calling the shots? Sometime ago I remember reading that a female rapper wanted to do positive lyrics, but execs weren't interested. It was only when she began to act out that she got the media attention she craved.

The PTBs in the media and recording industry are calling the shots. As a capitalist enterprise I would expect nothing less. But who are these African American front men and women who would sell their souls, like Judas sold out Jesus for 30 pieces of silver? Commercialized gangsta rappers have allowed greed to consume them. Like Sambo, the plantation overseer, they front for an industry that cares nothing about black children. If Jay-Z is right and only 10 to 20 rappers are truly making money, then the rest are fighting like crabs at the bottom of the barrel for a piece of a very small pie. This creates a dog-eat-dog mentality. They may do anything, including promoting harmful lyrics and lies to children, to succeed.

Possibly the biggest lie ever told in Hip Hop is the lie of ownership, that rappers have peeped the game and not sold out to "the man." Only a few have managed to do this. Most rappers are owned body, mind, and soul, and they must dance to the tune of their master. I can understand wanting to get paid, but as Luke 9:25 says, "And how do you benefit if you gain the whole world but lose or forfeit your own soul in the process?"

who's the boss?

Fortune magazine's tips to Edgar Bronfman, Jr., who sold his family's ownership of Seagram, TV, music, and film properties to Vivendi, include the following:

"Tip 4: We know you're a songwriter. But please don't flex your creative muscles by 'helping' Universal Music Group artists Eminem and Ja Rule with lyrics. That could be dangerous.

"Tip 5: Why not just scrap this whole entertainment thing and invest in what teenagers really care about: alcohol?"9

At one point during slavery, slaves outnumbered whites in the South two to one. Fearing that the Africans would rise up and rebel, the slick slave master put black overseers over the other slaves. These Judases were paid with extra food, tobacco, alcohol, water, and sex. I call this the Judas Factor.

Judas of Iscariot was one of the most famous mercenaries in history. One of the 12 apostles, Judas betrayed Jesus Christ to the high priests for 30 pieces of silver. While appearing to be a part of the crew, he was secretly working to destroy his people for a mere chance at some bling bling. He was possessed by greed, and what did it get him? Nothing. He committed suicide.

Today, music industry PTBs effectively use the Judas Factor to implement their economic and cultural rape of Hip Hop via an unholy alliance with rappers and Hip Hop moguls. Judases are mercenaries. Mercenaries have no loyalties except to their own interests and to those who cut their paychecks.

Jesus knew that Judas would betray him, and he said so at the Last Supper. Unfortunately, most of the brothas and sistas breaking bread at the feast of Hip Hop fail to realize that there are spies among us, selling out our culture and history while smiling in our faces.

Recently, within the past few years, Hip Hop summits and conferences, fronted by rappers and entrepreneurs, have entered the scene. Warning: these events serve as data collection opportunities for the major record labels. They may say they want to help youth, but their real agenda is to maintain and update their youth profile data. Why? To increase profits. The better they know youth attitudes, behaviors, and trends, the better they can sell to them. We need to come to grips with who really has the pimp juice and how the game is played.

Corporate PTBs approve of, or are actively involved in, the creation of the gangsta/whore/thug/bitch images we see in gangsta/Hip Hop music. They fund the production of these images at our expense. Just when you thought he had died with Eddie Murphy's Buckwheat (*Saturday Night Live*), the menacing black buffoon rises again.

Contrary to how they present themselves as self-sufficient and self-made, keeping it real gangsta rappers have bosses pulling their strings. Rappers report to corporate marketing execs and producers, who in turn report to senior bosses, boards, and trustees, who may be wealthy, elderly, male, and white—far removed from the ghetto experience but not from the monetary rewards generated by Hip Hop. These record industry bosses are friends with other bosses, who are friends with other bosses, and their wives do lunch and work out together at the country club. I imagine that the children of these bosses are nice and secure in their multi-acre ranches and gated communities while our children stare out the barred windows of the projects. While the sons and daughters of the bosses ride their ponies and attend the finest boarding schools, our children, the creative fuel of Hip Hop, have to board broken down buses to get to their substandard schools in the hood. It ain't right.

These financiers and financial beneficiaries of Hip Hop operate behind the scenes. We see their decisions playing out in the gangsta characterizations performed by their rapper front men and women, but these bosses remain invisible, so out of sight, out of mind. They are never questioned, so their edicts go unchallenged. They decide who's hot and who's not, whose face will appear on the front covers of the best selling magazines, blunts, guns, and prison stripes in tow. These far removed individuals will approve the next misogynist, violent, crime-ridden video, and they will ensure that it flows easily through all distribution channels and media. These same individuals banned the word wigger from entering the global consciousness and language of Hip Hop, sheltering and protecting their own children from low self-esteem and global disrespect while allowing nigger/nigga to proliferate in rap tunes.

We should be so diligent in presenting a positive image of our own intelligent, creative, and beautiful African children.

Hypocrisy 3—Role Models//Pimps, Hos, Pushers, & Spies

large & in charge

"Five giants—AOL/Time Warner, Walt Disney Co./ABC, Viacom, News Corp., and Bertelsmann—now control the equivalent of what 50 corporations dominated 20 years ago, according to *The New Media Monopoly*, the latest edition of renowned media critic Ben Bagdikian's book. Those five already control more than 80 percent of prime-time programming ... Corporate control of cable and satellite TV is even more striking, with monopolies representing 98 percent of all cable markets nationwide, and two companies controlling satellite TV."[10]

In addition to the top five corporations, in 2003, Vivendi Universal and General Electric Co. reached an agreement to merge Vivendi's Hollywood studio, cable TV networks, and theme parks with GE's NBC networks to the tune of about $13 billion in annual revenue.

"Today two music companies—Universal and SonyBMG—control more than 60% of music market shares in the world. The combined market shares of the 4 major record companies reached 95% of the Top 100 of 2003 best sellers. *The race for increased market shares and integration is taking place at the expense of the emergence of new talents, the renewal of new music genres, and creativity.*"[11]

There's been an assassination attempt on black creativity and artistic integrity, and the culprit is media and music industry consolidation. Consolidation is all about power and control. Further, how many black, brown, or economically oppressed individuals serve on the boards of the major record labels? Black creativity will never die, but it has gotten kicked to the curb. Because of the lack of diversity at the decision making level, only one type of image has been allowed to stand in the spotlight—the nigga/thug/gangsta/bitch/ho image.

In the 1980s, MTV was overwhelmed with complaints that gangsta rap videos were too misogynistic, violent, pornographic, and, in general, inappropriate for youth. Viewers issued an ultimatum: "Get that junk off the airwaves or we'll turn you off for good!" MTV responded by refusing to play many gangsta rap videos. Recognizing that one man's junk is another man's gold, however, BET aired the videos and the rest is history.

Multimillionaire rappers such as P Diddy, Russell Simmons, Jay-Z, and Master P grace the covers of magazines, but the low profile, multibillionaire corporate owners and trustees sign their checks. Some past and present good old boy chiefs and key players in the exploitation of ghetto youth include:

- Edgar Bronfman, CEO, Seagram Company Ltd.: Crown Royal, Chivas Regal, Polygram music label, and Universal Pictures.
- Sumner Redstone, Chairman/CEO, Viacom: BET, MTV Networks (MTV, VH1, Nickelodeon), Paramount Pictures, United Paramount Network, Showtime, Comedy Central, Infinity Broadcasting (180+ radio stations), 39 TV stations, Simon & Schuster, CBS. Produces and syndicates TV shows via Paramount Television, King World, and CBS Enterprises.
- George J. Mitchell (Chairman) and Michael D. Eisner (CEO/Director), The Walt Disney Company: ABC, significant stake in ESPN, stake in A&E Television Networks, Walt Disney Studios (Walt Disney Pictures, Touchstone, Hollywood Pictures, and Miramax), Walt Disney Parks and Resorts, Walt Disney Internet Group.
- Rupert Murdoch, Chairman/CEO, News Corp: publishes *The Times of London* and other newspapers and books through HarperCollins and other publishers. Fox Entertainment Group subsidiary holds FOX Broadcasting (TV network with 200 US affiliates) and 35 US TV stations, Twentieth Century Fox, and a stake in DIRECTV.

- Richard D. (Dick) Parsons, Chairman/CEO, Time Warner: AOL, Warner Bros., and a significant stake in Time Warner Cable.[12]

the bosses of hip hop

The Source (2004) reported that more than 20 percent of all Hip Hop CDs sold in 2003 were released under the Interscope Records umbrella (Geffen/A&M, Dream Works), which is overseen by chairman and CEO Jimmy Lovine. Interscope is in bed with Circuit City, K-Mart, Tower Records, Target, Best Buy, Transworld, Musicland, and Wal-Mart. Eighty percent of all Hip Hop CDs are sold through these eight companies.

Although there are a few successful independent labels, the Big Five—Universal, EMI Group, BMG, Warner, and Sony—have controlling interests in most. These corporations have bought or merged with many independent labels, and they now influence their creative output. The next time you hear rappers bragging about how they own a label ask yourself, "Who owns them?"

These major corporations are the marketing and distribution arms of the campaign to culturally colonize the world with Hip Hop. The figureheads may change, but the mission remains the same. These companies have masterminded the hijacking and kidnapping of Hip Hop culture. They create, promote, market, and distribute the Willie Lynch Traveling All Star Gangsta Rappers Road Show.

Make no mistake, Willie Lynch Gangsta Rappers may earn millions for their efforts, but their corporate masters earn billions—and we all know that a millionaire can't tell a billionaire what to do! As happy, well-fed slaves, Willie Lynch Gangsta Rappers appear to be suffering from Stockholm Syndrome: they voluntarily defend their overseers' behaviors and openly reject any rescue attempts. They love their kidnappers like a fat kid loves cake.

In the words of Harriet Tubman, "If I could have convinced more people that they were enslaved I could have freed thousands more."

Hypocrisy 3—Role Models//Pimps, Hos, Pushers, & Spies

The PTBs invest in the production of gangsta rap, then they invest their profits into government lobbying, political campaigns, and prison construction projects. They create the scary black gangsta then use our fear to pass zero tolerance laws, Rockefeller drug laws, and three strike laws that will condemn the futures of our children to hell.

Rappers can rhyme about killing black and brown people and poor white boys can rap about killing their parents, but they can't talk about the PTBs who exploit the ghetto just like they can't call a white child a wigger. It's time to pull the covers off the bed and expose those strange bedfellows that keep Judases fat and satisfied on the payroll.

please announce & post: job opportunities available

1. The Institution of Racism and Exploitation currently has several positions open for Judas rappers, gangsta/Hip Hop producers, directors, and wannabes. Candidate should be black, Latino, or poor white. Must be willing to help in the commercialization of gangsta rap and music videos.
2. Lottery Pick Rapper needed. Must be a franchise player with crossover appeal. Salary: High six figures. Minimum education/experience: Must have at least one year of rapping or acting experience. One year of junior high school or equivalent. Must have Pied Piper charisma, a criminal background preferred. Gang affiliation is accepted but not required. Old bullet wounds and battle scars preferred for street appeal and credibility. Frequent high-profile encounters with the law will secure future employment as a spokesperson for liquor companies.

house negroes & field hands

Attorney Bobby Joe Champion states the problem well:

"When rappers say they have a deal I cannot help but question, did they make a deal with the devil? We don't own much of anything in Hip Hop. As a collective, black folks continue to sell out and/or forfeit our musical power, geniuses, talents, and gifts. We don't own the look of Hip Hop anymore nor Hip Hop. When will we learn?"[13]

Artists sometimes call themselves slaves once they sign their record deals and realize the trap they've fallen into. The most famous was Prince. He went so far as to write the word "slave" on his cheek. Rapper DMX refused to deliver any more recordings to his label Def Jam.

"DMX over the years has made the label almost $50 million dollars, but received an amount in return that he called 'a loan.' 'The highest paid artist gets paid 18 cents on the dollar, its straight robbery,' DMX said. 'They still own your **music** and they ask for maybe 27 **songs** each album and they only use about 16 and give the rest away. It's straight robbery man, I can't be a part of it anymore.'"[14]

When it comes to the music business, there are three important copyrights: the sound recording, the musical compositions, and the packaging. In most cases, the record company owns the sound recording as well as all the artwork and packaging of the cover and CD booklet. This is different from the book publishing industry, where the author owns the copyright of the text and grants the publisher the right to distribute the book.

Musicians who sign a record contract always grant the record company the right to use their name and likeness on the packaging. Record companies insist on this to get around the artist's right of publicity and trademark.

Interestingly, artists complain about losing control over their creative output, but they give away all their rights! Fast talking execs start talking money and all the artist can hear is *kaching!*

hip hop c.o.d.

The Hip Hop state of mind now is C.O.D.—cash on delivery. Wu Tang called it C.R.E.A.M.: Cash Rules Everything Around Me. This means that the PTBs who have the cash and cut the checks rule everything and everyone around them.

Author Stephen Peters talks about how rich rappers pay cash for expensive things that often depreciate in value. They try to keep up with the lavish lifestyles of their new pro athlete and movie star friends, but if they want to keep what they earn, they must become smarter about managing their money and deals. A CD in the bank can become as valuable as a CD gone platinum.[15]

Endorsements are a lucrative income stream for rappers, but be warned: positive or conscious rappers need not wait by the phone. Only rappers who promote black-on-black violence, misogyny, drug consumption, and pimping will secure those deals. It's their reward for a job well done.

If you want to get paid, then act a fool. If you're willing to sell out your community, you'll get paid.

Coke, Pepsi, Nike, Reebok, NFL, NBA, Heineken, Courvoisier, McDonald's, Gap, Cover Girl, L'Oreal, Got Milk?, Pringles, JC Penny, AOL, ATD, Sears, Old Navy, Timberland, Helly Hansen, Ralph Lauren, Puma, Adidas, and Lugz pay top dollar to hard core Hip Hop entertainers. What happened to their All American image?

Missy Elliott is showing young black girls how to work it with her endorsement deals with the Gap. Old Navy countered with Lil' Kim. 50 Cent promotes his Reebok shoe line in print ads. Sean Combs caught a ride in the Pepsi big wheel. Lil' Bow Wow was eating Snickers for a minute. The list goes on.

Hypocrisy 3—Role Models//Pimps, Hos, Pushers, & Spies

Why would multinational companies hire menacing black gangsta faces to front their All American brands? Because gangsta rappers come with a ready made market, and it's a deal too lucrative to pass up, even for conservative companies and corporate whites who live far from the hood. The bottom line is always the profit line.

The next time you want to blast rappers for their ill behaviors and language, remember their masters, their wealthy corporate bedfellows. Roc-a-Fella Enterprises producer Damon Dash says, "People exploit us, and we exploit them back. If they're going to make a buck off us, we'll make a buck off them. That's just the way it's going to be."[16]

sista bosses: overseers or in control?

"Basically, I have teenage daughters, so I always listen to who's going on. Here's the situation: You got the presidents of BET, who's a black woman [Debra Lee] and the president of MTV, who's a black woman [Christina Norman], and the owner of one of the biggest radio station conglomerates [Radio One], Kathy Hughes, also a black woman. Yet the image of black women has never been in such a compromised position as it is right now."[17] **Chuck D**

African American women are in top leadership positions at several media empires that feed the viewing and listening habits of our children. They are:

- Debra L. Lee. President and CEO of BET Holdings, Inc., a multi-media entertainment corporation and the parent company for Black Entertainment Television (BET).
- Christina Norman. Formerly president of VH1, Norman was named president of MTV and MTV2. Under Norman's watch during the summer of 2006, black females were shown wearing leashes, crawling around on all fours, scratching

themselves, and defecating on a pet store floor in the cartoon *Where My Dogs At?*

- Cathy Hughes. Chairperson and founder of Radio One, which owns and/or operates 71 stations in 22 urban markets and reaches 14 million listeners each week. In January 2004, her company launched the cable channel TV One, aimed at African Americans. She is the first African American woman to head a firm publicly traded on a stock exchange in the United States.

These sistas are answerable to faceless boards and corporate masters, yet their leadership roles at BET, VH1, MTV, and Radio One means they should still be held accountable and responsible for adult pornographic content being marketed to children and the negative images of African Americans that have set us back pre-civil rights era.

"If people are asking for it, who's to say that it is wrong? If people don't like it, they should vote at the record store."[18]
Debra L. Lee, President and CEO of BET Holdings, Inc.

Good idea.

Chapter 14

Hypocrisy 4—

Grown Folks Business //
Tricks Are for Kids

"'Oh man, if my father saw this, he'd kill me,' says Nate Dogg, who's … thumbing through a girlie magazine. The L.A.-based singing roughneck's dad, you see, is a pastor in Clarksdale, Mississippi, who thinks his son's music is pure, uncut blasphemy. When he first heard 'Regulate,' Dogg's 1994 smash duet with pal Warren G., he threw it in the trash. 'I try to tell him it's just showbiz,' says the 32-year-old Dogg."[1] **Nate Dogg**

Sex is grown folks business, so what are our children doing messing around in grown folks business? Believe it or not, our children may be having more sex than we are. Think about it.

This is how children got into grown folks business: grown folks brought it to them. When commercialized gangsta rap replaced revolutionary rap, they brought an agenda of lyrical pedophilia with them.

Pedophiles are adults who sexually abuse children and/or create sexual arousal in children for self-gratification, which in the case of commercialized gangsta rap is financial. No healthy adult would expose their toddler, child, adolescent, or teen to some of the pornography that goes on in most gangsta rap tunes. Yet somehow our children know all about *BET Uncut*, and they can rap along with the music word for word.

Parents must monitor their children's viewing and listening, but this book is not about blaming the victims or their parents. I assume my readers are those caring, concerned parents, educators, counselors, and ministers who are doing the best for the children in their care. They know what they have to do.

On the other hand, it's unrealistic to believe we can stay awake and watch our children 24/7. When we're at work or asleep or the child is home alone or over at Pookie's house there are many opportunities to check out BET, MTV, VH1, log onto the Internet, and play with friends who have the latest X-rated CD or Hip Hop video game. We're not with them at school. We're not in every one of their conversations. So *stop blaming the victims!*

This section is about what rappers and the PTBs are doing to hypersexualize children in the throes of adolescent development. It will be years before we discover how this young generation will mature and what impact such widespread pornography will have on their development.

For years I felt like a lone voice in the wind. I've been told I didn't know what I was talking about and that I had too much time on my hands. My children sometimes think I've gone off the deep end.

Well I'm not alone anymore. Many other voices are now speaking out. *Essence* did a tremendous series in the magazine, and they are holding conferences on the impact of negative gangsta rap/Hip Hop around the country. Spelman College made history when the students protested against Nelly appearing on campus. That was a courageous step because when people stand against misogynistic Hip Hop they get ridiculed and shouted down. Ministers, educators, counselors, and service providers across the country have also been fighting for our children.

Commercialized gangsta rap makes the lies look like the truth. Ménage a trios sex, male gender bending, lesbian sex, and sexual violence make our children think this is what love is all about. Unless they're being taught otherwise, girls think they must automatically "put out" and boys think they deserve it. Girls think they can take it (and give it) like a man, and boys learn that down low ain't low down.

The truth is, the fans are not old enough to be consenting adults, and they're not mature or wise enough to walk away from harmful music that obviously fascinates them. If commercialized gangsta rap (and keep it real, a lot of R&B as well) was brought to trial, the movement would be convicted of the lyrical statutory rape of minors. Yet Hip Hop porn has been exported to the youth of the world as family entertainment.

Porn rap could only exist in a pornographic society. You can't walk out the door without hearing or seeing something blatantly sexual. In the hood, images on billboards, buses, store windows, viaducts, and abandoned buildings feature barely clothed women of all races, promoting everything from alcohol to toothpaste.

gender bending

Why is it that in most rap videos, we see male bonding but seldom healthy, wholesome male-female relationships? In the videos, only males have friendships with each other while females gangbang and catfight each other. This is classic Prolonged Adolescent Syndrome behavior. During childhood and adolescence, girls play with girls and boys play with boys. As they grow up, they start noticing the opposite sex. In rap videos, the only way a man notices a woman is if she's close to naked. Even a five year old who "hates" girls would have to stop and stare, and that they do.

One of the earliest videos that promoted this mentality was "Beat It" by Michael Jackson. The video depicts gangsterism, male bonding (in the complete absence of females), and symbolic group masturbation. Today's XXX, nasty videos make "Beat It" look innocent. If males and females are in scenes together, there's no love. She's simulating oral sex and more, and he's often on the receiving end of things.

Hypocrisy 4—Grown Folks Business//Tricks Are for Kids

Dirty dancing has always been a form of sexual expression, even in the days of the Arabian nights when the so-called Harem girls would dance before the sultan and remove their many veils. The dance of a thousand veils was the prelude to sex.

Today, veils have been replaced with daisy dukes, pasties, saggin' pants, and visible thongs. Lil' Kim leaves nothing to the imagination. In the rap business, Victoria's Secret is no secret.

skin is in

Hip Hop good girls Destiny's Child bared it all (so to speak) in their 2005 "Cater 2 U" video. Even the Christian of the group, sista Michelle, did as the Romans do while in Rome. I'm not judging, I'm just saying hmmm…

Rap stars train like athletes because they must stay in top shape. The rock hard bodies add to the sexual appeal and monetary rewards. I call these rap stars "enterletes," or entertainer-athletes. They have tremendous physiques, but we have to question why it's so important for rappers and singers to have such rock hard bodies. Is it just me, or does this seem strange? Think about Aretha, Luther, Barry, Lavert, Gladys, Jill, and so many other good looking, full figured singers who can bring the house down with their voices and star personalities. Do we love them any less because they have a few extra pounds and some love handles?

In rap videos, there seems to be an unwritten rule that manifests in plain view: male rap stars (who don't have rock hard bodies) must be clothed, while the video women and female rappers must wear as few clothes as possible. Fashion designers provide clothes for performers to wear to offset the cost of the video—although the enterletes don't need clothes because of their million dollar physiques. This sets the scene for male power and domination, female powerlessness and submission, and chaos and confusion in the minds and emotions of our youth.

Hypocrisy 4—Grown Folks Business//Tricks Are for Kids

porn rap

To perform in pornography, a rapper must be 18 years and older—or else he and the production company are in violation of the law. This means that only grown folks can be in pornographic videos. Check the hypocrisy and the lies being made to look like the truth. Only adults can perform in pornographic videos, yet rappers' lyrical rhyming styles and rebelliousness appeal to youth. I'll admit to liking a rap tune now and then, but for the most part, the over simplistic beats and nursery rhyme styles do not appeal to me. Why? *Because I'm grown!*

The music has been deliberately designed to appeal to children, but grown folks are perpetrating the fraud. No rapper would openly admit to being a pedophile, lyrical or otherwise, yet without question, the music can be sexually arousing to the primary audience, children. The hypocrisy is that the music is supposedly for grown folks—while every trick in the book is used to sexually tease, titillate, and trap our children.

Some rappers in the game are hitting 40 (plus), yet they're still like the Pied Piper to children. If the Pied Piper is teaching love for self, respect for others, respect of the sex act, and entrepreneurism, it's all good. But Hip Hop Pied Pipers have taken the low road.

Pornography is so entrenched in commercialized gangsta rap videos that we are now truly in a battle against principalities and powers, the realm of destruction. Children often appear in the background shots and group dance scenes in these lyrical porn videos. Have we no shame? Why do we allow our children to play with the nasty people?

In this section, I don't let up on the rappers and their crews who are serving as mercenaries and traitors against the community. They must be held accountable for their role in bringing sex directly to children. These reluctant role models will claim we have lost our minds. In the quote that opened this chapter, Nate Dogg tried to tell his father, the minister, that the music was "just showbiz." Just showbiz? Talk about a lie looking like the truth! What happened to keeping it real? I know it's showbiz, but our children, who can't fully tell the difference between fantasy and reality, think what they're seeing and hearing is real. That's the problem.

Chapter 15

Sex in the Hood

"When you raise a daughter you know that one day a man's gonna want her. I'll have to love mine and teach them to respect themselves. The main thing I'll stress to them is, 'Don't let any man dictate how much you value yourself.' I'll tell them to value themselves whether he's there or not. As long as they remember that, I'll have nothing to worry about."[1] **LL Cool J**

Brothers & Sisters, we've allowed a monster into our homes and communities. Like Cookie Monster on *Sesame Street,* the sex monster of Hip Hop consumes everyone in its path; it stalks our children like Jason. The sex monster is down with OPP (other people's privates), and like Cookie Monster, just can't resist the cookie no matter how hard he/she tries.

Normally a monster is a grotesque image, a creature that frightens, but the sex monsters of Hip Hop are some of the most physically beautiful, physically fit people in the entertainment industry.

The sex monster of Hip Hop has managed to frighten the pants off of parents, educators, and the church. The sex monster has moved from TVs and CDs into the hearts and minds of our children, adolescents, and teens. How many young children in your home, school, and church have been sexually titillated by rapper porn? Sad to report, too many to count, and at some point, children may cross the line and begin to do what they've been taught in the infomercials that pass as rap videos. With every new sexually explicit song, the sex monster captures new and younger prey.

The sex monster of Hip Hop was created by American slavery when our ancestors were used as sex slaves (for the sole pleasure of the white master). The virginity of black children, male and female, was routinely taken as a rite of passage among young white males. These acts of rape were ordained by their fathers. We can never forget that women and children (and men) were raped during the middle passage and on the plantation. These were the secrets never talked about but acted out and passed down through the generations. As the old saying goes, "You're as sick as your secrets."

To this day, sex is expected of us on all levels of consciousness, and we rush to accommodate. We readily dance to rap tunes that display black people as hypersexual beings. Review the lyrics and video images of a typical Hip Hop tune and prove me wrong.

no new 'miss new booty'

If white women are the standard of beauty, then African American women are the sexual standard in the pathological American mindset. Bubba Sparxxx thought he was singing a new song with his "Miss New Booty," but there is nothing new under the sun.

In 1810, an unfortunate young South African girl named Sara Baartman was abducted by white men and brought to London, England because they were fascinated by the size of her buttocks. Known as the Hottentot Venus, this unfortunate sista was put on display throughout Europe at pubs, fairs, museums, and universities because of her physical appearance. People paid her handlers (pimps by any other name) to touch her buttocks/booty. She eventually was forced into prostitution and died penniless at the age of 25 from STDs. Her skeleton was displayed in a Paris museum until 1974. Sara Baartman's remains were returned to South Africa in 2002.

During slavery, black female slaves (POWs) were frequently bought and sold based on the size of their buttocks and breasts. On the auction block, nude and greased up, they were forced to gyrate their body parts (especially the buttocks/booty), to attract potential buyers. Today, when sistas get paid to shake their buttocks/booty on rap/Hip Hop videos, they dishonor the memory of Sara Baartman and all those like her throughout the African Diaspora who suffered public humiliation. They are not getting over. They are on humiliating display, just like Sara. The more things change the more they stay the same.

decoding the secret lives of female gangstas

The sex monster of Hip Hop has taught an entire generation to negotiate its needs and wants via PMS (power, money, and sex). We all have theories on how and why our community is in such a constant state of sexual tension, and perhaps we can learn even more through the power of decoding and wordplay. In this chapter we'll uncover many hidden psychological, cultural, and historical motivations for our behavior in the loaded sexual arena. Decoding is not an exact science, but it does have the power to extract hidden messages from the psyche. As we work together, you, too, may uncover themes that relate specifically to you and your loved ones.

If all was good in the hood, a female's understanding of sex would be as follows:

S = **S**ecure it (protect the body)
E = **E**cstasy (pleasure the body)
X = **X**erox® (reproduce the body)

Females must secure/protect their bodies by choosing mates who will love and respect them and provide for their children. The female is the source of ecstasy and love in a male's life, and with him, she has the power to Xerox (copy) or reproduce life.

But all is not good in the hood. Commercialized gangsta rap emerged out of the gangbanging lifestyle, so it should be no surprise that the sex monster's influence can be easily found in gangs where sex is used to negotiate for survival needs, to achieve social and political goals (the oldest trick in the book), and to purchase drugs, weapons, and social status.

When female gang members are sexually sacrificed (prostituted) for the benefit of the gang, they learn to define and defend their view of sex and sisterhood within gang culture and the Hip Hop/ghetto matrix.

S = **S**hare it for esteem, sell for survival and income.

E = **E**ve syndrome—accept blame and endure physical and emotional pain.

X = (**E**)**x**change sex for companionship and love, even if it means risking your friendships with your sistas and your mental or physical health.

The sex monster principle strips the female gang member of the knowledge of self, and she goes into survival mode. The sex monsters of Hip Hop aggressively convince females that they can find their self-esteem while lying on their backs or on bended knee. I think not.

Throughout the history of street gangs in America there have been well kept secrets—secret rites, handshakes, passwords, hideouts, and knowledge. The truly scandalous secret is that sex/rape and sex "trains" are used to "jump in" new gang members. This rite of initiation bonds gang members together for life. It can also be used to blackmail members since sexual initiations are sometimes videotaped or viewed by other members.

The number of males in a sex train might be determined with a roll of the dice; the number could be as low as two or as high as 12. Students once reported to me that some girls are required to roll three dice at once, which means they could possibly have intercourse with 18 people in one night. If they should become pregnant, supposedly the baby belongs to the gang and will be financially cared for by the gang. Yeah, right. After more than 300 interviews with female gang members conducted over a seven-year period (1997–2004), no one ever told me that this promise was kept. In fact, females are highly disposable and are easily dismissed from the gang.

The same rite occurs within female gangs. If a female wants to join an all female gang, she might be made to perform oral sex or "bless" other female members via the roll of the dice.

> "I consider myself a gangbanger. I mean I've shot at niggas and they have shot at me. I guess you can say that's bangin. I got sexed into my set [gang] by older bitches and now I handle my business by sexing in my share of bitches, but it's done with love. That's why I'm not down with the fellas. They just be trying to pop some E and run a train on a bitch, bang you hard or rape ya and get your ass pregnant. F**k tha s**t." 17 year-old female, Washington, DC (November 2002)

Banging is the old 1960s slang for sex. Group connotes gang, thus gangbanging is group sex or an orgy. In sex initiations, female gang members are:
1. Sexed In
2. Sexed Out
3. Sexed Up
4. Sexed Down
5. Sexed Crazed

Clearly, the female role is to perform sexual favors. She may receive money for her services. Her self-esteem and self-worth are bankrupt. Her reputation and ranking in the gang increases with each of her sexual conquests. Female gangbangers are routinely oppressed within gang culture, which leads to depression. It is common for females in this situation to entertain suicidal thoughts. Gang affiliation or service to the gang can be hazardous to spiritual, emotional, and physical health.

decoding the secret lives of male gangstas

Male gangstas can eventually change if the desire is strong enough. They may be a member of the gang for life, but many have corrected their behaviors and now work to uplift the community.

1 Corinthians 13:11 says, "When I was a child, I spoke as a child, I understood as a child, I thought as a child; but when I became a man, I put away childish things."

Getting out of the gangsta mentality is hard, especially in the sexual arena. Clearly, we have low expectations of boys in the Hip Hop/ghetto matrix. We accept that irresponsible boys will grow up to be sexually irresponsible men.

If males were taught to value their bodies and to respect the female body, their psychosexual view would read as follows:

S = **S**ave it for marriage.

E = **E**mancipate yourself from unhealthy sexual conduct and thoughts.

X = (E)**x**amine the unknown potential/power of sex before you multiply with it. **X** is the Roman numeral for 10, thus keep the 10th commandment: "Do not covet your neighbor's wife."

They may think they're getting over, but males are also victimized by the sex monster. In the Hip Hop/ghetto matrix, as in the society at large, males are taught to avoid intimacy and emotional commitment at all cost. Masculinity is narrowly defined in terms of physical toughness and sexuality.

Males who participate in gang rites feast on the sexual benefits and liberties of gangbanging. They embrace the sexist, misogynistic doctrines of gang life. It appears that males in the Hip Hop/ghetto matrix view sex from the following psychosocial perspective:

S = **S**ee it.
E = **E**nter it.
X = (**E**)**x**it.

Hello! The message is clear. Males are conditioned early on to see women as sex objects and nothing more. They strategize to enter the vagina, and they learn, perhaps from their fathers (both present and absent), how to exit the "relationship" without guilt or shame. The psychosexual language of the male sex monster is violent: "Girl, can I hit that?" "Girl, let me smash that." "Girl, let me knock that out." "Girl, let me tap that a**."

In the Hip Hop/ghetto matrix, sex is a youth rite of passage. The Hip Hop monster does little to educate males on sexual morality and sex esteem. The research shows that teens are having sex as early as 12 and 13. Other studies seem to suggest that a backlash against the sex monster may be taking place, with youth increasingly choosing abstinence. Don't forget to acknowledge those youth who are trying to do the right thing.

Just as you can learn a lot about a person from his name or nickname, males' psychosexual attitudes are revealed by their names for the penis. My colleagues and I surveyed approximately 300 inner-city black males ages 10 to 13 in Chicago, Illinois. Sixty-five percent called their penis *dick*; 13 percent, *johnson*; 22 percent, *penis*. None called their penis *cock* (primarily used by white males) or *genitals*.

Twenty-four percent of the boys admitted they had sex at least once; not one child used a condom or any form of protection. Eighty-one percent believed that oral sex was not sex. Seventy-two percent said they had never been taught about their penis. Sixty-four percent said they had never discussed sex with a parent.[2]

In the general population, more than one-half of males 15 to 19 years old have had sexual intercourse. The older the teenager, the more likely he is to have had sex. Half of teenage males have had sexual intercourse by the time they reach their 17th birthday.[3]

We do not teach our boys to value their bodies. From an early age, boys learn that girls are "nice like sugar and spice." Boys are said to be like "snips and snails and puppy dog tails." A snip is a small, worthless piece of meat. A snail is associated with slime. A puppy can only grow up to become a dog, and a puppy tail is located just above his—you get the point.

The language of gangs reveals sex and violence, which is also reflected in gangsta rap. In secret ceremonial sex rites, male gang members are:

1. Beat In
2. Beat Out
3. Beat Up
4. Beat Down
5. Beating the System (so they think)
6. Beat On
7. Beat Off
8. Beat Dead (dead beats)

Violence is the key that opens the door to gang membership and acceptance. One must tolerate getting beat up and beat on. You must become a victim before making victims. All that beating symbolically suggests masturbation and that gangbangers (self-beaters) receive some level of *viogasmic* pleasure from violence.

Consider the following popular street argots as they relate to criminal behavior:

- Car jacking (stealing a car, using a weapon)
- Hijacking (stealing drugs to get high)
- New Jack attitude (criminal mentality)
- Jacked around (being manipulated)
- Jacked up (physically beaten)
- Jacking people (robbing others)

Apparently gangstas spend a lot of time jacking off, i.e., masturbating on some level of consciousness.

Thanks to Lil' Kim and 50 Cent, the penis has gone through a name change, from dick to magic stick. A magic stick is the same as a magic wand. Thus, males who identify and define their penis as magic sticks/wands cast their spells of seduction on females then disappear in a puff of smoke, leaving behind broken hearts and fatherless babies. This is all part of the world of illusion (vs. keeping it real).

The female may have thought the male was keeping it real when he said, "Baby, I love you." Little did she know that a lie was made to look like the truth, a rabbit was pulled out of a hat, and a magic stick/wand waved abracadabra. Now you see him, now you don't.

The truth is that some males are not comfortable loving anything other than their own magic sticks/wands (and possibly other magic sticks/wands). With a magic stick/wand (vs. a keeping it real penis), a male can imagine/pretend that his penis is bigger, more potent, and more powerful than it really is. This gives him some psychological comfort. The black male has not been trained to view his body, especially his penis, in a sacred way. As a result, you get 50 Cent's infamous line, "I'm into having sex/I ain't into making love."[4]

50 Cent's magic stick is about magical thinking, not God thinking, which leads to further mismanagement of the penis. Let's have fun with the following equation. Magic is synonymous with trick. The past tense of stick is stuck. Stuck connotes trapped. Put it all together:

Magic Stick = Tricked & Stuck (trapped)

We must teach young sistas that when they choose the magic stick/wand before marriage or have sex before even knowing the brotha, they will be tricked and stuck with the consequences from that magical moment—tricked into bed with an uncommitted man. Stuck with an unplanned and unwanted pregnancy, STD, and broken heart. Teach them to STICK to their principles and not get caught up in the magic/disappearing act!

Hypocrisy 4—Grown Folks Business//Tricks Are for Kids

Magicians never tell their secrets because this breaks the spell of the illusion. Now that the secret of the magic stick has been decoded, help young brothas and sistas to break the spell.

Magic stick/wand is loaded with occult (witchcraft) symbols and archetypes that penetrate the subconscious minds of youth. Historically, both the Africans and indigenous peoples of the Americas called the weapon (gun, bayonet) of the European invaders a magic stick. In the groundbreaking book *Isis Papers*, Dr. Frances Cress Welsing explained in detail how guns, canons, missiles, bombs, and other similarly shaped WMDs (weapons of mass destruction) are phallic symbols that cause death and destruction.[5] Like the gun, today's magic stick/wand, the penis, has become a real WMD in the hood.

Before you write me off as crazy, consider the following metaphor. The pen/penis is mightier than the sword/word. Within the psychology of gangsta rap, the pen is symbolically related to the penis. Lyrically, in gangsta rap, the penis is often the subject and object of the rapper's pen. Male rappers tend to live vicariously through their pens/penises. Thus, the rapper's pen/penis has the power to influence, impregnate, and change the course of a fan's thinking and life. Together, the pen and penis are potent WMDs, mightier than the sword and words of reason.

Rappers use their popularity to influence the sexual behaviors and attitudes of young males caught up in Hip Hop hype. Possibly male rappers openly brag in their writings (raps) about their blatant sexual mistreatment of females because of their unresolved fourth grade fear of girls/mama and sexual failure, including alcohol and drug-induced castration (impotence), premature ejaculation, and failure to please the female sexually.

Rappers/black males may fear failing in the area of family leadership (husband and father). Males in general fear commitment, but because males are not allowed to show fear, they brag about being a "dogg." As Job said, what they fear will come on them (Job 3:25). Think about it.

Hypocrisy 4—Grown Folks Business//Tricks Are for Kids

A male with a magic stick/wand complex allows his penis to control him vs. the other way around. Problem behaviors are the result:

- Eighty-seven percent of teen males who are two or more years behind in school for their age are sexually experienced.
- Three-quarters of teenage males with past criminal involvement, including being picked up by the police, arrested, or jailed, are sexually experienced.
- Three-quarters of teenage males who report using illegal drugs are sexually experienced.[6]

jailhouse rap

"Yeah, I guess you can say I'm on the DL, but I ain't gay. I roll through here maybe once or twice a month and I get mad loot. Men pay me just to be with me, and mostly talk. I don't do no favors. F**k that fag s**t. These bitches buy you the best of the best for really nothing. I got my females who treat me right cause I handle my business with them and my kids." **Athlete**, 22 years old, Washington, DC (November 2002)

Sex as a part of gang initiations and prison life is nothing new. I've always wondered why Elvis Presley recorded such an upbeat song about prison life because there's nothing upbeat about being incarcerated. Believe it or not, homoerotic relationships were hidden in plain view in the lyrics of his hit 1957 movie song "Jailhouse Rock": "You're the cutest jailbird I ever did see./I sure would be delighted with your company."[7]

Homoeroticism is a fact of prison and gang life, as well as gangsta rap. There are no healthy male-female relationships in gangsta rap, but there is a lot of male bonding. Boyz roll together, smoke blunts together, and do violence together (and girlz do hot tubs together). Are these tunes telling us that heterosexual love and marriage have become extinct in the hood?

Hypocrisy 4—Grown Folks Business//Tricks Are for Kids

Some males practice homosexuality as a way to survive in prison and/or the streets. Others are bisexual and are starting to emerge publicly and without shame. This is the so-called down low thug or down low brotha—straight by day, down sexually by night. Homosexual thugs are no more or less violent than their heterosexual counterparts.

Since gang members often go through prison's revolving door, it's no surprise that sex on the inside mimics sex on the outside. Sistas looking for a soldier or a roughneck, beware!

Male inmates who have sex with other male inmates deny on every level of consciousness that they are gay. In fact, just the mere suggestion that they are homosexual or bisexual can lead to violence. Down low brothas try hard to avoid the social stigma of being a homosexual. Some have labeled down low sex in prison "situational homosexuality" that fulfills the need for human touch and intimacy. Someone's in denial.

Sex in prison is achieved in several ways:
- Forcible rape (also occurs during gangbangs to cause humiliation)
- Consensual sex with another prisoner or staff person (guard)
- Conjugal visits (for married prisoners who meet certain guidelines)
- Extortion sex (blackmail or for protection)
- Initiation sex (as a means of gaining membership into a gang or cult)
- Group masturbation (hands only sex done as a group)
- Homosexual prostitution.

Homosexuality doesn't define down low; it's the sneaking around that makes down low *low down*. A predator is a predator whether gay or straight, and down low thugs appear to enjoy manipulating both groups. This has become a life and death issue for black females and children, who are now the fastest growing AIDS cases in the country. So now, when you watch a rap music video that features males bonding in camaraderie while the only female role is to dance sexually and simulate sex acts, you'll begin to see how the thug love lie has been made to look like true love.

love: gigagos & gigolos

gigolo: (noun) a man who receives money for sexual favors
gigago: (noun) female gigolo

"I rather be known as a gigago since I have the skillz to pull the heartstrings of any bitch (male or female) by going into their head. I get what I want or need and go. My game lets me be whatever I feel like being or being with." **19 year-old female,** Washington, DC (November 2002)

Young sistas in the hood are going for bad, mean mugging, and openly living the creed, "I'm a thug bitch." School educators and administrators often tell me about their challenges in disciplining young, aggressive, Hip Hop lesbian girls in middle school and high school. Even the appearance of discrimination will land administrators and faculty in court.

Parents don't want to believe their baby girl was suspended because of a fight over another girl (love/sex interest). It's time to get our heads out of the sand. Some of our girls are no longer riding in their boyfriend's Chevy. They are driving with an attitude, a gangsta lean, and a girlfriend—hello.

Research suggests these girls may have been abused, and they are determined to never be victimized again by males. Males are on their social menu but only as a piece of meat in the food chain. They frequently speak of males, particularly their brothers and fathers, with anger. Some play the field by stringing sugar daddies along, showing just enough flesh to catch the fish. This is called "faking" or "gig-in."

"I fake men, but I love women." **17 year-old female**, Washington, DC (November 2002)

Young males in the hood are going for bad as well. They have been trained to look for women who will finish the job their mothers started. This is a classic symptom of Prolonged Adolescent Syndrome. They want to be cared for, maybe because deep down they fear the real world. They look for females and males to accept their immaturity and mistakes in the same way their mothers did for so long. Thus, the playa longs to be somebody's baby.

> "I'm too young to settle down. That's why I let girls know from the jump no baby is going to make me stay with you. They get pregnant anyway. I got three that I know of." **18 year-old male**, Atlanta, Georgia

In response to each other's games, both males and females perpetuate cycles of mistreatment built on emotional, sexual, and financial manipulation. They play a deadly game of sexual gymnastics, jumping from bed to bed. From this they develop dysfunctional beliefs about sex, love, intimacy, marriage, employment, and childrearing. Their choice of music does little to correct their misconceptions.

the thug love creed

The following is the thug love creed:
- Buy a car instead of a house.
- Take your pit bulls to the veterinarian for annual check-ups before taking your children to the doctor.
- Buy yourself bling bling before buying your children school supplies.
- Know all about your boyz, but don't know anything about your children's school, teachers, friends, or progress in school.

- Name your children after alcohol brands and cars, but avoid giving them your last name.
- Spend time with your boyz rather than with your woman/women and children.

Having multiple sex partners indicates an inability to control the penis. The male has failed one of life's most precious tests. Teach young brothas that the body is a holy temple, and they must learn to value it. The penis is an energy source. It is so powerful it can generate/spark life, but that doesn't mean that males should be trying to give every female a charge! Male sexual energy will bring a special spark to marriage. It would be foolish to think you will not be tested/tempted one day, but with the right information, you can pass the test.

Men should never refer to their penis as "dick." Our penis/life source mimics the divine power of God in that it creates life, brings pleasure, and is powerful. To refer to it as a dick is evil to say the least, considering that dick means "old devil" and its origin comes from a fellow named Godfrey Derrick, an Englishman hangman who took life.[8]

A penis creates life; a dick (devil) takes life and performs outside the sexual laws of God. The sex monsters of Hip Hop don't want you to know that.

Sisters, don't let the devil into your life or your womb/sacred space. A man who readily uses dick probably curses like a devil during intercourse. Our children deserve to be conceived in a more positive, loving atmosphere.

equal time

"And God said to Adam, What hast thou done? And Adam with his head hung down, Blamed it on the woman." [9]
James Weldon Johnson

Female rappers are constantly rapping about their sexual powers and exploits, referring to their vaginas as the best compared to all the rest. Like their male counterparts, their genitals have also gone through a name change. "Ill nana" has been the term of choice within gangsta Hip Hop for some time now. Perhaps ill nana was the logical choice considering its hidden meaning:

Ill = sick
Nana = vagina/p**y
Put them together, you get: **Sick vagina (STDs)**

Rappers Lil' Kim and Foxy Brown made ill nana popular in the early 1990s. Their sexually explicit lyrics help us understand why STDs are out of control in the hood.

In 2001, a study by Ellen Yancey of Morehouse School of Medicine found that nearly half of low-income African American women surveyed in Atlanta did not use a condom during any sexual encounter during a two-month period, and 60 percent did not know their partner's HIV status. This in spite of the fact that nearly all black adults know how the HIV virus is transmitted, according to a study by the Kaiser Family foundation.[10]

Consider the following. The womb is the *first* resting place, a sacred place. Whoever enters the womb will be changed in some way. We have soul ties with and psychosexual memories of the people we intercourse with, which means they remain with us on some level.

The tomb is the *final* resting place, also a sacred place. Whoever enters will never leave it physically. Within the psychology of gangsta rap, the CNN on gang behavior, the womb is consistently linked to the tomb.

In female gangsta rap lyrics, life and death do a strange dance. Female rappers forget that their womb is a gift, a holy temple, and that it is not their duty to give every man some'n some'n. Such reckless behavior makes the womb a potential WMD, capable of killing babies before life has a chance, sending them to the tomb. We literally fight to come out of the womb, but we put up no fight to stay out of the tomb.

It appears that the sole duty of female rappers is to assist their male counterparts in undoing the sacred and holy meaning of the female womb. Where the music industry uses hundreds of male artists to execute their genocidal message, they need only a handful of female rappers to get the job done.

The few female rappers on the scene are exceptionally beautiful, articulate, intelligent, and sexy. They are perfect for this evil mission. The current females who enjoy national/global recognition are the more or less Active 10: Lil' Kim, Foxy Brown, Missy Elliott, Da Brat, Kahia, Remy Ma, Shawnna, Trina, Eve, and Jackie O. Some are worse than others. Some, like Queen Latifah, have matured and gone on to bigger and better things.

Unfortunately, the few who are still in the game have tremendous influence. They are rewarded with wealth, TV and movie deals, and endorsements in exchange for their antics, foul mouths, and influence on the attitudes, behaviors, values, and perceptions of females in the hood. Their lyrics pull our little girls out of the safe innocence of *Sesame Street* and into the dirty alleys of Main Street. This makes them (symbolically) social agents, spies, and mercenaries (economic hit women) charged with facilitating the demise of the black community.

According to the U.S. Bureau of the Census, African American adults and adolescents in 2003 had an AIDS case rate 10 times higher than whites. The CDC reports that black teens are more likely than whites to have had sex, more likely to begin at an earlier age (13), and more likely to have more than four partners by 18.

Like Method Man raps in Foxy Brown's tune, "Ill Na Na," "Who's got the illest p**y on the planet ... the Ill Na Na."[11]

under the spell

The thug love spell has made many women accomplices in crime, has made them bitter, hostile, and abusers of their own children. They are at times victims of domestic violence. To get a male, females are required to make sacrifices, and many do. They choose males over their children. They pay their hair stylist and manicurist to look good for the male before paying the rent. Often they must make ends meet without child support. These are common scenarios in the hood.

Thug love is violent, unforgiving, and demoralizing. Female rappers rhyme about thug love as if it is as wonderful and exciting as a Hollywood romance (and as unreal). Seldom do they rap about healthy relationships or commitment. In fact, they often try to top male rappers in lyrical vulgarity.

I often ask my female students the following question: How many of you are attracted to the thug type? Consistently, approximately 80 percent raise their hands.

These young females who don't know better are victims of multimillion dollar marketing campaigns and rap infomercials that are strategically designed to sway them to this mindset. As a result, they fantasize and romanticize the bad boys.

I then ask, "What is thug love?" Once again the answer is the same wherever I go: "It's being down for your man until the end. It's about keeping it real with your dogg (man)." At about this time I'm asking myself, what were you brainwashed with, Cheer or Tide? Let's break down thug love and see if it offers any clues to what's really going on.

Thug = Criminal
Love = Feelings
Put it all together and you have: **Thug Love = Criminal Feelings**

The female is more concerned with the feelings of her criminal (thug) boyfriend than herself and/or her children. She has no problem using her rent money to bail him out of jail or support his criminal conduct. Her feelings are stimulated, in part, by his thug, criminal ways. This speaks to the euphoric feelings some people get from associating with criminals. The female might actually be in love with the drama and not the man. The "good girls" of Hip Hop,

Destiny's Child, released a song to this effect in 2004 called "Lookin for a Solider." They sang, "I need a soldier that ain't scared to stand up for me."[12] The girls craved the drama the thug solider is famous for creating.

"I recently listened to a sister on the radio telling the DJ how she needed a man with a little thug in him," says my friend, Paul Scott, a minister in Durham, North Carolina. "It's sad compared to the sisters of previous generations who wanted a man to give her R-E-S-P-E-C-T. Whatever the answer, far too many of our young ladies are under the thug's magic spell."

In his lecture "Why Queens Tend to Love Fools," Dr. Ron Lewis says:

> "Counselors must often treat male juveniles referred by court services who have been diagnosed with a condition called 'Addictive Lifestyle Disorder.' The sad thing is that a lot of this behavior could be modified if the females were not so brainwashed. Instead, we have young males dealing with the disorder and their female partners are co-dependent on them. Instead of the female helping him out of the addiction, she becomes just as trapped as he is in the delusion. She becomes caught up in his reality when she could have helped him with her power of influence."[13]

People in general often allow addictions to sex and wealth to rule the heart and mind. However, within the Hip Hop/ghetto matrix, the magic spell of thug love complicates things. My students tell me all the time, "It's my body, I can do what I want to." Thug love is more than just an individual issue. It's a public health issue because few females wait out their partner's incarceration. Thus, whatever STD she received from him is now spreading. This is exactly how the latest AIDS epidemic among black females has flourished.

One interesting study that speaks to the deep levels of sexual deception and denial going on in the hood found that 34 percent of

African American men with HIV who have sex with men reported also having had sex with women—even though only six percent of African American women reported having had sex with a bisexual man.[14]

What you don't know can kill you. Teach young sistas that they can't go by how a brotha looks. They must develop the strength and courage to demand AIDS tests from potential sex partners and to use condoms every single time. Better yet, teach them to choose life, choose abstinence until marriage (and even then, both should get tested).

Incarcerated females are at risk as well.

> "Even though women are less likely to be incarcerated than men, incarcerated women are three times more likely to be HIV infected than incarcerated men. Almost two-thirds of women in prison are women of color. African American women are twice as likely as Hispanics and eight times more likely than white women to be in prison. Numerous studies have shown that the same behaviors that lead to incarceration put women at increased risk for HIV infection. Links between drug use, sex work, victimization, poverty, race, and HIV explain the prevalence of HIV infected women in prison."[15]

The sex monsters of Hip Hop don't want to discuss this. Their income depends on the sale of prison psychodrama and criminal behaviors to unsuspecting youth.

Chapter 16

Lyrical Felonies & Misdemeanors in Hip Hop

"BET markets their awards show as playing during prime time. Prime time usually means you're watching with your family and kids. Then the next thing you know, Destiny's Child is up onstage doing a lap dance. Did the decision to go from being a 'Survivor' to doing lap dances take place in some boardroom?"[1] **Chuck D**, Public Enemy, discussing the "virtual pedophilia" of sexual programming being targeted to youth

Most of us would consider "Magic Stick" and other gangsta rap tunes extreme, but believe it or not, there's a sub-segment of this music that takes us even deeper into the sickest corners of the rapper mind. These tunes are so low down that there should be a law. This is where my hypocrisy comes in because in principle, I don't believe in censorship. But my first responsibility is to children and my community. The songs you'll read about in this chapter should never have been produced or released. Be warned: this chapter is not for those with squeamish stomachs.

In an excellent study of gangsta rap lyrics, researcher Edward G. Armstrong, Murray State University, shows how the early songs laid the foundation for Hip Hop hate against women.[2] Some of the greatest offenders of this genre have been Dr. Dre, Snoop Dogg, Ice T, Ice Cube, N.W.A., Geto Boys, Eazy-E, MC Ren, Too $hort, Bushwick Bill, Willie D, and Eminem.

Some of these rappers have been rewarded for their pathologies with movie deals and awards. Eminem's *Slim Shady LP* won a

Grammy (1999) for best rap album although, as Armstrong notes, "Women are killed by guns and knives and by an innovative means, such as poisoning. Further, violent and misogynist lyrics are enhanced by an act of infanticide."[3]

lyrical rape

When a female doesn't submit sexually, what should a male do? Willie D in "Bald Headed Hoes"[4] and Too $hort in "Blow Job Betty"[5] advise raping the woman. In "Short Side," Too $hort says to beat the woman's "a**" with a billy-club." [6] How will a fourth grade boy who both hates and loves girls process this advice?

Anyone sick and disgusted yet? Well, there's more. In "She Swallowed It," N.W.A. teaches fans how to attack and rape a 14 year-old girl.[7] Ice-T, gangsta rapper turned big time mainstream actor, proposed sex "with Tipper Gore's two twelve-year-old nieces" in "KKK Bitch."[8] Armstrong believes Ice-T's statutory rape proposal was revenge against Tipper Gore's work with the Parents' Music Resources Center.[9]

"Nobody Move" by Eazy-E, "Ain't No Fun" by Snoop Dogg, and "Punk Bitch" by Too $hort all romanticize gang rape.[10] MC Ren in "Behind the Scenes" lyrically gang rapes ("ten niggas") a child and then violates her with a broomstick.[11] We know that children can't always distinguish fantasy from reality; when this song came out in the early 1990s, did little boys and girls know this was "just a song" when their older siblings, cuzins, and Hip Hop parents blasted it in the house or in the car?

In "Givin' Up the Nappy Dug Out," Ice Cube, another gangsta rapper turned mainstream actor, has "fourteen niggas" line up to rape an under age girl. Like Too $hort says in "She's a Bitch," "Fourteen, fifteen, all the way up/if she can bleed then she can f**k."[12]

With friends like these, who needs the KKK?

The following sobering statistics highlight the deadly reality of the above songs:

Hypocrisy 4—Grown Folks Business//Tricks Are for Kids

- About two out of 1,000 children in the U.S. were confirmed by child protective service agencies as having experienced sexual assault in 2003.[13]
- Among high school youth nationwide:
  - About nine percent of students reported that they had been forced to have sexual intercourse.
  - Female students are more likely than male students to report sexual assault (11.9 percent vs. 6.1 percent).
  - Overall, 12.3 percent of black students, 10.4 percent of Hispanic students, and 7.3 percent of white students reported that they had been forced to have sexual intercourse.[14]
  - Among college students nationwide, between 20 percent and 25 percent of women reported experiencing completed or attempted rape.[15]
- Among adults nationwide:
  - More than 300,000 women (0.3 percent) and more than 90,000 men (0.1 percent) reported being raped in the previous 12 months.
  - One in six women (17 percent) and one in 33 men (three percent) reported experiencing an attempted or completed rape at some time in their lives.
  - Rape usually occurs more than once. Among adults who report being raped, women experienced 2.9 rapes and men experienced 1.2 rapes in the previous year.[16]

the candy theory

Sexual predators often lure their young victims with the promise of something sweet, like candy. We teach our children not to play with the nasty people, and most of the time they listen and obey. However, our children are caught off guard when the predator is a trusted friend or rapper.

The sex monsters of Hip Hop use the candy trick all the time, and it works. Hip Hop artists are seen as friends, and their sexual lyrics are accepted as the norm. Their loyalty is established and maintained for years before the effects of the lyrical abuse are discovered.

Like most victims of sexual crime, the Hip Hop community is in denial. Candy is sweet and addictive, and too much can make you sick. Are we to believe that grown folk are the target audience for Hip Hop when so many rap tunes feature references to candy and sweets? Who are they kidding? The sex monster has one mission, and that is to keep our children in a hypersexual mode of thinking and behaving. Their sexual conduct has overwhelming consequences.

In rap tunes, candy and sex are synonymous. According to rapper 50 Cent, "When I say, 'I'll let you lick the lollipop,' little kids think it's literally a lollipop."[17] It looks like 50 Cent is having the last laugh on our children. Just the line "I'll let you lick the lollipop" is suggestive enough of oral sex, but with the sexual banter of Lil' Kim, the meaning of lollipop is clear: it's a penis.

The question is, do our children know this? Maybe, maybe not. Depending on their age and level of exposure to sexually explicit rap, they may know exactly what 50 Cent means by "lick the lollipop."

Pookie and Peaches may take 50's lyrics literally, but I guarantee, if they've seen the video and heard the song a million times in Uncle Ray Ray's car, if they've memorized the lyrics, the other verbal and nonverbal clues in the song will click together one day. They may already have.

This is no subtle aggression but an outright assault against our children. Back in the day, R&B and funk artists used double entendres to get their sex messages across. Today's rap artists are blatantly explicit.

From 1998 until the writing of this chapter, the sex monsters of Hip Hop have introduced summertime candy-laced sex songs for children each year like clockwork. Children as young as four have been rapping along with Pretty Ricky's "Juicy," D4L's "Shake Dat Laffy Taffy," 50 Cent's "Candy Shop," Lil' Kim's "Sugar (Gimme Some)," Kelis' "Milkshake"—the list goes on.

Hypocrisy 4—Grown Folks Business//Tricks Are for Kids

It's not enough that these sexually explicit songs play nonstop on the radio, BET, MTV, and VH1, our youth can now download them as ring tones into their cell phones. This is the epitome of Hip Hop love: bling bling, technology, and sexually explicit rap.

sadomasochism

In the 2003 mega hit "P.I.M.P." by 50 Cent and Snoop Dogg, black women are shown barely dressed with dog collars around their necks. The dog collars have chains (leashes) on them, and these women are being walked around like slaves or dogs (bitches). Hip Hop performer Boi of Outkast arrived at the 2003 MTV awards on a float with a semi-nude black female gyrating on a pole, which is a phallic symbol for an erect penis. Crunk music kings Lil John & the East Side Boyz scream in one of their hooks, "All you females crawl," symbolically calling females a bitch and blatantly humiliating all black women.[18]

Lyrical sadomasochism is widespread in gangsta rap. Sadism is the deriving of sexual pleasure from inflicting cruelty on others. Masochism is the deriving of sexual pleasure from being humiliated and abused. Gangsta rap features both sexual pathologies: someone is getting off on giving pain, and someone (usually a female) is getting off on receiving pain.

self-esteem?

Southern rapper Trina openly uses the title "baddest bitch." Mia X from the Dirty South clique uses the handle "boss bitch." East Coast rapper Lil' Kim refers to herself as "queen bitch." These sistas have flipped the script on self-esteem big time. They are teaching young black females to accept a type of anti-self-esteem, to take pride in being the best of the worst. This hurts black women as a whole.

After decades of sexism and mistreatment, Hip Hop females are flipping the sexual script as well. Consider the attitude of the beautiful but seriously misguided Remy Ma:

> "Last summer this Bronx guy was a male groupie type. I like male groupies; they'll do whatever you say for nothing. He had to bless my whole female crew, eating my p**y! Me and my friends f**k Niggas and disrespect Niggas. Treat them just like they treat us."[19]

In yet another interview Remy Ma says, "It's cool to be a fan, but for your own sake, don't be a groupie. We're going to tell everybody what we did with you."[20]

This psychosexual perspective of the female gangsta rapper was born out of a misogynistic male industry and a strange view of feminism. These ladies are voicing more than an opinion; they're expressing an attitude for the purpose of survival and acceptance in a sexist industry. They are gaining access but not freedom. As bell hooks says,

> "Women who have been abused and objectified have turned the tables and are now on the hunt. Eroticism is not pleasure-based. It is ruthless and violent, a tool to manipulate men and exact revenge on them by any means necessary. Black female sexuality is fictively constructed as 'bitchiness' and commodified in the music industry as sexual service for money, power and respect."[21]

Chapter 17

Dirty Dancing & STDs

"If a girl juke nasty, like, until I get me bricked up [erect penis], she got to handle my business since she made me that way. Every project chick [girl] at the dance knows what going down when they get you bricked up, dogg." **16 year-old male**, East St. Louis, Illinois

Dance and music are the heartbeat of African American culture, and new dances are created in the hood all the time. As soon as one shows up in the club, it quickly appears in urban areas across the country. The unwritten rule is that the city that gets the latest dance first leads, and all other cities are "late."

In the early to mid-1980s, breakdancing, the first official Hip Hop dance, came on the scene. I could get down on the dance floor with the best of them, but with the gymnastics of breakdancing I had to give it up to the young brothas.

Hip Hop dances come and go. While other youth were taking classes to learn how to breakdance, our children were busy creating the next dance craze. While breakdancing had an innocence about it, this new dance reflected the explicit sexuality of commercialized gangsta rap. It's called juking in Chicago, crunking in the South, and booty dancing, grinding, dooky booty, jacking, the nasty, and freak dancing in other parts of the country.

In crunk videos, nearly naked females perform lap dances on rappers and gyrate between the legs of other females. When crunk is played at the club, the dance floor turns into an orgy of couples simulating anal sex, oral sex, masturbation, and more.

Most of the complaints I receive from parents and school officials about youth dancing have to do with inappropriate touching and body positioning, mainly pelvis to pelvis and pelvis to buttocks. Take a trip down memory lane with me. Remember the Charleston, huckle-buck, jitterbug, hully-gully, and watusi? There was even a movie called *Dirty Dancing*. It was nearly impossible for a couple not to touch. During my teenage years, the bump and the freak were beyond risqué. Couples communicated sex in these dances via coordinated movements of the genital region. Today's youth are not the first to be thinking about sex while they dance.

Since the days of Elvis gyrating in the 1950s to Hip Hop, youth continue to redefine dirty dancing and social boundaries. Today, youth dancing appears to have one goal: sexual arousal. Dirty dancing is intensified with the use of alcohol and the so-called love drugs discussed earlier.

Crunking/juking is all about instant sexual gratification—no love, no commitment, no relationship necessary. Because crunking/juking takes place in seductive environments (low lights, smoky atmosphere), the club looks likes a brothel, a public orgy. Keep your children at home!

According to my friend and colleague Ron K. Harris, fights commonly break out at juke/crunk parties when a jealous boyfriend or girlfriend is found juking with someone else.

Youth in teen clubs, school proms, and homecoming dances have been discovered by shocked chaperones dancing themselves into a sexual frenzy, literally mounting one another on all fours. In a dance chain (gang bang?), dancers rub their backsides to the fronts of the dancers behind them in time to a pounding beat. This is no mere simulation but often foreplay to the actual act.

"The cute boys wanna dance with the girls with thongs and that's why we wear them. When a boy juke with you and you are bending over you can feel his sweat fall from his face on to your back or butt. It feels hot, like skin on skin. It gets you hot and before you know it you wanna go somewhere with him and get busy." **15 year-old**, Chicago, Illinois

Adult chaperones at high school dances have their hands full. Teens don't seem to understand what is and is not appropriate behavior on the dance floor. Even under the watchful eye of an adult, they'll try and simulate sex anyway. In Ohio, one high school now requires students attending dances to sign, with their parents, a form promising to not engage in sexual misconduct on the dance floor. At a school in Washington, DC, chaperones are armed with flashlights to shine on offending couples. At the extreme, a San Diego assistant high school principal was suspended after she inspected girls' underwear to make sure they were not wearing thongs.[1]

crunk mind control?

The dirty mouth of the dirty South, Nu South Crunk (Lil Jon, Nelly, David Banner, Bone Crusher, the Ying Yang Twins), has the entire nation dancing to a pounding new beat. I believe that the influence of Nu South Crunk on Hip Hop youth has trumped all other forms of rap. This variation of juking/crunking features a bass line and vibrating drumming techniques that overpower the melody line. These loud, low frequency vibrations and driving beats affect the pituitary gland. The pituitary gland produces hormones that control the sexual responses of males and females. It appears that Nu South Crunk has fine tuned the vehicle (rap music) to even more effectively deliver the theme of irresponsible sex to youth.

Crunk and gangsta rap as a whole have been engineered to influence the psychosexual development of black girls and boys trapped in the hood. When youth juke or crunk, they may be unaware of what their movements really mean or how they're being manipulated.

Dr. Gina M. Wingood, Emory University Center for AIDS Research, found that among a population of adolescent black females, the occurrence of health risk behaviors, STDs, and violence can be predicted according to their exposure to rap music videos.[2]

Wingood surveyed 522 single, poor, sexually active African American females, 14 to18 years old, from Birmingham, Alabama. The study looked at their music video viewing habits. Gangsta rap was preferred by 73 percent of the participants. The girls viewed about 14 hours of rap videos per week.

The results are disturbing. Wingood reports the following classic symptoms of Psychomedia Perpetrator Disorder (media copycatting):

> "Over the 12-month follow-up, 37.6% acquired a new sexually transmitted disease (chlamydia, trichomoniasis and gonorrhea), 4.8% hit a teacher, 12.1% reported being arrested, 14.8% had numerous sex partners, 44% reported using drugs (tranquilizers, marijuana, amphetamines, LSD, cocaine and crack), and 44.4% consumed alcohol. Compared with adolescents who had less exposure to rap music videos, adolescents who had greater exposure were 3 times more likely to have hit a teacher; more than 2.5 times as likely to have had multiple sexual partners; and more than 1.5 times as likely to have acquired a new sexually transmitted disease, used drugs and alcohol.
>
> "Thus, exposure to rap music videos, particularly gangsta rap, which is explicit about sex and violence and rarely shows the potential long-term adverse effect of risky behaviors, may influence adolescents by modeling unhealthy practices."[3]

The Rand Corp. surveyed 1,461 adolescents ages 12 to 17 nationwide in 2001 about their sexual behavior and how often they listened to sexually explicit, degrading music.[4] Youth were followed up one year and three years later. Information about listening habits and sex lyrics were analyzed to determine the frequency and type of sexual content youth were exposed to.

Hypocrisy 4—Grown Folks Business//Tricks Are for Kids

Here are the disturbing results: 17 percent had had intercourse at the beginning of the study, 29 percent at the first follow-up assessment, and 53 percent at the second follow-up.[5] Researchers discovered what we've known all along: youth who listen to a lot of music with degrading (or even non-degrading) sexual lyrics are at risk of having intercourse and other sexual activities too soon. According to Steven Martino, the psychologist who led the study,

> "These portrayals objectify and degrade women in ways that are clear, but they do the same to men by depicting them as sex-driven studs. Musicians who use this type of sexual imagery are communicating something very specific about what sexual roles are appropriate, and teen listeners may act on these messages."[6]

Gangsta rap lyrics and video images are infecting our youth during vulnerable developmental stages. Toddlers, adolescents, pre-teens, and teens were never meant to know so much about oral sex and hot tub ménage a trios.

Martino stated that furthermore,

> "It may be that girls who are repeatedly exposed to these messages expect to take a submissive role in their sexual relationships and to be treated with disrespect by their partners. These expectations may then have lasting effects on their relationship choices. Boys, on the other hand, may come to interpret reckless male sexual behavior as 'boys being boys' and dismiss their partners' feelings and welfare as unimportant."[7]

From the Too Little, Too Late file comes this report:

"Black Entertainment Television, partnering with the Kaiser Family Foundation, spent $15 million in donated air time last year to run public-service announcements encouraging teens to 'Rap It Up' and get tested—a potential inoculation against the nonstop bombardment of sexual music and videos."[8]

They must be joking. Black girls on a daily diet of crunk and gangsta rap run a high risk of engaging in the risky behaviors portrayed by their rapper role models in music videos. These girls would be shocked to discover that some of their idols don't smoke, are vegetarians, are married, and have children *with their wives*. But our girls don't know that. They think the videos are keeping it real.

'see, what had happen wuz ...'

TV puts pressure on all of us to keep up with the Joneses—or in the hood, the Pookies, Peaches, Pudd'ns, and them. Young people feel the pressure to make sexual conquests like never before.

The Hip Hop creed is to kiss and tell. Both males and females subscribe to this fourth grade behavior. I recently heard about one middle school where some seventh and eighth grade girls openly bragged about their sexual activities. What was once a shameful secret is now worn like a badge of honor. Go figure.

Females are viewed as tricks and consumed as treats. Hip Hop has no shame in its game of "nasty as you wanna be." It's time for women to fight back and say to the Hip Hop PTBs, "Game recognizes game." No more waking up in strange places, trying to explain to your love ones, "See, what had happen wuz ..." Hip Hop is a male dominated industry, and for females to try and match game for game is foolish.

Gangsta Hip Hop has corrupted the spiritual union between males and females. What should be an expression of love and life-long commitment has been reduced to a drunken one-night stand.

In "Where Are My Panties?" by Outkast,[9] a female speaks her inner thoughts as she wakes up still high from the night before, next to a man she doesn't know. She wonders what happened to her pant-

Hypocrisy 4—Grown Folks Business//Tricks Are for Kids

ies. She says to herself, "He's gonna think I'm a hoe." Then the male speaks his inner thoughts as he wakes up. (Watch out, here comes the set up!) He's thinking, "I don't think she a hoe. Just because a girl gives it up on the first night tells me she knows what she wants." He doesn't know her name, but after one night of having sex, he has decided she might have the qualities to be his future wife.

Young girls across the country are being seduced by this fantasy and thinking, "I'm down with this. Finally I can express my sexuality any way I want without consequences." They're also thinking, "Maybe he'll fall in love with me." They fail to understand that the game is about getting them out of their pants, on their knees, and convinced that it's their responsibility to serve a man in any way that pleases him. This scenario is being played out in every line, verse, and video frame. Teach girls to see the truth—that when they finally sober up, climb out of his bed, and find their panties, they will still be considered a ho.

too hot to handle

The complex psychosexual language system of Hip Hop provides clear connections between dirty dancing, sex, and STDs in the hood. Superstar rappers Missy Elliott and dirty south Hot Boyz made the terms "hot boyz" and "hot girlz" popular in the Hip Hop matrix. Let's break down these terms and see what the real deal is.

Hot Boyz	Hot Girl
Burned male	Burned female
Diseased male	Diseased female
Infectious male	Infectious female
Nasty boy	Nasty girl
Dirty male	Dirty female

A hot/diseased girl and a hot/nasty boy can only produce an infected baby. Think about it.

Hypocrisy 4—Grown Folks Business//Tricks Are for Kids

When you hear the word "hot" in a rap tune, you may think it means good, but think again. When a person finds out she has an STD, she says, "I've been burned." She refers to the person who infected her as "nasty" or "dirty."

Hot = burned = infected = diseased = nasty = dirty = filthy = ILLNESS

While the rates of some STDs, such as syphilis, have been brought to all time lows, others like gonococcal, genital herpes, gonorrhea, human papillomavirus, hepatitis B, trichomoniasis, bacterial vaginosis, HIV/AIDS, and chlamydia continue to adapt to treatment and spread through the population.

Sistas, do you still want a hot boy?

Hot boyz and hot girlz are flocking to chicken head parties. A chicken head party is an oral sex orgy given by mostly high school juniors and seniors. There you will see male on male, female on female, and all other combinations. In some parts of the country, a chicken head party is called a "rainbow party" because the females (or males) leave different colored lipstick marks on a male's genitals. It's common for three or four people to perform oral sex on one person at a time. Teens try to defend their behavior by saying "oral sex is not sex." Give me a break.

Favorite chicken head party songs include Khias' "My Neck, My Back" and 50 Cent's "Magic Stick." No wonder there's a high rate of STDs of the mouth among teens. The 13 to 19 year-old age group represents the largest group for STDs of the mouth. Approximately one-fourth of new infections are teenagers. Hip Hop kings and queens are like well-dressed assassins who are striking our youth right in their developmental stages, where it will be most effective.

From 1999 to 2002, 64 percent of heterosexuals who acquired HIV infections in the U.S. were females; sadly, the highest rate was in the 13 to 19 age group. Researchers think that the high rate of infected females is due to sexual contact with older males, who are more likely to be infected.[10] We must do a better job of protecting our girls from slick playas, pimps, and mack daddies!

One risky practice that may contribute to high rates of STDs among black teens is having sex buddies (a.k.a. "kut/cut buddies" or "shorties"). My generation calls them "maintenance men" or "booty calls."

> "It's nice to have a kut-buddy because you get a chance to practice, gain sexual experience without being committed. The person don't have to be cute, just as long as he knows what to do." **Teen**, Beaufort, South Carolina

> "Fat or chubby girls make the best f-buddies. They will drop it like it's hot anytime and want to press up on you like you're their nigga. All playas got a heavy girl on the down low somewhere—trust me on this one, Coach Powell." **16 year-old**, Oakland, California

Cut buddy "relationships" are widespread in the hood. They're the next step down from the sex games youth have played over the years—Spin the Bottle, Hide and Get It, Post Office, Touch the Booty, Doctor and Nurse, and House.

Although these games sound innocent, they have serious consequences, including unwanted pregnancies, rape, STDs, and loss of self-esteem. Despite the denial that follows the next morning about who and how many people you had sex with, the games can be addictive and you could end up playing again the next night.

In fact, the next time your child wants to sleep over at a cousin's or friend's house, think about it because sex games may be the reason. Talk to the adults in the home to make sure a responsible chaperone will be present.

Prevention specialist and educator Pam Shackleford weighs in with following:

"Familiarity sex is a real phenomenon not restricted to young people in the hood. My goal is to teach kids how to be responsible in social settings with the values they learn at home plus the ones I teach them in class. But, what do you do when they don't learn any at home? I guess it depends on how you look at it. Positive is a relative term. What I consider positive, you may consider outrageous. What you consider positive, I may consider ludicrous. Either way the fact is too many young people are looking for love in all the wrong places and many of those who are looking for love are still looking to be hooked up."[11]

hood rats

Hood rat is another animalistic term used to describe females in the Hip Hop/ghetto matrix. Let's decode.

Hood rat = neighborhood snitch, community disease carrier
Hood rats = community children

From the Eminem camp, rapper Obie Trice's rap tune "Hoodrats" tells the classic adolescent fantasy of two "unattractive" females fighting for Obie's attention and companionship while he is dining with another woman he describes as "beautiful." He publicly mistreats the so-called hood rats. In Obie Trice's world, hood rats are second class human beings and deserve humiliation.[12]

Within the Hip Hop/ghetto matrix, hood rat connotes a sexually nasty female and/or a female who has many children (like a rat has litters). The hood rat's main role in gangsta Hip Hop videos is to dress and dance provocatively and perform sexual antics. Apparently there is a difference between Rug Rats, the cute Nickelodeon cartoon characters, and hood rats as it relates to defining African American children in the hood. I often ask my students to write their definitions of Rug Rats and hood rats. Ninety percent associate African

American children with hood rats and affluent white children with Rug Rats.

Scripture puts a high priority on having a good name. Proverbs 22:1 says that "A good name is to be chosen rather than great riches." Thus, an evil name should be avoided at all cost.

A name can carry generational curses. Hip Hop artists under the guise of entertainment are inflicting a curse on the community for years to come. No group of people attacks their own via entertainment like black people. We teach the world to call our men niggas, our children hood rats, and our mothers, sisters, and daughters bitches and hos. Why should others respect us when we don't respect ourselves?

Hood rat speaks volumes to the psychosexual disdain many in the Hip Hop matrix have against black females. How do you kill a hood rat (neighborhood pest)? With popular hood poisons—heroin, crack, weed, malt liquor, and cigarettes, which may be laced with rat poison. Males and females use these substances to numb/medicate themselves against the perpetual cycles of violence and sexual abuse they must deal with in the hood.

Hood rats are seen as pests, regarded as disposable, and killing them is acceptable. This was on display big time in the sound track for Ice Cube's movie, *Friday*. 2 Live Crew contributed "Hoochie Mama," in which they rhymed, "Hoochie hoodrat is a hoe like her momma!"[13]

As a female disease carrier, hood rat symbolizes the high rates of HIV/AIDS and other STDs (from unprotected sex with multiple sex partners). Clearly, anyone who has intercourse with a hood rat becomes a dirty rat him or herself. Think about it.

Decoding hood rats will help us understand how the true potential of children is viewed in the hood. Consider the following: rats spelled backwards is "star"; hood indicates the location (community). The true destiny of our children is to become community stars; however, their star potential is kept hidden from them in the Hip Hop/ghetto matrix. Anyone who sees him or herself as a star will not behave like a rat (low life).

Hypocrisy 4—Grown Folks Business//Tricks Are for Kids

project chicks & more

Within the ghetto, the projects are government-funded places of residence; outside the ghetto, projects are known as "experiments."

Females who live in the projects and are caught in a cycle of perpetual poverty are experimental subjects (along with males and children of color). The outcomes of project experiments are freak discoveries—thus the following equations:

Project = Experiment = Freak
Project Chick = Freak Female

Chick is an argot for female; therefore, project chick connotes freak or freaky female (a.k.a. "nasty girl"). Old School star Rick James defined a freak as a girl you "don't take home to mother" in his song "Super Freak."[14] Clearly, when rappers call females freaks, they're saying they will perform freaky sexual tricks and treats without shame. Teach our girls that this is not a compliment!

"Gangsta Hip Hop, with its misogynist terms, has done more to set back black women's sexuality as well as sexual esteem than slavery. To identify any female group with animalistic terms speaks to a level of expectation and quality of life issues and the terms are dehumanizing. Both males and females in our communities have become desensitized to the seriousness of these terms: words have power beyond our comprehension. There is an old saying that goes, 'You can tell a lot about a society by the way it treats its women.' Something is dreadfully wrong when our daughters accept being mistreated as part of a creed to be down with Hip Hop, all in the name of keeping it real." **Robyn Price**, Executive Director, After School All Stars Program, Columbus, Ohio

Rappers have a long list of animal argots for females (typical fourth grade male psychology), including cows, heifers, hens, snakes, pigs, bird brains, bitch, chicks, fish, old goats, old bats, chicken heads, squirrels, and pigeons. These terms are hurtful to both black women and girls. Consider the following:

Chicken head. A chicken is considered to be a nasty animal because it will eat anything. Chicken head was introduced into the ghetto matrix around 1998. Describes females who give oral sex in order to support a drug addiction.

Squirrel. Introduced around 2003 or 2004. Describes females who stimulate the genitals (nuts) of men.

Pigeon. Describes females who perform oral sex and/or who are infected with an STD.

The community will only rise as high as its women. Obviously, crunk and gangsta rappers didn't get the memo. Male rappers' persistent name calling seems to suggest a hatred of women, including mama. This is a twist of the fourth grade developmental dynamic in which boys begin to separate from their mothers. In a healthy family, a boy begins to depend less on mama and more on daddy or another influential male. During slavery, however, boys were not allowed this rite of passage into maturity. To keep them safe, their mothers kept them close and immature. We see this playing out in the 21st century and glorified in the tunes of rappers.

Black rappers also appear to have an abstract Oedipus complex:
1. Kill the male/father figure.
2. Intercourse with the female/mother figure via sexually degrading animalistic female terms.
3. Fear castration, as witnessed by the constant holding of the penis. This is the legacy of slavery and the Jim Crow era.

Rap lyrics tell us that black males believe that the infected, disease carrying female/mother figure is a threat to his penis/sex life/ability to reproduce himself. To protect himself, he seeks oral sex, not intercourse, with her. Notice that many Hip Hop argots connote oral sex, which avoids pregnancy (but not disease).

Hatred, abuse, disrespect, rape, and/or murder of the black female. The black male/rapper lumps together all females in the hood, including his mother. His deep yearning is to marry someone other than his own mother figure because he sees females outside his community/race as disease free and safe for intercourse and reproduction. This is why there are so many women of other races in rap videos (although by association they, too, become infected). By being with females of other races, the black male believes he significantly lowers his chances of being castrated via HIV/AIDS and other STDs.

(Thanks to Cyrstal Harris, who contributed to this chapter.)

Chapter 18

Parent'Hood: A Divine Mission

By Crystal Harris & Alfred "Coach" Powell

"Children have never been very good at listening to their elders, but they have never failed to imitate them." **James Baldwin**, *Nobody Knows My Name: More Notes of a Native Son*

"Your children need your presence more than your presents." Rev. **Jesse Jackson, Sr.**

"Children are travelers in an unknown land and we are their guides." **Robert Fisher**

"We are family!" was the cry of black folk long before Sister Sledge sang it in the 1970s to uplift our community. The unwritten theme in the black family for the longest was "Family sticks together." If one of us got into a fight, then everybody had to fight. The cry was, "I'm gonna get my cuzins"—and it was on like popcorn.

You could always depend on family during illnesses, lack of cash, and matters of the heart. It was as if we had placed our collective hands on the Bible and swore before God to take care of family—blood, extended, and play cousins. We shared everything, including our clothes, food, beatings, hugs, and kisses.

Parents and grandparents ruled with an iron fist; they did not spare the rod, but their love was just as fierce. We went to church every Sunday, and we could not complain.

We survived the family secrets. At some point you found out that your auntie was your birth mother and your cousins were your brothers and sisters. Mr. So & So was your real daddy, your grandfather killed a man somewhere in the Deep South, the preacher laid hands on your pretty girl cousin more than he should have, the deacon played the numbers at your granny's house who sold a little corn liquor with the fish dinners, and your uncle had a boyfriend who played piano for the big church. Still we were family. Forgiveness back then was a golden rule as was dinner at six.

the home makers

It's all good in the hood—Parent'hood that is. There's no more important job than raising children. The terrain includes mountains and valleys, blue skies and cloudy days. Some people dream about becoming parents, others stumble into Parent'hood. No matter how you arrive, once there, you're left breathless. Parent'hood is a thing of beauty, despite all the challenges. To be a parent is a reward and a blessing.

Some will travel different roads on their journey through Parent'hood. Miracle Boulevard is always congested, and there's a fork in the road at Joy and Pain. The interstate exits are Peace Drive, Redemption Avenue, and Love Parkway. Parents and children who take a wrong turn sometimes end up at the back alley named Violence, the liquor store named Addiction, and the vacant lot at the intersection of Divorce and Misery.

The stress in Parent'hood can make you forget that children need love. In Parent'hood, you'll hear some parents say:

"I brought you into this world and I'll take you out."

"I'll knock you into the middle of next week."

"I'll knock you across a greasy floor and dare you to slide."

"Get your black a** over here, little nigga."

Thank God there are places to relieve stress in the Parent'hood. Around the corner on Believers Avenue is the WWJD (What Would Jesus Do) Recovery Center. On Imani Lane is the Brotherhood

Temple. Located at the intersection of Wisdom and Experience are billboards that read:

"Children are a gift from the Lord; they are a reward from Him" (Psalms 127:3).

"Train up a child in the way he should go, and when he is old he will not depart from it" (Proverbs 22:6).

Cars in Parent'hood have bumper stickers that read:

"The last four letters in parent spells RENT. As long as I'm paying the rent, I'm in charge."

"Role models—model the role."

There's help for young parents on Healing Drive, which is two blocks east of Hope Street. There you'll find Frances L, who advises, "Before going to bed, turn all your problems over to God. He's up all night anyway."

But what happens if you lose your way in Parent'hood? What if Frances L is out to lunch? This is how one man made a killing in the TV talk show business. Maury Povich is the master of exploiting the pain and confusion of young Hip Hop parents who have nowhere to turn.

ask maury

There was a time when "I went to the doctor's office" was the prelude to "Baby, I'm pregnant." Now she says, "I went to the Maury Povich Show and he said the baby's daddy is …"

Three times a day (in some markets) you can watch as Maury reveals to young males and females from the Hip Hop community the results of their DNA tests. The news is often shocking and painful to one if not both parties. Some young females are regulars on the show. There have been occasions where young females have had five, six, seven, and more males take paternity tests for one child.

Does Maury offer HIV testing while exploiting their sexual behavior and feeding the rest of the world the hypersexual stereotypes of young people, especially people of color?

According to the National Center for Health Statistics, the percentage of African American children born to married couples peaked at 70 percent after slavery. Today, 70 percent of black children are born out of marriage, half of whom live with single mothers.

African American children who have married parents have similar outcomes to white, suburban kids who have married parents. A healthy marriage contributes to a healthy child. Although many children are happier and better cared for in single parent families than in miserable marriages, separation and divorce are associated with poverty, poorer school performance, greater risk of teen pregnancy, and higher drug addiction and unemployment rates. Children of unwed parents are more likely to become unwed parents themselves.

Many unwed mothers and their children do fine, but the odds are stacked against them.

According to some estimates, 60 percent of all American children born in the 1990s (the height of Hip Hop) will spend some significant portion of their childhood in a fatherless home.

that's my baby daddy, maury

Maury should be hired by the U.S. government to find Osama Bin Laden because he can find fathers missing in action better than the females who are looking for them. There is an epidemic of child abandonment in America, mainly by fathers. The most uttered words by women on the Maury show are, "That my baby daddy, Maury," followed by, "He look just like him—same head, nose, and lips."

Back in the day, if a girl got pregnant, she was sent down South to stay with her grandmother. Either the boy was forced to marry her, or she would leave the child with the grandmother to be raised. Today, a high school female will bring her newborn to school so everyone can see how cute the baby is and so she can brag about who the daddy is. Heaven forbid someone says, "So and so wasn't the father." It's on, right then and there.

The sad reality is that the Hip Hop generation has bought into the idea that it's cool to collect baby daddies and mamas. Unfortunately, they have not bought into sexual abstinence, marriage, and children within marriage.

The monikers "baby daddy" and "baby mama" describe a faceless, uncommitted, and loveless connection with the other parent. Like nigger, these terms speak to our slave past when our ancestors were bred like animals and when young girls were forced to have children. They were mated with other POWs (prisoners of war), but they were also taken, issued out, and/or traded for the pleasure of the slave master, his sons, and the overseers. To be made pregnant against your will is traumatizing like any form of rape. So the women would refer to the child's father as "my baby daddy" because he wasn't her husband or lover. There was no so such loving connection. Baby daddy was faceless and absent, as are today's fathers in the minds of young sistas in the hood.

Black men were also traumatized. They were used as sex slaves to breed with women they had no feelings for or relationship with. They did not have a choice; they had to impregnate any and all females chosen by the master. The female could be a relative (unbeknown to him) who had been separated at birth and sold to a neighboring plantation. Or she could be another poor soul on his plantation. The odds of him impregnating his own sister or birth mother were high, which made him a potential motherf**r. This is why males often refer to sex as "f**king." This word might be used during a rape or a one-night stand—as well as "love making." He referred to his child's mother as "my baby mama" because she was not his wife or lover.

It's painful to hear young people in the hood brag about the number of babies they have (or think they have). At some point the children of these faceless encounters will grow up and recognize their true feelings about their parents', specifically their mothers', life choices. They may strike out at a sibling who has an involved father. They are often hostile towards their new stepfather or their mother's boy-friend.

"Step Daddy," by Hitman Sammy Sam, sheds a stereotypical view on this issue. His video depicts black children as insolent, attitudinal, and uncontrollable, specifically the little girl: "You aint my daddy!! SHUT UP!! ... You just mad cuz you aint my daddy!"[1]

'maury, man, she a ho'

Maury Povich has a production formula that never fails. On nearly every "Who's the daddy?" show, Maury shows a clip of the potential father speaking against the mother. The exact words may change, but the sentiment remains the same: "Maury, man, she a ho. Everybody done hit that in the hood." And on and on as he reads her sexual resume to the world.

Money always comes up as a major issue. She insists on the DNA test because she needs child support, and he claims she's just after his money. They're both right, and they're both suffering the negative impact of irresponsible sex on cash flow (Sexonomics). Their suffer-ing is real. Parents know how expensive it is to raise a child today from birth to college (and sometimes beyond).

While the viewer is being entertained by such trauma and drama, the child's future is being set. The damage has been done. These couples will probably never marry, putting their children at risk of repeating their own drama.

'you're the father!'

"When it comes to two year-old Pookie, you're the father!" These words are music to the ears of the mothers. They shout, "Nigga, where is my child support? I wanna get paid!"

According to the Annie E. Casey Foundation (2004), in 2001, only 30 percent of teen mothers received child support payments, and many studies have found that most eventually go on welfare.

The problem is not just economic. The father's absence significantly contributes to the social, emotional, and psychological under development of children. Consider the following statistics:

- 85 percent of children that exhibit behavioral disorders come from fatherless homes.
- 90 percent of homeless and runaway children are from fatherless homes.
- 71 percent of high school dropouts come from fatherless homes.
- 75 percent of adolescent patients in chemical abuse centers come from fatherless homes.
- 63 percent of youth suicides are from fatherless homes.
- 80 percent of rapists motivated by displaced anger come from fatherless homes.
- 70 percent of juveniles in state-operated institutions come from fatherless homes.
- 85 percent of incarcerated youth grew up in a fatherless home.[2]

The children of the Hip Hop era will spend part of their adulthood looking for their biological fathers. A common question children in the hood ask one another is, "Is that your daddy, who daddy that is?" It's painful.

Hip Hop artists B Rock and the Bizz made light of the situation in their summer hit, "My Baby Daddy." Their lyrics give us a peek into the suspicion, disrespect, and mistrust that characterize relationships in the hood: "When the phone click don't even try girl/Quit lying girl/You must think I'm stupid or either blind girl."[3]

Rapper Queen Pen wrote about being caught in a cycle of sexual betrayal, poverty, and violence in her song also entitled "My Baby Daddy": "So what he my baby daddy he don't do his child right/ Tryin to explain I got tears in my eyes."[4]

divine mission

Parenting is a divine mission. In an earlier chapter, we decoded sex within the context of a loveless exchange between two people. But when the context is spiritual, a God-given gift, the original purpose of sex is then revealed.

S is for seed, which comes from the male.

E is for egg, which comes from the female.

X marks the spot where the treasure is hidden and the source of pleasure is buried. X is also the symbol for the female chromosome. Given its placement as the last letter in sex, we are reminded that the female always has the final say in whether or not consensual sex will occur.

Have you noticed that the letter X is crossed? Perhaps the symbol is telling females that sex is not a problem as long as their legs are kept crossed—hello! So, my sistas, you bear the cross in more ways than you think.

Although she doesn't always know it, by nature a female is in charge of sex, which is why males have to ask for some'n some'n. Question: some of what? The first two letters in some are clues. What is the something a man is asking you to give away? Playing with the word "some," the first two letters are **s** and **o**. **SO** are also the first two letters of **SO**ul. Every time you have sex outside of marriage, you are giving away a part of your soul, the **U** you can never get back (the same is true for males). This is why sex is supposed to be reserved for your **SO**ul mate.

When men ask if they can have some, does this mean some or sum? Sum means total/all, as in "Can I have it all?" On a psychosexual level of consciousness, men intuitively know that all of it at once (sum/total) could kill us. Just small amounts put us to sleep. Can I get a witness?

Sometimes males ask, "Can I get a little piece?" Notice the psychosexual language—he didn't ask for all of it. As a female, you are giving a piece of your **SO**ul away. Thus, the wise sista does not give or receive sex outside of marriage, especially in the era of the down low/low down brotha.

We must teach our children, especially teens, about the power of celibacy, which is abstaining from intercourse, oral sex, and other behaviors that may lead to sex. Perhaps our children would do much better in school if they weren't so distracted by the drama and trama that comes from sex too soon.

Sex is both a physical and energy exchange. The male gives his spiritual energy and the female gives her soul energy (both are equally important).

Spirit + Soul = Love

That's why it's called making love. Remember, before God created Adam's soul mate, He put Adam into a deep sleep with some powerful (holy) anesthesia. Then He created Eve from a rib out of Adam's own body. When Adam awakened, he entered the womb/vagina of wombman/Eve. Her womb/vagina was as powerful as the holy anesthesia. That's why we go to sleep after making love to our wives. We can't help it. Every being that enters (husbands) or exits (babies) sleeps.

Let's revisit the letter X in sex. It is believed that women, at the height of sexual climax, dispense 10 times (X) more energy than men. X symbolizes power, and women have the power to cause a power shortage in men, which is why men must go to sleep after ejaculation.

The female has the power to evaluate after sex, and the male always seeks her approval after intercourse. "Between a 1 and 10, how did I rate?" Her answer can make or break his spirit.

Still not convinced? Every time a male enters the womb/vagina of his soul mate, they both encounter God. That's why, at the height of orgasm we say, "Oh, God" or "My God" (if you don't say it, you think it). It's as if you have just seen His face and you are greeting Him, the sight is so magnificent. God dwells in heaven, and this explains why men sometimes call their wives angels. Angels are the hosts of heaven; the womb/vagina of a wombman is the earthly host and should never be disrespected or fouled. Without a doubt, sex is God's business. The sex monsters of Hip Hop don't want you to know that.

Males involuntarily say "baby" or "oh baby" during sex. Well that makes perfect sense when you think about it. The act of intercourse produces what? Babies! And babies come from where? Heaven! So instead of shouting God's name, you simply called the name of a divine being, a baby, perhaps the baby you just created. That's why fathers tell their children, "I saw your lovely face before you were born." No matter how you cut it, you were in the presence of God.

Whatever name you shout at that moment, know this: if you don't believe you see God during intercourse, rest assured He sees you.

The word "intercourse" itself proves my point. Let's break it down. "**Inter**" connotes "**inter**nal/personal" or "**inte**grate." "Course" connotes "sexual lesson" or even "sexual path taken." (Am I going too far to say that course rhymes with coarse, which is exactly how rappers treat the sex act in their songs?) Thus, intercourse is both a "personal lesson" and a "sexual path taken together."

Females complain that men change for the worse after they have intercourse. Only after intercourse does a female learn a personal lesson, something she didn't know before she integrated her soul with his spirit, before he became an internal (physical) part of her. Then she realizes that the path taken was the wrong one, and the same is true for males who discover that the road they traveled has led to the wrong place.

Hypocrisy 4—Grown Folks Business//Tricks Are for Kids

Brother, if you think it's all about sex and not making love as 50 Cent's lyrics suggest, you need to consider the following: Man is made in the image of God (all faiths see God as perpetual Love). God made man by molding a piece of mother earth/nature (a female symbol) with care/love. He then took His breath/seed/life and blew His essence (Love) into the nostrils of man—that was an act of making love. Symbolically, man is full of God's love. Since God placed love into you and man is the image of God, you are then spiritually ordained and obligated to place Love (God) back into the womb of your mate and the hearts of your children.

The production of life is a God science—not magic. Thus, magic stick/wand is disrespectful within the spiritual context. As a man of God, you are supposed to make love, not just have sex. The feeling good part of sex is God's gift to you and a reminder to humans that God felt good making you during His act of love. Perhaps that's why a sexual climax is like God's love itself … simply overwhelming.

Testosterone is the hormone that expresses male traits in the body. Life itself is stored in the male's **test**icles. Every time a male ejaculates, he **test**ifies to or prophesizes new life. When the sperm engages a female egg, this is, because of the odds against its success, a **test**ament, tangible proof, of man's power to spark life. The child is considered a living **test**imony. When a man refuses to raise his own child, he fails the **test** of parenthood and manhood.

Chapter 19

Hypocrisy 5—

The Cross//The Beast

"First of all, I wanna give honor to God. I'm real religious. I know I sing a lot of crazy music, but I'm real religious. And I know this is God right here, that got me right here." **Missy Elliott**, 2002 Soul Train Awards

Whenever a gangsta rapper receives an award, the first thing he says is, "I want to thank God, Jesus, and my mother." Hanging across his chest is a huge eye-catching, custom-made, diamond-studded, platinum crucifix, maybe more than one. He may carry a chalice (Holy Grail goblet) with the words "ACT LIKE A PIMP" written on it. Yes, the same chalice used in the Christian faith for the consecrated, sacred rite of Mass (Eucharist) and/or Holy Communion. According to various legends, a chalice was used by Jesus either at the Last Supper or at the cross to contain His blood.

When asked to explain their vulgar lyrics, rappers will often say, "Only God can judge me," apparently referring to Matthew 7:1, "Judge not, that you be not judged." But we must question the hypocrisies.

How can gangsta rappers thank God for their success when their lyrics and video images are filled with profanity, pornography, violence, crime, hating on women, and drug abuse? This is the worse kind of hypocrisy—thanking God for success based on behavior He does not condone.

Just as symbols of success are craftily integrated with symbols of intoxication, Christian symbols are integrated with anti-Christian themes. Millions of children and teens are being lured away from having a true personal relationship with God, the very thing that could deliver them out of the harshness of ghetto life.

Gangsta rap has become an alternative religion (cult), and Hip Hop youth are buying it. We are in a real war against gangsta Hip Hop for the souls and spirits of our children. Since rappers have become the gods/idols of Hip Hop youth, we must address their version of spirituality that often hides behind the symbols of Christianity and, at times, Islam.

Gangsta rappers have twisted spirituality to suit their needs. Unless we teach our children differently, they will never know that the cult of gangsta Hip Hop goes against the principles held by most religions. Consider the following chart.

Religious Principles	Gangsta Hip Hop Principles
Giving, tithing	Taking, buying
Sex within marriage, monogamy	Promiscuity, multiple sex partners, orgies
Respect for the opposite sex	Misogyny, gold digging
Compassion	Coldness
Love	Lust, hate, fear, rage
Obedience, submission to God	Willfulness, submission to gang, crew
Modesty	Bling bling, g-strings, pasties, saggin
Humility	Pride
Peace	Violence
Turn the other cheek	An eye for an eye
Generosity	Greed

Hypocrisy 5—The Cross//The Beast

Since so many artists today appear to be coming from a Christian orientation, we will focus on Christian symbolism in the Hip Hop cult.

Gangsta rappers may wear the crucifix, but their lyrics, video images, and public persona have nothing to do with what Jesus taught. So why do these artists wear the cross? Why have the jewel-encrusted chalice and elaborately designed staff (cane) become the props of choice in booty-shaking music videos and publicity photos?

In 2005, rapper P. Diddy paid tribute to his fallen comrade, Notorious B.I.G., with his *The Notorious B.I.G. Duets: The Final Chapter* CD. His first release and video was "Nasty Girl," which featured P. Diddy along with Nelly and a host of others. The lyrics and video were equally raunchy. The video features the usual girls, half nude in a hot tub with P. Diddy, but what makes this video stand out from others is that P. Diddy wears a shiny Christian cross as he raps his explicit sexual lyrics.

Perhaps the crucifix is supposed to "bless" the lyrics, but make no mistake; scripture is clear about right and wrong sexual behaviors. There's a double message going on here that confuses young viewers who don't know any better.

Why do Hip Hop artists double cross their fans like this? How would a fourth grade boy internalize the conflicting images in P. Diddy's video? If he hasn't been taught about the cross, he probably does not know that the images are in conflict.

In the May 2005 issue of *Source* magazine, Ice T is shown sitting on a golden throne (priestly chair?) that is decorated with cherubs. He wears all black from head to toe (priestly garb?) and a necklace with a crucifix pendant. This image is suspicious and highly disturbing.

Are crucifix-wearing rappers devoted Christians? Are they ministers, priests, or missionaries? Or are these sacred symbols deliberately used in gangsta rap to confuse youth and express secret rites, secret group membership, and rank/hierarchy?

Rappers seem to have no problem bastardizing Christian symbolism, but we seldom see them bearing the symbols of other religions. When was the last time you saw the Islamic crescent moon and star in a rap video? What's up with that? The Islamic community wouldn't tolerate it. The message, unfortunately, is that the Christian community can be punked, pimped, and pushed around.

Some rappers try to justify wearing the crucifix by saying they are down with the same groups of people Jesus was down with, i.e., the poor, suffering, and downtrodden. Others say they wear the symbols to let people know that God has shown them favor. Still others say they wear them for spiritual protection from the gangsta game. Talk about hypocrisy! The cross symbolizes all that Jesus stood for—and against, including the gangstas (Pharisees and Sadducees) who had the people on economic and spiritual lock down. I believe the cross stands against the gangsta game, which is a tool of oppression.

Rappers who bear these sacred symbols break virtually every rule and principle in the Book. While promoting their foul lyrics and images, they are spiritually retarding and manipulating their young fans. Criticize the lyrics of a 50 Cent or a Lil' Kim and see how a fan will respond; they will shout you down in defense of their idol. Anyone criticizing these rappers will come under attack themselves. This happens to me all the time in workshops across the country. Thus, when rappers say "Only God can judge me" (and He will), they are really saying that *we* should not judge them, which lets them off the hook. This is a prime case of psychospiritual manipulation or reverse psychology.

Why the Hip Hop fascination with Christian symbolism? In the early days, you couldn't catch a rapper wearing a cross or any Christian symbol because Christianity was seen as "the white man's religion."

Around 1996 or so, the bling bling crosses and Christ heads began to appear in videos. As with most cases of Psychomedia Perpetrator Disorder, everybody started wearing them.

Is this just a fad, a fashion, or is it true faith? Fashions and fads are temporary, but true faith in God endures forever. If this is true faith, then more positive lyrics and images should begin to emerge out of Hip Hop. I have yet to see this change in rap, so I can only conclude that gangstas bearing sacred symbols is a fad, fashion, or maybe something worse, as implied by the "priest" picture of Ice T in all black and wearing a crucifix.

Are these rappers in league with the cross (Jesus), or are they in the hip pocket of the beast/devil/Satan? Their jewelry says Jesus, but their lyrics say the beast. This is hypocrisy of the most blasphemous kind. You can't have it both ways. As Jesus says in Matthew 6:24, "No one can serve two masters; for either he will hate the one and love the other, or else he will be loyal to the one and despise the other. You cannot serve God and mammon." To be clear, mammon is *money*.

Chapter 20

Hip Hop @ the Cross

"If you can get past the vulgar lyrics you will realize that these brothas don't have a clue about how life operates in the spiritual realm. In fact, most of them are so materialistic they wouldn't know any kind of spiritual force if it walked up and smacked them upside the head. I know of no God that would endorse what they say and do." **Dr. Ron Lewis**

As gangsta Hip Hop followers come of age and into spiritual maturity, the movement will find itself at a crossroad. Designed for children yet led by middle-aged men, gangsta Hip Hop will have to find new ways to hold onto their established base. One powerful way will be to compete against traditional religion to capture the imagination of young people.

We are entering the age of Holy Hop. The congregation of adoring, worshipful fans has been present all along. Donations have been put into the basket to the tune of billions. And within recent years, Holy Hop has taken a bold step forward with the appearance of religious, mythical, and mystical symbolism appearing throughout the Hip Hop/ghetto matrix.

reading between the lines

It's important that we define what we mean by symbol.

"A symbol is a term, a name, or even a picture that may be familiar in daily life, yet that possesses specific connotations in addition to its conventional and obvious meaning. It implies something vague, unknown, or hidden from us."[1]

We may *see* an image or read a word or phrase, but we *think* and *feel* on many, many levels. That's what is meant by the saying, "One picture is worth a thousand words." Nothing is what it appears to be. Everything stands for something else.

I deal a lot with symbols because I see them everywhere. When I wrote about how alcohol companies were targeting black youth with their subliminal advertising in *Message N/A Bottle*, I found many sacred and profane symbols in the ads. I've also found symbols throughout the Hip Hop/ghetto matrix.

The most popular symbols used in Hip Hop are Christian: the diamond crucifix, Holy Communion/Holy Grail goblet (pimp cup), and staff (cane). Rappers bearing these symbols are charismatic, smooth talking, and often have long, flowing hair. They say they're pimps, but in reality this is the subliminal and symbolic description of the black urban preacher. In the long history of black culture, the black preacher's rival has always been the black pimp, his personal devil. Why are these symbols being pushed on our youth? Why now? Is this a subconscious attack on black clergy, leadership, sexuality, and masculinity?

Let's look at these symbols in more detail.

Crucifix. The crucifix is the most important of all Christian symbols. This one simple "t" shape says it all: Jesus the Messiah, the Christ, worked miracles, died for our sins on a cross, defeated death, and ascended to heaven to be with the Father. For Christians, the crucifix represents the awesomeness of the life of Jesus and the sacrifice He made for us. It also symbolizes the burdens and persecutions we must sometimes bear in the name of the Lord.

For African Americans, the cross can have uglier meanings because of the way it was misused during slavery and Jim Crow.

Many Christians find it highly offensive and blasphemous when rappers casually wear crosses around their necks as fashion statements. It is even more amazing that their crucifix pendants are made of pure gold, diamonds, and/or platinum. Jesus represented the poor and disenfranchised. He told the rich man to sell all that he had and follow Him. In other words, if mammon is getting in the way of your righteousness/right behavior, then get rid of all bling, cash, cars, mansions, fur coats, hot tubs, designer gear, and diamond grills and follow Him. God wants us to prosper, but not at the cost of our souls. Rappers need to meditate on Matthew 19:24: "It is easier for a camel to go through the eye of a needle than for a rich man to enter the kingdom of God." Rappers may wear the crucifix and thank God at the Grammys, but their lyrics of sex and violence suggest mental confusion about what Jesus and the cross truly stand for.

Goblet/Chalice. All symbols can be interpreted in more than one way. Whether the goblet was used at the Last Supper or to contain Jesus' blood as He hung on the cross, this is a powerful symbol and has been responsible for legends, rumors, and the Crusades. The goblet used at Holy Communion carries this symbolic blood (wine, grape juice) of Christ. Witches also use the goblet in their ceremonies. When the jewel-encrusted goblet is featured in rap videos, presumably containing Courvoisier or Cristal, the holy idea of redemption of sins is twisted to satanically mean "sin with abandon."

Staff (cane). The staff symbolizes power, authority, and punishment. In Exodus 7, God tells Moses and Aaron to throw down the staff before Pharaoh, and it became a snake. Pharaoh's magicians did the same thing, and their staffs became snakes. But then Aaron's staff swallowed theirs whole. In the hood, we truly believe that if you spare the rod (staff, cane, switch/tree branch, belt, cord) you'll spoil the child. Parenting in the hood heavily depends on using the rod with force to discipline children. However, as it relates to the rapper, the true meaning of the symbolic cane is blindness. White canes are used by the blind all over the world. Think about it.

Historically, Hollywood has tried to connect the pimp to the preacher by portraying the preacher as a hustler and slick con man, thus ridiculing the charismatic, powerful voice of the Black Church.

The following compares media stereotypes of the pimp and the preacher. By no means is this an accurate portrayal of black male preachers today. If nothing else, these comparisons show how the black community continues to be under the surveillance of Hollywood.

Category	Preacher	Pimp
Clothing	Designer, expensive	Designer, expensive
Car	Large, expensive	Large, expensive
Hair	Short, neat, long, curled	Neat, long, curled, feminine
Charisma	Natural	Natural
Sexuality	Heterosexual, covert womanizer	Heterosexual, overt womanizer
Language	Hypnotic rhymes	Hypnotic rhymes
Mode of operation	Theology	Pop psychology
Admirers	Women, men	Men, women
Grooming	Impeccable	Impeccable
Character	Spontaneous	Flamboyant
Jewelry	Designer	Designer
Leadership skills	Powerful, respected	Powerful, imitated, intimidating
Relationship with white authority	Threatened, black-mailed, controlled via scandal	Controlled and kept out of prison
Economic status	Doing very well	Well to do
Persona	Charismatic	Charismatic

Hypocrisy 5—The Cross//The Beast

My high school students say that Snoop Dogg's persona fits the above description perfectly. His latest CD projects, *Welcome To Tha Chuuch: Tha Album* and *Boss'n Up* (the first so-called pimp musical), prove their assessment. Ron Isley (Isley Brothers) personifies the pimp style in his Mr. Biggs persona. Gangsta rapper David Banner praised the pimp role with his crunk mega hit, "Like a Pimp." Nelly gave tribute with his hit "Pimp Juice." 50 Cent teamed up with Snoop Dogg and Bishop Don Magic Juan to idolize the lifestyle of pimps in their smash hit "P.I.M.P." I ask you, is this entertainment or entrainment?

Earlier I defined entrainment as the tendency for two separately vibrating bodies to come together so that they vibrate in harmony. Now let's take this idea even deeper. In street psychology, entrainment is when sexually stimulating rap tunes vibrate *against* the normal hormonal, developmental states of children, adolescents, and teens. They are being sexually stimulated *out of phase*, which creates an artificial harmony or resonance with the values and behaviors promoted in commercial gangsta rap.

Let's decode "entertainment."

Enter	=	from the outside to the inside
tain	=	reminiscent of "taint," as in poison or polluted
ment	=	suffix that indicates the act or process of doing something; a state or condition

Thus, gangsta Hip Hop entertainment and entrainment is the process of rap lyrics and video images entering into the body, mind, and spirit and creating an internal condition of poison/pollution. Roman 12:2 says, "And do not be conformed to this world, but be transformed by the renewing of your mind, that you may prove what is that good and acceptable and perfect will of God."

According to Christian scripture, which these rappers appear to represent, we have two choices: either we are conformed to this world, or we are transformed by the renewing of our minds. If you are conformed to this world, then your mind has not been renewed to the things of God—which means it has been entrained to the things of the beast. Gangsta rappers are not serving Christ or the cross; they are serving the beast. Youth who are entertained by gangsta rap 24/7 are being conformed to this world (the beast) through the process of entrainment, and their indulgence in risky behaviors is bearing witness.

blaxploitation

The pimp-rapper fantasy has been the backbone theme for rappers such as Jay-Z, Too Short, Ice T, Biggie Smalls, Big Daddy Kane, Tupac, and many more. In the 1970s, the image of the pimp-hustler was at its height. The leading symbol from that era came from the movie *Superfly*. Hollywood subliminally linked Superfly to the Black Church by naming the main character Priest. The same trick was utilized in the movie *The Mack*. The main character's name was Goldie, in which *God* can be easily found. Goldie was held in high esteem like a false idol or god made of gold. Like Jesus, both Priest and Goldie had disciples who denied and betrayed them. Rent these movies and check out the pimp-preacher similarities for yourself.

the p.i.m.p. cup art project

The 2003 "P.I.M.P." video featuring 50 Cent and Snoop Dogg had a powerful influence on a group of fifth grade black boys I was asked to speak to at an elementary school in Dayton, Ohio. Some were failing their classes, but the most immediate problem I had to deal with was the stealing of Styrofoam cups from the cafeteria. "What do you need Styrofoam cups for?" I asked.

I thought I'd seen everything, but what these boys showed me was one for the books. They had decorated the cups with colored markers and earring studs, and they wrote on them phrases such as PLAYA

4 LIFE, PIMP OF THE YEAR, and DIRTY SOUTH (mind you, they live in the Midwest). In addition to the P.I.M.P. cup art project, many of the young boys put aluminum foil grills over their teeth to imitate the platinum fronts of their favorite pimps and rappers. Several fights had occurred among them over which girls in the school were their hos. The girls didn't even know they were being fought over. Needless to say, I was livid.

Are young boys in school fantasizing about having a future career as a pimp one day? Thanks to gangsta rap, the pimp has become confused with the sexual predator, but we must tell our children that they are not the same. A pimp is an individual, usually a man, who manages the daily work of a prostitute and takes a percentage (if not all) of her earnings. Top pimps on the street have many women working for them.

On the other hand, sexual predators hunt the opposite sex not for love, maybe for money, and definitely for sport. Both pimps and sexual predators leave the community devastated with broken hearts, broken families, STDs, and the perpetuation of the slave master's sick legacy.

I asked the boys, "Where did you get the idea to make a pimp cup and to pretend to be a pimp?" They said they got the idea from rap videos. When I asked which artists influenced them the most, they said 50 Cent and Lil John & the East Side Boyz.

The pimp mindset continues to be highly associated with black male rites of passage. In a stunning move, The Academy of Motion Picture Arts and Sciences, at their 78th Annual Academy Awards, gave an Oscar to Memphis-based rap group Three 6 Mafia for their hit "It's Hard Out Here for a Pimp," from John Singleton's movie, *Hustle & Flow*. Further proof that we must fight to protect our children from the lies of gangsta Hip Hop and mass media.

pimping in the name of God

In the "P.I.M.P." video, 50 Cent stands before the elder pimp to be "blessed" into the pimp game. The meeting is brought to order with the chant, "chuuch, chuuch," another link to the Black Church. The word "preach" is also used in Hip Hop. They need to quit. Even world renowned pimp from Chicago, Pimpin Ken, said, "Pimps need to quit using the word church and using God's name in vain. You cannot lead a whole generation of people astray."[2]

In the pimp game, pimps take on church related monikers, such as Reverend, Angel, Savior, Choirboy, Bishop, Priest, and Preacher. Some monikers have hypersexual, feminine undertones, such as Sugar, Sweet/Sweetness, Candy, Sexy, Chocolate, Pretty Tony, Darling, Cute, Baby, Delicious, Diamond, Little Pearl, Precious, Honey, Love, Tasty, Gorgeous, and Puddin. The more macho street monikers include Big Daddy, Big Papa, Little Pimp, King Pimp, Sugar Daddy, Stud Man, Big Man, Big Dog, Big Balla, Slim, Slick, Dollar Bill, Ice Baby, Mack, Big Time, Big Money, Sir, and Mister. All pimp monikers create an ever-present double consciousness regarding black men.

Snoop Dogg openly pushes the pimp-church connection with his highly publicized relationship with his spiritual adviser, Bishop Don Magic Juan, a former pimp from Chicago. A self-ordained minister with his own reality TV show in the works, Juan allegedly gave up the street pits for the pulpit. Given that Snoop's mother is an ordained minister herself, is this relationship truly spiritual? I'm just raising the question.

sacrilegious hip hop?

According to Stephanie Mwandishi Gadlin,

> "The overall predominant pseudo-religious theme in today's rap music is Christianity. It seems to have replaced popular Islamic doctrine in the late '80s and early 1990s. Lyricists such as DMX, Dead Prez, Leaders of a New School, Brand

Nubian, Nas, Common and the Black Eyed Peas, among many others, have all effectively used religious symbolism in their music."3

In order to keep this section in perspective, it is important to begin with the following scripture from Ephesians 6:10, 12, and 13:

> "Finally, my brethren, be strong in the Lord and in the power of His might. For we do not wrestle against flesh and blood, but against principalities, against powers, against the rulers of the darkness of this age, against spiritual hosts of wickedness in the heavenly places. Therefore take up the whole armor of God, that you may be able to withstand in the evil day, and having done all, to stand."

Pushing religious themes, symbols, and archetypes has become standard practice in the music industry. Remember when blues and jazz were called the devil's music by religious fundamentalists? Heavy Metal has been labeled satanic or devil music. In the hood we said those white boys—Ozzy Ozborne, Black Label Society, Marilyn Manson, Slipknot, Coal Chamber, Six Feet Under—must be crazy. Promotions and stage designs all support claims of satanic worship.

In black culture, religious symbols moved beyond the church, mosque, and temple to Hip Hop when rappers began playing the God and devil cards. Hip Hop artists are going all out, using religious symbols and lyrics to win over and manipulate young fans. Sister Gadlin brilliantly submits the following points:

> "Hell sells! Apparently the mostly young, white and suburban consumer of rap music isn't all that interested in supporting artists that can express something beyond their own subjugation. Thus some Hip Hop activists have launched various campaigns to push conscious rap sales beyond what can be generated by radio and video play. Which leads one

to yet another question: Can music alone save the soul of a generation that often defines itself as 'lost, unloved and abandoned?' As young people grapple with their spiritual identity, cultural critics must be mindful not to pimp even the lowest Hip Hop prostitute. We can condemn and examine the sin, without judging the sinner. In other words don't kill the messenger—unless he's holding it down with a semi-automatic complete with hollow points. Some people will be quick to denounce my observations as religious zealotry. They will undoubtedly say that the Bible itself is full of tales of blood and gore, death and destruction, sexual immorality and persecution and therefore rap music is no different. However, those biblical lessons aren't the end of the story. Holy Scripture is not only designed to present a historical, theological and geographical understanding of God (who is to be worshiped) and the so-called devil (who is to be rebuked), but is first and foremost designed for readers to make a choice between good and evil."[4]

Let's look at some of the psychospiritual symbolic messages created by Hip Hop artists. There are too many to mention, so only a handful of notable rap groups and artists will be discussed.

Cypress Hill. This 20-year veteran Hip Hop group uses graveyards, dark colors, crosses, caskets, gothic letters, skulls, bones, and skeletons to portray melancholic and morbid themes. CD titles include *Till Death Do Us Part*, *Skull & Bones*, and *Black Sunday*. This group is truly focused on the dark side, which should be no surprise considering their name. Unlike the evergreen, which is viewed as a symbol of immortality, the cypress is a tree that represents death and mourning in Western symbolism. In Greek mythology, the cypress is the tree of Hades/hell. In Christianity, the gloomy "god" of hell is Satan. In Roman mythology, the cypress tree was often planted at the top of a hill in a cemetery, connoting life after death. On the inside of the CD covers, Cypress Hill shows half human demons and skeletons. Clearly this group has a death fixation. This is Hip Hop?

Bone Thugs-N-Harmony uses themes from the dark side to push murder, alcoholism, and marijuana consumption. Their name can be decoded follows:

Bone = Death
Thugs = Criminals
Harmony = Union

Perhaps it's the duty of this group to bring death and criminals into union (harmony) with those considered to be devils or demon angels. The group utilizes backward writing on their CDs, forcing the reader to hold the lyrics up to a mirror to read them. This is witchcraft. Like Cypress Hill, Bone Thugs-N-Harmony is pictured on the inside of their *Eternal 1999* CD cover as half human, half skeleton.

Ja Rule. The rapper takes his name from the Rastafarian name for God, which is Jah. Decoded, his name means "God rules," "God has the power," or "God is the controller." This was his label name during his time at Murder Inc. On his 1999 CD, *Ja Rule: Venni Vetti Vecci*, the rapper is seen praying in front of the famous Christ statue in Rio de Janeiro, Brazil. On the cover he sports a shiny Christian cross around his neck.

Ja Rule's song "187 Motha Fucka Baptiss Church" paints the Black Church as a sexual den of sin. In the skit, the pastor's name is Rev. Lust. The deacon shouts out, "That ho bite me," suggesting she was performing oral sex on him in church.[5] Number 187 is police code for homicide; thus the decoded message reads, MURDER THE BLACK BAPTIST CHURCH.

Ja Rule was raised as a Jehovah's Witness. He says,

> "… the religion is so strict, it is very different. I went through a lot of phases and studied many religions—I came to a conclusion: I am not into religion, I am spiritual and

have whatever relationship with God, you do not need the middlemen."[6]

Is Ja Rule serving the beast by symbolically killing the church? Will you trust your children to him?

Hypocritically Ja Rule says he's not into religion, yet he consistently uses Christian symbols and themes. His latest album is entitled *JA Rule–Exodus*. Now he's Moses? What's up with that? If this brotha attacked other faiths the way he strikes out at Christianity, he would never have gotten roles in *Half Past Dead, Scary Movie 3, The Fast and the Furious,* and *Assault on Precinct 13*. He and other rappers hate on Christianity because they know they can get away with it. Unlike the Muslims who protested en masse when the prophet Muhammad was depicted as a cartoon, there are no consequences when Christianity is blasphemed.

The 2002 CD cover for *Ja Rule: The Last Temptation* features the rapper leaning against a church wall. Sunlight streams through a stained glass window. His back, which is turned to the camera, features tattoos of two large golden heads of Jesus and two large Christian crosses. The inside cover features other pictures of a spiritual-religious nature, including Ja Rule being baptized (cleansed) in a lake and Ja Rule holding a giant snake (traditional symbolism for Satan) while wearing the gold Jesus head figures around his neck.

The cover of Ja Rule's *Rule 3:36* CD reads, "He who believes in Ja shall have everlasting love. He who does not shall not see life but the wrath of my vengeance."[7] The writing style mimics the original King James version of scripture, which adds to the confusion. Is this Christianity or not?

It is not. Doesn't Ja Rule know that God declared vengeance as his own (Deuteronomy 32:35)? Is this brotha committing blasphemy or what? His words steal from John 3:36: "He who believes in the Son has everlasting life; and he who does not believe the Son shall not see life, but the wrath of God abides on him." Ja Rule is pictured on the inside cover with his hands in a praying position. This is Hip Hop?

DMX. DMX, which stands for Dark Man X, is another rapper with psychospiritual CD titles: *It's Dark and Hell Is Hot* and *Flesh of My Flesh, Blood of My Blood.* The title of the latter CD comes from Genesis 2:23: "And Adam said: 'This is now bone of my bones and flesh of my flesh; She shall be called Woman, because she was taken out of Man.'"

The cover and inside jacket of *Flesh of My Flesh, Blood of My Blood* features the mother of all rapper religious symbols. DMX is featured covered in blood with his head placed in the middle of the letter M, which serves as subliminal devil horns (or the bent, open legs of a woman). He is shown praying in a bathtub full of blood. He performs a duet ("The Omen") with self-described antichrist superstar Marilyn Manson. DMX ends the CD with a profound song titled "Ready to Meet Him." It's not too difficult to guess who "him" is.

The most disturbing lyrics DMX offers are from his song "Bring Your Whole Crew." They describe a bloody act of necrophilia, or sex with a corpse.

Brothers & Sisters, if your children have this CD, throw it in the garbage right away.

Earl Simmons is DMX's real name. Is DMX an act or is necrophilia what the real Earl Simmons is all about? Why is he putting this out there for impressionable young minds and spirits to absorb? I know "shock and awe" is a common marketing practice, and Hip Hop artists frequently use it. If you want to shock the black community, just say anything devil/beast related. Does this brotha have any limits, conscience, or biblical knowledge? Sexual boundaries are present throughout most spiritual texts, including the Bible. These boundaries are designed by God to protect us from the unseen forces of darkness. Participation in such activities can easily lead to demonic possession.

DMX is rumored to be retiring from the rap game to go into the ministry. Whose ministry would that be? In his song "Let Me Fly," DMX raps about selling his soul to the devil.

"We do not war according to the flesh, for the weapons of our warfare are not of the flesh, but divinely powerful for the destruction of fortresses" (2 Corinthians 10:3–4).

By the way, speaking of the spies among us, in June 2004, Earl "DMX" Simmons crashed his SUV into a gate at Kennedy Airport. He admitted he was on Valium. Forget that in post-9/11, all he got was 60 days for crashing into Kennedy Airport. Guess how he identified himself to the parking lot attendant after the crash? He told him he was an FBI agent.[8] I don't think you heard me. *Earl Simmons got 60 days for impersonating an FBI agent after he crashed into a major international airport located in New York in post-9/11 America.* Of all the things Earl Simmons could have said, FBI agent is the first thing that came to mind. Last time I heard, Valium doesn't make you delusional, just sleepy. Hmmm…

using God & hip hop to sell out

> "For a good tree does not bear bad fruit, nor does a bad tree bear good fruit. For every tree is known by its own fruit. For men do not gather figs from thorns, nor do they gather grapes from a bramble bush. A good man out of the good treasure of his heart brings forth good; and an evil man out of the evil treasure of his heart brings forth evil. For out of the abundance of the heart his mouth speaks" (Luke 6:43–45).

In an ad for Candy shoes, Lil' Kim is barely clothed (as usual). Her arms, which are lifted out to each side, are surrounded by lights that resemble the Christian cross. At the foot of the "cross" are 12 female "disciples" wearing nun habits. Now you tell me, is all that really necessary to sell a pair of shoes? Are they selling us shoes or an abstract message about our sole/soul? The ad is not that difficult to decode.

In an ad that depicts a rapper as a spiritual idol, one of Hip Hop's genuine kings, Rakim, is selling Hennessy cognac. That's right, the king of ghetto yak rhymes is being used to sell alcohol to youth just like Tupac, Biggie, and Snoop Dogg did via their psychospiritual techniques.

In the ad, Rakim appears to be crucified in abstract on a cross like Christ. (Puff Daddy/P Diddy was also featured Jesus-like in one of Nas' videos, nailed to a cross.) Rakim's head is shaved and his eyes are closed. His arms are draped over a microphone stand that lies horizontally across his shoulders. His head hangs downward, suggesting defeat. One of the many messages here could be, "The king of conscious Hip Hop is dead." Rakim is one of the few rappers who barely uses profanity. You'd be hard pressed to find 10 curse words in all of his songs put together. Unfortunately, since his marriage with Hennessy, he used nigga/nigger on a recent CD—a symbol of defeat. The mixed messages are deafening. He understands violence and other problems in the hood, but he fails to recognize the alcohol industry's contribution. This will only serve to confuse young people.

In another ad, a female rapper is depicted sitting on the lap of the beast/devil in the midst of hell. Is this Hip Hop? The caption reads, "Here I Come." The feet and legs on the chair are those of a goat. The rapper's feet rest atop two human skulls. On either side of her are two burning joints, all this amidst flowing lava. And why is she wearing sun glasses? To conceal her identity? It's getting hot in here, Brothers & Sisters!

Nas depicted himself as an Egyptian pharaoh/god on his CD titled *I AM*. I AM translates in both Hebrew and Greek as God (Exodus 3:13–14). Nas also recorded a CD titled *God's Son*. Now which is it? Is he God or is he God's Son, also known as Jesus? In 1999, Nas recorded the *Nastradamus* CD. Nostradamus, born Michel de Nostredame, was a famous seer/psychic who lived during the Middle Ages. So is Nas now saying he's a prophet (a false one)? Are we detecting a theme here? According to the Holy Quran, "He is God, the one and only God. He is eternal, absolute. He begetteth not nor is He begotten and there is none like unto him" (Al-Quaran Ch 112).

The Hip Hop nation should read Matthew 24: 5: "For many shall come in my name saying, I am Christ; and shall deceive many."

Rap idols appear to the have power to resurrect and reincarnate. Tupac Shakur and Christopher "Biggie Smalls" Wallace were two prolific rappers who flirted with both religious and secular themes before their premature deaths some 180 days apart (as in 180 degrees before the cycle/circle was completed). Both had deep insights into life after death.

Biggie Smalls was often pictured wearing a cross around his neck. One photo showed him sitting on a gold throne with a crown of jewels on his head, suggesting he was a priest and/or royalty. Biggie never got the chance to explore his religious beliefs in public, though his *Born Again* CD features him wearing a Jesus head on the end of a gold chain. His *Ready to Die* and *Life After Death* CDs and cover art offered a glimpse into his view of his own mortality.

Tupac's pen often showed his spiritual depth in songs like "Only Fear of Death," "Thug Angel," "Thug Mansion," "Hail Mary," "I Wonder If Heaven Got a Ghetto," "How Long Will They Mourn Me?" "Blasphemy," "If I Die 2night," "Gotta Make It to Heaven," "Only God Can Judge Me," "Ain't Mad at Cha," and "So Many Tears." In "Good Life," Tupac raps that he sold his soul to the devil.

One of the first CDs released after Tupac's death was *Makaveli*. On the cover is an illustration of Tupac being strung up on a cross much like that of Christ. The image and CD concept gave birth to the 2003 soundtrack and motion picture *Resurrection*. Tupac's CD titles also boast psychospiritual themes (*2Pacalypse Now, Me Against the World, Until the End of Time, Still I Rise, It Was Written*).

Islamic hip hop?

Since 9/11, Islam has received nothing but negative press in the U.S. Islam is a one God, monotheistic faith based on the Quran. Islam demands that followers submit to Allah, the Arabic name for God. *Shahadah* (to bear witness that there is only one God, Allah, and that Muhammad is his messenger), daily prayer, annual fasting, giving of alms, and making the holy pilgrimage to Mecca are the cornerstones of the faith.

In the beginning of Hip Hop, there was Islam. No history of Hip Hop can forsake this fundamental truth. The debate is whether rappers who claim to be Muslim are true followers of Islamic law. Possibly a Muslim brother or sister will write that book someday.

Like Christianity, Islam was also snared in the PTBs' wicked net of evil. For example, on the December/January 2003 cover of Russell Simmons' *One World* magazine, Lil' Kim was featured wearing lingerie underneath a burqa. Her waist, legs, and breast were exposed as she stared into the camera with her blue eyes. Whatz up with that? Mr. Simmons follows Eastern spirituality (yoga, Buddhism). Does his faith allow him to disrespect other faiths?

In 1999, Def Jam, the record label founded by Simmons with which he continues to have influence, released the CD *Chyna Doll* by female rapper Foxy Brown. That CD features a sexually explicit track targeted at Islam titled "Hot Spot." This is blasphemous.

It has become a fashion statement within Hip Hop for non-Muslim men to wear kufis, the Islamic prayer caps, the way non-Christian rappers wear diamond-studded crosses. Culturally, Muslims are not driven by materialism or excess sexual behaviors, the main tenets of Hip Hop. For the most part, Islam and Hip Hop contradict, with one heading toward purity and the other toward getting paid.

Islamic and Christian rappers sound alike in part because the two religions grew out of the same Judaic root. The major difference is in how rappers pay respect (or not) to the Almighty. For example, Christian rappers refer to Jesus Christ as JC in their lyrics, but Muslim rappers revere Allah and Islamic concepts. Secular rappers who use Christian symbols blaspheme the faith; Islamic rappers use their faith to deal with injustice, which is the way Hip Hop began. Only time will tell if the forces of evil are successful in destroying positive Islamic influences in Hip Hop as well.

Hypocrisy 5—The Cross//The Beast

the bottom line

Knowing God and playing God are two different things. Many of today's Hip Hop stars seem to have a God complex. For example, Jay-Z has referred to himself in song as "Hova," "Hov," or "Ova." In his 2003 video entitled "Encore," his audience chants "Hova" while making an upright triangle (pyramid) with their hands. "What's the big deal, and how is this a God complex?" you may ask.

Hova/Hov/Ova are taken from Jehovah, which is the Old Testament name for God. In fact, one of Jay's nicknames is "J-Hova." Hello! Only Jay-Z knows what he believes, but the Hova/Hov/Ova link to Jehovah, combined with his new *Kingdom Come* CD make his intensions suspicious.

Many in Hip Hop agree with the Five Percenters (offshoot of the Nation of Islam) that the black man is God (Jehovah) on earth. In Christianity, the upright triangle (pyramid) is symbolic of the Holy Trinity (God the Father, God the Son, God the Holy Spirit). The triangle is the symbol for God in Judaism as well. According to Jay-Z's followers, this is his symbol for dynasty. Symbolically speaking, the fans (followers) of Jay-Z can also be called "Hova Witnesses"—or better yet, sheep. Holla back at me if I'm wrong.

Consider the first and second of the Ten Commandments (Exodus 20 and Deuteronomy 5):
1. I am the Lord thy God: Thou shalt not have strange gods before me.
2. Thou shalt not take the name of the Lord thy God in vain.

I recommend that the brothas and sistas of commercialized gangsta Hip Hop who have set themselves up as gods and priests over Hip Hop youth repent their sinful ways. Repent before it's too late.

hidden messages

(Thanks to Yaves M. Ellis, "The Street Pastor," for contributing the following report.)

After hearing that G. Craig Lewis of EX-Ministries in Texas had found encoded messages in the lyrics and beats of secular artists, I began to do my own research. I had heard of a producer/DJ named DJ Danger Mouse who manipulates songs by mixing old classic records with rappers' a cappella vocals and decided to investigate.

While searching the library, music stores, and Internet, I found DJ Danger Mouse's *The Grey Album*, in which he overlaid lyrics from Jay-Z's *The Black Album* onto samples from The Beatles' *White Album*.

The Grey Album features a song entitled "Interlude." The song startled me because it sounds like a rock band slowly playing backwards, but every once in a while you clearly hear Jay-Z rhyming at normal tempo, "Lord forgive him, he got them dark forces in him" and "I can introduce you to your maker." Remember, Jay-Z calls himself J-Hova.

I wondered why some of the music was playing in reverse and at an altered speed while Jay-Z's lyrics played normally. So I took the CD to the studio and copied the song format (wav file) into Cubase SX 3, a recording software program that lets you record, sequence, and produce a number of medias. My goal was to undo the reversal so that I could hear the lyrics and music clearly.

I processed "Interlude" and reversed the altered song. What I found was alarming.

The song begins with a man saying "six six six," which we know from the Bible is the mark of the beast (Revelations 13:8). Some 30 seconds later, we hear pianos, more decoded sounds, and then a voice we believe to be Jay-Z's saying, "murder murder Jesus," followed again by a man slurring, "six six six."

I don't know if Jay-Z had any knowledge of this remix or if he even said these words in that particular sequence. But I am sure that secret messages were inserted into *The Grey Album*, to be hidden from those who may not try to uncover the true meaning behind the music.

Hypocrisy 5—The Cross//The Beast

Chapter 21

St. Hip Hop

"Next time I'm in the club everybody screaming out (Jesus Walks)/God show me the way because the devil trying to break me down (Jesus Walks)/The only thing that I pray is that my feet don't fail me now."[1] **Kanye West**, "Jesus Walks"

"I feel that the last word is always God, but Pac saved my life. He's my ... Pac saved my life."[2] **Marion "Suge" Knight**

Kanye West has racked up numerous award nominations since his 2004 debut, including 10 Grammys. "Jesus Walks" walked away from the 47th Grammys with Best Song and Best Rap Recording, a long shot for a song that, according to *USA Today*, was destined to never get airplay.[3]

During the 1960s, LSD-tripping hippies worshipped idols of every shape, substance, and rock star. Has Hip Hop likewise become a religion, and are rappers its high priests? Has Hip Hop/Holy Hop reached a level of sainthood in the hood?

Today, the Christian church faces an invasion from the forces of Hip Hop, so this is an important question. Youth and young adults are demanding that the church allow elements of Hip Hop to be infused into church practices and services. Why is it that no other faith faces this challenge?

Over the past four years, I've talked to at least one hundred pastors about Hip Hop's invasion of the church. From my discussions, two disturbing ideas emerged:

1. Hip Hop is becoming a major cult or minor religion.

2. Hip Hop doctrine and beliefs are contrary to orthodox Christianity.

Author Fritz Ridenour, in his book *So What's the Difference?*, says,

> "1 Corinthians 15:3, 4 is a 'plumb line' for measuring the difference between Christianity and other faiths … In one of the shorter books of the Old Testament God says: 'Look, I am setting a plumb line among my people' (Amos 7:8). A plumb line is a tool still used today by masons to make sure they lay up a brick wall straight and true."[4]

And what is this plumb line? That "Christ died for our sins according to the Scriptures, and that He was buried, and that He rose again the third day" (1 Corinthians 15:3–4). The life, death, and resurrection of Jesus form the centerpiece of the faith, and this sets Christianity apart from other religions and belief systems.

Don't be fooled by appearances. Wearing Christian jewelry does not mean you're a Christian. "Beware of false prophets, who come to you in sheep's clothing, but inwardly they are ravenous wolves. You will know them by their fruits" (Matthew 7:15–16). Rappers are the prophets of Hip Hop, and only by their fruit (words, deeds) can we know whether they are false prophets or not. Given Jesus' allegiance to the poor and disenfranchised, a huge diamond-encrusted cross could be a symbol of a false prophet.

Is Hip Hop a mere social movement, or is it a religion or cult?

A religion is "an institution to express belief in a divine power."[5] A cult is "a group of people devoted to beliefs and goals which are not held by the majority of society, often religious in nature."[6]

Hip Hop appears to fit both definitions. It has a system of beliefs and practices, but the beliefs and goals of gangsta Hip Hop are out of touch with most of society as well as mainstream Hip Hop.

As a cult, Hip Hop is most disturbing. Remember the 900 (plus) people in Guyana who followed Jim Jones' order to drink the poi-

Hypocrisy 5—The Cross//The Beast

soned Kool-Aid in 1978? Millions of children, adolescents, and teens around the world are following their high priests and drinking the various poisons rappers love to rap about. The foul images and lyrics of gangsta Hip Hop are just as lethal to spirit, mind, and body as poisoned Kool-Aid.

Hip Hop has included symbols and themes from Christianity, Islam, Judaism, Rastafarianism, Buddhism, Hinduism, the Hebrew Israelites, Five Percenters (Nation of Islam offshoot), and Christian Science in rap lyrics. God is called by many names in the music, including JC (Jesus Christ), Allah, Lord, Creator, Yahweh, Mother-Father God, King, Jehovah, and Jah.

The problem most Christian ministers have is that Hip Hop constantly redefines Christianity with the tenets of other faiths, putting Christian orthodoxy in danger. Christians have always separated right (true) beliefs from various kinds of heresies, and the Hip Hop doctrine is viewed as a heresy.

trust thee not

What does the Hip Hop generation believe? Although Hip Hop recognizes the Bible as sacred, they also believe that many Christian scriptures have been tampered with. Thus they refuse to limit their knowledge to the Bible. Rap takes from the Torah (Judaism), Holy Quran (Islam), and The Book of Coming Forth by Day and the 42 Declarations of Innocence (Egyptian Book of the Dead).

Christian ministers are concerned with performers who seek their own glory. They have a problem with rap performances that serve as entertainment vs. true ministry. What makes Christian Hip Hop hard to trust is its delinquent cousin gangsta rap, which is brutal and profane. Is it only a matter of time before Christian Hip Hop, realizing that "blood is thicker than water," edges back to its gangsta roots, like rapper Ma$e went from rapper to preacher back to rapper with hard core group G-Unit?

Hypocrisy 5—The Cross//The Beast

But Hip Hop asks, "Why should we accept a religion that was handed down by slave owners, kidnappers, murderers, and rapists?" Like Black Nationalists, the Hip Hop generation sees a white Jesus as the symbol of white supremacy.

> "How can Mel Gibson in 2004 make a movie about Jesus the Christ [*The Passion of the Christ*] and no one in the movie be black or a person of color? Mel Gibson knew he had to satisfy the spiritual-psyche of white people and that people of color, especially black folk, are happy with the distortions of the story of Christ in spite of the scriptures. In my opinion, this is a mental disorder invoked by fear. It was common for the slave master to use scripture to frighten black people then and now. Even as free black people all over the world, we still interpret the scriptures via the eyes and culture of Europeans only." **Rev. Dr. Allen K. Blackshear**, Atlanta, Georgia

As the late Dr. Bobby Wright once pointed out, the Ku Klux Kan is primarily a Christian organization. Remember, Pope Pius XI blessed the Italian planes and pilots on their way to bombing Ethiopian men, women, and children.

Today's generation wants church on its own terms. Hip Hop bucks tradition and questions the source of spiritual information. That alone frightens the elders and churchgoers. As a workshop participant said,

> "I had to change my membership to a church that met my spiritual needs. As a 22 year-old, I just couldn't take singing those old hymns slave owners wrote from the late 18th century. It was different before I went to college and became enlightened about black history. Besides, I'm young and I need and want to enjoy the music and the presence of the Lord. I know a lot of young adults who feel the way I do."[7]

What many fail to understand is that Christianity originated in the deserts and cities of northern Africa, now known as the Middle East. Christianity is an authentic African religion. Slave-owning Europeans bastardized the faith by picking and choosing scripture that served their evil goals. Slave-owning Arabs did the same with the Quran. Slave owners did not practice the true Christian faith, and they certainly didn't follow Jesus' lead.

Jesus out the box?

The Black Church has played a significant role in African American culture. In fact, gospel music, a globally recognized art form in its own right, has impacted secular music, including R&B, soul, and Country Western.

The Black Church arose out of the same streets as Hip Hop, and in some respects may have more in common than either is willing to admit. Except for a handful of throwback churches, they both believe that Jesus, Mary, and the angels were black, or at the very least not white. Hip Hop youth aren't afraid to ask the tough questions. They are not a passive generation that will just allow you to whitewash a question. They have no problem with checking your sources. They come armed with research and are ready to debate the major questions facing the Black Church today such as:

- What color is God?
- Is Jesus a black man?
- Why are all the angels white?
- Was Mary, Jesus' mother, an African?
- Why don't white churches fight racism?
- Why does God only bless white people?
- Has there ever been a pope of color?
- Why do black churches still feature white images of Jesus?

The Holy Hop movement wants answers now, not next week. These young members of the faith are black, white, brown—all colors of the human rainbow. Needless to say, many ministers are shaking in their boots.

Ultimately, Holy Hop wants Jesus out the box. Seemingly the church is not ready for that and probably won't be for a long time to come.

hip hop preachers & rappers

Black entertainers who come from the church often struggle with whether to sing secular or sacred music. Some, like Al Green, do both. Rappers are no different. In fact, some have left the stage for the pulpit and the church. Run of Run DMC became a minister. Kurtis Blow, another MC from the 1980s, is presently serving Christ. Kurtis Blow is one of the founders of The Hip-Hop Church at two Harlem, New York, parishes. Christopher "Play" Martin of Kid and Play and Cheryl "Salt" James of Salt-n-Pepa' use God's Word to minister to young people.

For awhile, rapper Ma$e stopped glorifying money, sex, and drugs to rap about respectable and godly topics. After selling millions of CDs, Ma$e became Pastor Mason Betha. He left the rap game because he believed that rap was corrupting young people with sexual and violent lyrics.

Ma$e returned to secular Hip Hop in 2003, but he said he was still a minister. His 2004 comeback tune was "Welcome Back" (from Diddy's *Bad Boy* CD). "Keep It On" encourages girls to not take their clothes off. He has even rapped about tithing.

Then the blacksliding began. In 2005, Ma$e signed with 50 Cent and G-Unit and immediately returned to his former hardcore "Murda Mase" persona. His new singles—"Return of the Murda," "300 Shots" (dissin' former G-Unit member The Game), and "Check Cleared"—are filled with profanity. Ma$e refers to R&B artist and ex lover Brandy as a ho. It seems the prodigal son has left the house again.

Can you say Hip Hop hypocrisy? A few Christian rappers claim Matthew 11:12 as an anchor for their edgy approach ("The kingdom of heaven suffers violence, and the violent take it by force"), but shooting your brother in the back was not what Jesus had in mind.

Ma$e has played into the hands of all those who distrust Christian Hip Hop by returning to a den of sin. He appears on the January/February 2006 cover of *XXL* magazine with the G-Unit family, who look thugged out. Ma$e, the Christian of the group, sports a G-Unit medallion while 50 Cent and another rapper sport Christian crosses. Can you say whatz up?

MC Hammer returned to his church ministry roots as well. Hammer grew up in a religious environment and was no stranger to spiritual endeavors. He is now an evangelist; his shows consist of prayer, preaching, and gospel singing. He can often be seen on Christian television networks like TBN. Will he stay the path, or will money, sex, lies, and videotape pull him back into the sin game? We can only pray for him.

As Hip Hop attempts to merge with Christianity, we must deal with the contradictions that Hip Hop poses for a Christian lifestyle. Despite a wealth of good intentions, be warned: Some Christian Hip Hop artists aren't worth adding to your CD collection. They mix egotistical posturing with violent themes.

shall they overcome?

For many church folk, Christian Hip Hop artists are guilty by association (with gangsta Hip Hop). Christian metal bands had to deal with the same suspicion because of the satanic themes in heavy metal tunes by artists such as Led Zeppelin and ACDC.

Can the Black Church move beyond style to the message of Holy Hop? Bobby Hill, founder of Vanguard Ministries, says, "We often confuse the content and the wineskins. We should be conservative fundamentalists when it comes to content and liberals when it comes to containers."[8]

Hypocrisy 5—The Cross//The Beast

Throughout this book I have criticized how commercial gangsta rap targets children, adolescents, and teens. In Christian Hip Hop, this appeal to youth is actually a blessing. Christian Hip Hop may be the only way to reach youth and make the church relevant to them. Christian rap (carefully selected) can be a good introduction to the social gospel of Jesus preached by Dr. King and others. In this sense, rap is tapping into its original purpose of empowerment and protest against racism, poverty, and other social ills. Like the civil rights movement of the 1960s, Hip Hop needs religion and spirituality to provide a moral compass.

But does the church need Hip Hop to reach youth? Since youth are our future, does the church need Hip Hop for its own survival?

Since Hip Hop is where our children live today, I believe it's better to love Holy Hip Hop than hate on it. The generation gap doesn't need to be any wider than it is right now. Christian rap may be providing the golden opportunity to reclaim our children. Think about it.

holy hip hop here to stay

Christian rap is going the way of gangsta rap—commercialization. Brothers & Sisters, get out your full armor of righteousness because you know what that means. Money, power, and corruption. The church must stay on top of the situation and provide ongoing guidance to young artists who are trying to do the right thing. Check out some of the developments that have occurred over the past few years:

- The *Holy Hip Hop: Taking the Gospel to the Streets* CD received a Grammy nomination for Best Rock Gospel album of 2004. A variety of Christian Hip Hop artists are showcased.
- *Charisma* magazine's May 2003 cover story read, "Get Ready for the Hip-Hop Revolution. The music is loud, and the beats are strong, but Christian hip-hop artists say they're using this unorthodox sound to reach a generation for Christ."

Hypocrisy 5—The Cross//The Beast

- The evangelistic efforts of Youth Entertainment Studios in Norfolk, Virginia, include training youth to produce rap music.
- Christian artists Kirk Franklin and DC Talk were guest performers on stage with Rev. Billy Graham.

These are not necessarily bad developments. Let's just stay on top of it this time to prevent Christian rap from going the way of gangsta rap.

the mandate

"'The medium is just as important as the message,' said Dale Fincher, a Los Angeles-based staff writer and apologist specializing in youth culture and the arts with Ravi Zacharias Ministries. 'The medium can wash out the message,' Fincher said. He emphasized he does not believe Christians can make hard and fast rules about music. But they must be careful not to create one more disposable item with a message that becomes just as disposable. 'A lot of people are good at popular culture, but not at theology,' Fincher said."[9]

Some Christians believe we should not be so quick to embrace a genre of music that represents a culture of violence and profanity. But given the growing list of Christian acts and ministries that cater to Hip Hop youth, the question is not whether or not Hip Hop has a place in the church but how it will be integrated.

The Black Church finds itself caught between a rock and a hard place. If we resist Hip Hop, we risk losing a large and growing membership. If we embrace Hip Hop and its gangsta influence, how do we reconcile the teachings of Jesus with the gangsta theology of getting paid, profanity, hating on women, fornication, and an eye for an eye? This issue is at the heart of what divides traditional worship and the new. Many elders take offense at the loose dress code and language of Hip Hop, but values and behaviors are the greater problems we must deal with.

Some youth ministers have said, "If you can't join 'em, beat 'em." The number of Hip Hop churches is growing. Crossover Community Church (Assemblies of God) in Tampa, Florida, the Universal Fat House in New Jersey (pastored by rapper B.B. Jay), and Church Without Limits in Pickering, Ontario, offer "a variety of classes from DJ-ing to rapping to break dancing."[10]

How do we reconcile the gangsta influence in Christian rap and the theology of Jesus? What would Jesus do? Based on His actions in scripture, I believe Jesus would open his arms to those who have glorified fornication, drugs, and materialism and then welcome them into the fold. He would love them unconditionally.

Then I believe he would say, "Go and sin no more."

Christian Hip Hop must begin to honestly deal with the problems in its own house. It can't just be about getting paid. It must become a force for positive social change.

Christian Hip Hop can no longer allow brethren gangsta rappers to lead young people astray. Jesus said, "Whoever causes one of these little ones who believe in Me to sin, it would be better for him if a millstone were hung around his neck, and he were drowned in the depth of the sea" (Matthew 18:6). Christian Hip Hop must stop apologizing for and being defensive about the evil turn the music has taken. It must take a strong stand against gangsta rap and the record industry for targeting youth with pornographic adult content. Christian Hip Hop must follow Jesus' lead, or it can't call itself Christian.

Christian Hip Hop comes out of a movement that has no trust or respect for elders. I have seen this same attitude among some Christian rappers and Hip Hop ministers. Arrogance and disrespect for elders are against God's law. Throughout scripture God tells us to respect our parents. If you're sick, ask for an elder in the church to pray for you. The church needs the energy of youth, but it also needs the wisdom of the elders. Both must come together to make the body of Christ whole and effective in the world.

the negotiation begins ...

Church tries to get young people to act old. Youth are expected to act like their grandparents and enjoy their grandparents' music. Instead of aggressively countering gangsta Hip Hop, we were busy building mega churches whose arms weren't big enough to take in those who were trapped in the Hip Hop/ghetto matrix.

Youth are sick and tired of playing church. They are tired of going to boring services and hearing what they think is irrelevant information. Young people are searching for ways to escape the sinful spell of gangsta Hip Hop in their own ways, and we were no different back in the day. With their driving beats and lyrical hooks, Christian Hip Hop artists attract youth and young adults who have been entrained to love phat beats. So let the negotiation begin here. Let them have their beats and unique sound. So what if it doesn't sound like "Amazing Grace." The content is what's important. What are they saying about Christ's life and message?

When Kirk Franklin came out with the smash single "Stomp," it was a revelation. Youth could be reached, they just needed music and a ministry they could relate to. Franklin has attracted younger listeners to the gospel message like few others have been able to do.

Is the real issue Hip Hop or fear? Jesus can and will use the least of these to save souls. The church ignored the Hip Hop generation for years, but they are coming home and are knocking at the door to a different beat. The time is now. Will the church embrace the Hip Hop generation or allow them to be led astray by gangsta rappers?

graffiti scriptures?

Every religion has its holy book to record its history and beliefs in writing. Is graffiti the holy book of Hip Hop?

The graffiti writer and aerosol artist find inspiration in everyday ghetto life. The Hip Hop community embraces graffiti because it allows for freedom of speech and self-expression. Presidential candidate Howard Dean commissioned New York graffiti king Keo to tag a wall for his presidential campaign to try and draw Hip Hop votes. It didn't work, but the point was made.

Graffiti, which consists of "tagging" (painting) your name, your group's name, or artwork on public property is nothing new. Graffiti tagging took place during war times with famous slogans such as "KilRoy was here." Graffiti from World War II has even been discovered in Roman catacombs. Some of the earliest and most sophisticated graffiti ever created were the hieroglyphics written by the ancient Egyptians (Africans).

Hip Hop's code of conduct is written on brick walls, viaducts, and billboards throughout the hood. Epitaphs for beloved dead gang members are written there. Art as intricate as that of the most famous European masters describe scenes of poverty and destruction. Lettering (fonts) resemble the gothic lettering of the Catholic Church. Graffiti has long been linked to gangs, vandalism, and all kinds of criminal activity, yet you can't deny the feeling of reverence that permeates.

Most modern graffiti emerged out of inner city African American and Latino gang culture. Just as the church has fractured into many dominations and factions over the centuries, gangs split into different sects, with each promoting its own theology, language, values, rites, and rituals. The most popular street gangs have some form of religious art hidden inside their logos or gang signs. The Jewish Star of David, the Islamic crest, and the Christian cross (upright, sideways, and inverted) all appear in graffiti. There are pitch forks, angel wings, skulls, crossbones, and devil figures. These images create a strong mystique in the consciousness of Hip Hop youth.

Even gang names are linked to deity symbolism: Bloods, Lords, Kings, Prince of Darkness, Disciples, Devils, Hell's Angels, Nation, People, and Folks. The last three names could be arranged to read: "Chosen Folks for the People of God to move a Nation." Also, the Folks, Nation, and People all have sects with the surnames of lords, disciples, and kings.

Hypocrisy 5—The Cross//The Beast

Memorial graffiti murals of rappers Big Pun, Jam Master Jay, Biggie Smalls, and Tupac Shakur appeared in inner cities from New York to Compton. Graffiti is a basic element of Hip Hop culture, and many believe it to be the most authentic and consistent. In fact, some Hip Hop churches offer graffiti contests.

As some youth complain about the difficult language in the Bible, oddly enough, the same complaints are made by adults when they try to read and understand Hip Hop graffiti. The mixture of Latino and African American argots, symbols, and colors makes decoding graffiti difficult. Graffiti can be so complex that most police gang units are required to take a course to learn how to read it.

The influence of the church is starting to have a positive effect on young graffiti artists who are now being hired to create advertisements and script biblical verses on buildings, including some churches. Gospel graffiti has grown over the past decade. Some churches now teach gospel graffiti classes.

In my talks to knowledgeable brothas and sistas about religion and Hip Hop, a friendly argument has emerged regarding which city, coast, or region has the best graffiti. I don't take sides because I've seen graffiti with beauty and deep emotion all over the country.

Hypocrisy 5—The Cross//The Beast

Part 3

Rescuing Our Children

Chapter 1

Redefining the Revolution

By Kevin Britton (©2005)

"If revolution had a movie, I'd be theme music."[1] **Common**, "The 6th Sense"

Whenever I have a chance to speak casually to groups of teens or young adults about Hip Hop music and culture, I like to conduct an informal, admittedly unscientific survey: I ask each person to raise his or her hand if they've heard of Jay-Z, Ludakris, Nelly, Lil Jon, 50 Cent, Jackie-O, and other icons of mainstream, commercially popular rap music.

Not surprisingly, all hands are proudly raised high.

I ask them to keep their hands raised until they hear an artist or group they don't recognize, and I continue with names such as Foreign Exchange, K-OS, Immortal Technique, Zion I, Living Legends, the Hieroglyphics, and Crown City Rockers.

By this time, most (if not all) hands have been lowered, further evidence of the stronghold that mainstream popular culture has on the minds of our children.

The fact that music video rotations and radio station playlists contain virtually no Hip Hop music that can be considered "positive" is hardly a coincidence. During a political era governed by ultra-conservative social values and staunch religiosity, one has to wonder how it's possible that rappers who include overt references to criminal activity, violence, and objectification of women in their lyrics are propelled to superstar/spokesmodel status while others who promote self awareness, political involvement, and spirituality are completely dismissed and eliminated from mainstream popular culture.

Over the course of the last ten years, "cultural hijackers" (ad execs and marketing analysts) have perfected their methods of extracting the spirit and soul from Hip Hop culture and selling it back to us via overpriced, intentionally baggy jeans, plastic basketball shoes, and platinum teeth. The Telecommunications Act of 1996 removed the limitations on the number of stations a single company could own across the country, bringing an end to the programming diversity that only local, community-based music directors could offer. In addition, we've witnessed countless debates about sexuality and violence in Hip Hop culture; we've also seen senate committee hearings, lawsuits, Hip Hop summits, town hall meetings, and useless attempts to boycott an industry that generates more than $10 billion in annual revenue.

It's time to "clear the channel." We cannot change Hip Hop until we change ourselves. Only when we resurrect the wisdom, strength, and beauty of our ancestors within ourselves can we understand that popular music does not, and cannot, shape our reality.

One way to accomplish this shift in thinking is to reinforce the significance of the origins of Hip Hop culture from West African storytelling to South Bronx street parties. If today's young Hip Hop fans understood that rap music once served as the voice for largely disadvantaged and disenfranchised African American and Latino youth, then perhaps they would recognize its current potential as a vehicle for political commentary and social change. Fortunately, in our Hip Hop elders, we have a living blueprint for re-creating this cultural phenomenon. Pioneers such as Afrika Bambaataa, Kool Herc, Grandmaster Flash, Run-DMC, Public Enemy, Rakim Allah, Richie "Crazy Legs" Colon, and others should be considered generals in the battle for the minds of our children.

In many ways the current state of Hip Hop culture is analogous to the popular Matrix trilogy. And while we have no Neos, there are plenty of "agents" who are prepared to die in order to protect the grand illusion (i.e., the "get rich or die trying" mentality) that the creators of this matrix feed to our children on a daily basis. Interestingly, the trilogy makes references to an underground city called Zion, where freedom fighters attempt to hack into the Matrix's reality-altering signal. How fitting is it that most of today's positive, socially-relevant music is also underground?

Though you would never know it by watching BET or eMTyV (as revolutionary Hip Hop pioneer Chuck D has called it), there are scores of artists rocking mics and raising consciousness well below mainstream media's radar screen. Lyrics about education, responsible sexual behavior, raising our children, and respecting the women in our lives can be found within songs representing the often overlooked positive Hip Hop movement.

While the evening news is quick to lead with headlines about heated exchanges and escalating violence between rival rap groups, you'll never hear about the annual Black August Hip Hop Concert series featuring nationally known artists such as Mos Def, Talib Kweli, Saigon, Jean Grae, and others. We've heard quite a bit about the growing number of new HIV/AIDS cases within the African American community; yet we hear little about Common's "Knowing is Beautiful" AIDS awareness campaign. It's not likely that conservative talk show hosts will discuss how grassroots organizations such as the Third Eye Movement and Ricanstruction use Hip Hop music and culture as a conduit to promote critical thinking and community/political involvement. Nor is it likely that national retail music chains will carry (or prominently display) CDs by positive artists like Philadelphia's Hezekiah, Oakland's Mystic, LA's One.Be.Lo., or the Texas-based Strange Fruit Project.

Now is the time to bring positive artists such as these to the forefront of Hip Hop culture. Once we begin supporting positive, independent music that reflects our worldview, the monopoly that a few media companies and record labels have over our airwaves will not be able to compete with the voice (and choice) of the people.

Not long ago, as I was browsing for CDs at an independent music store, a man who appeared to be in his mid-to late-50s approached me and asked for my help with choosing several current Hip Hop releases. He was interested in purchasing only positive, socially-relevant music by artists similar to Gil Scott Heron and The Last Poets.

A friend in his early 20s recently told me that he grew tired of the negative lyrics and images promoted by gangsta rap CDs. He's traded them in and now purchases only positive Hip Hop, neo-soul, and classic jazz.

I know a young mother who actively engages her teenaged daughter in discussions about how women are portrayed in popular rap songs and videos.

And speaking of girls, my four-year-old daughter asked me to explain what a Nubian was after listening to a verse from a Watusi Tribe CD.

Imagine, a child learning about African history and culture from a rap song!

The redefinition has begun.

Chapter 2

Hip Hop Survival

"Brother, brother, brother, there's far too many of you dying."[1] **Marvin Gaye**, "What's Going On"

Survivor, the hit "reality" TV show, puts contestants in remote locales with no food or water and expects them to survive the elements and each other. Sounds like life in the hood, doesn't it?

This chapter is a guide to surviving the Hip Hop/ghetto matrix, which can be a jungle sometimes. Hip Hop youth—in fact, all youth—believe they're invincible, and middle-aged rappers won't tell them the truth. When was the last time you saw a rapper driving a Rolls or Ferrari with his seatbelt on? Even beyond alcohol, tobacco, drug abuse, and unprotected sex, youth take unnecessary risks. Many of the accidents that occur during the pre-teen and teenage years, as well as the sicknesses and diseases that manifest during the adult years, can be prevented.

Brothers & Sisters, share this chapter with all the young people you know and love. You may save a life.

survival eating

(Thanks to Valerie E. Robinson, who contributed "Survival Eating.")
Survival eating has been the focus in the African American community, and minimal attention has been paid to the nutritional value of foods purchased or eaten. More than 60 percent of African Americans are overweight, compared to 54 percent of the general U.S. population. As of 2003, African Americans are 13 percent of the population in America but have twice the incidence of diabetes and heart

disease as that seen in adult Caucasians. Obesity is killing blacks in epidemic proportions. An estimated 77 percent of black women are overweight, and 49 percent are considered obese. Black men are 60 percent overweight while an estimated 20 percent are obese.

We know that something is wrong with our youth when we see them wearing clothes that reveal bodies that are overweight, obese, and underweight. Our young women between the ages of 12 and 18 are wearing garments that show very large breasts and mid sections (stomachs) that hang over their pants or protrude through their clothing. They walk very slowly and are quickly out of breath due to not being in shape. Some appear to be puffy and congested with unhealthy toxins. Our young men are either overweight or underweight. We see many of them wearing layers of clothing two or three sizes too big. Beneath the clothes are usually unhealthy bodies.

What and how our youth eat on a daily basis is called survival eating. Many of our inner-city youth live in households where there is only one parent who is providing all of their basic needs, shelter, clothing, and food. Many of these single run households are maintained by one paycheck.

The parent is usually too tired from working all day to cook on a daily basis and will allow the children to eat whatever they can find or purchase from the neighborhood carryout or McDonald's.

There are many survival stories of single parents purchasing McDonald's for breakfast (Egg McMuffins, pancakes) on the way to school, providing children with money for lunch at a local carryout or school lunch store (steak and cheese sub sandwich with French fries or chips and soda). Dinner is the neighborhood Chinese carryout (fried chicken wings with French fries and mumbo sauce with a soda). Our children don't consume enough water. Some teenagers inform me that they can't recall if they honestly consume eight glasses of water per day.

The child is then bombarded with messages from television and billboards of unhealthy snacks (cookies, candies, potato chips, cakes and pies, ice cream, pizza, etc.). Black prime time television contains

60 percent more food and beverage commercials, more images of candy and soda, and more obese characters than general prime time television, report researchers at the University of Chicago Children's Hospital in a study presented at the joint meeting of the Pediatric Academic Societies and the American Academy of Pediatrics.

This cycle takes place on a daily basis in many of our households. The Sunday meal at Grandma's house is probably a cultural, traditional meal that is greasy, fattening, overcooked and has excessive sauces. Portion control is not encouraged. This is where the cycle of overweight and obesity is started and maintained within the black community.

As a people, we have learned to use food as a symbol of wealth and power. We celebrate birth and death with it, and we even medicate ourselves with it. Food is used as a coping tool by people caught in the cycle of poverty. African Americans convey love through food. Meals and times of breaking bread are avenues of socialization in African American families and communities.

Our children are being set up for serious health risks before they reach young adulthood. We are seeing hypertension, strokes, type two diabetes, and higher incidences of weight related arthritis in the knees and ankles. According to research, many are predisposed to obesity and other health risks that can be prevented. If the cycle of overweight and obesity is not addressed with practical solutions, this generation will bombard our healthcare system and funeral homes.

The recommended dietary guidelines for Americans to combat overweight and obesity include a healthy assortment of foods, including vegetables, fruits, grains, especially whole grains, fat-free or low-fat milk products, fish, lean meat, poultry, and beans.

The American food guidelines further emphasize the importance of choosing foods that are low in saturated fat and added sugars most of the time and, whatever the food, eating a sensible portion size. It is also recommend that everyone be more active throughout the day and get at least 30 minutes of moderate physical activity most, or preferably all, days of the week.

Our youth should become more active in their daily routines. Participate in activities that will cause the use of the physical body versus sedentary activities (computer games and cable television).

It may surprise youth to know that some of their favorite Hip Hop superstars are vegetarians. They know the importance of good health—despite the fact that they often rap about consuming things that are not healthy for you. Some rappers are good at making their lies sound like the truth as it relates to the Hip Hop diet. Consider the following: Nelly's Pimp Juice contains the same vitamins B-6, C, and B-12 you can get by eating an orange. Rapper Ice T's Liquid Ice contains 66mg of caffeine and is loaded with sugar. Can you say buzz-ville? Red Bull is quite the rage on the Hip Hop scene, but with only vitamins B-6 and niacin, it contains little to no nutrients. Piranha has guarana, which is a stimulant guaranteed to cause your heart to race. Blue OX energy drink has 25 grams of sugar. A natural cure for a sweet tooth would be delicious fresh fruits.

a smile to die for

"Got 30 down at the bottom, 30 mo at the top
All invisible set in little ice cube blocks
If I could call it a drink, call it a smile on da rocks
If I could call out a price, let's say I call out a lot
I got like platinum and white gold, traditional gold."[2] **Nelly,** "Grillz"

Teenagers, young adults, and some grown folk, too, line up at the mall like children eager to have their picture taken with Santa Claus to get removable grillz (fronts) into their mouths. Perhaps they want to look like their favorite rappers, Paul Wall, Nelly, Lil Jon, Master P, and Trick Daddy. Gold and platinum grills are popular within Hip Hop right now, and some are easy and cheap to get. But be warned: you get what you pay for.

In the late 1990s, gold and platinum went from around the necks of gangsta rappers and Hip Hop youth to inside their mouths. Radio One gives out a "Dirty" award each year to rappers with the best grills (no joke). Some rappers probably have more money in their mouths than in their bank accounts. Reportedly, rappers David Banner and Lil Jon spent $25,000 (plus) on their oral jewelry.

During the blues and jazz era, entertainers who had gold and sliver teeth were considered the coolest of the cool, the hippest of the hip. Metal teeth were, and continue to be, a status symbol.

Hollywood and the media show thugs, pimps, prostitutes, criminals, and black men with shiny gold and sliver teeth. In movies, the bad guy often sports a silver tooth. Now Hip Hop artists are conforming to the stereotype in their videos.

Wait before you hate. Rappers and Hip Hop youth have the right to wear grills and diamond-studded teeth, but they should know about the negative connotations they carry. Youth wearing grills will not be hired to run IBM, no matter how smart they are.

Wearing grills can also be hazardous to dental, overall physical, and mental health. State Representative Joe Heckstall (D-Atlanta) proposed a bill that would require merchants who fit customers for grills to have a dental license. Heckstall told the *Atlanta Journal-Constitution* that it is unsafe for an unlicensed person to do the procedure.[3]

The human body generally does not tolerate metals well. Gold, platinum, and titanium are the best tolerated, but

> "... all other metals should be strictly avoided as they have many toxic effects when accumulated in the body. Combinations of metals in restorations generate weak electrical currents in the mouth because of their constant contact with saliva, an excellent electrolyte. These weak currents are stronger than the electrical fields generated by the brain and in some people lead to mood and personality changes."[4]

I interviewed Dr. Llaila Afrika, author of *Nutricide and Holistic Health,* about this issue because our children are so fascinated by bling bling teeth that they do not consider the dangers of wearing foreign metals in their mouths. Dr. Afrika said that youth in the hood are purchasing what amounts to unregulated costume jewelry that may have been manufactured with trace amounts of lead by-products. Poisoning from lead by-products can cause permanent brain and bone damage, depression, aggressive behavior, and low sperm count in men.

Q. Dr. Afrika, I often see young men put their grills in their pockets, only to put them back into their mouths without washing the grills or their hands. What do you want them to know?

A. The mouth is a breeding ground for germs, and dirty grills increase the chances of infection. Grill wearers tend to get small cuts in their gums when they remove the grills quickly and frequently. Putting grills on the nightstand before going to sleep allows moisture from the saliva to contribute to rust and mold.

Q. Is there any danger with covering or capping the teeth?

A. Capping or covering the teeth denies the teeth and gums of much needed oxygen. Youth whose teeth haven't matured should never wear grills because the grills place extra weight and stress on the teeth and gums, in time causing them to weaken, shift, and bleed. Another issue is the food, plaque, and tartar that get trapped underneath the grills, which contributes to tooth decay and halitosis.

Q. Are you at risk when you allow a non-dentist to place anything into your mouth, specifically foreign metals like gold and platinum?

A. Yes, they are trying to make a sale. It's their job to say they are safe, but they are not dental hygienists. They are giving you prefab grills, but one size doesn't fit all. After you try one on and decide you don't like the fit, what do you assume they do with it? They just wipe it off and put it back until the next buyer comes along. There are no laws to regulate these products. In rare occasions, platinum and gold in the mouth have been linked to asthma, blurry vision, sinusitis, allergies, migraine headaches, and other symptoms in people who suffer from chemical or metallic sensitivities. No one in the mall will warn you of these rare but real medical possibilities.

Q. What about the quality of the gold or platinum used to make the grills?

A. Superstar rappers can afford to buy real metals that have been medically treated and custom made for $1,000 and up. If something goes wrong, they can afford the best dentists and doctors. The average teen is purchasing removable grills made from cheap scrapes surrounded by rhinestones ranging from $29.95 to $300.

Q. What should parents be aware of?

A. Consider that these things have been sitting in a plastic bag under a bright lamp; that combination alone can be deadly. The toxicants from the heated plastic bag are now integrated with the cheap metal by-products.

Q. Any parting tips to pass on to the village?

A. Just a few:

- Don't do drugs anyway, but especially don't take the designer drugs Sextasy or Ecstasy while wearing a grill. These drugs cause people to grind their teeth. The pressure from the grinding could cause the rhinestones or cheap glass to break and be ingested into the body.
- Use soap and warm water to clean your grill. Don't clean your grill with isopropyl alcohol or jewelry cleaner.
- Don't wear a grill if you have mercury fillings. Grills can scrape off mercury particles from the fillings and can cause problems.
- Don't smoke anyway, but especially when wearing a grill. The intense heat produced by cigarettes (tobacco and marijuana), cigars, and pipes may cause the cheap grill metals to chemically react and create toxicities in your body.

- If you must wear grills, limit it to about two or three hours a day and never sleep with them on overnight.
- Treat grills like your toothbrush. Get rid of them after 90 days.

driving under the influence of hip hop

"You can't drive down the street nowadays without having to blow your car horn just to have the young people move their cars. They stop and hold conversations in the middle of the street with their friend who is also stopped on the other side, heading in the opposite direction. If you dare ask them to hurry and move, they give you the dirtiest look. These are the same young people who take up two parking slots when they park." **Retired African American teacher** (67 years), Dayton, Ohio

Driving Under the Influence (DUI) and Driving While Intoxicated (DWI) are well known, and now there is Driving Under the Influence of Hip Hop (DUIHH). DUIHH is seasonal here in the Midwest. On the first day of nice spring weather after a long and snowy winter, it's on.

On the main strip you'll find young people driving Hip Hop style. This includes:
- Weaving in and out of traffic.
- Driving while talking on a cell phone.
- Playing bass-thumping music so loud the truck shakes.
- Sitting so low in the driver's seat it appears the car is driving itself.
- Watching a small TV built into the dashboard while driving.
- Hanging feet out of the windows.
- Hitting the switches, causing the vehicle to bounce up and down.
- Last but not least, smoking dro/weed with a 40 on the seat.

Unlike Driving While Black (DWB), these folk are rarely stopped by the po po. Driving under the influence of Hip Hop can be as intoxicating as alcohol—and as dangerous. Amazingly, there are always passengers in the car enjoying the foolishness. I have lost far too many student athletes to DUIHH. We must teach young people that a car mishandled can become a weapon and a casket. Cars are not toys. Or as we say, "Drive to arrive."

spinners & dubs get luv

"I'm a neighborhood trend setter, getting that cheddar
Nobody does it better, I'm a cash money go-getter
Looking clean riding spinners, on these Lone Star streets."[5]
Paul Wall, "Know What I'm Talkin' About"

My son (18 at the time) informed me of the unwritten rule as it relates to whips (cars) in the hood. He said, "Spinners and dubs get a brotha luv [love], kisses, and hugs. That's why a brotha got to keep his wheels clean. Now pass me the Armorial, Pops."

Rappers love to buy all kinds of spinning, sparkling, singing rims for their tires. The flashier, the more expensive, the better. Brothas in the hood buy rims, too, but at what price? They can't pay rent or child support, but somehow they find the cash to buy their car jewelry.

Wait before you hate. I'm talking from experience. My wife and I have rescued our share of female family members and students who were struggling to pay for baby and educational expenses while the boyfriends, who never seem able to help out beyond bringing an occasional birthday gift, somehow manage to buy tire rims and other car toys.

Custom-made dubs/spinners are made here in my hometown of Dayton, Ohio, by the Dayton Wheel Products company. This company has put us on the Hip Hop map. I've witnessed students risk being late for class just to run to the parking lot to check their tire rims.

On any given day, you can see young men in the waiting room of Dayton Wheel Products with the impatience of an expectant father. They drive their new baby out of the shop with tender loving care. I've watched them drive through the hood, proudly showing off their new wheels/babies.

Unfortunately, the arrival of spinners to Dayton also brought violence like wheels spinning out of control. Young people in the hood understand that their wheels can attract the wrong crowd, so they carry weapons to protect themselves. Dubs/spinners have become a target for thieves, which have led to assaults and occasionally death in cities across the nation. Within Hip Hop, dubs/spinners are to die for, literally. Dubs, blades, shoes, sneakers, and Twinkies (street slang for custom wheels) are status symbols made popular by athletes and gangsta rappers. Spinners are always featured in Hip Hop videos and are the subject of rap tunes, like the following popular staple in our locker room:

> "I'm ridin' spinners, I'm ridin' spinners, they don't stop
> I'm ridin' spinners, I'm ridin' spinners, I'm rollin'
> Pedal to the metal then STOP *[Brakes]*
> Take another sip from the syrup then STOP *[Brakes]*."[6]
> **Three 6 Mafia**, "Ridin' Spinners"

buckle up

> "Buckle up means I love you, buckle up means I really care
> Buckle up means I love you, buckle up means you're a friend."[7] **Alfred "Coach" Powell**, "Buckle Up"

In our rites of passage classes, Marlon Shackelford and I ask young men to view the driving scenes in rap videos. What do they notice?

"The whips and girls were sharp."

"They were smoking blunts."

"The music was loud."

"The driver wasn't looking at the road."

In every class they miss the most important thing: no one—drivers nor passengers—in rap videos wear safety belts. Driving Hip Hop style is high risk. In 2001, 16.1 percent of African American teens said they rarely or never used a safety belt as a passenger, compared to 13.6 percent of white teens and 14.5 percent of Hispanic teens. Even though African American and Hispanic male teens drive fewer miles than white male teens, they are twice as likely as whites to die in a crash.[8] This is why I say to our rites of passage group, "I once knew a dude whose name was Cool. He looked like you. He refused to wear a safety belt, and all they found were his shoes."

Motor vehicle crashes are the leading cause of death for people 15 to 24 years old in the U.S. In 2001, 68 percent of 18-to 34-year-old male vehicle passengers who were killed or severely injured in crashes were not wearing safety belts. Fifty-four percent of the women 18 to 34 years old who were killed or severely injured in crashes were not buckled up.[9]

Our youth are dying because they want to look cool and because they feel invincible. Only a fool is willing to die for the sake of looking cool. All we need to do is buckle up and respect the rules of the road. Demand that your driving teens buckle up, or take away their driving privileges.

gun play

"Brotha, brotha, you said you were out to have some fun
Why in the hell did you bring a gun?
Don't go to your grave no slave."[10] **Alfred "Coach" Powell,**
"Why Did You Bring a Gun?"

People love to tell me, "Guns don't kill people, people do." But life in the hood is not a chicken or egg question. Here parents cry to the beat of gun shots. The Hip Hop persona was born with a gun in its hand. Gangsta rap videos and mainstream media constantly hype the connection between gun play and Hip Hop. Rappers on CD covers and magazines are always toting guns or pretending to. Hip Hop loves guns, and gun makers and sellers love Hip Hop.

The gun is by far the most romanticized weapon in rap music. Ice Cube rapped,

> "Just like a jimmy hat's used for protection
> I use my nine when suckers start to flexin
> Cause if you run up and try to play mine
> I'd rather have a A.K. than a f**king canine."[11]

And who will ever forget "It Was a Good Day" also by Ice Cube:

> "Drunk as hell but no throwin up
> half way home and my pager still blowin up
> today I didn't even have to use my A.K.
> I got to say it was a good day."[12] **Ice Cube**, "It Was a Good Day"

Black males die of hand gun violence more than any other group. Gun play took out legendary rappers Tupac and Notorious B.I.G., among many others. Among 10 to 24 year olds (prime Hip Hop years), homicide is the leading cause of death for African Americans, the second leading cause of death for Hispanics, and the third leading cause of death for American Indians, Alaska Natives, and Asian/Pacific Islanders.[13]

To avoid violence, teach children how to:
1. Stay in situations that are violence free.
2. Avoid circumstances likely to be violent.
3. Learn healthy ways to express anger.
4. Understand that guns and poverty equal death.
5. Recognize actions and words that trigger anger.
6. Be an active listener; try to understand what the other person is saying.

7. Think of peaceful ways to resolve arguments.
8. Handle conflict so they can manage it better as adults.
9. Seek professional help if they can't work out problems.[14]

act like you know

If I had a dollar for the times I've heard a parent or teacher say to Pookie and Peaches, "You better act like you know!" I'd be rich. If I just had a nickel for the times I've said it myself. I have no idea who invented the catchy phrase, but it works.

The following "act like you knows" should be mastered by young people to survive day-to-day life in the hood.

- When a fight breaks out at school or a party, *act like you know* and run in the opposite direction. Never run to trouble!

- If someone is smoking dro/dope in the car, *act like you know* and get out ASAP. Not only will you get a second hand (contact) high, if you're stopped by the police you may get arrested as an accomplice, even if you're not smoking. Use your cell phone and call somebody to pick you up.

- Brothers, listen up: if you're in a car with a known gang banger and he pulls into a bank parking lot, places a ski mask on his head, tucks something into his waist, then says to you, "I'll be right back," please *act like you know*. Don't stick around.

- If the police officer tells you to freeze, *act like you know* and do what he says.

- If your friend takes money out of the offering tray at church, *act like you know* and pray a special prayer for her.

- If your friend doesn't have a drivers license and picks you up in a car that has a screw driver in the column (because the car is stolen), *act like you know* and get out of the car. You don't want to get arrested as an accomplice.

- Brothers & Sisters, if he/she leaves someone else for you, *act like you know* and move on before it happens to you.

- Sisters, if you're dating a guy in school and he keeps forgetting your name, *act like you know* and move on.
- Brothers, if on a first date the girl asks if you love her because she loves you, *act like you know* and move on.
- Sisters, if the guy pressures you to have sex and you are faithfully committed to remaining a virgin until marriage, *act like you know* and move on.
- Brothers & Sisters, if after sex you say to yourself, "How did this happen? I don't know how it happened. It just happened!" then *act like you know* and make sure you don't put yourself in a situation for it to happen again (that is, until the time is right).
- Sisters, if your date keeps begging for a little some'n some'n, *act like you know* and tell him he's getting noth'n noth'n.
- Brothers, if the girl keeps grilling you on your bank balance, your cash stash, and what kind of car you drive, *act like you know* and move on from the golddigger.
- Brothers, if you think *no* means *yes*, go to a dictionary and *act like you know*. No means NO!
- Sisters, if you ask your date about his faith and he says, "I don't listen to Faith since Biggie Smalls died," *act like you know* and go home.
- Sisters, if you ask your boyfriend what he got on his ACT test and he says, "I don't like to act, I keep it real yo," *act like you know* that he won't be a brain surgeon and make a wise decision to move on.
- If your ex asks you to appear on Jerry Springer or Maury Povich with them, *act like you know* and say no—unless you want your business on national TV!
- If you have a crush on a person who is overweight and you think he or she is good looking, please don't say, "I think you're PHAT." *Act like you know* that phat sounds like fat and this is an insult.

- If you give your number to someone and she doesn't call or return your phone calls, *act like you know* and leave her alone.
- Sisters, if your boyfriend hits you, promise yourself he will never do it again. *Act like you know* and press charges.
- Parents, if your child comes home in new gear and shoes you didn't buy and has money but no job, *act like you know* and handle your business.
- If your parents warn you that if you act a fool in school they will too, *act like you know* and chill out.
- Parents, if your daughter is a pre-teen or teenager with a boyfriend you have never met, *act like you know* and handle your business.
- If you notice your friend is giving away personal items and cracking jokes about suicide, please *act like you know* he is depressed and get help.
- Students, school is your job. *Act like you know* that you can't afford to be fired from your J.O.B.!
- If friends joke about bringing guns to school, *act like you know* and TELL SOMEBODY.
- If your school tells you to never come back, *act like you know* and get your act together.
- If you're getting high before, during, and after school, *act like you know* and get help today.
- If you're a bully and your victim finally says to you, "It would be in your best interest to not bully me ever again," it's best that you *act like you know* that he has just snapped. Better leave him alone.
- If you need someone to read this book to you, *act like you know* and find someone to teach you how to read. Illiteracy is no joke!
- Sisters, if you love rappers who call females degrading terms, *act like you know* how to get some self-esteem and put on a song that treats you like a queen.

- If you're tempted to call someone a nigger/nigga, dogg, bitch, or ho, *act like you know* and resist temptation. We are calling on all Africans of goodwill to never call a brotha or sista out of their name again.

Chapter 3

SugarStrings: Music Education for the Hip Hop Generation

By Donna Marie Williams

"When the music changes, so does the dance." **Nigerian Proverb**

"When I auditioned for my high school band the band director was excited because my father was known to be a great musician. When he heard me, he said 'Are you sure you're Ellis's son?'" **Wynton Marsalis**

"Music can change the world." **Ludwig Van Beethoven**

We know that gangsta rap stimulates the emotions of young people in often negative ways, but what if there was a way to use children's innate love of music to stimulate and enhance higher emotions, cognitive functions, academic performance, and overall self-worth?

Music is a core academic subject of the No Child Left Behind Act of 2002 (Title IX, Part A, Sec. 9101-11)—yet, drastic reductions in funding for music education in public schools across the country are wiping out music and other arts programs. For example, in California, there has been a 50 percent decline in the percentage of students in music education programs, from 18.5 percent in 1999–2000 to 9.3 percent in 2003-2004.[1]

Music programs have been virtually wiped out in urban areas. It may be a stretch to correlate this void with escalating drop out rates and low reading and math scores on national tests, but I believe it is one important risk factor among many that conspire against African American children.

A close friend lives in an affluent suburb, and her daughter attends public school there. Beginning in kindergarten, assemblies are filled with music and students singing. In fourth grade, students are encouraged to join the school choir. Both band and orchestra are offered to fifth grade students; wind, string, and percussion instruments are brought in so students can learn about each one and then choose the one they like the best. Thanks to an aggressive district-wide grants writing program, the cost of instruction is minimal. Parents only pay for books and instrument rental. Those who cannot afford to pay can receive support.

Compare my friend's experience to my own. I've had to beg and borrow to pay for private lessons for my daughter. Why? Because in the inner city, except for a handful of progressive schools, there is no such thing as music education. Students might sing the national anthem and/or "Lift Every Voice and Sing," but that's about it. Music education has been virtually dismissed from public schools. As a result, all our children know is what they hear on the radio. I give the U.S. Department of Education, state education departments, and urban school districts an F for this scandalous state of affairs.

Like any other African American teen, my daughter loves rap, but she has also been exposed to a wide range of musical genres through her music training and concert outings. She actually enjoys listening to classical, jazz, and gospel music.

In the suburb where my friend's daughter began her love of music, the tax base and aggressive grants writing program provide funding for music and other arts programs. In urban school districts, the tax burden can be equally high but the will and dedication to funding arts programs don't seem to exist. Individual schools must raise funds on their own for arts instruction. In impoverished communities, schools are trying to meet basic academic and safety needs. Music is not seen as a necessity, so mostly it goes to the back burner.

Yet, we must find a way because music *is* a necessity. Music can become an effective antidote to low academic performance and student behavioral problems. Our brains are wired for music. We marvel at our children's ability to sing songs from beginning to end with rhythmic, lyrical, melodic, and harmonic perfection. Without an appreciation for music theory, music performance, and different musical genres, a vacuum has been created in our child's lives—and negative gangster rap has rushed to fill the void. We can't complain about gangster rap without being prepared to replace it with music instruction and quality music choices.

If we want African American children to improve reading and math scores on national tests, music education is a no brainer.

- In 2001, students participating in music scored higher on the SATs than students with no arts education. Students with coursework/experience in music performance scored 57 points higher on the verbal and 41 points higher on the math than did students with no arts participation. Students in music appreciation scored 63 points higher on verbal and 44 points higher on the math than did students with no arts participation.[2]

- A study of 237 second grade children used piano training and newly designed math software to demonstrate improvement in math skills. The group scored 27 percent higher on proportional math and fractions tests than children that used only the math software.[3]

- A University of California (Irvine) study showed that after eight months of keyboard lessons, low income second graders went from scoring in the 30th to the 65th percentile on the Stanford 9 Math Test. Second graders were performing sixth grade math![4]

- The best engineers and technical designers in the Silicon Valley industry are, nearly without exception, practicing musicians.[5]

- Physician and biologist Lewis Thomas found that 66 percent of music majors who applied to medical school were admitted, the highest percentage of any group. For comparison, 44 percent of biochemistry majors were admitted.[6]
- A study of 7,500 university students revealed that music majors scored the highest reading scores among all majors including English, biology, chemistry, and math.[7]
- In an analysis of U.S. Department of Education data on more than 25,000 secondary school students, researchers found that students who report consistently high levels of involvement in instrumental music over the middle and high school years show "significantly higher levels of mathematics proficiency by grade 12." *This observation holds regardless of students' socioeconomic status.*[8]

Music education can have a positive impact on the behavior of Hip Hop students as well.

- Secondary students who participated in band or orchestra reported the lowest lifetime and current use of all substances (alcohol, tobacco, illicit drugs).[9]
- According to statistics compiled by the National Data Resource Center, students who can be classified as "disruptive" (frequent skipping of classes, times in trouble, in-school suspensions, disciplinary reasons given, arrests, and drop-outs) total 12.14 percent of the total school population. In contrast, only 8.08 percent of students involved in music classes meet the same criteria as "disruptive."[10]

Even with budget cuts, music *must* be reincorporated into schools, or we'll have to deal with another generation of technology-driven music vs. skills-driven music. The ideal would be to provide choir, music theory, and instrument instruction for band and orchestra. Schools lacking the commitment and/or resources still have no excuse to ignore this most important program. The Singing Schools of Hungary prove that schools with no budget for music education can still incorporate music into the curriculum. A Zimbabwe proverb says, "If you can walk you can dance. If you can talk you can sing." Anyone can open their mouths and sing a tune.

I know from my own years of studying piano that music creates discipline, a sense of responsibility, and mastery, which contributes to self-esteem. Interestingly, I wasn't great in math during my elementary and high school years, but in college, that part of my brain just seemed to turn on, which was a pleasant miracle. I think piano lessons, daily practice, recitals, and singing in the high school choir had something to do with it.

the case of sugarstrings

What is SugarStrings (www.sugarstrings.com)? you may ask. In 2004, my two sisters and I brought together our young daughters, who were then Suzuki method students in violin, viola, and cello, into a classical music trio to experience the joy of harmonizing with family. Soon requests to perform began to pour in from churches, schools, and organizations, and SugarStrings was born. Other talented African American children have performed with the cousins as well.

I include the SugarStrings story here because we parents believe that music education and stage performance have contributed to our children's high academic performance, self-esteem, and self-confidence. Mira (8 years, violin and viola) earned straight 8 and 9 stanines on the Iowa Test of Basic Skills. Adé (9 years, violin) is home schooled and has won numerous competitions, including the Walgreens National Concerto Competition, in which she was the 2005 winner of the Early Music Category. Last year, my daughter Ayanna (14 years, cello) scored in the top three percentile nationally in math on the Iowas and was accepted into one of the top high school honors programs in the country.

To borrow Coach Powell's love of formulas, the following is the secret to the children's success:

Faith in God + Music Education + 100% Involved Parents = Successful Children

Daily individual practice, ensemble practice, weekly music lessons, and summer music camps are mandatory in our family—and scholarships play a large part in our financial planning. Ultimately, the benefits far outweigh the sacrifices. We believe that providing music lessons is the greatest gift we could give our children, no matter what career they eventually choose.

I imagine some readers may argue for sports education, which can be equally powerful in developing the innate talents of children. Our girls love basketball, tennis, volleyball, and gymnastics. I promote music education for children, however, because the focus of this book is a form of fallen music that has taken over the minds of our children. We must fight fire with fire.

Stevie Wonder once said, "Music at its essence is what gives us memories." If our children only have pornographic rhymes to dance to, what kinds of memories will they have as adults? What kind of adult will this generation become? It's our responsibility to create a musical atmosphere in our community that is positive, emotionally uplifting, and cognitively stimulating.

If your child's school is still in the dark ages about music education, don't let that stop you from raising the energy of your home's musical environment. Play jazz, classical, and gospel music. Share a little Old School (the clean songs) with them. Censor gangster rap or any other genre of music that stimulates the lower emotions in your child. And under no circumstances should young children watch gangster rap videos—ever.

orchestrate a solution

1. If finances make it difficult to pay for private music lessons, offer to barter services. Smaller music schools may go for it.
2. Seek out scholarship opportunities with larger music schools. Some have aggressive grants writing programs to fund scholarships and reduced fee programs.
3. If your child's public school doesn't have a music program, offer to work with the administration to develop a course or write a grant. If you have music ability, volunteer to direct a choir or teach your instrument to select, self-motivated students.
4. Contact the music department at a local college to see if there might be a good music student who would be willing to teach your child at a reduced rate. Most college students could use the extra cash.
5. Talk to your pastor about starting a music program at your church. One church in Chicago provides free string instruction to children who are members of the church. At another church, some generous musicians regularly give of their time and talents to teach music to children for free. This is an excellent way of incorporating a positive spirituality in music instruction, which is painfully lacking in popular music.
6. As a community, reach out to your district administration and board of education via letters, petitions, and telephone calls. Attend public meetings. Let them know that music and the arts are important to a child's overall development and that you won't take no for an answer.

"It's sad to see musically untrained youngsters shucking and jiving for a bit of money and fame. Most could never dream of succeeding in a serious artistic setting like a church choir, dance ensemble or jazz band, places that require study, discipline and hard work. Many would be swiftly laughed off the stage."[11] **Errol Louis,** *New York Daily News*

Chapter 4

Gateways to Heaven: Enhancing Prevention Programs

Lyrically speaking, *100 percent* of our youth have been approached to use drugs via gangsta rap infomercials, and this marketing has gone on nonstop *their entire lives*! We should throw a parade for those who have found the strength to resist the pressure. We must teach our children to run from the lyrical pusher the same as they would run from the street pusher.

In the prevention world, we often talk about the various gateways to risky behaviors. Alcohol is a gateway to irresponsible sex, which is a gateway to STDs. Gangsta rap is also a gateway to irresponsible sex, alcoholism, drug abuse, and violence.

It's easy to see a gateway as negative, but in this chapter, let us think of it in a more positive light. Instead of gateways to hell, we're going to strategize some gateways to heaven.

In my workshop and forthcoming book, *Caterpillars in the Hood: A Survival Guide for Hip Hop Youth,* I make the case that our communities can be heaven on earth, but we've got to put the **neighbor** back into the **hood** so that we can have **neighborhoods** again. Then the **vill**age will no longer be **ill**/sick. Our children will no longer be in danger. Brothers & Sisters, we can do this.

I've attended many prevention conferences over the years. We go over the statistics of death, sickness and disease, poverty, unemployment, poor academic performance, homicide, and crime. It's easy to forget the vision.

Prevention planning and implementation should always keep the view of heaven in front. The power to rescue our children is within

342

us—even more so when we work together. As Jesus says in Matthew 18:19–20,

> "Again I say to you that if two of you agree on earth concerning anything that they ask, it will be done for them by My Father in heaven. For where two or three are gathered together in My name, I am there in the midst of them."

What can one man or woman do? you may ask. It's true that the PTBs have deep pockets—but we've got the love. No one loves our children like we do. And love trumps money every time.

here comes the judge

Unfair drug laws have placed a disproportionately high rate of African Americans in prison, but the one thing America did right was to invent the drug court system. I've done my share of work in the drug courts, and I'm glad to report that they work! Drug court is on the cutting edge of making change.

Drug courts give people who really want to kick their addiction the opportunity to do so. Drug court helped save the lives of my sister, friends, and some former students. Those who choose to work the system quickly realize it's no cakewalk, but they receive the treatment they need. There are a lot of court TV shows; I wonder if there will ever be a drug court show?

Drug court clients learn that only they are responsible and accountable for their choices and actions. To participate, they must agree to completely abstain from alcohol and illegal drugs. Clients are monitored frequently via in-person court hearings.

Best of all, clients must have a W-2 tax-paying job, and they must complete a program of education and/or vocational training.

The benefits of a typical drug court are as follows:
- Reduces emergency room, hospital, and medical costs.

- Reduces domestic violence.
- Reduces felony and misdemeanor crimes.
- Decreases use of public assistance.
- Eases court, jail, and prison overcrowding and costs.
- Breaks the cycle of addiction.
- Gains control of life patterns and decisions.

open the door

We can enhance our prevention and intervention programs by making sure they include entertaining gateway activities that lead to positive peer relationships, an appreciation for positive music, and natural ways of enjoying life. Why focus on entertainment when there are so many devastating problems facing our youth? In the Hip Hop/ghetto matrix, only the music and Hip Hop culture matter to our children. So we must take our weapons to this battlefield because that's where our children live.

There are many gateways to positive behaviors that we can expose our children to. Our programs shouldn't be just about preventing negative behaviors but promoting a positive lifestyle. So many people (me included) fail at dieting because we fail to make a lifestyle of it. Just saying no to sweet potato pie is not enough to make you lose weight. You must say yes to exercise, eight glasses of water per day, fruit, vegetables, etc. to lose the weight.

Same thing with prevention planning. Programs that focus on saying no will not be as effective as programs that focus on yes. If we tell young people not to do drugs, what will replace the high? What are some positive gateways to a sober, drug-free life?

If we don't want young people to engage in risky sexual behaviors, how should we fill their down time? What legal and lucrative money making opportunities can we expose them to that will be more attractive than crime?

The following are entertainment gateways that can empower youth to lead safe and drug-free lives. Gangsta rappers have commanded the attention, imagination, and leisure time of our youth for too long. The following are fun and wholesome alternatives to the negative activities presented in gangsta rap.

1. Arts and sports activities
2. Chaperoned parties, card games, skating parties, etc.
3. Unique ways to present academics such as Know Your Heritage, Hip Hop Trivia competitions, and Academic Olympics (school vs. school, church vs. church)
4. Chaperoned nature trips (hiking, rock climbing, camping)
5. Chaperoned dance contests with strict guidelines
6. Chaperoned fashion shows with strict guidelines
7. Christian rap concerts
8. Chaperoned boys only/girls only sleepovers
9. Rap battles/competitions with strict guidelines
10. Video game competitions
11. Organized mall expeditions
12. Community volunteering. They may not like the idea at first, but eventually they'll get into helping others. Very necessary for this self-centered culture.
13. Supervise money making activities, e.g., washing cars, making/selling jewelry and crafts, producing CDs, etc.
14. Enroll youth in a television production course at your local cable access station. They will enjoy making and viewing their own television programs. Supervise content.

sexual abstinence

My editor and co-writer, Donna Marie Williams, wrote the book *Sensual Celibacy* to start a new discussion with adult women about celibacy and sexual behavior. Since youth today have been exposed to so much pornographic adult content in commercialized gangsta rap, we adopted her strategies for youth.

Let's define our terms. A virgin has never had sex. Youth today think they're slick. They say that since sex is intercourse, oral sex is not sex. Many use this to rationalize having oral sex so that they can technically remain virgins. That's bull. I don't buy into the technical virgin idea. Either you've had sex and all related sexual behaviors, or you haven't.

"So, Coach Powell, is kissing sex? Is holding hands sex?" As you're working with youth, you'll have to use your better judgment. They'll ask those kinds of questions because it's human nature to try and get away with things. As a rule of thumb, sex is intercourse and all other genital contact. I call it as I see it based on the level of risk. A peck on the cheek and holding hands may not necessarily lead to sex. However, tongue kissing, frontal contact, and juke dancing have a higher risk factor.

The following Passionmeter adapted from *Sensual Celibacy* can help youth understand how innocent (and not so innocent) behaviors can lead to sex:

> **talking** → **holding hands** → **eye gazing** → **sweet talk** → **kissing** → **tongue kissing** → **dancing** → **grinding** → **clothes coming off** → **clothes off** → **doing the deed** [1]

What's the difference between abstinence and celibacy? According to Donna, "…'abstinence' is a catchall for the act of self-denial. You can abstain from anything—eating red meat, drinking alcohol, and having sex. 'Celibacy,' on the other hand, specifically refers to abstention from sexual intercourse."[2] Sexual abstinence and celibacy are basically the same thing.

To help youth, we must create a climate of wholesomeness in our communities. This may be difficult with all the billboards featuring barely clothed women in the hood and our neighbors doing window-shaking musical drive-bys down the street. Still we must try. The following are some prevention and intervention strategies to help Hip Hop youth resist temptation:

- Strongly and frequently advocate for virginity and sexual abstinence (celibacy). Talk openly about sex to your children in developmentally appropriate ways. You have to fight fire with fire. Just as our youth are constantly approached to use alcohol and drugs via rap infomercials, they are being stalked by the sex monsters of commercialized gangsta Hip Hop.

- Help youth be successful in setting and keeping sex goals:
  - No sex until marriage, *period*!
  - No means no, absolutely not, no way, talk to the hand, leave me alone, you must be joking, are you crazy?, get out my face!
- Parents, raise your expectations. Often we hedge our bets with our children. We tell them to wait on sex while giving them a condom just in case. In these dangerous times, they do need to know how to prevent pregnancies and STDs, but that should not be our first line of defense. Virginity and sexual abstinence are the bottom line expectations.
- Don't let youth dance to inappropriate rap tunes.
- Don't let youth put inappropriate songs on their cell phones, PCs, lap tops, iPods, etc.
- Help youth become aware of sexual triggers in lyrics and music videos so that they can become responsible for their behavior. Sexual triggers can be anything that stimulates the desire to have sex. They are most powerful at the subliminal level. Sexual triggers can also include certain types of dancing, conversation (lines), clothes, shoes, perfume/cologne, gifts, money, and cars. No more "it just happened," "I don't know what happened," or "see, what had happened was …" No more accidental sex.
- Help youth resist sexual pressure (lines, macking, golddigging, etc.) via ongoing discussion and role play.
- Set and enforce household dating rules. Our youth are dating much too soon, which may explain why they are having sex much too soon. Also, chaperone your teen's dates.
- No double standards for males and females. It's insanity to continue teaching our boys to sow their wild oats while teach-

ing our girls to wait for their prince. The same sexual abstinence rule applies to both males and females. Teach youth to
have respect for one another.

- Model responsible behavior to youth (no more "do as I say").
- Deal with your own inner conflicts about young people having
  sex. Maybe you think it's hypocritical to advocate abstinence
  because, perhaps, you were not so responsible. Many (okay,
  most) of us fall into that category. Doesn't matter. The world
  is a lot different today than it was back in the day. Today, teen
  sex is a life and death issue.
- If you yourself are dating, consider waiting until the relationship is serious before allowing the person to meet your children. Also, don't allow casual dates to sleep over at your house.
  This puts your girls and boys at emotional and even physical
  risk. It also puts you in a hypocritical light. Model the role.
- Help youth strengthen their sexual abstinence via church
  involvement, community service, sports, the arts, music
  instruction, and, most importantly, daily prayer and meditation. A personal relationship with God can save us if we trust
  Him. Especially powerful for males, read Luke 4 to see how
  Jesus resisted temptation.
- Form and monitor a single gender support group for teens.
- Never stop talking about the lyrics and images in gangsta rap.
- Teach youth the difference between love and lust. Let the fol-
  lowing scripture be our guide on the subject:

"Love is patient, love is kind.
It does not envy, it does not boast, it is not proud.
It is not rude, it is not self-seeking, it is not easily angered, it
keeps no record of wrongs.
Love does not delight in evil but rejoices with the truth.
It always protects, always trusts, always hopes, always perse-
veres.

Love never fails." (1 Corinthians 14:6, New International Version)

best practices in prevention programming

As I reviewed the literature on prevention planning, I found that the most effective youth programs—whether the focus was preventing violence, poor academic performance/dropping out, teen pregnancies, STDs, violence, or substance use—employed the following village-oriented best practices:

1. Include the entire community—schools, churches, law enforcement, medical professionals, libraries, businesses, and media. Adults can serve as mentors, trainers, leaders, chaperones, and counselors.
2. Focus on the whole family. We can't develop a child apart from his/her family.
3. Focus on the whole child. A child is composed of mind, body, and spirit. All aspects must be considered when developing and implementing prevention programs.
4. A healthy village has a coordinated approach to raising children. Community organizations and institutions are all on the same page regarding the child-centered approach.

rap literacy

Earlier, I mentioned that one of the reasons substance abuse and alcoholism are so entrenched in Hip Hop is because the symbols of intoxication (blunts, pipes, alcohol) are expertly woven with the symbols of sex and success (mansions, cars, women). This is a lie made to look like the truth, and most children lack the cognitive ability or maturity to make the distinction.

Help youth separate the symbols of sex, wealth, and intoxication. The truth is, drinking, doing drugs, and having irresponsible sex can lead to poverty.

Churches, teach youth to separate Christian symbols from gangsta values, themes, and images. Just because rappers wear Christian jewelry doesn't make them Christian.

Chapter 5

Raising Hip Hop Scholars

"I'm not comfortable being preachy, but more people need to start spending as much time in the library as they do on the basketball court. If they took the idea that they could escape poverty through education, I think it would make a more basic and long-lasting change in the way things happen. What we need are positive, realistic goals and the willingness to work. Hard work and practical goals." **Kareem Abdul-Jabbar** (Ferdinand Lewis Alcindor, Jr.), 1990

Educators do many things, and one of the toughest jobs they do is teach. Being a good teacher requires knowledge, patience, commitment, healing, allies, flexibility, cultural sensitivity, and forgiveness.

Every educator should declare the classroom a learning zone. Education takes place when a teacher teaches and a student learns. It's the teacher's responsibility to set the tone, expectations, and timeline for the success of each student. Remind your students everyday that failure is not an option. Remind yourself that each student's grade is a reflection on your ability or inability to educate effectively.

These may seem like obvious statements, but you'd be surprised at how many teachers today get into the profession because of the regular paycheck, health insurance, short hours (so they think), summers off, and pension. These educational mercenaries are the ones who tell our children, "I got mine." They could care less.

Like the ministry, teaching is a calling. Think long and hard before going into this career because some days, it's only the calling that will keep you going. The stress can be unbearable. The hours are long, and there will be times when you'll get no support—not from your principal, parents, media, community, and least of all the students. There must be a love for teaching children, or else you'll burn up mentally, spiritually, and physically.

I have a friend who teaches first and second grades in the hood. Many of her students were born drug-addicted and have high-sugar, junk food diets. They're being raised in single parent homes and foster care. Some have fathers, mothers, uncles, aunts, siblings, and cousins in prison. Some of their parents are on crack. They live in public housing.

My friend's students are some of the best dressed children in the city, but because they don't come to class prepared to learn, they're often failing in reading and math. These are the same children who can recite verbatim the words to the latest gangsta rap tune.

Behavioral problems on a daily basis get in the way of teaching and learning. This sista believes that even in the primary grades, black children have already learned to distrust adults and this prevents learning.

Rebellion against authority is not only a Hip Hop value but also a part of childhood development. Yet, have we ever seen a generation that so disrespected authority that they didn't believe their teachers? When I was a child, I unquestioningly accepted most of what my teachers told me. And if I didn't, I kept my opinions to myself. Today's children question er'thing, including the relevance of school to their lives.

I hear all the time from students, "I hate school" and "Why do I have to learn this?" They are failing school because they do not believe education has anything to do with getting paid. Hip Hop doesn't value traditional education like we did.

It's easy to become frustrated with this generation. Their values are not our values. They can be attitudinal and disrespectful. On the other hand, they are our children, and they still need us and seek our guidance, just on their own terms.

school is my job. i can't afford to be fired!

In workshops I have my students chant, "School is my job. I can't afford to get fired from my J-O-B … baby!" Then I tell them that no one can keep a job with a punctuality, attendance, or attitude problem.

I then have students answer the following questions with a show of hands, but without calling out any names (which they always do).

1. How many of you know people who come to school and you wonder why they bother?
2. How many of you know people who use curse words in every sentence at school?
3. How many of you know people who get high before, during, and after school?
4. How many of you know people who love to blame the teachers and the school when they fail?
5. How many of you know people who sleep all day in school?
6. How many of you know people who never ever (never ever) do homework?
7. How many of you know people who gossip and spread rumors all day in school?
8. How many of you know people who bully other people and appear to be angry all the time?
9. If you were a teacher, how many of you would have lost your job by now and why?
10. How many of you know people who know every word to the top 10 rap songs but can't complete their alphabets without missing a few?

I tell students that it's okay to laugh at a joke but never cool to *become* the joke. The world has been conditioned to put all jokes to the side. Have you become the joke? Hmmm …

I then ask the silent audience the following:

1. When I asked those questions, did your classmates think of you?
2. Do your classmates see you as a joke?

I tell students they won't be teenagers the rest of their lives, and what they do now becomes the history they'll have to live with for the rest of their lives.

Part of my job is to get students to believe in the power of education, so it's at this point I get on my soapbox.

Coach's Soapbox

Excellent Education + Excellent Attitude = Editude™

Since many of you have developed a negative attitude towards education, I encourage you to get an *Editude*, which is education with attitude. Hip Hop students already have attitude. Now just roll those eyes and jump bad on that lab assignment, research paper, math formula, book, or vocabulary test, and you will be unstoppable.

Being a proud, high achieving scholar is having an Editude. Students have Editude when they are not ashamed to participate in after school academic clubs or compete in math and science fairs. Students with Editude hold their heads high when they are awarded honor roll certificates or when they receive A's on difficult tests. Students with Editude help other students who may be struggling in a subject.

Students with Editude have high self-esteem that is based, not on the clothes they wear, but on their A style in math, science, English, geography, social studies, and the arts. They respect their teachers and demand an education from them. They turn off the TV when there's homework to be done. Most importantly, students with Editude are never ever (never ever) ashamed to be young, gifted, and black!

Eldridge Cleaver once said, "All people are due equal education and everything else that goes along with maintaining a healthy society. You're either part of the solution or you're part of the problem."

From the moment the first African ancestors arrived in America, every effort has been made to dummy us down, portray us as stupid, classify us as ignorant, and deny us an education. During slavery, blacks were punished for learning how to read and write. For 400 years, our ancestors risked their lives learning how to read and write. The whites who taught them were fined, imprisoned, and shunned; blacks were whipped and even killed. It was never America's intention to educate you on equal terms with whites.

I believe the Hip Hop generation is the most talented generation of blacks since our arrival in America, but you lack appreciation for the sacrifices our ancestors made so that you can learn. This may be the most unappreciative, ungrateful generation yet. You think you're getting over when your teachers pass you and you still can't read, write, or compute—but you're only hurting yourself.

You'd better get an Editude, and get your education! Nothing less than an A is acceptable. The next time you get less than an A, look at yourself in the mirror, put your finger in your own face, and say, "Oh no you didn't just get a B (C, D, or F). Oh … no … you … didn't!" Then answer, "So what you gonna do? Huh? Think you bad?" Say to your own self, "I'm gonna turn off the TV. I'm gonna stop dissin' the teacher. I'm gonna hit the books. I'm gonna do some extra credit. I'm gonna get my education. Oh, it's on!"

Everyone blames teachers and parents for your failure, but who's responsible for coming to school and being ready to learn? You are. Who's responsible for paying attention to the teacher? You are. Whose job is it to take good notes and read every day? Yours. Who's responsible for doing homework and studying for quizzes and tests? You are. If you're not doing your job, then you have no one to blame but yourself.

It's not good enough to get a Most Improved certificate at the next assembly. Every one of you should be on the Honor Roll, the Principal's List, and the National Honor Society.

Students, you must fight for your education like the ancestors did. This is your responsibility. How dare you go to school, surrounded by millions of dollars worth of knowledge and not make an effort to get at least fifty cent worth! Don't you know that nine out of ten of the 11,000 youth in adult detention facilities have, at best, a ninth grade education?[1]

i brought my hip hop to school

Back in the day, the typical things a child brought to school was a ruler, pencils, erasers, crayons, notebooks, paper, glue, a pencil sharpener, an apple for the teacher, and a good attitude. Nowadays, the book bags of Hip Hop students are loaded with iPods, CD players, Game Boys, cell phones, two-way pagers, an occasional weapon, and an attitude that says, "You ain't taking my stuff no matter what the rules of the school say."

When teachers ask students why they brought their cell phones to school, they say their parents told them to do it. Children in the hood don't always ride to school on the yellow bus. They walk through gang territories, past liquor stores and crack houses. They take public transportation through dangerous routes. They leave and come home to an empty house. Under these conditions, parents have found that cell phones and pagers are a good way to maintain contact with their children. They may give some type of medical excuse to get around the rules. More and more school districts are allowing cell phones just as long as they stay off during class time.

Still, I see students in school hallways talking on their cell phones. Cell phones today come with iPods, cameras and video recorders, text messaging, and pagers (a.k.a. sidekicks). Don't let a cell phone come up missing. Then it's on. Accusations lead to fighting and threats made by both students and parents.

I call this, "Bringing your Hip Hop to school."

These are the toys and tools of Hip Hop youth, and for many, playtime is all the time, and class time becomes show and tell time. According to educators in the hood, these toys are major distractions and slow down the educational process. They create an atmosphere that is more social than educational.

According to the unwritten rules of poverty, when you get a new toy you have to show it off. "Look at what I got" or "I got one first" is what this mindset is all about (at least that's how it was for me). It's the very reason why our children cut school to be the first person in line at the mall at 10:00 am to buy the new Nike Michael Jordan basketball shoe. I witnessed this on many occasions in the 1990s. The student would purchase the shoes then rush back to school and brag about being the first in the school (or the hood) to have them. This is about status. And if someone accidentally steps on the shoe, all hell breaks out.

odd or simply hip hop?

How much time does a teacher waste telling students to pull up their pants? Or to put away their iPods, CD players, or Game Boys (now!)? Remember the days of teachers telling students to throw away their gum? There's no comparison.

Hip Hop loves to defy authority. Youth call this behavior "acting hard," which is a survival technique in the hood. Students trapped inside the Hip Hop/ghetto matrix find it easier to maintain this hard persona/attitude instead of shifting back and forth from hard to nice, which is mentally exhausting.

Teachers ask, "Why are they so angry? Why do they fight all the time? What is their problem?" This persona/attitude is necessary to survive life on the street. Looking hard at the correct times can save your life as well as lead to your demise; it's a double edged sword.

The look appears threatening and disrespectful, and police and prison guards refer to it as "reckless eyeballing." Students with the look are often diagnosed by school psychologists as suffering from "Oppositional Defiant Disorder" (ODD). ODD is a pattern of negative, hostile, and defiant behaviors lasting at least six months, during which four (or more) of the following behaviors occur:

1. Loses temper.
2. Argues with adults.
3. Defies, refuses to comply with adults' requests, rules.
4. Deliberately annoys people.
5. Blames others for mistakes, misbehavior.
6. Is touchy, easily annoyed by others.
7. Is angry, resentful.
8. Is spiteful, vindictive.[2]

ODD behaviors are identical to the typical Hip Hop creed of acting and looking hard. Hip Hop behaviors also mimic clinical depression. So this is why your angry black male child who's been acting out in school gets thrown into special ed. He's been diagnosed with a psychiatric disorder, when all he's doing is responding in the sanest way he knows to conditions that are beyond his control. These children may be saner than the rest of us who keep accepting sub-level conditions in the hood as normal. Think about it.

the fear factor

Fear Factor is more than a hit TV show. It's a dirty secret of education in America's inner city schools. Who's afraid of the big bad black kids? Teachers are, that's who. The students know this, and they work it for all it's worth. This is a sad reality. They think they're getting over, but they're not. No one wants to discuss this dirty secret, but we'd better start talking.

In my teacher workshops I survey inner city white teachers on the issues of school and race. I ask them for candid statements as it relates to their fear of working with black students. Here's what some teachers had to say:

> "Anxiety more so than fear. I can only speak for myself. I do have colleagues who are petrified of the neighborhoods they teach in more so than the students themselves." **36 year-old white male high school teacher** (Columbus, Ohio)

> "Students can't learn when they're angry. Many of my black boys are angry and violent for no apparent reason, and I just can't understand why." **54 year-old white female middle school teacher** (Youngtown, Ohio)

> "You hear rumors about gang affiliations and you never know how the students are going to respond to your disciplinary referral and whether or not they will retaliate. That brings about stress and fear." **31 year-old white female high school teacher** (Detroit, Michigan)

> "The only thing I really fear is that people buy into the stereotypes about black kids. I have taught in majority all white school districts before coming here and I can honestly say black children are no worse or better than any other group I've taught over my 22 years of education. Kids are kids, and if you're a dedicated teacher then you know fear cannot be a part of your curriculum." **50 year-old white male high school teacher** (Trotwood, Ohio)

> "I fear a great deal of these parents more than I do the students. Parents come in very loud, occasionally threatening, very accusatory, trying to intimidate you. They never deal

with the issue such as their child's behavior." **39 year-old white female** (St. Louis, Missouri)

Black children occasionally feel obligated to implement the following rules of the hood while in school or when confronted by authorities:

1. Don't take any stuff off of anyone, at any time, or at any place. Stand up for yourself.
2. If someone hits you, hit them back.
3. Teachers don't care, especially white teachers. They only want to expel you, put you in detention, or worse, special ed.
4. Represent your people/crew/set/gang/family at all cost.

Cultural differences play a role, too. At home, black children are taught to stick up for themselves. When they get to school, they seem belligerent to white teachers. When the white teachers react, the black students feel targeted.

> "Teachers and staff stereotype us—our backgrounds and where we live and the types of the things that go on in our neighborhood—like we're more likely to steal and fight. It's like they expect us to do stuff wrong. Instead of helping us out, they just go ahead and accuse us of doing something."[3] **17 year-old African-American senior**, Withrow International High School

Over the years I have been summoned to classrooms to calm angry black children when white teachers could not diffuse the situation. With an authoritative voice, in seconds I am able to restore order. White teachers are more than capable of handling classroom problems, but they don't want to appear racist. Some have told me, "They respect you because you're a coach" or "They just won't listen to me."

The bottom line is, the classroom is the educator's domain, and only he/she is held accountable for teaching students; within legal and policy boundaries, handle your business.

i didn't drop out—i got pushed out

"Don't push me cuz I'm close to the edge." That could be the battle cry of thousands of black males as schools push them out the door and they lose focus—but not before a parent or teacher gave up on them first. Family crises, a lack of self control, and poor choices of friends started the downhill slide, but they always believed an adult would be there to help them. Finally, at the edge of the cliff, they felt pushed over.

These students come from dysfunctional families, and at least one other sibling has similar behavioral issues. Everyone is relying on the already stressed out single parent to step up to the plate, which is a bit naïve, but the system is not designed to handle such situations.

If I had a nickel for the number of times a student believed an intervention plan made it impossible to succeed I'd be rich. Zero tolerance policies handcuff school administrators and counselors, restricting their options. One referral for tardiness or discipline is enough to void the agreement and lead to suspension.

African American students are suspended and expelled more than any other group. Unfortunately, removal from school has become a rite of passage for young people, and school districts seem to be unwilling to implement alternatives. Based on my work with schools, I have compiled the following top 10 reasons African American secondary students are suspended or expelled from public schools. The list is not flattering and would easily apply to other groups if all things were equal.

1. Disruptive conduct, insubordination
2. Tardiness, truancy
3. Physical assaults, fighting
4. Cutting class

5. Theft
6. Verbal assaults, threats
7. Intoxicated (alcohol, drugs)
8. Sexual harassment
9. Trespassing
10. Weapons possession

Absenteeism is detrimental to student achievement, promotion, graduation, self-esteem, and employment potential. Students who miss school fall behind their peers in the classroom. This leads to low self-esteem and increases the likelihood that at-risk students will drop out of school.

> "Some six million students throughout America are currently at risk of dropping out of school. High school dropouts are unable to enter the workforce with the necessary skills to meet the demands of the nation's global economy. American business currently spends more than $60 billion each year on training, much of that on remedial reading, writing, and mathematics."[4]

counted out

The dropout problem is much worse than statistics indicate. Students who fail to receive diplomas are often not counted as dropouts by school districts and states. Even the hardest hit urban districts report dropout rates much lower than they really are. Such was the case in Chicago, Illinois, in 2004. State officials claimed that 70.7 percent of high school students graduated, but only 54 percent walked the stage. Even worse, only 39 percent of African American males graduated![5] Can anyone say Hip Hop suicide? Is this the legacy of Hip Hop and the African American community as a whole? Did the ancestors who sacrificed so much for education die in vain?

The University of Chicago's Consortium on Chicago School Research exposed the Illinois State Board of Education's scandalous reporting. According to consortium researcher Elaine Allensworth, "Illinois' method of calculating graduates is so prone to manipulation that 'there could be some schools cooking the books' here."[6]

The findings presented in this report spotlight the failure of public schools to educate students:

- The national graduation rate is 68 percent, with nearly one-third of all public high school students failing to graduate.
- Tremendous racial gaps are found in graduation rates.
- Students from historically disadvantaged groups (American Indian, Hispanic, and African American) have little more than a 50-50 chance of finishing high school with a diploma.
- By comparison, graduation rates for whites and Asians are 75 and 77 (respectively) percent nationally.
- Males graduate from high school at a rate eight percent lower than female students.
- Graduation rates for students who attend school in racially segregated, impoverished urban school districts lag 15 to 18 percent behind their peers.[7]

dropping out: warning signs

I have witnessed students standing outside the school building in the parking lot, in the early A.M., in the cold, only to turn around and head home or downtown just to hang out. This ritual may occur maybe three times a week. The students' behavior is consistent. They get up early in the morning, come to school, but don't go into the school building. Then they have the gall to attend a school dance or sporting event that evening.

Certain groups of young people are more likely than others to leave school before graduating. While not everyone in these categories drops out, paying special attention to the needs of students from these groups can keep some of them in school.

- Students in large cities are twice as likely to leave school before graduating than non-urban youth.
- More than one in four Hispanic youth drop out, and nearly half leave by the eighth grade.
- Hispanics are twice as likely as African Americans to drop out. White and Asian American students are least likely to drop out.
- More than half the students who drop out leave by the 10th grade, 20 percent quit by the eighth grade, and three percent drop out by the fourth grade.
- Nearly 25 percent of dropouts changed schools two or more times, with some changing for disciplinary reasons.
- Almost 20 percent of dropouts were held back a grade, and almost half failed a course.
- Almost one-half of dropouts missed at least 10 days of school, one-third cut class at least 10 times, and one-quarter were late at least 10 times.
- Eight percent of dropouts spent time in a juvenile home or shelter.
- One-third of dropouts were put on in-school suspension, suspended, or put on probation; more than 15 percent were either expelled or told they couldn't return.
- Twelve percent of dropouts ran away from home.[8]

reasons why youth drop out

Both school problems and personal problems factor into why students drop out.

- Didn't like school in general or the school they were attending.
- Were failing, getting poor grades, or couldn't keep up with school work.
- Didn't get along with teachers and/or students.
- Had disciplinary problems, were suspended or expelled.

- Didn't feel safe in school.
- Got a job, had a family to support, or had trouble managing school and work.
- Got married, got pregnant, or became a parent.
- Had a drug or alcohol problem.[9]

what did you do in school today?

On a typical day parents ask their children several questions about their school day.

"What did you do in school today?"

"Nothing," says child.

"You've been gone for eight hours and you did nothing?" Child shrugs.

"Do you have any homework?" asks parent.

"NO!" says child with a straight face.

"I called the school and they said you had homework."

A moment of silence, then, "I done it in school," the child says.

"How are your grades?" asks the parent.

More silence, then the child says, "I guess they're cool, I mean straight."

"What do you mean you guess?" says frustrated parent.

"In three of my classes we have subs and the rest we haven't really done nothing because the books aren't in yet," says child. "That's why we don't have any homework." Parent throws up hands and goes to fix dinner.

This is the sad account of students trapped in poor schools across America. Hollywood has captured the spirit of failure in movies such as *Lean On Me, The Substitute (1&2), Cooley High, The Principal, Dangerous Minds,* and *Coach Carter.* These movies depict the urban youth's struggle against the odds and how education can save even the toughest cases.

Failing schools have one thing in common: all the ingredients for producing what I call poor "school esteem" are present. Poor school esteem is created by litter in the hallways and school grounds, filthy restrooms, poor lighting in classrooms, under staffing of certified teachers, low expectations of students and staff, high suspension rates, little or no after school activities, unruly classroom behavior, poor academic reputation, and little or no parent participation. Poor school esteem promotes a failing culture so that the students who are more than capable of excelling choose not to. They say, "Everybody's failing," as if to justify their poor performance. Has failure become a rite of passage for urban students? If so, what kind of life prospects are they passing into?

In their smash hit "City High Anthem," rap artists City High convey the emotions of poverty-stricken youth. The song is a wake up call.

> "They just gave up on our entire generation
> So we were all pushed to the side cuz we didn't see the world
> through our teachers eyes
> When all we needed was a little bit of motivation
> But because we wore our pants saggin' y'all labeled us gangstas
> And said we wasn't worth the time."[10]

how parents can help prevent dropping out

Parents, working with school administrators, counselors, and teachers, can help their children stay in high school:

- Get tutoring for students in crisis. Consider this an urgent priority.
- Students' personal problems may be too much for parents to handle alone. Get professional help.
- Help students prioritize school, work, and family obligations.
- Have students talk to people who dropped out so that they can understand the consequences of such an action.
- If students become pregnant or parents, help find school and social programs that will meet their special needs.

- If all else fails, help students find a GED program and encourage them to stay with it until they get a GED diploma.[11]

hip hop in academia

Thanks to Angela W. Peters, PhD, who contributed "Hip Hop in Academia."

"We have a powerful potential in our youth, and we must have the courage to change old ideas and practices so that we may direct their power toward good ends."
Mary MacLeod Bethune, 1955

In urban schools across the country I see first-hand the impact of gangsta Hip Hop on student behavior. Schools often ask me to come and "fix" their students, but I tell them it will take more than one motivational speech, workshop, or counseling session to reverse the gangsta Hip Hop curse on our children.

No Child Left Behind has focused on math and reading to the neglect of the development of the whole child. Schools need a complete program of sports, the arts, creative methods, relevant coursework, and high expectations to develop children. Suburban schools provide all these and more for their children. Why don't we?

*The following essay by Dr. Angela Peters bears witness to the fact that education is still the best deal in town, so our children must succeed in school. This is not an option. **Coach***

The type of students we see in academia is predicated on the secondary school system from where they graduated. If secondary teachers and administrators follow Stephen G. Peters' model of "capturing, inspiring, and teaching," students will become well-rounded, mature, focused, and eager to absorb and display knowledge in a post-secondary environment. However, if the student barely made the grade in middle school and skated by on charm in high school, then our job as college professors involves more than just teaching. We must analyze, critique, back up, and motivate while laying a foundation of knowledge that will sustain the environment, peer pressure, distractions, and lack of momentum.

College students who were not "captured" in high school by a caring and stimulating teacher (or administrator) are difficult to save from the rhyme, rhythm, and bling bling of Hip Hop. If college students have not been taught discipline and respect, then the loose, tight, and provocative clothing worn in Hip Hop videos will be their garments of choice (even if they were brought up in the church or their university has a strict dress code). If college students have not been taught how to study, take notes, and focus in secondary school, then Hip Hop songs and videos promoting getting high, cutting class, dropping out of school, and having sex with numerous partners will distract them and serve as their daily teachings. If students were not strengthened holistically, spiritually, and academically prior to college, their weak minds can be easily infiltrated with the glamour, glitz, and unrealistic fantasies promoted by commercialized Hip Hop.

As a scientist and chemistry instructor, I must be able to communicate difficult concepts. We in the sciences must be able to promote the results of our research through oral and posted presentations at national meetings. I am concerned about students who, influenced by the degrading lyrics of Hip Hop, have poor verbal and writing skills. If students cannot articulate their thoughts and ideas to the public, then they may never make it to the corporate board room where the big decisions are being made. They will not be present at the negotiating table where high stakes and stocks are being discussed.

When teaching this generation, our job in academia is to show by example that at any time the bottom can fall out from under a million dollar a day rap star. He will be left with bills, depression, and the IRS hounding his door. However, the rap star who holds a college degree (even an Associates degree) has something to fall back on, and the window of opportunity is opened.

We must show by example that inappropriate lyrics and videos are not to be retained and rehashed as a learning tool. Yet, positive Hip Hop lyrics and videos can be the key to teaching math or spelling through rhyme. Secondary and post-secondary institutions must work together to ensure that our children are receiving the highest quality education. We must help them pursue and achieve their higher education degree.

Chapter 6

Welcome to Nellyville

"Rebuilding the Black community will involve gaining control of our own education, economics and law enforcement. Many people are tricked into believing that an education refers solely to attending the system's schools, but to educate means to prepare and inform people about controlling their community."[1] **Chuck D**

I've blasted rappers in *Hip Hop Hypocrisy*, but I'll be the first to say that when the brothas and sistas get it right, we should give them credit where credit is due. Since the first time I heard the song "Nellyville" blasting in our locker room after winning the city league football championship, I've been wishing I could take all my students and loved ones who live in the ghetto and move there.

In this song, Nelly recognizes the wisdom of the African saying, "It takes a whole village to raise one child" and that the village is very ill and can never come to age if we do not work to change things. Though I'm hard on rappers, I have to give it to them when their brilliance is allowed to shine through in their music, as in "Nellyville." The lyrics take us to a higher plane of life. Nellyville should be named the capitol of the Hip Hop nation. Nellyville is what we should aspire to. This is how we should all be living.

how u livin where u livin?

"Welcome to Nellyville, where all newborns get a half-a-mil'
Sons get the tan DeVille, soon as they can reach the wheel

And daughters, get diamonds the size of their age–help me
out now
One year get one carat, two years get two carats
Three years get three carats, and so on into marriage
Nobody livin average, everybody jang-a-lang
Nobody livin savage, e'rybody got change
Even the paperboy deliver out the back of a Range
It's not a game, it's a beautiful thang."[2]
Nelly, "Nellyville"

What I love about "Nellyville" is that it goes against all the roman-
ticizing of oppressive ghetto conditions usually found in rap music.
"Nellyville" gives us a vision of how life should be for *all* African
Americans, not just one rapper showing off bling bling. The song
harkens back to the day when ghetto and social conditions were pro-
tested by artists such as Marvin Gaye ("Inner City Blues-Make Me
Wanna Holler," "What's Going On," "Mercy Mercy Me"), Donny
Hathaway ("The Ghetto"), Edwin Starr ("War"), and Stevie Wonder
("Village Ghetto").

You should never forget where you come from. I recently visited
my childhood home, and as I stood quietly on that busy street corner,
childhood memories came flooding into my mind, causing tears of
joy and pain.

Those were the days when I lived in a real neighborhood, not a
hood. This was a place where people truly cared for one another.
Neighbors watched out for us, and they corrected and protected us
from others as well as ourselves.

Sad to say, my Lower Dayton View neighborhood has been
reduced to a hood, ghettofied and left to die. The neighbors have
all left. Homes are boarded up or are mostly rental properties now.
Broken glass and dreams litter the streets.

Black people have always managed to turn ghettos into loving,
respectable communities, so there's hope for communities that go the
way of Lower Dayton.

Decoded, community reads "common-unity." Communities are made up of love, cultural laws, mutual respect, and leadership. The safe environment of community promotes healthy emotional, physiological, psychological, and spiritual development. This is what the Hip Hop generation must learn if they are to survive and thrive.

It's no secret that codes for the black community are "inner city," "urban," "projects," "crack house," and "gang territory." Rappers use "hood," "ghetto," and occasionally "village." The black community is the only place in America where the minority is seen as the majority.

With the widespread use of these terms, we develop a psychological kinship with victimization, which is a dysfunctional state of silent depression. Why do we say we hate being victims but love those things, people, and places that victimize us? Hip Hop youth like to say, "It's all good in the hood." The truth is it's not all good in the hood! The only hood where it's all good is in childhood and adulthood. To speak of the hood as all good is the foolish thinking of the victim loving his victimization.

the black family in nellyville

> "Imagine blocks and blocks of no cocaine, blocks with no gunplay
> Ain't nobody shot, so ain't no news that day
> Ain't nobody snitchin, they refuse to say
> Every month—we take a vote on what the weather should be
> And if we vote it rains—know how wet we want it to be
> And if we vote it snow—know how deep we want it to get
> But the sun gon' shine 99 percent, in Nellyville."[3]
> **Nelly**, "Nellyville"

In order to fully appreciate Nellyville, let's take a trip back in time and revisit the 1965 Daniel Patrick Moynihan Report, "The Negro Family: The Case for National Action." Sadly, although the report described the crisis of the black family in 1965, the same report describes *in essence* the Hip Hop/ghetto matrix today. The village is ill because the family is broken. Moynihan wrote,

> "The fundamental problem ... is that of family structure. The evidence—not final, but powerfully persuasive—is that the Negro family in the urban ghettos is crumbling."[4]

Out of their victimhood, our apologists and social scientists responded by saying the African family is matriarchal—but ask any single mother how she feels about raising children by herself and she will tell you the story of her life. They say the extended black family is African and it keeps the community strong. Is it strength for generations of women in a family, from the great grandmamma to the teenage mother, to raise the children while the men are standing on the corner unemployed or playing out their Prolonged Adolescent Syndrome?

We didn't like it when Moynihan said it (and we still don't), but our families have crumbled. Some 70 percent of black children are being born out of marriage and raised by a single parent, usually the mother (sometimes the grandmother). This is a recipe for poverty and disaster. The village is ill, and we are in denial. Our ancestors, who, after slavery, went searching far and wide for their wives, husbands, and children, must be turning over in their graves to see today's high unwed pregnancy rate, high rates of children in foster care, the multitudes of children in the hood who are being raised by gangs, and the Maury Povich exploitation of our pain.

> "A national effort is required that will give a unity of purpose to the many activities of the Federal government in this area, directed to a new kind of national goal: the establishment of a stable Negro family structure."[5]

Moynihan's national effort never happened, but if we can keep Nellyville in the spotlight to give our youth a vision to hold on to, then we will heal our community. Nelly blessed us with a beautiful picture of how life can and should be for the many who feel hopeless and forgotten.

Like Nelly rhymed,

"No unexpectancy, like teenage pregnancy
And physical mental attraction your only ecstasy
Your own destiny, create your own recipe."[6]
Nelly, "Nellyville"

who changed the theme song?

At some point our theme song as a people changed. Our song used to be "Eyes on the prize," "Black power," and "We shall overcome." After the deaths of Dr. King and Malcolm X, black folk could be heard humming TV sitcom theme songs. Two in particular were "Good Times" (*Good Times*) and "Moving On Up" (*The Jeffersons*).

We were told that living in the projects, merely surviving the night, or making the payments on a rat infested apartment in a violent community was somehow "good times." Every time that song would play, my father would tell us,

"That jingle is for white folks, not us. Be careful of the words you embrace. If you embrace that song, you'll never see yourselves living outside the projects. You'll be living in a hostile place for the rest of your lives. That ain't no damn good times."

Consider the lyrics:

"Temporary lay offs. Good times.
Easy credit rip offs. Good times.
Scratchin' and surviving. Good times.
Hangin in a chow line. Good times.
Ain't we lucky we got 'em? Good times."

Dave Grusin and Andrew Bergman, "Good Times"

Saying good times to such ungodly conditions creates pathology and romantic delusions about the hood. Now, let's sing the song again, but this time substitute "bad times" for "good times." Teach the children the truth! This will help us change our perspective on the ghetto—only then can we keep our eyes on the prize: Nellyville.

'give the people what they want'

Nothing bothers me more than to hear recording industry PTBs say they are giving the people what they want. Who are these people? Far too many black folk accept this lame excuse. Where do these people live, and give us their names. We, the real people, want to know!

The spies among us believe they know us more than we know ourselves. We need to become private. You don't hear other groups airing their dirty laundry in rap tunes 24/7. When was the last time you saw a tobacco company handing out free cigarettes in affluent suburbs and taking surveys? Yet the PTBs of all industries come to the hood, stake us out, take notes, and make plans to take our money.

Hip Hop is now 30 (plus) years old, and the themes have not changed. Who said youth want sex, violence, addiction, and drama 24/7 in their Hip Hop music? Who are these people?

The PTBs assume that these so-called people who want this so-called entertainment are mainly black youth. This is not necessarily true. Insiders say the number one consumers of Hip Hop are middle-class white males, 16 to 30 years old. Whites run Hip Hop, from the business executives at major labels to the suburban teen consumers. Black youth and rappers are merely the creative fodder.

when rappers get it right: hip hop pledge

On October 16, 1995, approximately one million black men gathered at the Mall in Washington, DC, for the historic Million Man March. Minister Louis Farrakhan delivered the keynote address, "Toward a More Perfect Union." As he concluded, he had us recite a Pledge of Atonement.

As we launch the biggest rescue mission in recent memory—the saving of our children from the destructive elements of the Hip Hop/ghetto matrix—let us use this pledge (adapted for this generation) as our guide. As we abide by these principles, we will heal our children, ourselves, and our community.

HIP HOP PLEDGE OF ATONEMENT

I, _____, pledge that from this day forward, I will strive to love my brother/sister as I love myself.

I, _____, from this day forward will strive to improve myself spiritually, morally, mentally, socially, politically, economically, and educationally for the benefit of myself, my family, and my people.

I, _____, pledge that I will strive to build businesses, build houses, build hospitals, build factories, and enter into international trade for the good of myself, my family, and my people.

I, _____, pledge that from this day forward I will never raise my hand with a knife or a gun to beat, cut, or shoot any member of my family or any human being except in self-defense.

I, _____, pledge from this day forward, I will never abuse my wife by striking her or disrespecting her, for she is the mother of my children and the producer of my future. I, _____, pledge to never disrespect my husband for he is the father of my children and the producer of my future.

I, _____, pledge that from this day forward, I will never engage in the abuse of children, little boys or little girls, for sexual gratification. But I will let them grow in peace to be strong men and women for the future of our people.

I, _____, will never again use the "b" word to describe any female, but particularly my own black sister. I, _____, will never again use the "n" word to describe any member of my race.

I, _____, pledge that from this day forward I will not poison my body with drugs or that which is destructive to my health and my well being.

I, _____, pledge from this day forward that I will support black newspapers, black radio, and black television. I will support black artists who clean up their acts and show respect for themselves and respect for their people and respect for the heirs of the human family.

I, _____, will do all of this, so help me God.

final thoughts

Confined by unjust laws, addictions, convictions, and sickness, NEIGHBORHOOD cradles her children nonetheless with love and tries to protect them, as best she can, from HIV/AIDS, police raids, crime, violence, and misery. As the hood struggles to become a NEIGHBORHOOD, she strives to reclaim her dignity and fights for her children.

The Hip Hop generation was the first ever to sleep days and stay up all night—still she loves her children.

They have been drugged, mugged, and thugged in their pursuit of riches, bling bling, stacks, crack, and any and all things declared phat—and still she loves them.

She hurts when her Hip Hop manchild accepts being called nigga, dogg, pimp, baby's daddy, crackhead, playa, and hustler. She longs to see him grow into full manhood.

She cries when her Hip Hop daughter accepts being called bitch, ho, chickenhead, and ill nana. All she wants is for her daughter to be respected and called a woman.

Her children fight, lie, do drugs, sleep with men they don't know, and refuse to pay child support—and still she loves them.

Her sons have been both low down and down low. Her daughters wear pasties and g-strings in broad daylight. And still she loves them.

NEIGHBORHOOD doesn't need apologists and social scientists to excuse her children's behavior. She knows the best remedy is a dose of tough love, unconditional and 24/7.

The hypocrisies have put her children to sleep, but as she becomes NEIGHBORHOOD, she knows her children are waking up to the truth, and the truth is setting them free.

As NEIGHBORHOOD grows up, the black family experiences *umoja*/ unity. As the black family gets stronger, so does NEIGHBORHOOD.

NEIGHBORHOOD is no longer putting up with black-on-black hate. She's bringing her children together in Black-on-Black Love.

NEIGHBORHOOD longs for the day when she hears her son rap, "Don't ya'll believe the hype. I love life, my children, and my wife, and I will fight for what is right."

She smiles because she knows one day her daughter will say, "I love my husband, my children, and myself. My family is strong and I'm building a nation."

~ ~

As I look back through my history I see African kings pointing at me, telling me to pick up the flame and keep fighting the good fight, because we're going to win. I am an African man who lives in America, and I can do more than make three point shots, touchdowns, and jokes.

They gave us the crack pipe, the cameras, and lights so that we would lose ourselves in the fame. It's not about fame but the *flame* of all those who stood and sang, "We shall overcome" or "We are over-coming."

I promise you, I will hold up the legacy.

I'll tell the truth about the hypocrisies in commercial gangsta Hip Hop and how they have deceived an entire generation with lies that are made to look like the truth.

I'll prove they didn't successfully drug, mug, and thug us all.

I refuse to let the real Hip Hop fall.

Endnotes

Preface: My People Are Destroyed for Lack of Knowledge

1. "Viral Marketing," Wikipedia. <http://en.wikipedia.org/wiki/Viral_ marketing>.
2. Young Y. (July 20, 2006). "'Gangsta lit' poisons black audiences," *USA Today*. <http://www.usatoday.com/news/opinion/editorials/2006-07-20-young-edit_x.htm>.
3. Eckholm E. (March 20, 2006). "Plight Deepens for Black Men, Studies Warn," *The New York Times*. <http://www.nytimes.com/2006/03/20/national/20blackmen.html?ex=1300510800&en=57e0d1ceebcbc209&ei=5090>.

Introduction: A Unique Generation

1. "Rap," *Encarta Africana*. <http://www.africana.com/research/encarta/tt_153.asp>.
2. Stanton JR. "The Last Poets' Umar Bin Hassan Enthralls Hip Hop 101," *Chicken Bones: A Journal*. <http://www.nathaniel-turner.com/lastpoetsumar.htm>.
3. Jones A. (Feb. 20, 2002). "Black gold: Entrepreneurs cash in as image controversy lingers," *Variety.com–Award Central 2002*. <http://www. variety.com/index.asp?layout=awardcentral2002&content=jump&nav=naacp&jump=article&articleid=VR1117861081&categoryid=1187>.
4. Hughes A. (May 2002). "From New York to Nepal, Hip-Hop has become America's leading culture export," *Black Enterprise*. <http://www. blackenterprise.com/Archiveopen.asp?source=/archive2002/05/0502-23.htm>.
5. Lewis R. (2000). "Captured Minds." Lecture series, tape #1. Raleigh, NC.
6. George Clinton. (1982). "Atomic Dog," *Computer Games*. Capitol Records.

7.   The American Heritage® Dictionary of the English Language, Fourth Edition. (2000). Houghton Mifflin Company.

Part 1: Get the Hell out the Hood
Chapter 1. Framework for Understanding Hip Hop Youth
1.   Packaged Facts, a division of MarketResearch.com. (July 2003). "Urban Youth: An Elusive, but Lucrative, Population to Target for Consumer Goods Marketers." <www.packagedfacts. com/editor/viewcontent.asp? prid=244>.
2.   "Stages of Intellectual Development in Children and Teenagers," Child Development Institute. <http://www. childdevelopmentinfo.com/development/piaget.shtml>.
3.   "Stages of Social-Emotional Development in Children and Teenagers," Child Development Institute. <http:// childdevelopmentinfo.com/development/erickson.shtml>.
4.   Byrd A, Solomon A. (Jan. 2005). "What's really going on: entertainment insiders, thinkers and consumers candidly discuss hip-hop's outlook on Black women's sexuality," *Essence*. Essence Communications, Inc. <http://www.essence.com/ essence/takebackthemusic/whattheyresaying. html>.

Chapter 2. Types of Rap
1.   BrainyQuote.com. <http://www.brainyquote.com/quotes/ keywords/rap. html>.
2.   Ibid.
3.   Ibid.
4.   Public Enemy. (1990). "Fight the Power," *Fear of a Black Planet*. Def Jam.

Part 2: Trapped in the Matrix
Chapter 1. Hypocrisy 1—Keeping It Real//Flippin' the Script
1.   Amber J. (March 2005). "Dirty dancing: Take Back the Music, part two," *Essence*. Essence Communications, Inc. <http:// www.essence.com/essence/takebackthemusic/dirtydancing. html>.

2. Dooms R. "Howard Student Proud to Win P.I.M.P. Scholarship," Black College Wire. <http://www.blackcollege wire.org/culture/050718_pimp-scholar/>.

Chapter 2. Making Lies Look Like the Truth

1. Williams B. (Oct. 20, 2003). "Ghettopoly: an American phenomenon. By our capitalistic rules, even a foul game can be fair play," WorkingforChange. <http://www.workingfor-change.com/article.cfm? ItemID=15839>.

2. Awadu KO. (2000). "The Reoccurring Themes of Hip Hop" (interview with Alfred "Coach" Powell). Long Beach, CA.

3. Wright BE. (Dec. 1, 1985). *The Psychopathic Racial Personality and Other Essays.* Partners Publishers Group, 2nd ed.

4. Powell A, Shackleford M, Harris K, Lewis R, Adams H. The Reoccurring Themes & Images in Hip Hop Videos study.

5. Ibid.

6. Adams III H. (Spring 2003). "The Public Health Risks of Rap Videos," *Creativity* (Arts and Humanities Magazine of the Sutherland Community Arts Initiative). pp. 30–31.

7. Press release. (July 25, 2005). "Sony Settles Payola Investigation: Company Acknowledges Problems; Agrees to Sweeping Reforms," Office of New York State Attorney General Eliot Spitzer. <http://www. oag.state.ny.us/press/2005/jul/jul25a_05. html>.

8. Ibid.

9. Friedman R. (Nov. 22, 2005). "Warner Music Payola Scandal," Fox News. <http://www.foxnews.com/story/0,2933,176348,00.html>.

Chapter 3. Hip Hop Mind Control

1. Key WB. (1973). *Subliminal Seduction: Ad Media's Manipulation of a Not So Innocent America.* New York: Signet Books.

2. Davey D. "Nigga or Nigger," *Davey D's Hip Hop Daily News.* <www. daveyd.com/nigaornigpol.html>.

Chapter 4. Words of Deadly Persuasion

1. Cadenhead R. (Feb. 23, 2006). "Actor Tries to Trademark 'N' Word," Wired News. <http://www.wired.com/news/technology/0,70259-0. html>.
2. Thompson B. (May 2006). "Gettin' Some: Bubba Sparxxx," *XXL Magazine.*
3. Scott-Heron G. (1999). "Evolution (and Flashback)," *Evolution (and Flashback): The Very Best of Gil Scott-Heron.* RCA.
4. Akbar N. *Papers in African Psychology*, Mind Productions & Associates. p. 100.
5. Stuckey S. (1976). *"I want to be African": Paul Robeson and the Ends of Nationalist Theory and Practice. 1919–1945.* Los Angeles: Center for Afro-American Studies, University of California.
6. Middleton P, Pilgrim D (Ferris State University). (2005). "Nigger (the word), a brief history!" The African American Registry®. <http://www. aaregistry.com/african_american_ history/2420/Nigger_the_word_a_ brief_history>.
7. Ibid.
8. Weatherford CB. (May 4, 2000). "Japan's bigoted exports to kids." *The Christian Science Monitor*, p. 9.
9. Christie A. (1939/1978). *Ten Little Niggers.* Great Britain: William Collins Sons & Co. Ltd. Glasgow.
10. Middleton. The African American Registry®. <www.aaregistry. com>.
11. Powell A. "Are niggas born or made?" (entry questionnaire).
12. Nas. (2000). "Favor for a Favor," *I Am.* Sony.
13. Akbar N. (2004). *Akbar Papers in African Psychology.* Mind Productions. p. 94.
14. Queen Latifah. (1993). "U.N.I.T.Y.," *Black Reign.* Motown.

Chapter 5. Poetry in Motion

1. Ballou B. (Nov. 7, 2004). "Hip-hop fans turn to original gangstas: Sinatra & pals," BostonHerald.com. <http://news.bostonherald.com/> (archives).
2. Dickinson D. (1993). "Music and the Mind," *New Horizon's on the Beam.* <www.newhorizons.org>.
3. Hill ME. *The Effects of Heavy Metal Music on Levels of Aggression in College Students.* <http://clearinghouse.mwsc.edu/manuscripts/194. asp>.
4. Arnett JJ. (1996). *Metal Heads: Heavy metal music and adolescent alienation.* Boulder, CO: Westview Press Incorporated.
5. Lil' Flip. (2004). "Sunshine." Sony BMG.
6. Juvenile. (2000). "Slow Motion." *Juve the Great.* Universal.
7. Waymer W. (2005). "The More Things Change, the More Things Stay the Same: Observations on Hip Hop Music." Permission granted to excerpt unpublished essay.
8. Jefferson M. (Oct. 13, 2004). "Blackface Master Echoes in Hip-Hop." *The New York Times.* <http://www.nytimes.com> (archives).
9. "Rap," Encarta Africana. <http://www.africana.com/research/encarta/tt_ 153.asp>.
10. Juvenile. "Slow Motion."
11. Ibid.
12. DJ Waxy Fresh. "Breakbeat explanation." <http://www.djwaxyfresh. com/Breakbeat%20Explanation.txt>.
13. Adams III H. "The collective effect of gangsta hip hop," *Creativity* magazine.
14. Kaplan A. (1987). "*Rocking Around the Clock: Music Television, Postmodernism and Consumer Culture.* New York State University at Stonybrook. New York: Routledge, Inc.
15. Wolfe L. (1999). "Turn Off Your TV" (pamphlet), reprinted from *The New Federalist.*

16. Tanner L. (April 5, 2004). "TV Linked to ADHD. Young Children Who Watch TV May Face Risk of Attention Problems," *Associated Press.*
17. Wolfe. "Turn Off Your TV."
18. White JL, Cones III JH, Cones JH. (1999). *Black Man Emerging: Facing the Past & Seizing a Future in America.* New York: W.H. Freeman & Company.

Chapter 6: Hypocrisy 2—Bling Bling//Poverty in the Hood

1. Jadakiss. (2004). "Why." *Kiss of Death.* Ruff Ryders/ Interscope.

Chapter 7. Africa: The Origin of Bling

1. Kanye West. (2005). "Diamonds from Sierra Leone (Remix)," *Late Registration.* Roc-A-Fella Records.
2. Lil' Kim. (1996). "Queen Bitch," *Hardcore.* Atlantic Records.
3. Doebele J. (Feb. 26, 1996). "RA brand is born," *S Forbes.* p. 65.
4. Associated Press and Reuters. (July 17, 2000). "Diamond industry reacts to charges that it's letting trade in 'blood diamonds' pay for African wars," CNN.com. <http://archives. cnn.com/2000/WORLD/europe/07/17/belgium.diamond. congress/>.
5. Kanye West. "Diamonds from Sierra Leone (Remix)."
6. Jones S. (Aug. 21, 2005). "Kanye West, hip-hop's writer-in-residence," USAToday.com. <http://www.usatoday.com/life/ music/news/2005-08-21-kanye-west-inside_x.htm>.

Chapter 8. Ghetto Life: Not So Fabulous

1. Nelson H. (Nov. 1994). "BIG: rap's next big thing—rapper The Notorious BIG—Interview," *Interview.*
2. Doyle R. (March 2004). "Rise of the Black Ghetto: How to create an American version of apartheid," *Scientific American.* <http://www. sciam.com/article.cfm?colID=19&articleID=0000 4E57-B832-101E-B40D83414B7F0000>.

3. Vail K. (Dec. 2003). "The Urban Challenge: Against the Odds in City Schools," *American School Board Journal.* <http://www.asbj.com/specialreports/1203Special%20Reports/S3.html>.

4. National Campaign to Prevent Teen Pregnancy; Centers for Disease Control and Prevention, *2001 Youth Risk Behavior Survey*; National Center for Health Statistics, Births: *Final Data for 2002*; "The Reproductive Health of African American Adolescents, from the Joint Center for Political and Economic Studies, 2003. As reported in "This Is My Reality: The Price of Sex," Motivational Educational Entertainment and the National Campaign to Prevent Teen Pregnancy, January 2004.

5. Associated Press. (Oct. 9, 2003). "'Ghettopoly' game causes outrage." CNN.com. <http://www.cnn.com/2003/US/10/09/ghettopoly.ap/>.

6. Joe. (2001). "Ghetto Child," *Better Days.* Jive.

7. "'Ghettopoly' game causes outrage."

8. Herbert B. (Oct. 17, 2003). "An Ugly Game," *The New York Times.* As posted on Truthout, <http://www.truthout.org/docs_03/101803J.shtml>.

9. Miller, SB. (Oct. 27, 2003). "Hip-hop product portrayals divide black community," *The Christian Science Monitor.* <http://www.csmonitor. com/2003/1027/p01s02-ussc.html>.

10. Encarta® World English Dictionary, Microsoft Corporation. 1998-2004.

11. Ibid.

12. Ibid.

13. Ibid.

14. Ibid.

15. Ibid.

16. Ibid.

17. Ibid.

18. Grandmaster Flash. (1982). "The Message," *The Message.* Elektra Records.

19. Encarta® World English Dictionary.
20. Young Jezzy. (2005). "My Hood, *Let's Get It: Thug Motivation 101*. Def Jam.

Chapter 9. Hypocrisy 3—Role Models//Pimps, Hos, Pushers, & Spies

1. Christian MA. (Aug. 5, 2002). "Nelly: hot rap star sounds off on being no. 1, his pop appeal and the role of an entertainer," *Jet*.
2. Berman E. (Dec. 1996). "What's new at the dogg house?–interview with rapper Snoop Doggy Dogg–Interview," *Interview*. Brant Publications, Inc.
3. Amber J. (March 2005). "Dirty dancing: Take Back the Music Series," *Essence*. Essence Communications, Inc. <http://www.essence.com/essence/takebackthemusic/dirtydancing.html>.
4. Ibid.
5. Ibid.
6. Ibid.
7. Berman E. "What's new at the dogg house?"

Chapter 10. Fear of a Gangsta Planet

1. Adams III H. (Spring 2003). "Public Health Risks of Rap Videos," *Creativity* (Arts and Humanities Magazine of the Sutherland Community Arts Initiative), pp. 30–31
2. Imperioli M. (April/May 2004). "Hip hop, Hollywood and the art of the modern gangster," *Complex Magazine*.
3. Huff A, Mills R. (1999). *Style over Substance: A Critical Analysis of an African American Teenage Subculture*. Chicago: African American Images. p. 13.
4. Imperioli M.
5. Adams III H. "Public Health Risks of Rap Videos." p. 30–31.
6. Muhammad C. (Jan. 10, 2003). "Rap COINTELPRO XII—The 'War On Drugs' Meets the Hip-Hop Economy."

BlackElectorate.com. <http://www.blackelectorate.com/articles.asp?ID=780>.

7. Rhee JK. (2000). "The New School Hip Hop Revolution." <www. aainnovators.com/Archives/Articles/New%20School %20Hip%20Hop-JKRhee.htm>.

8. "Black on Black Crime Statistics," Black on Black Crime Coalition. Center for Healing Hearts and Spirits. <http:// www.hhs center.org/bonbstat.html>.

9. Louis E. "Not on our block," *New York Daily News.* <http:// www. nydailynews.com/news/ideas_opinions/story/361028p-307615c. html>.

10. Ibid.

11. Knoedelseder W. (1993). *Stiffed: A True Story of MCA, the Music Business, and the Mafia.* New York: HarperCollins.

12. Davis D. (May 2003). "Hip Hop and the Po Po" (PowerPoint presentation). East Orange, NJ: PAL Program.

Chapter 11. The Intoxication of the Hip Hop Generation

1. N.W.A. (1988). "Express Yourself," *Straight Outta Compton.* Priority Records.

2. Webb G. Series of articles throughout 1996 in the *San Jose Mercury News* about the CIA's alleged involvement in the crack trade in African American communities.

3. Special Report to Congress: Cocaine and Federal Sentencing Policy. (February 1995). U.S. Sentencing Commission. Washington, DC.

4. Grandmaster Melle Mel. (1998). "White Lines," *White Lines and Other Rap Classics.* Rhino Flashback.

5. Music 365. (April 28, 2000). Eminem Interview: "Oh Yes, It's Shady's Night," <http://www.eminem.net/interviews/shadys_night/>.

6. Nas. (1999). "Nas Is Like," *I Am.* Sony.

7. Missy Elliott. (2001). "X-Tasy," *Miss E ... So Addictive.* Elektra/Wea.

8. Jones M. (2005). "Still Tippin," *Who Is Mike Jones?* Asylum Records.
9. Xzibit. (1998). "Shroomz," *40 Dayz & 40 Nights.* RCA.
10. "DJ Screw," Wikipedia. <http://en.wikipedia.org/wiki/DJ_Screw>.
11. National Survey on Drug Use and Health. (2003). Substance Abuse and Mental Health Services Administration.
12. Ibid.
13. Kanye West. (2005). "Celebration," *Late Registration.* Roc-a-Fella.
14. Busta Rhymes. (1997). "Get High Tonight," *When Disaster Strikes.* Elektra/Wea.
15. Big Tymers. (2002). "Get High," *Hood Rich.* Cash Money.
16. "Youth Smoking." Cancer Trends Progress Report–2005 Update. National Cancer Institute, U.S. National Institutes of Health. <http://progressreport.cancer.gov/doc_detail. asp?pid=1&did=2005&chid= 21&coid=202&mid=>.
17. Soldz S, Huyser DJ, Dorsey E. (Oct. 2003). "The cigar as a drug delivery device: youth use of blunts," *Addiction.* 98(10):1379–86.
18. Wallace Jr. JM, et al. (Nov. 1999). "The Epidemiology of Alcohol, Tobacco and Other Drug Use among Black Youth," *Journal of Studies on Alcohol.* 60(6):800–809.
19. "The NHSDA Report: Alcohol Use by Persons Under the Legal Drinking Age of 21." (May 9, 2003). National Institute on Drug Abuse Substance Abuse and Mental Health Services Administration. Rockville, MD: Office of Applied Studies.
20. Miniño AM, et al. (2002). "Deaths: Final Data for 2000," National Vital Statistics Reports 50. No. 15: Table 27.
21. National Center for Health Statistics Vital Statistics System, "10 Leading Causes of Death, United States 2000, Black, Both Sexes," in WISQARS Leading Causes of Death Reports, 1999–2000 (cited May 18, 2003); American Medical

Association, "Facts about Youth and Alcohol" (cited April 8, 2003).

22. Roberts DF, et al. (1999). "Substance Use in Popular Movies and Music," Center for Substance Abuse Prevention.

23. DuRant RH, et al. (1997). "Tobacco and Alcohol Use Behaviors Portrayed in Music Videos: A Content Analysis," *American Journal of Public Health 87.* No. 7: 1131–1135.

24. Vedantam S. (Sept. 10, 2003). "Severe Steps to Curb Teen Drinking Urged: Alcohol Industry Denounces Report," *Washington Post.*

25. Afroman. (2001). "Because I Got High," *The Good Times.* UMVD Labels.

26. J. Kwon. (2004). "Everybody Getting Tipsy," *Hood Hop.* Arista.

27. "An Imperial History." Courvoisier website. <http://www. courvoisier. com/en/100_imperial.asp>.

28. MacLean N. (Dec. 16, 2004). "Bring on the bling—rappers give Cristal and Hennessy street cred," *San Francisco Chronicle.* <http://www.sfgate. com/cgi-bin/article.cgi?file=/c/ a/2004/12/16/WIGNCAC0AG1.DTL>.

29. Parker E. (Sept. 11–17, 2002). "Hip-Hop Goes Commercial: Rappers Give Madison Avenue a Run for Its Money," *Village Voice.* <http://www.villagevoice.com/news/0237,parker,38205,1. html>.

30. Lawton C. (July 14, 2003). "Napoleon's nightcap gets good rap from hip-hop set," *The Wall Street Journal.*

31. Busta Rhymes. (2002). "Pass the Courvoisier." Bmg Int'l.

32. Strong N. (May 13, 2004). "Jermaine Dupri New Owner of Vodka Company," AllHipHop.com. <http://www.allhiphop. com/hiphopnews/?ID=3169>.

33. Jay-Z. (2000). "Excuse Me, Miss," *Blueprint 2: The Gift & The Curse.* Roc-a-Fella.

34. MacLean N. "Bring on the bling."

35. Ibid.

36. U.S. Department of Health and Human Services. (1998). Tobacco Use among U.S. Racial/Ethnic Minority Groups–African Americans, American Indians and Alaska Natives, Asian Americans and Pacific Islanders, and Hispanics: A Report of the Surgeon General.
37. Ibid.
38. Maine AG. (March 31, 2004). "Kool Cigarettes Target Blacks," Associated Press.
39. King C, Siegel M. (2001, 345). "The Master Settlement Agreement with the Tobacco Industry and Cigarette Advertising in Magazines," *New England Journal of Medicine*. pp. 504–511.
40. Associated Press. (Aug. 30, 2006). "U.S. Report: More Nicotine in Cigarettes," *The New York Times*. <nytimes.com> (archives).
41. Mowery PD, Brick PD, Farrelly MC. (October 2000). Legacy First Look Report 3. Pathways to Established Smoking: Results from the 1999 National Youth Tobacco Survey. Washington DC: American Legacy Foundation. Also included in the "Smoking and Teens Fact Sheet," American Lung Association. (April 2006). <http://www.lungusa.org/site/pp.asp?c=dvLUK9O0E&b= 39871#two>.
42. "Nicotine Craving and Heavy Smoking May Contribute to Increased Use of Cocaine and Heroin." (Feb. 2000). National Institutes of Health and the National Institute on Drug Abuse.

Chapter 12. Spies Among Us

1. Perkins J. (2005). *Confessions of an Economic Hit Man*. San Francisco: Berrett-Koehler.
2. "Cryptanalysis," Wikipedia. <en.wikipedia.org/wiki/Code breaking>.
3. Davis D. (April 18, 2004). "Everything You Need to Know about Hip Hop" (workshop presentation). East Orange, NJ.

4. Interview with Tyrone Powers, PhD. Dr. Powers is the author of *Eyes to My Soul: The Rise or Decline of a Black FBI Agent* (Dover: The Majority Press, 1996).

5. "50 Cent Appeal Fails (Nov. 29, 2005)." Australia: News 2005. <http://www.melonfarmers.co.uk/inau05a.htm>.

6. Matthew A. (Aug. 7, 2005). "His Name Means Money: 50 Cent." *New York Daily News.* <http://www.nydailynews.com/ entertainment/music/story/335269p-286421c.html>.

7. Reuters. (Nov. 23, 2005). "50 Cent: 'Bulletproof' Game OK for Kids."

8. Thomas K. (Nov. 14, 2005). "Anniston Joins the Guys," *USA Today* as cited on <www.vincevaughn.com/archives/cat_ news_etc.html>.

9. Miller D. (Jan. 5, 2004). "Digital Sin Signs 50 Cent; Rapper Will Appear at AVN Adult Entertainment Expo," AVN.com. <http://www. avn.com/index.php?Primary_Navigation=Artic les&Action=Print_Article&Content_ID=66432>.

10. Davis D from the Sept. 2004 lecture, "The Beat Goes on and on to the Break of Dawn."

11. Snoop Dogg. (1993). "Gin and Juice," *Doggystyle.* Death Row.

12. Rodriguez K. (Nov. 29, 2005). "Rock & Roll Hall of Fame Overlooks Hip-Hop Nominees," NobodySmiling.com. <http://www.nobody smiling.com/hiphop/news/85430.php>.

13. Jones T. (June-July 2006). "Is 'Hoopz' Really In Love, Got Game? Or Is She Just Playin'?" *Black Men.* p. 34.

Chapter 13. Who's the Boss?

1. George N. (1998). *hip hop America* (New York: Penguin Putnam), p. 57.

2. Samuels A. (Nov. 22, 2004). "The Reign of Jay-Z," *Newsweek.* MSNBC News. <http://www.msnbc.msn.com/id/6471859/ site/newsweek/>.

3. "40 Richest Under 40." (Sept. 20, 2004). Fortune.com.

4. Leeds J. (Dec. 26, 2004). "Directions 2004: The Most Merchandised; $50 Million for 50 Cent." *The New York Times*. <www.nytimes.com> (archives).

5. "Rock's Rich List," VH1. <www.vh1.com> (archives).

6. Robert. (Aug. 30, 2004). "Ja Rule and MTV Hit with Lawsuit," Rap News Network. <http://www.rapnewsdirect. com/0-202-259408-00.html>.

7. "Trina's Home Facing Foreclosure: Yes, the house featured on 'Cribs'." (Jan. 6, 2005). Lee Bailey's www.EurWeb.com. <http://eurweb.com/story.cfm?id=18188>.

8. Bracelin J. (June 4, 2003). "Ricky Streetz: Prison and bullets can't keep a hardened rapper down," Cleveland Scene. <http://www.clevescene. com/Issues/2003-06-04/music/ soundbites.html>.

9. Leonard D, Wheat A. (June 9, 2003). "Take Two: What has the younger Bronfman learned from his first reign?" Fortune. com. <http://money. cnn.com/magazines/fortune/fortune_ar chive/2003/06/09/343960/index.htm>.

10. Taiara CT. (July 14, 2004). "Invasion of the Media Snatchers," *SF Bay Guardian*. Posted on <http://www.media-alliance. org>.

11. "Music Indies Launch Anti-Concentration Campaign." (March 17, 2005). Impalasite.org. <www.adbusters.org>.

12. Bills L. (2005). Hoover's Fact Sheets. *Fortune*. <www.fortune. com> (archives). Austin: Hoover's, Inc.

13. Attorney Bobby Joe Champion interviewed by Alfred "Coach" Powell. (2001). St. Thomas, Virgin Islands. People of Color Conference.

14. Strong N. (March 23, 2004). "DMX Refuses to Record for Def Jam," AllHipHop.com. <http://www.allhiphop.com/ hiphopnews/?ID=2973>.

15. Peters S. (2004). "A CD is More Than Something in the Music Department" (lecture series).

16. Berfield S. (Oct. 27, 2003). "The CEO of Hip Hop," BusinessWeek Online.com. <http://www.businessweek.com/magazine/content/03_43/b3855001_mz001.htm>.
17. Murphy K. (June 2006). "Fight the Power with Public Enemy's Chuck D," *King Magazine*. p. 166.
18. Byrd A, Solomon A. "What's really going on," *Essence*.

Chapter 14. Hypocrisy 4—Grown Folks Business//Tricks Are for Kids

1. Weingarten M. (Dec. 2001). "Nate Dogg: This Dogg is A Rapper's Best Friend," *Interview*. Brant Publications, Inc.

Chapter 15. Sex in the Hood

1. George N. (Feb. 1996). "LL Cool J's love jones—rapper/actor keeps love as theme of music," *Essence*.
2. Powell A, Harris R. (2004). The Historical Mistreatment of the African American Penis Survey.
3. Darroch JE, et al. (1999). "Age Differences between Sexual Partners in the U.S," Family Planning Perspectives. 31(4), 160–167.
4. 50 Cent. (2005). "In Da Club." *Get Rich or Die Tryin'*. Interscope Records.
5. Welsing FC. (1991). *The Isis Papers*. Chicago: Third World Press. p. 136.
6. Darroch JE. "Age Differences between Sexual Partners in the U.S."
7. Performed by Elvis Presley, composed by Jeff Alexander. (1957). "Jailhouse Rock," from the movie *Jailhouse Rock*. MGM.
8. Hendrickson R. Encyclopedia of Word and Phrase, 2nd edition QPB. p. 207.
9. Bell JC. (1995). *Famous Black Quotations*. New York: Warner Books. p. 41.

10. Boykin K. (May 15, 2002). "Anatomy of a Media Frenzy: The Down Low on the Down Low." <www.keithboykin.com/arch/000476.html>.

11. Foxy Brown & Method Man. (1996). "Ill Na Na." *Ill Na Na.* Def Jam.

12. Destiny's Child. (2004). "Lookin for a Solider," *Destiny Fulfilled.* Sony.

13. Lewis R. (Jan. 2004). "Why Queens Tend to Love Fools" (lecture tape).

14. Montgomery JP, Mokotoff ED, Gentry AC, Blair JM. "The extent of bisexual behaviour in HIV-infected men and implications for transmission to their female sex partners." AIDS Care 2003; 15:829–837. As reported in "Fact Sheet: HIV/ AIDS among African Americans." (Feb. 2006). Center for Disease Control and Prevention. <http://www. cdc.gov/hiv/topics/aa/resources/factsheets/aa.htm>.

15. Infectious Diseases in Corrections Report (formerly the HEPP Report). (2000). "HIV Infection Among Incarcerated Women." <http://www.idcronline.org/>. As reported in "Fact Sheet: HIV/ AIDS and African American Women." (Oct. 22, 2004). Black Women's Health Imperative. <http://www.blackwomenshealth. org/site/News2? page=NewsArticle&id=6594>.

Chapter 16. Lyrical Felonies & Misdemeanors in Hop Hop

1. "Public enemy's Chuck D urges students to be decisive." (Nov. 3, 2005). Diverse Issues in Higher Education.

2. Armstrong EG. (2001). "Gangsta Misogyny: A Content Analysis of the Portrayals of Violence Against Women in Rap Music, 1987–1993." *Journal of Criminal Justice and Popular Culture.* vol. 8(2) pp. 96–126. <http://www.albany.edu/scj/jcjpc/vol8is2/armstrong.html>.

3. Ibid.

4. Willie D. (1989). "Bald Headed Hoes." *Controversy.* Rap-A-Lot/Priority.

5. Too $hort. (1987). "Blow Job Betty." *Raw, Uncut And X-Rated.* 75 Girls.
6. Too $hort. (1987). "Short Side." *Raw, Uncut And X-Rated.* 75 Girls.
7. N.W.A. (1991). "She Swallowed It." *Efil4zaggin.* Ruthless/Priority.
8. Ice-T. (1992). "KKK Bitch." *Body Count.* Sire/Warner Brothers.
9. Armstrong. "Gangsta Misogyny."
10. (a) Eazy-E. (1988). "Nobody Move." *Eazy-Duz-It.* Ruthless/Priority. (b) Snoop Doggy Dogg. (1993). "Ain't No Fun." *DoggyStyle.* Death Row/Interscope/Atlantic. (c) Too $hort. (1990). "Punk Bitch." *$hort Dog's In The House.* Jive/RCA.
11. MC Ren. (1992). "Behind The Scenes." *Kizz My Black Azz.* Ruthless/Priority.
12. Too $hort. (1987). "She's A Bitch." *Raw, Uncut And X-Rated.* 75 Girls.
13. Department of Health and Human Services (U.S.), Administration on Children, Youth, and Families. Child maltreatment 2003 (online). Washington: Government Printing Office; 2005 (cited April 5, 2005). <www.acf.hhs.gov/programs/cb/publications/cm03/>.
14. Centers for Disease Control and Prevention. Youth Risk Behavior Surveillance—United States, 2003. MMWR 2004;53(SS-02):1–96. <www.cdc.gov/mmwr/PDF/SS/SS5302.pdf>.
15. Fisher BS, Cullen FT, Turner MG. (2000). "The sexual victimization of college women," Washington: Department of Justice (US), National Institute of Justice. Publication No. NCJ 182369.
16. Tjaden P, Thoennes N. (2000). Full report of the prevalence, incidence, and consequences of violence against women: findings from the national violence against women survey. Washington: National Institute of Justice. Report NCJ 183781.

17. Klosterman C. (April 2005). "Hard Candy," Spin.com, p. 77.
18. Lil Jon & the East Side Boyz. 2002. "Get Low." Kings of Crunk. TVT.
19. *XXL* magazine. July 2003. pp.121–122.
20. Barone M. (Sept. 2005). "Tongue Lashing." *King* magazine. p. 118.
21. hooks b. (1992). *Black Looks: Race and Representation*. Boston: South End Press. pp. 68–69.

Chapter 17. Dirty Dancing & STDs

1. Whitcomb D. (May 1, 2002). "Girls Made To Pass Underwear Test to Enter CA High School Dance." Reuters Limited.
2. Wingood GM, et al. (March 1, 2003). "A Prospective Study of Exposure to Rap Music Videos and African American Female Adolescents' Health," *American Journal of Public Health*. Vol. 93, Issue 3, 437–439. <www.ajph.org/cgi/content/citation/93/3/437>.
3. Ibid.
4. Martino SC, Collins RL, Elliott MN, Strachman A, Kanouse DE, Berry SH. (Aug. 2006). "Exposure to Degrading Versus Nondegrading Music Lyrics and Sexual Behavior Among Youth." *Pediatrics*, Vol. 118, No. 2, pp. e430–e441.
5. Ibid.
6. Ibid.
7. Ibid.
8. Kalb C, Murr A. (May 15, 2006). "Battling a Black Epidemic," *Newsweek*. <http://www.msnbc.msn.com/id/12665721/site/newsweek/>.
9. Outkast. (2003). "Where Are My Panties?" *Speakerboxxx/The Love Below*. La Face.
10. The Body: Heterosexual Transmission of HIV—29 States, 1999-2002. Center for Disease Control. HIV/AIDS

Surveillance Report, 2002. Vol. 14. <www.cdc.gov/hiv/stats/hasrlink.htm>.

11. Pam Shackleford interviewed by Alfred "Coach" Powell. (May 2003). Survey on the historical mistreatment of the African male penis.

12. Obie Trice. (2003). "Hoodrats," *Cheers*. Interscope Records.

13. 2 Live Crew. (1995). "Hoochie Mama," *Friday: Original Motion Picture Soundtrack*. Priority Records.

14. Rick James. (1992). "Super Freak. *Street Life*. Motown.

Chapter 18. Parent'Hood: A Divine Mission

1. Hitman Sammy Sam. (2003). "Step Daddy," *The Step Daddy*. Umvd Labels.

2. "Stats and Facts." (2003). Children of Incarcerated Parents National Forum.

3. B Rock & Bizz. (1999). "My Baby Daddy," *Porkin' Beans & Wienes*. Tony Mercedes.

4. Queen Pen. (2001). "My Baby Daddy," *Conversations with Queen*. Motown.

Chapter 20. Hip Hop @ the Cross

1. Jung CG. (1964). *Man and His Symbols* (New York: Laurel). p.3.

2. Clark J. (April 2004). "Pimpin Ken Game Over," *The Source Magazine*. p. 84.

3. Mwandishi GS. (Aug, 21, 2003). "Hip Hop Holy Trinity," *Christianity Today Magazine*. <www.stinkzone.com/cgi-bin/archives/000043.html>

4. Ibid.

5. Ja Rule. (1999). "187 Motha Bucka Baptiss Church." *Venni Vetti Vecci*. Def Jam.

6. "Ja Knows, Ja Rules," AskMen.com.

7. Ja Rule. (2000). *Rule 3:36*. Def Jam.

8. The Associated Press. (Oct. 25, 2005). "Rapper DMX Faces Prison After Guilty Plea," as reported on ABCnews.com. <http://abcnews.go. com/Entertainment/LegalCenter/ wireStory?id=1250707>.

Chapter 21. St. Hip Hop

1. Kanye West. (2004). "Jesus Walks," *The College Dropout.* Roc-a-Fella.
2. "Suge Speaks Out about Tupac." (Sept. 20, 1996). MTV.com, <http://www.mtv.com/news/articles/1434031/19960920/ story.jhtml>.
3. Jones S. (Aug. 21, 2005). "Kanye West, hip-hop's writer-in-residence." USA Today.
4. Ridenour F. (2001). *So What's the Difference?* (Ventura, California: Regal Books, A Division of Gospel Light).
5. WordNet ® 2.0, 2003 Princeton University.
6. "Cult." Wikipedia. <en.wikipedia.org/wiki/Cult>.
7. Marsha Hicks interviewed by Alfred "Coach" Powell. (Jan. 6, 2004). Milwaukee, WI.
8. Brown WJ, Fraser BP. (Jan. 5, 2001). "Hip-Hop Kingdom Come," *Christianity Today.* <http://www.christianitytoday. com/ct/2001/001/4.48.html>.
9. Sailhamer S. (Feb. 2005). "Holy Hip Hop genre brings gospel to urban America," ChristianExaminer On the Web. <www.christianexaminer. com/Articles/Articles%20Feb05/ Art_Feb05_07.html>.
10. Gaines AS. (Aug. 2002). "Get Ready for the Hip-Hop Revolution." *Charisma Magazine.* <http://www.charismamag. com/display.php?id= 6337>.

Part 3: Rescuing Our Children
Chapter 1: Redefining the Revolution

1. Common. (2000). "The 6th Sense," *The Light/The 6th Sense.* Universal.

Chapter 2: Hip Hop Survival

1. Marvin Gaye. (1971). "What's Going On," *What's Going On.* Motown.
2. Nelly. (2005). "Grillz," *Sweatsuit.* Umvd Labels.
3. Seymour Jr. A. (Feb. 27, 2003). "Bill restricts who can do gold teeth," *The Atlanta Journal-Constitution.*
4. Duggan JW. "Toxic Metal Syndrome: The Great Dental Debate: Structure and Function Vs Toxicity." *The Holistic Alternative.* <http://www.carondevita.com/dentaldebate.html>.
5. Paul Wall. (2004). "Know What I'm Talkin' About," *Chick Magnet.* Paid in Full.
6. Three 6 Mafia. (2003). "Ridin' Spinners," *Da Unbreakables.* Sony.
7. Powell A. (2006). "Buckle Up," *School Is My Job* (workshop).
8. Youth Risk Behavior Survey. (2001). Centers for Disease Control and Prevention.
9. Annual Assessment of Motor Vehicle Crashes. (2001). The National Highway Traffic Safety Administration.
10. Powell A. (2006). "Why Did You Bring a Gun?" *School Is My Job* (workshop).
11. Ice Cube. (1991). "Man's Best Friend," *Death Certificate.* Priority Records.
12. Ice Cube. (1992). "It Was a Good Day," *The Predator.* Priority Records.
13. "Groups At Risk (2006)." Youth Violence Fact Sheet. Center for Disease Control. < http://www.cdc.gov/ncipc/factsheets/yvfacts.htm>.
14. Haynie RL. "Real Men, Real Issues: What African American Men Need to Know." African American Health. School of Medicine, Case Western Reserve University.

Chapter 3. SugarStrings: Music Education for the Hip Hop Generation

1. "The Sound of Silence: The Unprecedented Decline of Music Education in California Public Schools: A Statistical Review," compiled by the Music for All Foundation in cooperation with music and arts education organizations in California and around the country. <http://music-for-all.org/sos.html>.

2. College-Bound Seniors National Report: Profile of SAT Program Test Takers. (2001). Princeton, NJ: The College Entrance Examination Board.

3. Graziano A, Matthew P, Shaw G. (March 1999). "Enhanced learning of proportional math through music training and spatial-temporal training." *Neurological Research 21*.

4. Shaw G. (March 15, 1999). Neurological Research. University of California, Irvine.

5. Venerable G. (1989). "The Paradox of the Silicon Savior," as reported in "The Case for Sequential Music Education in the Core Curriculum of the Public Schools," The Center for the Arts in the Basic Curriculum, New York.

6. "The Comparative Academic Abilities of Students in Education and in Other Areas of a Multi-focus University," Peter H. Wood, ERIC Document No. ED327480. Also reported in "The Case for Music in the Schools," *Phi Delta Kappa*. (February 1994).

7. Ibid.

8. Catterall JS, Chapleau R, Iwanaga J. (1999). "Involvement in the Arts and Human Development: General Involvement and Intensive Involvement in Music and Theater Arts." Los Angeles, CA: The Imagination Project at UCLA Graduate School of Education and Information Studies.

9. Texas Commission on Drug and Alcohol Abuse Report. Reported in the *Houston Chronicle*. (January 1998).

10. Based on data from the NELS:88 (National Education Longitudinal Study), second follow-up. (1992).

11. Louis E. (Oct. 22, 2006). "All rhyme, no reason for rap world's modern minstrels," *New York Daily News.* <http://www. nydailynews.com/news/col/story/463962p-390396c.html>.

Chapter 4: Gateways to Heaven: Enhancing Prevention Programs

1. Williams DM. (1999). *Sensual Celibacy: the Sexy Woman's Guide to Using Abstinence for Recharging Your Spirit, Discovering Your Passions, Achieving Greater Intimacy in Your Next Relationship.* New York: Fireside (Simon & Schuster). p. 159.
2. Ibid, p. 19.

Chapter 5. Raising Hip Hop Scholars

1. Shaughnesy MF. (April 17, 2006). "An Interview with Samuel Halperin and Nancy Martin: About 'Turning Around Drop Outs,'" EducationNews.Org. <http://www.educationnews.org/ writers/michael/An%20Interview_with_Samuel_Halperin_ and_Nancy_Martin.htm>.
2. Chandler J. "Oppositional Defiant Disorder (ODD) and Conduct Disorder (CD) in Children and Adolescents: Diagnosis and Treatment." <http://www.klis.com/chandler/ pamphlet/oddcd/oddcdpamphlet.htm>
3. Mrozowski J, Byczkowski J. (Feb. 22, 2004). "Black students disciplined more: Difference blamed on stereotypes, culture, poverty and behavior," *The Cincinnati Enquirer.*
4. Alliance for Excellent Education fact sheet. <http://www. all4ed.org/publications/Economy%20Factoids%20for%20W ebsite.doc>.
5. Rossi R. (Feb. 3, 2005). "Fewer city high school grads than claimed," Suntimes.com. <http://www.consortium-chicago. org/mediacontacts/citations/020305_suntimes.html>.
6. Ibid.
7. Swanson CB. (Feb. 25, 2004). "Who Graduates? Who Doesn't? A Statistical Portrait of Public High School Graduation.

Class of 2001." Urban Institute. <http://www.urban.org/url. cfm?ID=410934>.

8. Information from two digests published by the ERIC Clearinghouse on Urban Education: "School Dropouts: New Information about an Old Problem" by Wendy Schwartz and "The Impact of Vocational Education on Racial and Ethnic Minorities" by Francisco Rivera-Batiz.

9. Ibid.

10. City High. (2001). "City High Anthem," *City High*. Interscope Records.

11. Rivera-Batiz, Schwartz.

Chapter 6. Welcome to Nellyville

1. Chuck D. (1998). *Fight The Power: Rap, Race and Reality*. Delta Publishing.

2. Nelly. (2002). "Welcome to Nellyville," *Nellyville*. Umvd Labels.

3. Ibid.

4. Office of Policy Planning and Research, United States Department of Labor. (March 1965). "The Negro Family: The Case for National Action." <http://www.dol.gov/asp/ programs/history/webid-meynihan. htm>.

5. Ibid.

6. Nelly. "Welcome to Nellyville."

For more information on Coach Powell's programs, please visit www.acoachpowell.com.

Index

106 & Park 56, 58
2 Live Crew 71, 261, 399
50 Cent xvi, 48, 61, 77, 102, 116, 155, 156, 161, 178, 191, 194, 195, 196, 197, 198, 199, 200, 204, 216, 233, 248, 249, 258, 275, 279, 285, 286, 287, 305, 306, 315, 393, 394, 395

Abner Louima 88
academic performance 30, 128, 335, 337, 339, 342, 349
act like you know 331, 332, 333, 334
Africa 2, 39, 82, 115, 116, 117, 118, 165, 226, 304, 386
African American community xiii, xiv, xvi, 47, 125, 189, 190, 317, 319, 362
Afrika Bambaataa 4, 31, 149, 316
Afro-Latino 19, 61
Agatha Christie 79, 128
Agent provocateur 189, 190, 200
AIDS 93, 102, 131, 141, 165, 236, 241, 243, 244, 253, 258, 261, 264, 317, 377, 396, 399
alcohol xv, xviii, 12, 23, 33, 52, 63, 130, 137, 141, 147, 157, 162, 168, 169, 174, 175, 176, 178, 179, 180, 181, 182, 183, 187, 191, 198, 208, 209, 221, 234, 239, 252, 254, 282, 294, 295, 319, 325, 327, 338, 342, 343, 346, 347, 349, 362, 365, 390, 391, 403
alias 192, 195
Alizé 176
Amadou Diallo 88
American Idol 160, 161
American Music Awards 47
American Tobacco Company 78
Amilcar Cabral 169, 182
AOL/Time Warner 211
artificial harmony 54, 285
A Tribe Called Quest 86
autonomic nervous system 106

Bad Boy Records 154
bass line xviii, 253
Bernie Mac 119, 143
Bertelsmann AG 83
Bert Williams 109
BET xvi, 7, 46, 47, 55, 56, 57, 58, 66, 112, 140, 141, 148, 155, 170, 175, 179, 212, 217, 218, 220, 245, 249, 317
BET's Rap City; The Bassment 56, 57
Big Tymers 167, 172, 191, 390
Bill Cosby 67
bitch 34, 45, 53, 59, 62, 65, 70, 71, 72, 89, 90, 91, 92, 93, 94, 101, 103, 115, 205, 209, 211, 229, 237, 246, 249, 263, 334, 378, 386, 397
black-on-black crime 5, 52
black-on-black love xix, 32, 378
black-on-black violence 36, 216
black arts movement 2, 55, 103
Black Church 3, 284, 286, 287, 291, 304, 306, 308
Black Panthers 82, 189
black power movement 2, 39
bling bling 10, 66, 69, 70, 93, 102, 111, 114, 115, 116, 147, 191, 201, 209, 238, 249, 277, 279, 324, 368, 371, 377, 386
blood diamonds 118, 386
Bloods 160, 164, 311
blues 1, 7, 87, 98, 170, 289, 323, 371
blunts 108, 162, 168, 172, 173, 181, 210, 235, 329, 349, 390
BMG 60, 213, 385, 392
Bobby E. Wright vii, 169
Bob Johnson 191
Bone Thugs-n-Harmony 167, 170, 290, 291
break dancing 184, 309
Brown & Williamson 183, 184, 185, 186
Bubba Sparxxx 75, 226, 384
Busta Rhymes 171, 179, 390, 392

C-Murder 161
call-and-response 5, 33

candy xix, 9, 168, 172, 186, 187, 197, 202, 247, 248, 288, 294, 321, 398
candy shop 9, 197, 248
Cane 144, 163, 278, 282, 283
capitalism 38, 112, 158, 206
cartoons 9, 29, 108
Cash Money Millionaires 115
Cathy Hughes 218
Cecil Rhodes 117
Cedric \"The Entertainer\" 119
celibacy 273, 345, 346, 403
cerebral cortex 97
Chaka Khan 99
chalice 144, 276, 278, 283
Champagne xvi, 177, 178, 181
chicken head 33, 258, 263
child development 27, 382
Chris Rock 67, 119
Christian 50, 92, 119, 164, 179, 222, 276, 277, 278, 279, 282, 285, 291, 292, 294, 297, 300, 301, 302, 303, 304, 306, 307, 308, 309, 310, 311, 345, 349, 384, 387, 388
Christina Norman 217
Chuck D viii, 202, 217, 245, 317, 370, 395, 396, 404
CIA 63, 147, 164, 203, 389
cigarettes 52, 167, 171, 183, 184, 185, 186, 187, 261, 325, 375, 392
cigars 39, 52, 108, 162, 172, 173, 181, 325
civil rights movement 5, 39, 55, 103, 307
cocaine 52, 126, 131, 132, 147, 154, 163, 164, 165, 166, 167, 172, 196, 254, 372, 389, 392
Cognac 171, 172, 177, 178, 179, 182, 294
COINTELPRO 85, 389
comedy 16, 67, 120, 212
conscious rap 32, 173, 216, 289
consumerism 46, 125, 189, 191, 206
Country Western 33, 69, 70, 175, 304
Courvoisier 171, 178, 179, 216, 283, 391, 392
crack 52, 119, 126, 127, 147, 153, 154, 155, 163, 164, 165, 166, 167, 171, 172, 186, 190, 195, 254, 261, 352, 356, 372, 377, 379, 389
Crips 160, 164

Cristal 113, 178, 181, 182, 205, 283, 391
crucifix 8, 11, 276, 278, 279, 280, 282, 283
crunk 33, 59, 107, 249, 251, 252, 253, 256, 263, 285, 398
Cypress Hill 86, 290, 291

Da Brat 241
Damon Wayans 74
dancing 20, 81, 98, 184, 222, 251, 252, 253, 257, 309, 346, 347, 383, 388, 398
Daniel Patrick Moynihan 372
Dave Chappelle 67
David Banner 107, 253, 285, 323
David Chang 52, 126
Death Row (Tha Row Records) 154
DeBarge 99
DeBeers 117
Debra L. Lee 217, 218
decode 95, 104, 110, 129, 260, 285, 294
Def Comedy Jam 120
deoxyribonucleic acid (DNA) 93
Destiny's Child 94, 95, 222, 243, 245, 396
diamonds 8, 112, 115, 117, 118, 283, 371, 386
Diana Ross 99
Dick Gregory viii, 3
DJ 4, 5, 56, 60, 105, 169, 170, 184, 185, 243, 298, 309, 385, 390
DJ Kool Herc 5
DJ Screw 169, 170, 390
DMX 215, 288, 292, 293, 395, 400
dogg 48, 50, 71, 72, 77, 81, 89, 90, 91, 92, 93, 94, 95, 96, 103, 105, 139, 142, 144, 146, 148, 160, 178, 191, 201, 219, 223, 234, 242, 245, 246, 249, 251, 284, 285, 286, 288, 294, 334, 378, 388, 393, 395, 397
Don L. Lee (Haki Madhubuti) 3
Donna Marie Williams x, 125, 335, 345
Don Redman 171
Dr. Dre 14, 77, 105, 167, 204, 245
Dr. Seuss 98, 104, 110
Driving Under the Influence (DUI) 326
Driving Under the Influence of Hip Hop (DUIHH) 326
Driving While Black (DWB) 327
Driving While Intoxicated (DWI) 326
drop out 113, 336, 361, 362, 364, 403

Drug Court 343
drug culture 8, 37, 123
Drug Enforcement Administration (DEA) 164
drug laws 214, 343
drugs xv, 32, 37, 41, 52, 54, 93, 121, 132, 141,
    147, 148, 151, 154, 156, 157, 162, 166,
    168, 169, 170, 171, 172, 176, 187, 188,
    191, 194, 197, 198, 205, 228, 232, 235,
    252, 254, 305, 309, 325, 338, 342, 343,
    344, 347, 349, 362, 377, 378, 389
drums xviii

Earth Wind and Fire 96
Ebonics 9, 33, 177
economic hit man 189, 393
economy 2, 7, 13, 157, 362, 389, 403
Ecstasy 147, 167, 168, 169, 172, 227, 325,
    374
Eddie Murphy 67, 119, 209
education 19, 25, 41, 51, 104, 111, 112, 122,
    123, 142, 143, 145, 146, 147, 198, 214,
    317, 335, 336, 337, 338, 339, 340, 341,
    343, 351, 352, 354, 355, 356, 358, 359,
    362, 363, 365, 367, 369, 370, 396, 402,
    403, 404
educators v, xiii, xix, 2, 20, 50, 53, 110, 143,
    146, 220, 225, 237, 351, 357
Elijah Muhammad 55
Elvis Presley 235, 396
EMI Group 213
Eminem 87, 91, 167, 180, 204, 208, 245, 260,
    390
entertainment xix, 2, 7, 14, 33, 40, 55, 58, 67,
    74, 85, 109, 131, 140, 142, 152, 154, 156,
    160, 188, 197, 205, 208, 212, 217, 221,
    225, 255, 261, 285, 302, 308, 344, 375,
    382, 387, 393, 400
entrainment 15, 53, 54, 61, 142, 285, 286
epidemic xiv, 29, 54, 243, 268, 320, 399
Erik H. Erikson 20
Eve 137, 228, 241, 273

Fannie Lou Hamer 169
fantasy 24, 29, 59, 106, 108, 142, 150, 173,
    224, 246, 257, 260, 286
fashion 2, 14, 39, 66, 83, 114, 116, 190, 193,
    222, 279, 280, 282, 297, 345

Federal Communications Commission 59
Flava Flav 202
Foxy Brown 240, 241, 297, 396
funk 4, 33, 99, 106, 143, 248

gangbanging xiv, 52, 71, 139, 154, 227, 229,
    230
Gary Byrd 5
Gary Webb 164
gender bending 25, 45, 220, 221
George Clinton 9, 71, 96, 102, 382
ghetto xiv, xix, 1, 2, 5, 13, 20, 29, 38, 40, 41,
    47, 52, 53, 54, 67, 72, 85, 87, 88, 89, 91,
    93, 94, 98, 106, 112, 113, 114, 116, 119,
    120, 121, 126, 127, 128, 129, 131, 132,
    137, 138, 149, 150, 156, 157, 159, 165,
    181, 189, 190, 192, 201, 210, 214, 228,
    230, 231, 243, 260, 261, 262, 263, 277,
    281, 282, 294, 296, 310, 319, 344, 357,
    370, 371, 372, 373, 375, 376, 386, 387
ghetto fabulous 112, 116, 132
Ghettopoly 52, 126, 127, 128, 383, 387
Gil Scott-Heron 3, 76, 384
goblet 276, 282, 283
God x, xiii, xviii, 8, 11, 37, 46, 51, 64, 72, 90,
    91, 92, 93, 94, 97, 98, 111, 118, 122, 150,
    166, 200, 203, 233, 239, 265, 266, 267,
    272, 273, 274, 275, 276, 277, 279, 280,
    281, 283, 285, 286, 287, 288, 289, 290,
    291, 292, 293, 294, 295, 296, 297, 298,
    300, 301, 302, 304, 305, 309, 311, 340,
    348, 377
gold 8, 70, 74, 116, 117, 148, 176, 184, 202,
    212, 277, 283, 286, 292, 295, 296, 322,
    323, 324, 325, 381, 401
Good Times 374, 375, 391
gospel 2, 21, 33, 97, 98, 106, 107, 304, 306,
    307, 310, 312, 336, 340, 400
graffiti 5, 184, 310, 311, 312
Grammys xvi, 46, 283, 300
Grand Master Flash & the Furious Five 6
Grandmaster Melle Mel 166, 390
grills 283, 286, 322, 323, 324, 325, 326
guns 35, 52, 71, 123, 126, 149, 151, 156, 210,
    234, 246, 329, 330, 333

H. "Rap" Brown 3
harmony 54, 97, 98, 167, 170, 285, 290, 291
Harriet Tubman 39, 169, 213
Hennessy 171, 180, 294, 295, 391
heroin 147, 155, 172, 261, 392
Hip Hop/ghetto matrix xiv, xix, 20, 29, 85, 94, 98, 106, 138, 189, 190, 192, 228, 230, 231, 243, 260, 261, 281, 282, 310, 319, 344, 357, 373, 376
Hip Hop market 6, 198
history 1, 2, 6, 10, 15, 31, 32, 39, 55, 76, 77, 82, 95, 143, 146, 149, 161, 176, 182, 188, 192, 193, 201, 202, 203, 207, 209, 212, 220, 228, 282, 296, 303, 310, 318, 354, 378, 384, 391, 404
hit xvii, 8, 35, 58, 61, 62, 70, 83, 91, 94, 104, 107, 113, 114, 132, 133, 142, 147, 163, 166, 167, 168, 171, 176, 179, 189, 231, 235, 241, 249, 254, 270, 271, 285, 287, 319, 355, 358, 360, 362, 366, 393, 394
ho 36, 53, 58, 61, 62, 70, 130, 131, 132, 139, 211, 257, 270, 291, 305, 334, 378
homosexual 35, 236
hood (neighborhood) 1, 89, 121, 126, 128, 133, 134, 135
hood rat 33, 260, 261
Hottentot Venus 226
Hpnotiq 171, 176, 177, 178
Hunter Adams III ix, 59, 107
Hurricane Katrina 51, 199

Ice-T 159, 246, 397
ice cream 9, 89, 119, 320
Ice Cube 14, 77, 159, 245, 246, 261, 322, 330, 401
ill nana 240, 378
Image Awards 47
incarceration xvii, 15, 131, 153, 198, 201, 243, 244
infomercials xv, 55, 58, 85, 106, 108, 170, 225, 242, 342, 347
In Living Color 120
institutionalized racism xix
irresponsible sex 51, 55, 69, 125, 153, 253, 270, 342, 349
Islam 277, 296, 297, 298, 302

J. Anthony Brown 119
Jackie O 241
Jackson 5 99
Jadakiss 114, 191, 386
James Brown 55, 82, 98
James Byrd 88
Ja Rule 168, 205, 208, 291, 292, 394, 400
Jay-Z 14, 27, 77, 90, 96, 148, 167, 178, 180, 181, 182, 191, 200, 204, 208, 212, 286, 297, 298, 299, 315, 392, 394
jazz 1, 2, 21, 32, 87, 97, 98, 106, 107, 170, 289, 318, 323, 336, 340
Jean Piaget 20
Jermaine Dupri 180, 181, 392
Jesus xix, 11, 38, 117, 142, 208, 209, 266, 276, 278, 279, 280, 282, 283, 286, 292, 294, 295, 296, 297, 299, 300, 301, 302, 303, 304, 305, 306, 307, 308, 309, 310, 343, 348, 400
jewelry xvi, 38, 39, 115, 116, 144, 159, 184, 280, 284, 301, 323, 324, 325, 327, 345, 349
Jezzy 133, 388
Jim Crow 74, 263, 282
J Kwon 176
John Hendrick Clarke 45
juke dancing 346
Juvenile xv, 101, 104, 201, 364, 385

K.C. and the Sunshine Band 99
Kahia 241
Kanye West 31, 115, 117, 142, 167, 199, 200, 300, 386, 390, 400
keep it real 41, 45, 54, 81, 115, 150, 221, 332
KKK (Ku Klux Klan) 150, 151, 152, 246, 397
Kool and the Gang 99

Latino 9, 19, 61, 98, 113, 144, 166, 206, 214, 311, 312, 316
Lil' Bow Wow 113, 216
Lil' Flip 101, 385
Lil' Kim 14, 70, 115, 159, 178, 191, 207, 216, 222, 233, 240, 241, 248, 249, 279, 294, 296, 386
Lil' Romeo 45, 113, 181, 203
Lil Jon 107, 191, 253, 315, 322, 323, 398
Lil Mack 45

limbic system 97
Llaila Afrika ix, 324
LL Cool J 225, 395
Lovebug Starski 4
Luke 1, 71, 191, 208, 294, 348
lust 36, 68, 69, 100, 117, 145, 201, 277, 291, 348
lyrical rape 246

Ma$e 191, 302, 305, 306
Ma'at 137
Mack vii, ix, 3, 45, 48, 49, 143, 144, 259, 286, 288
Mafia 146, 147, 148, 149, 168, 287, 328, 389, 401
magic stick 9, 22, 198, 233, 234, 235, 245, 258, 275
Malcolm X 39, 73, 127, 169, 189, 374
Malt liquor 63, 113, 126, 131, 177, 178, 186, 261
Marcus M. Garvey 169
marijuana 52, 71, 108, 126, 147, 167, 170, 171, 172, 173, 196, 202, 254, 290, 325
marriage xix, 28, 36, 52, 69, 101, 125, 126, 144, 158, 230, 233, 235, 238, 239, 244, 268, 269, 272, 273, 277, 295, 332, 347, 371, 373
Martin Luther King, Jr. 102, 165
Marvin Gaye 96, 319, 371, 401
Master P 14, 45, 46, 77, 120, 191, 209, 212, 322
materialism 5, 21, 46, 55, 114, 125, 189, 191, 206, 297, 309
matrix xiv, xix, 2, 12, 13, 20, 29, 41, 43, 47, 53, 54, 74, 85, 87, 91, 94, 96, 98, 100, 106, 120, 138, 156, 165, 189, 190, 192, 228, 230, 231, 243, 257, 260, 261, 263, 281, 282, 310, 316, 317, 319, 344, 357, 373, 376, 383
Maury Povich Show 267
McLoughlin Brothers 78, 128
melody 97, 98, 253
memory v, 32, 74, 82, 97, 99, 100, 101, 102, 171, 201, 227, 252, 376
mentacide 55, 62
menthol 184
Message N/A Bottle 12, 63, 83, 176, 282

Michael Jackson 27, 28, 99, 221
milk shake 9
Million Man March 376
minister vii, viii, 223, 243, 288, 305, 376
misogyny 55, 71, 216, 277, 397
Missy Elliott 14, 168, 216, 241, 257, 276, 390
Mo'Nique 119
mole 189
MTV 7, 46, 47, 55, 56, 108, 112, 175, 179, 198, 205, 212, 217, 218, 220, 249, 394, 400
MTV Cribs 112, 205
Murder Inc. 149, 154, 291
music education 335, 336, 337, 338, 339, 340, 402
music videos 1, 7, 29, 34, 35, 37, 48, 58, 59, 70, 106, 108, 121, 140, 141, 153, 155, 162, 175, 214, 254, 256, 278, 347, 391, 398
Mystikal 161

Na'im Akbar ix, 77, 90
NAACP 75, 381
Nas 77, 85, 149, 167, 288, 294, 295, 385, 390
Nate Dogg 219, 223, 395
Negro 76, 77, 81, 82, 89, 372, 373, 404
Nelly 14, 46, 48, 49, 138, 140, 176, 204, 220, 253, 278, 285, 315, 322, 370, 371, 372, 373, 374, 388, 401, 404
New Orleans 51, 115, 200
nguzo saba vii, 137
nicotine 185, 186, 187, 392
nigga xix, 35, 47, 50, 52, 53, 59, 62, 65, 73, 74, 75, 76, 77, 80, 81, 84, 85, 86, 87, 89, 90, 91, 95, 161, 168, 180, 210, 211, 259, 266, 271, 295, 334, 378, 384
Niggaz With Attitude 86
nigger xix, 50, 52, 73, 74, 75, 76, 77, 78, 79, 80, 81, 84, 85, 86, 87, 88, 89, 90, 103, 129, 210, 269, 295, 334, 384
Nikki Giovanni 3, 70, 103
No Child Left Behind Act of 2002 335
no snitching 54, 134, 135, 152
Notorious B.I.G. 77, 119, 145, 178, 191, 278, 330

obesity 320, 321
Obie Trice 260, 399
Ohio Players 99
Old School xviii, 6, 9, 48, 86, 96, 98, 99, 101, 102, 107, 201, 262, 340
Oppositional Defiant Disorder (ODD) 403
Outkast 249, 256, 399

P. Diddy 14, 96, 113, 178, 179, 278
pandemic xiv, 106
P and L Theory 68
Paramount 155, 212
parents v, xiii, xv, xix, 2, 9, 11, 20, 21, 23, 24, 30, 46, 47, 50, 52, 53, 64, 66, 67, 69, 94, 98, 103, 109, 113, 117, 120, 128, 131, 132, 134, 139, 141, 143, 146, 159, 163, 164, 175, 197, 214, 220, 225, 237, 246, 252, 253, 265, 266, 267, 268, 270, 309, 320, 325, 329, 333, 336, 339, 340, 347, 352, 355, 356, 357, 359, 365, 366, 399
Parliament Funkadelic 99
Paul MacLean 97
payola xviii, 60, 61, 64, 383
pedophiles 135, 219
pimp xv, 1, 3, 29, 45, 47, 48, 49, 50, 58, 75, 90, 91, 102, 126, 139, 144, 146, 148, 162, 164, 209, 276, 282, 284, 285, 286, 287, 288, 289, 322, 378, 383
pimp cup 162, 282, 287
platinum 8, 39, 70, 75, 116, 148, 173, 202, 216, 276, 283, 287, 316, 322, 323, 324, 325
playa xv, 3, 29, 45, 48, 95, 144, 159, 238, 286, 378
player 144, 145, 214
poetry 2, 3, 32, 96, 98, 101, 102, 103, 188, 385
Pokemon 79
pornography 9, 46, 147, 219, 220, 223, 276
poverty xv, 2, 10, 15, 32, 38, 41, 51, 52, 67, 88, 107, 111, 112, 114, 115, 119, 122, 125, 126, 133, 134, 137, 138, 145, 153, 156, 166, 182, 244, 262, 268, 272, 307, 311, 321, 330, 342, 349, 351, 357, 366, 373, 386, 403
preacher xviii, 3, 266, 282, 284, 286, 288, 302

prevention 14, 27, 174, 181, 185, 259, 342, 344, 346, 349, 387, 391, 396, 397, 401, 403
prison xvi, xvii, 16, 23, 37, 52, 68, 69, 83, 94, 121, 122, 123, 125, 146, 155, 159, 164, 210, 214, 235, 236, 244, 284, 343, 344, 352, 358, 394, 400
profanity 65, 66, 67, 68, 69, 143, 276, 294, 305, 308
Prolonged Adolescent Syndrome 20, 27, 28, 45, 57, 83, 114, 169, 221, 238, 373
promiscuity 5, 148, 156, 206, 277
Psychomedia Perpetrator Disorder 27, 29, 30, 54, 106, 254, 279
PTBs (powers that be) xviii, 6, 34, 51, 74, 121, 189
Public Enemy 6, 202, 203, 245, 316, 382, 395, 396

Queen Latifah 6, 27, 91, 241, 385
Queen Mother Moore 169

R&B (rhythm and blues) 2, 4, 32, 33, 60, 106, 126, 170, 221, 248, 304, 305
racism xix, 5, 32, 77, 88, 134, 137, 146, 147, 165, 188, 214, 304, 307
rape 72, 93, 151, 169, 209, 221, 226, 228, 229, 236, 246, 247, 259, 264, 269
reality 11, 22, 23, 29, 34, 40, 55, 59, 61, 63, 74, 106, 107, 108, 112, 142, 148, 162, 178, 203, 224, 243, 246, 269, 282, 288, 316, 317, 319, 358, 387, 404
Redd Foxx 67
Redman and Method Man 109
Remy 171, 241, 250
Remy Ma 241, 250
Reticular formation 97
rhythm 7, 9, 97, 98, 102, 368
Richard Pryor 67, 119, 156
Rick James 99, 262, 399
Ricky Smiley 119
rite of passage 226, 231, 263, 361, 366
RJ Reynolds 184, 186
Robert Pittman 108, 109
Rodney King 88

role model xiv, 7, 11, 47, 108, 135, 138, 139, 140, 141, 144, 147, 155, 181, 223, 256, 267, 388
Rosa Parks 169
Rug Rats 260, 261
Run-DMC 202, 316
running trains 71
Russell Simmons 14, 48, 179, 191, 212, 296

safety belts 329
saggin' 20, 27, 28, 83, 84, 96, 116, 128, 143, 202, 222, 366
Sara Baartman 226, 227
Satan 93, 168, 280, 290, 292
Scarface 85, 146, 149
self-esteem 25, 84, 116, 142, 210, 228, 229, 249, 259, 334, 339, 354, 362
Sesame Street 104, 110, 167, 225, 241
sex xvii, xviii, 26, 28, 32, 33, 34, 35, 36, 38, 41, 47, 49, 51, 52, 54, 55, 59, 60, 61, 66, 67, 69, 71, 72, 90, 91, 97, 98, 100, 101, 104, 123, 125, 131, 139, 141, 144, 153, 162, 167, 168, 169, 176, 178, 181, 188, 192, 193, 194, 198, 199, 209, 219, 220, 221, 222, 223, 225, 226, 227, 228, 229, 230, 231, 232, 233, 235, 236, 237, 238, 239, 241, 243, 244, 246, 247, 248, 251, 252, 253, 254, 255, 257, 258, 259, 260, 261, 263, 264, 269, 270, 272, 273, 274, 275, 277, 283, 287, 291, 293, 305, 306, 319, 332, 342, 345, 346, 347, 348, 349, 368, 375, 387, 395, 396
sex monster 225, 226, 227, 228, 230, 231, 239, 244, 247, 248, 274, 347
Sexonomics 125, 270
sexual abstinence 269, 345, 346, 347, 348
sexual triggers 347
Shania Twain 70
Shawnna 241
Sigmund Freud 59, 90
Sinbad 67
single mother 122, 268, 373
single parent 29, 122, 268, 320, 352, 361, 373
situational homosexuality 236
slavery xix, 2, 76, 81, 83, 98, 100, 145, 148, 163, 209, 226, 262, 263, 268, 282, 355, 373

Sly and the Family Stone 99
Snoop Dogg 48, 50, 77, 96, 105, 139, 142, 144, 146, 148, 178, 191, 201, 245, 246, 249, 284, 285, 286, 288, 294, 388, 393, 397
sobriety xix
social entrainment 54
social service providers xiii, xix
Sojourner Truth 39, 169
Sonia Sanchez 3, 103
Sony 14, 60, 83, 213, 383, 385, 390, 396, 401
Sony BMG 60, 385
Soul Train Awards 46, 276
Source xix, 46, 87, 130, 156, 159, 161, 213, 227, 239, 272, 278, 303, 381, 399
Source Awards 46
spirituality xix, 31, 37, 38, 47, 89, 193, 277, 297, 307, 315, 341
spy 188, 189, 191, 192, 193, 194, 197, 199
staff (cane) 278, 282, 283
STDs (sexually transmitted diseases) xviii, 93, 131, 137, 153, 169, 181, 226, 240, 251, 254, 257, 258, 259, 261, 264, 287, 342
stereotype 323, 360
Steve Harvey viii, 67, 119
Stevie Wonder 96, 340, 371
subliminal 15, 56, 63, 83, 95, 108, 171, 177, 282, 292, 347, 384
Sugar Hill Gang 6
SugarStrings 335, 339, 402
Suge Knight 154
surveillance 123, 147, 154, 284, 397, 399
sweets 186, 248
symbolism 9, 92, 190, 196, 278, 279, 281, 288, 290, 292, 311
symbols xv, 9, 21, 22, 55, 63, 84, 92, 102, 145, 158, 162, 234, 277, 278, 279, 280, 282, 283, 289, 291, 292, 297, 302, 312, 328, 349, 399

The Emotions 58, 96, 335, 366
The Geto Boys 86
The Jeffersons 374
The Last Poets 3, 4, 103, 149, 318, 381
Three Six Mafia 168
Tommy Hilfiger 116
Too Short 71, 286

Top 40 xvii, 175
Total Request Live 56
Trace Adkins 70
Trick Daddy 167, 322
Trina 205, 241, 249, 394
Tupac Shakur 74, 77, 191, 295, 312
TV (television) xvi, 7, 8, 13, 21, 25, 29, 46, 48, 52, 53, 56, 57, 58, 61, 66, 67, 82, 99, 105, 107, 108, 109, 124, 190, 200, 203, 208, 211, 212, 218, 241, 267, 288, 319, 326, 332, 343, 354, 355, 358, 374, 386

Universal 5, 83, 208, 211, 212, 213, 309, 385, 401
Universal Zulu Nation 5

VH1 105, 175, 203, 204, 212, 217, 218, 220, 249, 394
Viacom 55, 58, 155, 211, 212
Vibe 56, 153, 154, 159
video games 28, 29, 108, 190, 195, 198
village vii, 32, 62, 67, 136, 137, 143, 325, 342, 349, 370, 371, 372, 373, 391
violence xvii, xviii, 2, 5, 8, 9, 14, 15, 27, 32, 33, 35, 36, 51, 52, 55, 59, 61, 67, 72, 73, 79, 81, 91, 93, 107, 119, 120, 121, 122, 127, 133, 134, 137, 142, 147, 149, 152, 153, 154, 155, 156, 159, 174, 176, 190, 191, 196, 197, 201, 216, 220, 232, 235, 236, 241, 254, 261, 266, 272, 276, 277, 283, 295, 306, 308, 315, 316, 317, 328, 330, 342, 343, 349, 375, 377, 397, 398, 402
violence prevention 14, 27, 174
viral marketing xiii, 381

Walt Disney Co./ABC 211
Warner 60, 83, 211, 213, 383, 396, 397
Warner Music Group 60
weapons xv, 1, 2, 11, 39, 51, 98, 123, 169, 228, 234, 293, 328, 344, 362
Welcome Back, Kotter 99
white supremacy 35, 160, 303
Whodini 6
wigger 52, 87, 88, 89, 129, 210, 214
Willie Lynch 213
Will Smith 27

WMDs (weapons of mass destruction) xv, 1, 11, 234
Wu-Tang Clan 109

Xzibit 167, 168, 390

Ying Yang Twins 107, 253

Zero tolerance 166, 214, 361

978-0-595-41909-8
0-595-41909-7